Velocities of Change

Velocities of Change

Critical Essays from *MLN*

Edited by
Richard Macksey

The Johns Hopkins University Press
Baltimore and London

The Johns Hopkins University Press, Baltimore, Maryland 21218
The Johns Hopkins University Press Ltd., London

Library of Congress Catalog Card Number 72-12343
ISBN 0–8018–1494–4 (clothbound edition)
ISBN 0–8018–1495–2 (paperbound edition)

Library of Congress Cataloging in Publication data
will be found on the last printed page of this book.

Contents

                                 Poulet and the Reader's Share

Alan Bass   341   *"Literature"/Literature*

                     355   Other Critical Essays from *MLN*

                     356   Contemporary Criticism: Selected Readings

                     359   About the Contributors

                     365   Index

V ELOCITIES OF CHANGE ❧ RICHARD MACKSEY ❧

Farewell to an idea . . . The cancellings,
The negations are never final.

—Wallace Stevens

I

"Of all the cants that are canted in this canting world,—though the cant of the hypocrites may be the worst,—the cant of criticism is the most tormenting!" [*Tristram Shandy*, vol. III, chap. 12] There is a paradoxical edge to Laurence Sterne's outburst, written in a century that made fine arts of both hypocrisy and criticism. For his own allegedly confessional fiction constitutes both an extended, penetrating criticism of the novel itself as a mimetic form and, at the same time, a subtle exploitation of the devious rhetoric of bad faith (both the author's and the reader's) in the interests of exhibiting " sincerely " the disguises of the self.

Yet there is a curious modernity about this complaint from 1761. Of the making of criticism there would seem to be no end, but in our own time most criticism has become ominously institutionalized as a by-product of an academic industry that at times seems to have goals totally alien to the elucidation of literary texts. (Indeed, the recent passing of Edmund Wilson, a critic allied by choice to another, nonacademic marketplace, leaves a void almost larger than the man.) The inflationary pressures of the modern academy, where more is better, are notorious, and so too is the narrowing circle of readers for whom much professional criticism is written, readers who may in fact be primarily interested in recycling it back into their own critical production line. In France critical fashions seem to change with the rapidity of *haute couture* and the " book of the decade " appears regularly every six months.

The works of criticism that lead to significant and pervasive changes in the way we read literature or understand the nature of literary language are rare in any generation and often are initially misunderstood and subsequently vulgarized by their epigones. The

problems of writing a narrative account of critical theory in our
time extend well beyond the initial task of identifying the genuinely
important works. Perhaps it is only in retrospect that we can
assess the place of truly seminal works. Even the briefest litany of
highly original and influential titles would suggest some of the
difficulties of situating them within a cultural and historical description: Gundolf, *Shakespeare und der deutsche Geist* (1911); Lukács,
Die Theorie des Romans (1920); Richards, *Principles of Literary
Criticism* (1924); Shklovsky, *O teorii prozy* (1925); Benjamin,
Ursprung des deutschen Trauerspiels (refused as dissertation,
1925); Mukařovsky, *Máchův Máj: Estetiká studie* (1928); Empson,
Seven Types of Ambiguity (1930); Raymond, *De Baudelaire au
surréalisme* (1933); Bachelard, *La Psychanalyse du feu* (1938);
Paulhan, *Les Fleurs de Tarbes* (1941); Blanchot, *Faux pas* (1943);
Bataille, *Sur Nietzsche* (1945); Auerbach, *Mimesis* (1946); Leavis,
The Great Tradition (1948); Poulet, *Etudes sur le temps humain*
(1949); Barthes, *Le Degré zéro de l'écriture* (1953); Goldmann,
Le Dieu caché (1955); Frye, *Anatomy of Criticism* (1957); Girard,
Mensonge romantique et vérité romanesque (1961); Derrida, *De
la Grammatologie* (1967). (One might remark that the historian's
task is further complicated by the fact that the majority of the
books in this arbitrary list are, excluding academic exercises and
works in other disciplines, the authors' first substantial publications.) In any critical accounting one would also have to consider
the shaping significance of certain writers whose reputations lie
in other provinces of literature—Proust and Valéry, James and
Eliot, Sartre and Borges.

While we tend to measure the turnings of the critical path by
the appearance of new *theoretical* statements about the nature of
literature and the reader's task, it would be foolish to neglect the
impact on critical practice of those rare major works of *scholarship*
that open new points of access to the text as well as comprehensive
visions of Western culture and values. One thinks immediately of
contributions such as those made by Lovejoy and his associates in
the history of ideas, by Curtius, Auerbach, Spitzer, and other stylistic
critics drawing on a rich tradition of philological scholarship, by
R. S. Crane and his fellow neo-Aristotelians at Chicago, by literary
historians of various learning and generous perspectives, such as
C. S. Lewis, Hugo Friedrich, Paul Hazard, Mario Praz, Jean Seznec,
and D. C. Allen. Currently, the historical "archaeologies" of

Michel Foucault are having a profound effect in unsettling some of the most closely held assumptions of literary critics about cultural change and intellectual contexts. Any tentative critical survey would also have to weigh the significance of another sort of scholarly achievement, less influential perhaps as a *method* but almost as rare as the preceding examples—a work that effects a thorough revaluation and "re-reading" of an individual author. Here one might cite G. Wilson Knight and, more recently, C. L. Barber on Shakespeare, Starobinski on Rousseau, Damon or Frye on Blake, Wasserman on Keats and Shelley, or Hillis Miller on Dickens and Hardy.

We are justified in asking, however, whether any such cursory census of original works (culled from the vast detritus of derivative books, sensible and absurd, which are appearing exponentially to fill our libraries and, presumably, our understanding) can rescue us from Sterne's impatience and disclose, by itself, a means of calibrating what Stevens called the "velocities of change" in modern critical judgment. Even if the possibility of a history of modern criticism must for the moment remain moot, how in fact could we recognize a new Kant of criticism amid the ceaseless babble of critical cant?

One of the most familiar ways to escape the problems of an intrinsic history of criticism is to turn to one or more of those extrinsic disciplines that, in the eyes of the beholder, seem to have supplied the methodological or metaphysical foundation for each critic's characteristic posture. Thus, to shift the descriptive categories is merely to defer the question of history, but it does afford a received vocabulary and handy means of discriminating "schools" and "influences" (often unperceived by the critics themselves).

The dependence of critical argument on anterior philosophic positions was evident at least as long ago as the old dispute between Plato and Aristotle about the nature and function of poetry. Much critical practice can in fact be sorted out with respect to implicit philosophic paradigms. Thus, Kant with the famous questions by which he launched his transcendental philosophy would seem to have inaugurated the very *possibility* of modern literary criticism. And, thanks to the long shadow of Coleridge, he remains alive among Anglo-American critics. It is easy to demonstrate the pervasive influence of Croce early in this century, not only on Italian critics but (through Collingwood and others) on their English-speaking colleagues. Similarly, one could study the impact of Bergson's philosophy of process and temporality on the critics of the *N.R.F.* Much American criticism in our century owes a devious if profound debt to the pragmatism of John Dewey (and this may help to account for some of the surprising if unsystematic ways American critics seem to have anticipated cherished assumptions of contemporary European "structuralists"). A revival of neo-Kantian aesthetic reached literary critics through Cassirer and, in this country, Susanne Langer, while the re-reading of Hegel inspired by Kojève's Sorbonne lectures in the late thirties affected a wide spectrum of postwar French critics. As early as 1931, Roman Ingarden's *Das literarische Kunstwerk* brought phenomenology into contact with European critical practice. The influence of Heidegger, early and late, on literary theory is still very much with us, and H.-G. Gadamer's *Wahrheit und Methode* (1960) succeeded in articulating a systematic application of the Heideggerian hermeneutic to problems of interpretation.[1] Similarly, the later Wittgenstein of the *Philosophical Investigations* (1953) and John Austin's (also posthumous) *How to Do Things with Words* (1963) have given new directions to Anglo-American criticism with notions like "family resemblance" and "performative utterance." Both Sartre and Merleau-Ponty, inheritors of several of the traditions noted above, have moved with a Gallic freedom between technical philosophy and critical enterprises. Finally, at the present moment no philosopher seems more firmly situated at the center of most Continental literary controversy than Friedrich Nietzsche, thanks in large part to his sweeping deconstructions of the philosophical tradition itself.

While such tentative genealogies of philosophical presuppositions may be useful in demonstrating otherwise unsuspected similarities and differences among practicing critics, the philosopher and the

---

[1] Gadamer's philosophical hermeneutics marks a decisive break with the methodological hermeneutic tradition of Schleiermacher and Dilthey. It has certain common causes with the temporal approach of the "demythologizing" theologians of the New Hermeneutic—Bultmann and his disciples Gerhard Ebeling and Ernst Fuchs. All of them have been subjected to an extended critique from the older tradition of "objectively valid interpretations" by Emilio Betti in *Teoria generale della interpretazione* (Milan: Giuffrè, 1955) and subsequent polemical writings. In the United States E. D. Hirsch has taken up Betti's plea for "validity in interpretation."

critic obviously operate within very different modes of discourse and under very different functional constraints. The critic, if he is to function at all, must address and seek to integrate alien texts— and these in turn are as often as not freighted with alien concepts— even though, like the philosopher and the poet, he feels the need to create (again in Wallace Stevens's phrase) "confidence in the world." Yet it is a mediated world he is exploring, and part of his training involves a certain forgetfulness of his own conceptual baggage.[2]

Every discourse or discipline clearly has its own rules of evidence and changing budget of questions, both urgent and inadmissible. In fact, one of the most fascinating problems in the sociology of knowledge is the relation of the unasked, uncited, or unproved to the presiding *episteme* or paradigm of a given investigation. (Relevance and repression would be key terms in the interpretation.) Yet other disciplines besides philosophy have been advanced as specula for studying the changing features of critical theory. Thus, in the early years of this century, when sociology seemed for many the most vital academic discipline in France and Germany, there was a temptation to discover the basic orientation of literary critics in their implicit social theory and manipulation of social categories. (A revival of this metacritical game concurrent with the burgeoning of anthropological theory in our own time could be found in the peculiar seduction of descriptions borrowed from ethnology.) Again, few critics in our century have completely escaped the challenge of Freud's contribution to interpretation. There is a corresponding tendency to see in many critics and schools the lineaments of Freud himself or of Jung or Binswanger or Lacan or some other interpreter of the Freudian text.

The one discipline, however, that for contemporaries seemed to afford the most plausible mirror for critical theory is that concerned with the same medium as literature, the study of language itself. The slogan could be found in Mallarmé's dictum that "poetry is written with words not ideas" and the program in

---

[2] Many readers have observed the hazards for critics of traveling with too much philosophic luggage. Leo Spitzer once proposed a "negative reading list" for our younger scholars; his proscribed authors reflect the fashions of the time (1957) but include several philosophers who were central to his own critical formation: Buber, Bergson, Dilthey, Freud, Heidegger, Ortega, Sartre, Scheler, Spengler, Unamuno.

Valéry's insistence that literature is a systematic extension of "certain proprieties of language." But language is also situated at the intersection of philosophy and criticism. And the investigation of its proprieties is a common concern of much otherwise unrelated contemporary philosophy that has left its mark on modes of interpretation. One immediately thinks of the reflections on language in Husserlian phenomenology, the later thought of Heidegger and Wittgenstein, English ordinary language analysis, and neo-rationalism. A similar preoccupation with problems of language could be traced in recent theological hermeneutics as well as in those influential "human sciences" considered above, anthropology and psychoanalysis. Through the pioneer lectures of F. de Saussure linguistics was the first discipline to suggest a "structural model" for synchronic analysis. The subsequent work by Trubetzkoy, Jakobson, Hjelmslev, Benveniste, and others developed methodological tools capable of a high degree of formalization in the diacritical ordering of linguistic elements. Literary critics, like their colleagues in other fields, were understandably drawn to the distinctive lexicon of linguistics and to sometimes strained applications of binary, differential analysis. (Most extrinsic uses of structural linguistics derived from Jakobson's phonetic models and his complementary notions of metaphor and metonymy. The relative independence of phonetic and semantic elements, however, posed both practical and theoretical problems for literary critics.) [3]

Similarly, and more recently, work in generative grammar has had profound consequences for any general theory of literature and seems to suggest possible reassessments of older theories of language. Thus, we may have witnessed a possible revolution (or counterrevolution) in both philosophy and literary theory as a consequence of Chomsky's rehabilitation of linguistic universals through his transformational notion of "deep sense." The very metaphysical issues the language analysts had claimed to decon-

[3] For a brief discussion of the theoretical implications for the other human sciences of recent inroads on the privileged linguistic model, see "The Space Between" [Preface to the 1972 edition], *The Structuralist Controversy*, ed. Macksey and Donato (Baltimore: The Johns Hopkins Press, 1972). For an ambitious attempt at a more highly formalized mathematical model for the human sciences (and a resolution of some of the unresolved discontinuities in linguistic description), see René Thom, *Stabilité structurelle et morphogenèse: essai d'une théorie générale des modèles* (Reading, Mass.: W. A. Benjamin, 1972), especially Chap. 13.

struct through a scrupulous theory of descriptions, the transformational linguists seem intent on reconstituting into legitimate philosophic problems. (Chomsky's own historical arguments may be vulnerable, but the possible implications of his linguistic model for the reinstitution of Descartes and Leibniz in discussions of "mind" are challenging.)

Yet the moment when linguistics could claim to provide a theoretical methodological model and a matrix for the understanding of all critical descriptions may well have passed. Many would quarrel with the privileged status afforded binary oppositions (an analytic tool conveniently adapted to the potentials of the digital computer, if not to reality, which also demonstrates its analog components). As often noted too, the relative subordination of semantic elements and their formalization poses obvious problems for the student of literary texts. While work in semantic descriptions continues, we are still lacking a general theory of context. But perhaps the most powerful attack on the adequacy of modern linguistics to supply a metacritical model has come from a general critique of the sign itself by French analysts like Derrida, Foucault, and Deleuze.

Traditionally language has supplied a convenient provocation to speculations about origins, a preoccupation that seems to haunt much modern criticism. From this issue and from the differential character of the Saussurean sign, an element of "deferred presence," Derrida has launched a far-reaching deconstruction of our traditional metaphysics of presence. For many critics this has precipitated a conceptual crisis of language itself. (Alan Bass discusses the implications of Derrida's critique in the last essay of this volume.)[4] To translate the problems of identifying and situating critical discourse in terms of a more adequate theory of linguistic description would seem, for the moment at least, only to multiply the problems and raise the conceptual stakes.

---

[4] A reader of a recent review that brought the "conceptual crisis of the sign" to bear on a work of traditional critical history supplied the following Cole Porter response:

It's de-centered,
    It's De-leuzean,
It's de-latest,
    It's de-mystified,
It's De-riddian deconstruction—
    It's depressin'!

II

The essays collected in this volume are directed toward some of the issues sketched above, but their collection proposes a much more modest assay of contemporary literary criticism. The collection reflects the changing postures of a diverse group of critics within a continuing practical context. One could imagine, for instance, a review of critical theory that limited itself to the pragmatic norm of examining a few widely influential texts that had shaped the *teaching* of literature for a large number of students. Such a pedagogical mirror could try to measure the velocities of critical change against the pages of texts from Lanson to Brooks and Warren, or from Richards's *Practical Criticism* to Wellek and Warren.

An even more obvious context within which to follow the course of critical theory is the pages of a single journal or review. As this is the context chosen for the present volume, it may be useful to distinguish some of the kinds of journals that normally serve as coherent critical vehicles. An initial distinction might be made between general reviews and scholarly journals (which, for the contributors, is ordinarily a distinction between those who get paid and those who get promoted). Clearly, the review is normally more responsive to a larger and less initiated audience. Traditionally at least, the prose may be clearer and the theoretical issues more cloudy. In many social instances, however, this distinction between the popular and the academic will not hold. (Roland Barthes describes in his essay collected here an " ideological " criticism which evolved outside the walls of the academy and its journals but which has subsequently become doctrinal in many of our universities.)

There are a few reviews that seem to have been directed, usually with a degree of violence, at a single issue or a unique historical moment. One thinks of *Blast* (1914-15) or Wyndham Lewis's *The Enemy* (1927-29). More common are those critical reviews that reflect the shaping hand of a single, strongly committed critic who determines both the tone and the doctrine. An extreme case would be Karl Krauss and *Die Fackel* (1899-1936), although for some years, after the departure of Gentile, Croce exercised a similar control over *La Critica* (1903-). There is a tendency to think of *The Criterion* (1922-39) as the lengthened shadow of T. S. Eliot and of *Scrutiny* (1932-53) as the natural extension of Dr.

Leavis, though both of them encouraged several generations of critics who began as disciples. Other reviews could more justly be seen as the product of a small, congenial, and relatively coherent group of critics. Supreme among such would be the *N.R.F.* of the early years, under Rivière, Thibaudet, Gide, Ramon Fernandez, and DuBos. (The *Imago* [1912-38] and the *Blätter für die Kunst* (1892-1919) performed similar functions for the Freudian circle and that of Stefan George and saw the same number of defections.) In the United States, the *Kenyon Review* (1939-70) was for a number of years the house organ for the New Critics. More recently, *Tel Quel* (1961-) has come to stand for a certain strain of critical terrorism emanating from Paris.

Scholarly journals have by custom less pronounced features, although they frequently reflect the critical judgment (or aberrations) of a single editor of long tenure. (In this country, Basil L. Gildersleeve first set the pattern for personal editorial continuity with his regular department, "Brief Mention," in the *AJP* [1880-].) Equally commonly the scholarly publication may reflect a "school" or a "method" with a persistence which is more than a match for that of the little magazines. Although it would be hard to define the "character" of the *PMLA*, it probably remains the most representative and symptomatic portrait of the present state of academic letters in America.

The essays in this volume have been drawn from the pages of *MLN*, an academic journal coeval with *PMLA* but one which has always been closely associated with one university, Johns Hopkins, and which has never been burdened by the responsibility to be thoroughly "representative." Throughout its history, however, it has been closely associated with contemporary criticism in Europe and with a certain fascination for "method."

Although all the essays in the present collection date from the last thirty years (and most of them from the last twelve), they are, in a sense, inscribed within the longer history of the journal. The points of difference from the earlier, philological decades of *MLN* may seem more marked in these essays than any elements of continuity, yet they may still be read against the longer narrative of eighty-seven years as changing views of the rôle of literary language and the historical imagination.

III

The early history of *MLN* is one chapter in German scholarship's triumphant colonization of the United States during the last quarter of the nineteenth century. Founded in 1886, a decade after Johns Hopkins itself, *Modern Language Notes* was one manifestation of President Gilman's program to translate the European higher learning to this country. His new university was animated by European-trained scholars and European ideas; it introduced the " seminary " and the laboratory as methods, the rigors of " scientific " research, and the notion of an international community to which it was responsible. As one guarantee of this emerging community, Gilman stressed the importance of scholarly journals and publications to enlarge the audience of the research seminar. Not accidentally, his institution—generally granted the claim to being the first American graduate university—was also the first to encourage a wide array of new scholarly journals and the first to sponsor a university press.

A. Marshall Elliott, the founding editor of *MLN*, came to Hopkins as an associate in Romance Languages with the pioneer group that Gilman had gathered in 1876. Significantly, he came from eight years of study and travel in Europe and initially regarded modern Romance languages as secondary to his interest in Sanskrit and comparative philology. In 1883 he was instrumental in the establishment of the Modern Language Association and served as its first secretary and, subsequently, as its president. Although it was some years before his contributions to the new university caught Gilman's eye, Hugh Hawkins could say of Elliott that " most Romance-language scholarship in America traces to the department . . . he erected at Hopkins." [5] His new journal, which was to publish learned articles and reviews in English, German, and Romance languages (as well as other items of pedagogical and topical interest " to answer the needs of the day ") , had a senior model in the *American Journal of Philology*, founded at Hopkins by Gildersleeve six years earlier. And the aspirations of classical philology, translated into the study of modern languages, were to play a large role in characterizing the critical attack for many years. Thus Elliott proposed in the first issue to give the journal " as scientific

[5] *Pioneer: A History of the Johns Hopkins University, 1874-1889* (Ithaca: Cornell University Press, 1960) , p. 160.

a character as possible, considering the present status of modern language study in America." Some years later he was to define the aim of philological " science " as " an orderly progression from the known to the unknown, from the special to the general, a strict observation of the facts of living speech and then the induction is recorded regardless of traditional authority." [6] For seventeen years—according to C. C. Marden—he had the magazine printed in a shed behind his house, while the editing and most of the folding, sewing, wrapping, and addressing were done in his library. In 1903 the production was assumed by the J. H. Furst Co., which still prints *MLN*.

The personality of Elliott was to dominate the magazine until 1916, when J. W. Bright assumed the editorship and gave the journal the form it was to retain until 1962. In that latter year *MLN* began a new stage in its career, with an enlarged format, a greater emphasis on extended articles, individual issues devoted to each of the major Romance and Germanic languages and literatures, and an annual comparative number. (The English faculty was henceforth largely occupied with *English Literary History*, founded in 1933 as the journal of the Tudor and Stuart Club.)

The year of *MLN*'s foundation, 1886, was to prove a most significant one in the diffusion of the new academic industry. Elliott and his colleagues of the Modern Language Association also launched the *PMLA* as the organ of their new group. Mandell Creighton founded the *English Historical Review*; the vicomte de Vogüé published his pioneer study, *Le Roman russe*; and Ferdinand Brunetière (shortly to visit Hopkins as the first Turnbull Lecturer) completed his *Histoire et littérature*. The grand design of the *New English Dictionary* was two years old and the *Dictionary of National Biography* had just completed its first year. (Although these were the academic achievements most characteristic of the time, one could note a few rather more subversive events that were ultimately to transform the times: Jean Moréas and Gustave Kahn founded *Le Symboliste; Les Illuminations* of Rimbaud appeared; Nietzsche published *Jenseits von Gut und Böse*; and Dr. Sigmund Freud turned his scientific attention from neurology to psychiatry.) But perhaps the most symptomatic event of 1886 in the context of academic literary theory was the publication of the second and

[6] *The Johns Hopkins University Circulars* **X** (1891) : 59.

definitive edition of August Boeckh's posthumous *Encyclopaedie und Methodologie der philologischen Wissenschaften* (ed. Bratuschek and Klussmann). This ambitious claim to methodological objectivity was to be the monument of nineteenth-century systematic philological hermeneutics, the " china egg " of German linguistic scholarship against which Ezra Pound was later to rail.

Boeckh had been a student of F. A. Wolf (1759-1824), who had laid the foundations of modern classical philology, while his study of Plato had been directed by Friedrich Schleiermacher (1768-1834), the father of scriptural hermeneutics. Although Boeckh began the series of lectures that was to form the *Encyclopaedie* at Heidelberg in 1809, he was to continue to expand and redact the text during the fifty-four years that he held the chair of eloquence at the new University of Berlin. It was during this busy half-century that the new disciplines of "scientific" philology and hermeneutics evolved, leaving their mark on Boeckh's synthetic effort. Thus, K. K. F. W. Lachmann (1793-1851), through the impulse of A. W. Schlegel (1767-1845), refined a method for the establishment of critical texts; Jacob Grimm (1785-1863) and his brother Wilhelm (1786-1859) opened new areas of investigation in Folkpoetry and comparative mythology and laid the groundwork of Germanic philology; Franz Bopp (1791-1867) developed the new field of comparative philology; while F. C. Diez (1794-1867) performed a similar service for Romance philology. In the fields of interpretation, Wilhelm von Humboldt (1767-1835) in the philosophy of language, Schlegel in literary history, Heymann Steinthal (1823-99) and Moritz Lazarus (1824-1903) in ethnopsychology, F. K. von Savigny in jurisprudence, and the generation of Niebuhr (1776-1831), Leopold von Ranke (1795-1886), and J. G. Droysen (1808-84) in historiography all contributed to the Romantic welling up of a search for method that was to be the common concern binding together the humane disciplines. This was the inheritance of Boeckh, and it was in a very real sense the scholarly burden laid on *MLN*'s first editor and contributors.

Boeckh stated the rigor and veridical ambitions of his enterprise at the very beginning of the *Encyclopaedie*. Philology coincides with history in the broadest sense—linguistic, social, intellectual, institutional; it comprehends the knowledge of what man has made. It is cumulative and systematic in its methods:

The concept of a science or scientific discipline is not expressed through counting, piece by piece, what comprises it. This assertion seems, in fact, to be axiomatic; yet many people are accustomed to view philology merely as an aggregate. . . .[7]

Philology proceeds inductively, using " facts " established by related disciplines, and seeks to attain an " encyclopaedic " view, formulaically stated as "the knowledge of what is known " (*Erkenntniss des Erkannten*). In its pursuit of knowledge, philology bears a reciprocal relationship to philosophy:

> Nevertheless this opposition is not absolute, for all knowledge (*gnosis*), as Plato wisely realized, is, from a higher, speculative point of view, reknowing (*anagnosis*) ; and philology must attain to the same knowledge that philosophy has reached by speculation.[8]

The instruments of understanding are dual: *hermeneutics*, which aims at " absolute understanding," and *criticism*, which seeks " relative understanding " (or judgment between works) . Both activities can be analyzed into further dualisms, first of objective and subjective conditions from which the understanding proceeds, and then into grammatical and historical as well as individual and generic interpretations or judgments. Although later theorists such as Dilthey, Simmel, and Wach would refine the address of Boeckh's hermeneutics, it remains a monument to a faith in method and the " objectifications " of science, an emblem of one phase in the collaboration of linguistics, history, and philosophy.

The early years of *MLN* clearly reflect the same scientific aspirations grounded in linguistic and historical preoccupations. Thus, in the first anniversary number (January 1887) , Elliott writes: " We hope to make such selections as tend more and more toward the development of the scientific spirit. The disciplinary value of

---

[7] *Encyclopaedie* . . . (Leipzig: Teubner, 1886) , p. 1: Der Begriff einer Wissenschaft oder wissenschaftlichen Disciplin wird nicht dadurch gegeben, dass man stückweise aufzählt, was in derselben enthalten sei. Dies scheint sich zwar übermässig selbst zu verstehen; aber die Philologie sind Viele gewohnt nur als Aggregat zu betrachten. . . .

[8] *Ibid.*, pp. 16-17: Doch ist dieser Gegensatz nicht absolut, da alle Erkenntniss, alle γνῶσις nach Platon's tiefsinniger Ansicht auf einem höheren speculativen Standpunkt eine ἀνά~νωσις ist, und indem die Philologie reconstructiv auf dasselbe gelangen muss, worauf die Philosophie von entgegengesetzten Verfahren aus gelangt.

literary criticism will accordingly be emphasized. . . ." (What he characterizes as "popular" and opposes to "scientific" seems to have to do with pedagogy, an early if rival concern in the journal.) Early issues feature work by historical linguists like Henry Sweet (whom Gilman hoped to lure to Hopkins) and Gaston Paris and reflect, in their emphasis on the earliest stages of modern languages, the familiar Romantic preoccupation with origins.

At its worst, the insistence on the rigors of the philological method could lead to a kind of standardized scholarly "production" all too familiar a few generations ago, while the historicism could mean an abdication of critical sensibility. (Carrington Lancaster, who introduced the *Index* to volumes 1-50 (1886-1935), could somewhat defensively assert, "As scholars are sometimes accused of concerning themselves primarily with minor authors, it may be of interest to note that the seven writers who received the largest amount of space in the subject-index are, in order, Shakespeare, Chaucer, Goethe, Milton, Spenser, Dante, and Voltaire.")

At its best, this first vision of language and critical method could aspire to a total view of civilization and a command of its languages. It was dedicated to a scrupulosity of attention, an honesty in assessing detail, an alert historical awareness, and a sense of obligation to a community of scholars. While such ideals have a distant plangency, there are certain ironic echoes of the past in much that has been published here recently—a renewed preoccupation with language (although now synchronic rather than diachronic in focus), a fascination with analytic method (although dialectics seems to have replaced causality as the category of analysis), and, finally, further speculations about the possibility of a "science" of literature (or "textuality").

IV

The essays in this collection are not arranged chronologically but rather are divided into two general sections. The first, "The Fictions of Criticism," introduces theoretical statements from a number of different perspectives. Thus, each of them may be read in parallel with another in the section (for example, Donato and Kermode on the claims of structuralism), and others are actually part of a continuing dialogue (for example, Barthes and Girard or Hartman and Miller). The first essay, by Lionel Gossman, introduces the topic of the social context of literature, the burdens of ideology and history, and the aims of literary education (issues not totally alien to the first issue of *MLN*). The second essay, by Edward W. Said, raises complementary and equally urgent questions about textuality and literary authority. A number of the frankly polemical essays reflect debates that extend well beyond the confines of any single journal.

The second general section, "Critical Profiles," includes ten portraits of influential literary theorists, arranged by critic approximately chronologically. (The essay by Leo Spitzer on Hugo Friedrich was, as its form indicates, originally an extended review, but its digressive-progressive form illustrates a genre in which Spitzer felt peculiarly at home and free to develop his own insights.)

Many of the contributors have been directly connected with the editorial board of *MLN* (Spitzer, Girard, Gossman, De Man, Donato, Hart), while others, like Barthes, Derrida, Goldmann, Raimondi, and Kermode, have been visiting members of the Hopkins faculty. Still, it would be foolish to suggest that there is visible a "party line", an impression which the most casual reading can dispell. In fact, one question that is more likely to occur to the reader is, what critical concerns unite those contributors who have been colleagues and collaborators? Clearly they are frequently separated by both critical vocabularies and critical preoccupations.

Amado Alonso, student of Menéndez Pidal, and Leo Spitzer, student of Meyer-Lübke, are the most direct bridges to *MLN*'s philological past. And yet, in their insistence on the newer concerns of stylistics, they are most conscious of that part of the past that had ossified. Similarly, both Roland Barthes and René Girard are products of traditional French training (in the latter case, at the Ecole des Chartes), but both are fully aware of the paradoxes of liberation from the same tradition.

V

Although modern criticism has seemed to flourish in a climate of continuing crisis (real or imagined) and the polemical edges of many of the critics gathered or discussed in this volume are all too obvious, we might here attempt a few irenic observations about issues that underlie apparent change. Simply put, there is not so much disagreement among conflicting critical theorists as there might seem to be, if only the following metacritical tasks have been faced: (a) the discrimination of the major critical *questions*; (b) the definition of the *subject* of study (whether it be the "work," text or context, creative pretext or post-literary consequences); and (c) the discrimination of which critical *languages* are being invoked. Now the recurrent critical questions seldom occur in isolation, but one reason for the total deafness of one critic to another while attending to the same text is often that they are primarily concerned with answering very different though equally complex questions. A preliminary—admittedly partial— census of basic critical questions would include the following queries directed to either textual parts or wholes; for the sake of rapid recognition, each critical attitude can be tagged with a familiar pejorative label:

1. ONTOLOGICAL: What is the literary work's nature and mode of existence? The answer may involve the discrimination of strata and may implicate a number of the questions below. (" Metaphysical Gas ")

2. EPISTEMOLOGICAL: How can we " know " the work; what is its " cognitive content," its kind of " truth "? (" Jesting Pilate ")

3. TELEOLOGICAL: What is the function and purpose of the work (in, for example, the good society, the Marxist state, the ideal university)? (" Philistinism ")

4. ARCHEOLOGICAL: What is the source or origin (*arche*) of the work, and how can we describe its genesis? (" *To Hen* or the Eggs ")

5. DESCRIPTIVE: What can be said about the intrinsic characteristics of the work (text) itself—about (a) its phonetic aspects; (b) its semantics of either simple or complex units; (c) the relations between phonetics and semantics? This question is usually extended to include most semiotic, stylistic, and rhetorical analysis. (" Lemon Squeezing ")

6. INTERPRETATIVE: What can be said about the extrinsic relations of the work to the " real " world—about (a) theme; (b) thesis? (" Heresy of Paraphrase ")

7. PERFORMATIVE: How can one reenact or " perform " the work in the richest sense? This generally involves related questions about " optimal " reading and the critic's identification with the text. (" Critical Histrionics ")

8. NORMATIVE: How is the work to be judged by the application of explicit or implicit standards, by canons such as unity, complexity, originality, moral seriousness, and so on? ("Praising and Blaming")

9. HISTORICAL: How can the work as an "event" be related to other events, artistic and otherwise? The principles of organization for an historical account may be any of the following: (a) *annalistic*, a simple chronological sequence of works; (b) *organic*, integrating each work to a governing value, norm, convention, or analogue seen diachronically; (c) *dialectical*, introducing another level of necessity where the work is related to an underlying causal factor or factors, such as determining economic, social, political, linguistic, or psychological structures; (d) *narrative*, the "continuity of a sequence of distinct events connected causally by whatever individual men or groups of men, through a period of time, happened to do with respect to the element constituting the continuum of change" (R. S. Crane), specifically by the discovery of "plots" in the changing relationships between the author and his materials, techniques, forms, or ends. This last approach may include a history of artistic "kinds" as well as of devices, conventions, preoccupations, and uses (all implicating other questions in this budget). ("Pre-artistic Antiquarianism")

10. PSYCHOLOGICAL: How is the work related to mind (feelings, ideas, obsessions, repressions)? Apart from studying the representation of "psyches" or "types" within the work, this question is generally directed toward two quite different aspects of the artistic process, one preconstructive and the other postconstructive, namely—

    GENETIC: How did the author's mind operate in creation and shaping up of the work (Cf. question 4)? ("The Intentional Fallacy")

    AFFECTIVE: How does the mind of the audience respond to the work (Cf. question 7)? ("The Affective Fallacy")

11. APPRECIATIVE: How does it grab you? The celebration of the work—always in danger of lapsing into narcissism. ("Impressionism")

12. METACRITICAL: How does the work reveal certain im-

plicit or explicit critical assumptions, metaphysical presuppositions, controlling views of the sphere, limits, and uses of
art? (" The Shadow of a Shadow or Plato's Fourth Bed ")
Not all of these questions have in any given period been considered
interesting, appropriate, or even decent—as some of the pejorative
labels may indicate—but clearly the choice of critical language and
the vector of the critic's attention will in part be a function of
which question or questions he is valorizing. And since not all
texts respond equally well to individual questions, the same matter
of privilege may well help to determine the choice of text (though,
in an ideal critic, the reverse should probably be the case).

In situating the actual subject of discussion, the locus of the
critic's attention, the following schematic, however primitive, may
have some heuristic value. The familiar quadripartite division of
critical issues into an *author-audience* axis and a *" work "-" world "*
axis lends itself to a rather Cartesian system of coordinates. Each
extremity of the expressive-pragmatic and objective-mimetic axes
can be associated with a characteristic critical metaphor that tends
to dominate the discourse. (Thus, in the representation here, the
metaphorics can be derived from the familiar images of the lamp
and the performance, the organism and the mirror.) The horizontal axis, moving from preconstructive to postconstructive concerns, may be described as diachronic, while the vertical axis is
concerned with synchronic relationships, moving from endotelic to
ectotelic concerns. At each extremity of the coordinates significant
distinctions can be made that help to characterize critical presuppositions and presiding critical questions. One can thus distinguish
collective and individual concerns at either end of the horizontal
axis and epistemological or formal distinctions at either end of the
vertical.

Now the limitations of such a procrustean system of coordinates
are all too obvious. Few critics or critical theories will stay pinned
for very long at any one point in the scheme, and most are concerned with what could be described as vectoral relationships between points. Somewhat more seriously, an adequate descriptive
system would have to introduce a third dimension to account for
the relative " distance " that the critic assumes in the process of
interpretation and the sequential dynamics of his " framings " of
his subject. The fact remains, however, that a discrimination of the
executive critical questions and a situation of the relevant critical

CRITICAL COORDINATES

"Interpretative Fallacy"
WORLD(S) : "History"
Mimetic [MIRROR]

Truth Theory: { verisimilitude
coherence
essence: { Universal
Type

Referent: { external
internal
supernal
absent/displaced

Community: (congregations)
Community: { Cult
Taste
Communion

AUDIENCE
[PERFORMANCE] Pragmatic   O   [influences]

Identity: { Rite
Impression
Catharsis: { homeopathic
allopathic

Aim: { Prodesse
Delectare
Movere

Reader: { Canonical Expectations
Canonical Deflections

Extrinsic

RECOGNITIONS
CONVENTIONS
OBSERVING
MAKING

WORK(S) : "Poetry"
Objective [ORGANISM]

Autotelic: { Textual
Locutionary
Stylistic: { Phonetic
Semantic: { categorematic
syncategorematic
Rhetorical

Generic: { Oeuvre (Author)
Models (Canon)
Genres (Types)

Diacritic: { Periodicity
Contextuality
Intertextuality
"Formalistic Fallacy"

(collectivities)
Community: { Linguistic
Historic
Sociological
Ideological
Philosophic: { Unit—Idea
Weltenschauung

AUTHOR
Expressive [LAMP]

O

Identity: { [Empty Subject]
Psychological: { Constructive
Archetypal
Gestaltist
Phenomenologic: { Cogito
Dasein
Body-Subject

empathy/imitation
abstraction/formalization
expression: { feeling
desire
cognition: { intuition
sensuous concept

Genesis: { play
illusion
protreptic

[sources]

Extrinsic

subject can go a long way in helping us to distinguish significant change in the theory of literature from the faddish confusions of hermetic talking at cross purposes.

VI

We might well conclude with a question raised by two kinds of critical language—and by two kinds of critical approach to language. It may be argued that these two approaches are ultimately irreconcilable in a single critical discourse. One descends, in its classic form, from the historical moment we have identified with the foundation of *MLN*. The other characterizes much contemporary " structuralist " activity—at least in its logocentric phase. The modern impulse is to see all texts as synchronous sign systems, related dialectically in terms of part and whole but secreting no " veiled " or hidden meanings. The traditional language of interpretation is, on the other hand, that achievement of nineteenth-century *Geisteswissenschaften*, hermeneutics. Even the most alert of modern critics is apt to retain traces of its inheritance.

For that century which began with Schleiermacher's universal investigations of evidence and language and closed with Dilthey's " hermeneutic circle " could be said to have invented interpretation in its modern sense. Although the elucidation of meaning from human artifacts is as old as the conscious preservation of canonical texts and monuments, the nineteenth century—with its embarrassment of interpretative systems in history, theology, arts and letters—discovered many of those reflexive paradoxes which have made modern hermeneutics such a profoundly self-conscious enterprise. The nineteenth century witnessed radical shifts in the language of traditional philosophy, a new emphasis on the reciprocal relation of theory and practice, and the symptomatic burgeoning of what Henry Aiken has called " that gaudiest of metaphysical disciplines," the philosophy of history.

But it was also precisely the period when the *sign*, in thinkers otherwise as diverse as Marx, Nietzsche, and Freud, was given its ambiguous hermeneutic value as both the object and the instrument of interpretation. Even words themselves (by which we investigate meaning) had, as Nietzsche demonstrated in his famous etymology of *agathos*, received the impress of interpretation. This implication of the sign in the interpretation exposed the possibility of infinite regression in any search for the origins of meaning, whether in history, language, or the psychoanalytic process. Further, the new, relativistic hermeneutics discovered analogous circularity in the reflexive implication of the interpreter in his initial act of interpretation as well as in the relationship of part and whole in the totalizing act of the critic. These basic paradoxes generated many of the issues which recur in this volume—the question of origins, the relation of text and context, the status of the subject and of language, the degree of mediation or alienation in artistic expression. To attempt to step outside the interpretative process and its circles, to return the sign to its place among signs, was the adventure awaiting the twentieth century in its fascination with general linguistic and semiotic systems, an enterprise already being prepared by that nineteenth-century Hopkins scholar, C. S. Peirce. But as a number of contemporary theorists such as Gadamer have insisted, such an ambition would be to divorce understanding from the contingency of the particular experience in the search for method; and this would be for the same theorists the end of interpretation as such.[9]

*   *   *   *   *

The final words should be those of editorial gratitude: to Jo Champlin, who helped with the gathering of the essays; to Catherine Macksey, who bore the major burden of the translations; to Joanne Allen of the Hopkins Press, who so patiently bore with the editor's vagaries; to Elias Rivers, the General Editor of *MLN*; and finally to Earl Wasserman, a generous if skeptical colleague with whom the constitution of this book was first discussed.

1973

[9] To the "scientific" aspirations of *MLN*'s contributors, early and late, Gadamer might supply a suitably skeptical epilogue. Writing of Heidegger's discussion in *Holzwege* of Hegel's notion of experience, he concludes: "Die Dialektik der Erfahrung hat ihre eigene Vollendung nicht in einem Wissen, sondern in jener Offenheit für Erfahrung, die durch die Erfahrung selbst freigespielt wird." *Wahrheit und Methode* (Tübingen: J. C. B. Mohr, 1960), p. 338.

I. The Fictions of Criticism

Literary Education and Democracy

L̲ITERARY EDUCATION AND DEMOC-
RACY ᷩ BY LIONEL GOSSMAN ᷩ In a classical
article, published in Holland in 1929, Pyotr Bogatyrev and Roman
Jakobson undertook an important reconsideration of the relation
between written and oral literature.[1] Rejecting both the Romantic
reverence for folklore as communal creation and the opposing view
that all folk literature is " gesunkenes Kulturgut," [2] they found in
the linguistics of Ferdinand de Saussure a model on which a more
adequate theory of folklore creation and folklore tradition might
be built. Against the positivist and neo-grammarian view that only
individual speech acts are real, while everything else is philosophical abstraction, a view that is easily compatible with the theory of
"gesunkenes Kulturgut" in folkloristics, they set Saussure's view of
language as a unity of "langue" and "parole," of the system of
language and of individual realizations of it, the former being as
"real" as—because the condition of—the latter. When specific,

[1] "Die Folklore als eine besondere Form des Schaffens," *Donum Natalicium
Schrijnen*, Nijmegen and Utrecht, 1929, pp. 900-13. The ideas set forth in this
paper were to some extent adumbrated by Cecil Sharp (*English Folk Song:
Some Conclusions*, 1907, and the introduction to *English Folk-Songs from the
Southern Appalachians*, 1917), and they have been confirmed, on the whole,
by subsequent scholarship; cf. notably Albert B. Lord, *The Singer of Tales*,
Cambridge, Mass., 1960 and Lord's contribution to *Four Symposia on Folklore*,
ed. Stith Thompson, Bloomington, 1953, pp. 305-15. Bertrand Bronson has
criticized Sharp's notion of tradition as a debate between individual creativity
and the censoring control of the group on account of its obvious evolutionist
bias. Tradition, he claims, is not opposed to but built into the creation of
individuals, so that individual creation does not seriously transgress the framework prescribed by tradition ("The Morphology of the Ballad Tunes," *Journal
of American Folklore*, 1954, 67: 1-14). This refinement of Sharp's position seems
compatible with the views of Jakobson and Bogatyrev.

[2] Summed up in the statement of Hoffmann-Krayer, "Das Volk produziert
nicht, es reproduziert" (cf. Hans Naumann, *Primitive Gemeinschaftskultur*,
Jena, 1921, p. 5). A version of this view is at least as old as Scott ("Introductory Remarks on Popular Poetry" in the 1830 edition of *Minstrelsy of the
Scottish Border*, ed. T. F. Henderson, Edinburgh, 1902, 1: 8-15). It is still
widely accepted among non-specialists of literature (Charles Lalo, *L'Art et la
vie sociale*, Paris, 1921, pp. 142-45, puts it forward as a fact). Alan Dundes
has made what he calls the "devolutionary premise in folklore theory" the
subject of a general survey of the ideologies underlying folklore studies in
Journal of the Folklore Institute, 1969, 6: 5-19.

individual exploitations of the speech code are sanctioned by the community, they become part of the general linguistic resources of the community, and thus, in a way, part of "langue." Language, in short, is a constant interchange, of varying intensity, between the speech acts of individuals and the linguistic system, which alone makes these acts possible and through which alone they have any chance of survival. In folklore, according to Jakobson and Bogatyrev, a similar relation obtains between individual performances of folk works and the works themselves.

Individual performers of folklore works may well give an individual rendering of their models.[3] Only those variations which the community finds acceptable, however, Bogatyrev and Jakobson claimed, are integrated into the work and taken up by subsequent poet-performers. In contrast, the written work, even though it meets with indifference or misunderstanding on its first appearance, survives as a potentiality which may be, and, as some celebrated cases in literary history testify, often is realized at a later date by subsequent generations of readers.

Bogatyrev and Jakobson did not deny that individuals contribute to folklore works, but they questioned our tendency to consider these in the same way as products of written literature. To us, they argued, a work is born at the moment its author writes it down on paper; correspondingly, the moment at which the oral work is objectified—" performed ": in other words—is taken by us to mark its birth, whereas in reality it becomes part of folklore only by being admitted into the tradition by the community. At the birth of folklore, in short, there is not an anonymous author, but a collective one. Though this position seems close to that of the Romantics, it differs from it in that the Romantics merely applied

---

[3] One should distinguish between free-form and fixed-form types of folklore—tales, for instance, on the one hand, and proverbs, on the other. Only the first category is subject to modification by individual performers. In addition, Bogatyrev distinguishes between "active-collective" and "passive-collective" works of oral poetry. The former category includes works which can be performed by all members of the community (cradle-songs, ceremonial songs, etc.), the latter includes those works which are performed by specialized—often quite rare—members of the community, though the whole community considers them its spiritual heritage. The evolution of the tradition is different in the two cases, according to Bogatyrev, and should be studied separately; "Über die Rolle von Sänger, Zuhörerschaft und Buch bei der Überlieferung und Veränderung epischer Lieder," in *Sowjetische Volkslied- und Volksmusikforschung: ausgewählte Studien,* ed. E. Stockmann, *et. al.,* Berlin, 1969, pp. 187-201.

an individual notion of authorship to the collectivity, whereas Bogatyrev and Jakobson are arguing that folklore creation requires a different and more comprehensive notion of authorship itself.

Above all, the folklore work, according to Bogatyrev and Jakobson, should not be seen as an individual objectification. Saussure's categories of "langue" and "parole" help us to understand the real nature of the folklore work for, like "langue," the folklore work has an impersonal existence as a complex of norms, a kind of scenario, which individual performer-artists bring to life in their own particular versions. In contrast, the written work perpetuates a particular "parole" and successive readers can go to it directly. In other words, previous "performances" or "readings" are only one ingredient in the reception of literary works, whereas they constitute the very being of folklore works, which exist and are known only through them.

Not the least important aspect of the argument developed by Bogatyrev and Jakobson is their conception of folklore and written literature as two distinct, albeit communicating systems, which determine the character of individual works within the systems. Thus they admit that much folk material is indeed "gesunkenes Kulturgut," the product, originally, of individual artists in the written tradition—though it could be shown that the original material is not always of notable artistic merit and may even be itself a degraded version of a folk work, as with certain broadsides of the sevententh and eighteenth centuries [4]—but the question of origins, they held, is irrelevant. What counts is not the origin of the materials, but the function of the borrowing, and the processes of selection and transformation of the materials borrowed. And here the folk is as creative in adapting "art" materials to its system as the cultivated artist is when he adapts folk materials. Both transformations—say, Beethoven adapting Scottish and Irish folksongs, and the people as it "zersingt," in the contemptuous phrase, an art song—are acts of creation. Most importantly, the theory expounded by Bogatyrev and Jakobson implies that the "same" work outside of folklore and inside it constitutes two different artistic phenomena. They illustrate this point by a discussion of Pushkin's poem "Gusar" (The Hussar). Here the folk motifs taken over by the cultivated writer impart a flavor of naivety

[4] See an interesting short study of *The Bold Soldier of Yarrow* by Norman Cazden in *Journal of American Folklore*, 1955, 68: 201-209.

to his poem, but this very naivety is a sophisticated artistic phenomenon.[5] When Pushkin's poem went back into folklore in the
Russian popular play *Tsar Maximilian*—similar in some respects
to the traditional English pantomime—its subtle ironies were lost.
Assimilated to the esthetics of the popular play, it became virtually
a different work.[6]

*   *   *   *   *

Of the many suggestive points made by Bogatyrev and Jakobson
in their article, I should like to single out two which seem to me
of considerable importance for literary culture in general: 1) that
oral "literature," unlike written, is synchronic, and 2) that while
literary texts enjoy a degree of autonomy and fixity unknown to
oral works, they must still be actualized by successive individual
readers. I should make clear from the outset that as the focus of
my interest here is literary education, I shall be more concerned
with some aspects of the literary culture than with others, with the
relation of poets and poetic works to the community or public,
rather than with modes of composition or the structural characteristics of written and oral works.

It could, I think, be argued, that it is here that the crucial
difference between the oral and the written is to be found. Lord
and others have pointed out, of course, that the structure of individual written and oral works is significantly determined by the

[5] On the distinction between primitive and simple, see I. Lotman, *Lektsii po
struktural'noi poetike*, 1964, Brown University Slavic Reprints, Providence, 1968,
pp. 52-55. Simplicity, according to Lotman, can be perceived only against a
background of complexity or ornamentation: "Artistic simplicity is more complex than artistic complexity, for it appears as a simplification that occurs later
than and against the background of complexity." In English poetry, the
practice of Wordsworth and the theory laid out in the Preface to the *Lyrical
Ballads* illustrate Lotman's point well. Similarly, W. K. Wimsatt, comparing
the Scots of Fergusson and that of Burns, clearly implied that Burns' "naive"
language is in fact more complex in its artful simplicity than the "literary"
English against which its readers read it ("Imitation as Freedom, 1717-1798,"
New Literary History, 1970, 1: 215-36). See also B. Hrushovski, "On Free
Rhythms in Modern Poetry," in *Style in Language*, ed. T. A. Sebeok, M. I. T.
Press and John Wiley, New York, 1960, pp. 173-90: Hrushovski argues that free
rhythms, though they may professedly aim at more "prosaic" or "speech-like"
effects, often have a more "rhythmical" and less "prosaic" impact than many
metrical texts. It has long been held—since Rousseau and Herder at least—that
prose, apparently more simple, is a later development than poetry and a more
complex one; cf. recently Northrop Frye, "The Critical Path," *Daedalus*, 99,
1970: 268-342, at p. 317.

[6] Bogatyrev returns to this problem in the article cited note 3 above.

mode of composition imposed on the poet by his medium and by his relation to his audience.[7] It is also likely that it is rare—perhaps impossible—for a great artist in the oral tradition to be a great writer. By all accounts the abbé Galiani was a brilliant raconteur, but it was Diderot who wrote his anecdotes. Nevertheless, it is possible to exaggerate the difference between oral and written compositions, and in order to focus our attention on the points that seem most important for my present topic, it may be appropriate to recall, as Lord himself did in a note to the *Singer of Tales,* that from certain points of view literature—verbal art would be a more accurate expression, but it is also a clumsy one—can be regarded as a continuous field accommodating a variety of different practices and different esthetic values not finally reduceable to a simple oral/written dichotomy.

Jakobson himself has defined poetic language in general as that in which the principle of equivalence (relations of similarity and dissimilarity, of synonymity and antonymity) is " promoted to the constitutive device of the sequence," and this definition may be taken as valid for both written and oral compositions.[8] In the numerous studies that have been made of the working of repetition and metaphor—the principal devices which, in a variety of forms, establish relations of identity and difference in poetic discourse— no significant distinction is made between oral or traditional materials and written ones.

Repetition and refrain, for instance, which characterize folk works and oral compositions, are also found in more sophisticated verse. In her recent book on *Poetic Closure,* Barbara H. Smith observes that Wyatt obtains some of his effects by " allowing a refrain to remain constant but altering its significance in succeeding

[7] Cf. for instance, Richard Müller-Freienfels, " Zur Psychologie und Soziologie der Schrift," on the possibility offered by writing of an overview which the spoken language does not allow. (*Beiträge zur Gesellungs- und Völkerwissenschaft, Prof. Dr. Richard Thurnwald zu seinem 80. Geburtstag gewidmet,* ed. Ilse Tönnies, Berlin, 1950, pp. 297-312).

[8] " Linguistics and Poetics " in Sebeok, 1960, p. 358. See also Roger Fowler, " Linguistic Theory and the Study of Literature," *Essays on Style and Language,* ed. R. Fowler, London, 1966, pp. 1-28. Fowler is skeptical of the possibility of finding features that will distinguish " literature " from " non-literature," but he also rejects as irrelevant the distinction between oral and written. Whether language uses noises in the air or marks on paper as its substance, he argues, its form remains the same, and it is form that both the linguist and the literary critic are interested in, not the physical representation of form.

stanzas through the material that precedes it." [9] This is the same
principle that operates in a popular song such as *Corn Rigs are
bonie* or in ballads such as *Lord Randal* or *Fine Flowers in the
Valley*. The forms of repetition are, of course, varied, ranging from
very simple ones, as in the examples referred to, to complex ones
which are only half-consciously perceived by the reader and which
occur not as refrains or even as repetitions of words or phrases but
at the phonemic level only. The principle of operation is always
the same, however: repetition establishes links and equivalences; it
draws together and, at the same time, because it is never absolute—
the context has always changed—it subtly separates and establishes
difference. The greater the approximation to identity, indeed, the
more sharply whatever elements of difference remain will be thrown
into relief. Paratactic structure, it is true, remains more characteristic of folk and oral poetry—and Kernodle suggests that it is characteristic of popular theatre too—allowing as it does infinite inter-
polation and substitution of similarly structured verses and requir-
ing no complex back and forth scanning for the perception of the
pattern, but whether the poem's structure is paratactic, sequential
or associative, to borrow some of the terminology used by Mrs.
Smith, does not substantially alter the poetic function of repetition.

From the point of view of esthetics, as from that of poetics,
the distinction between oral and written as such does not seem to
be fundamental. Esthetic categories cut across the oral-written
boundary, to which they correspond only in part. Jan Mukařovsky,
for instance, distinguishes between two terms of the esthetic—the
"normative" or "structured," in which poetic diction is strictly
codified and the category of the esthetic in general is clearly defined
and delimited, and the "functional" or "unstructured," which is
more free and adventurous, and which aims to blur the boundaries
between art and life, artistic language and everyday language. The
former is socially supported and relatively stable, it aims at order,
harmony and euphony, and because of its strict codification, it
carefully controls the energy of its individual components; the latter
is bound to smaller units of expression, it privileges the word—that

---

[9] Chicago, 1968, pp. 62-63. See also the discussion of repetition in Lotman,
op. cit. Jeanroy considered that the earliest refrains were fragments of different
works from those in which they were inserted, so that from the outset, in his
view, the refrain introduced a kind of counterpoint into the song. (Cf. G. Lote,
Histoire du vers français, t. 2, Paris, 1951, pp. 186-89.)

" Pandora's box from which all the potentialities of language fly out," as Barthes was to put it [10]—over all grammatical relationships, subverts established esthetic and linguistic categories, and opens the literary discourse to new and unpredictable possibilities of meaning. In some periods, according to Mukařovsky, the structured esthetic may predominate, in others the unstructured, but there cannot be one without the other, since literature requires the presence, in some measure, of both.[11]

In similar vein Roland Barthes defines literature as a world which is full of meaningful signs but which resists any conclusive statement of its meaning, which constantly invites and encourages interpretation, in other words, but which can never be definitively interpreted ("emphatiquement signifiant, mais finalement jamais signifié").[12] This general "anthropological" character of literature, he holds, can accommodate quite widely varying kinds of literary practice. The literary devices or *signifiants* can be strictly codified, as in classical literature, or left to seek their fortunes, as in modern poetics.[13] They can be brought close to denotation or impelled to the outermost limits of meaningfulness, where they initiate "a discourse full of gaps and full of lights, filled with absences and over-nourishing signs, without foresight or stability of intention." But literature can never become a purely denotative system, nor a completely open one. It must always be suspended

[10] *Writing Degree Zero,* transl. Annette Lavers and Colin Smith, London, 1967, p. 54.

[11] Cf. "The Esthetics of Language," in *A Prague School Reader on Esthetics, Literary Structure and Style,* ed. Paul Garvin, Washington, D. C., 1964, pp. 31-69. In his *Letters on the Esthetic Education of Man,* notably letter 15, Schiller was already insisting on the dialectical unity, in the esthetic, of what he called "form" and "life" (corresponding approximately to Mukařovsky's categories of normative and functional). The tendency to absolutise the functional in modern esthetics has been criticized by René Wellek (Sebeok, 1960, pp. 415-16), by Lotman (notably in his criticism of Shklovski, *Lektsii po struktural'noi poetike,* 1968, pp. 156-59) and by Michael Riffaterre, "Stylistic Context" in *Essays on the Language of Literature,* Boston, 1967, pp. 430-41, at p. 431.

[12] "Littérature et signification," *Tel Quel,* 1964, 16: 3-17, on p. 9.

[13] Cf. Auerbach's contrast in the first chapter of *Mimesis* (1946) between the Homeric style—"fully externalized description, uniform illumination, uninterrupted connection, free expression, all events in the foreground, displaying unmistakable meanings"—and that of Genesis—"certain parts brought into high relief, others left obscure, abruptness, suggestive influence of the unexpressed, 'background' quality, multiplicity of meanings and the need for interpretation. . . ."

somewhere betwen the two poles of specific meaning and meaning-
lessness. " The play of signifiers can be infinite, but the literary sign
itself remains fixed: from Homer to the tales of Polynesia no one
has ever transgressed the simultaneously signifying and deceiving
nature of this intransitive language which ' doubles ' the real (without ever reaching it) and which we call ' literature.' "

Barthes adds that in certain periods great value may be placed
on literary techniques that openly display the "deception" of
literature, its artfulness, while in others the emphasis may be on
clarity, simplicity and the concealment of art. It does, indeed, seem
likely that where the community is experienced as essential and
the individual appears secondary, the emphasis in poetic theory
may be on clarity, the observation of established conventions, and
the revelation of the fundamental likeness or universality of things,
and that where the individual is experienced as concrete, while
the community appears abstract, the emphasis will be on openness
of meaning, on poetic invention, and on the creation of new and
unexpected relations of likeness whose purpose is to subvert the old
ones.[14] Significantly, however, Mukařovsky argued that a "normative" esthetic was characteristic not only of folk literature but of
classical literature also. On his side, Barthes points out that in
periods when audience and artist form part of a single, relatively
homogeneous group, sharing the same values and the same language, the writer will be less aware than he is in periods when
the public and its language are divided, of literature as an object,
of his writing as something distinct from its instrumental function.
In this respect, classical literature in France had, according to him,
some of the characteristics of a folk culture in that it " postulates
the possibility of dialogue, it establishes a universe where men are
not alone, where words never have the terrible weight of things,
where speech is always a meeting with others." " Classical literary
language," he goes on, " is a bringer of euphoria, because it is immediately social. There is no genre, no written work of classicism
which does not suppose a collective consumption, akin to speech;

---

[14] The displacement of grammatically homologous rhymes and the increasing
preference, since the Renaissance, for rhyming morphologically dissimilar words
is a simple illustration of such a shift within the context of rhyming practice.
rhyme itself being, of course, historically conditioned (see Jean Cohen, *Structure
du langage poétique*, Paris, 1966, pp. 81-86). English critics have frequently
observed that Pope is a virtuoso at varying the grammatical forms he reconciles
in rhyme.

classical literary art is an object which circulates among several persons brought together on a class basis; it is a product conceived for oral transmission, for a consumption regulated by the contingencies of society." [15]

Like Mukařovsky, the Soviet scholar Iurii Lotman explicitly relates the esthetics of folk literature and the esthetics of classicism. Lotman distinguishes between an esthetics of "identity," which constantly reaffirms identity against difference, the permanence of order against the vagaries of change, and an esthetics of "opposition," which aims to frustrate the reader's expectations and to force him to consider in the work of art a different model of reality from the one he set out with. An esthetics of identity is common, in Lotman's view, to folk culture, medieval culture, and the culture of classicism, while most modern movements—baroque, romanticism and realism—are characterized by an esthetics of opposition.[16] At no point in Lotman's discussion does the oral-written distinction assume any importance at all.

It might be supposed that, on the one hand, the autonomy and individuality of the writer (as opposed to the rhapsode or performer) and, on the other, the autonomy and fixity of the written text (as opposed to what one might term the oral " programme ") radically distinguish the written and oral poetic traditions. On inspection, however, these two criteria appear less stable than one might have thought.

The solidity of the " author " has been dissolving for some time in the crucible of psychology, sociology, and literary history itself. The boundaries between the " writer " and all those, dead and alive, with whom he is in communion, for instance, are less clearly defined than they once seemed to be. Many texts themselves appear to be elaborations and combinations of other texts. Among the author's various manuscripts, representing different stages in the creation of the final text that passes for the work, and among the

[15] *Writing Degree Zero*, p. 55. Cf. Sartre, *Qu'est-ce que la littérature* (1948), ch. 3.

[16] Lotman also distinguishes between esthetic structures with predominantly intratextual relations, which are thus perceived as artistically complex (medieval art, folklore, baroque, romanticism), and esthetic structures with predominantly contextual relations, which are perceived as artistically simple (classicism and realism). The distinction cuts across and complicates that between the esthetics of identity and the esthetics of opposition, but it still ignores the boundary between oral and written; cf. Lotman, *op. cit.*, p. 179 *et passim*.

various editions of printed texts themselves, where should we look
for the "true" embodiment of the author, the version that best
fulfills "his" intention? The thing we call the work may be one
crystallization of a scenario or program, of which there were other
crystallizations, some preserved, though not easily visible, others
erased, accidentally or deliberately.[17] Besides, the mere graphic
recording of a *parole* does not commit us to a belief in a substantial
and autonomous self behind it or incorporated in it. It remains
arguable at least that there is no original individual essence supporting the *parole* and embodying itself in it. This position is fully
assumed and made explicit, in fact, by some modern writers, such as
the German poet, quoted by Hans Blumenberg, who prefaced a
collection of his poems with the comment: "If some lucky lines on
the pages of this book are successful, may the reader please forgive
me the discourtesy of having usurped them. Our playing—yours
and mine—is not very different: the circumstance that you are the
reader and I the composer of these exercises is trivial and accidental."[18] The point of the comment is surely that the work is no
closer to—or more alien from—the subjectivity of the author than
that of the reader.

The autonomy and individuality of post-Renaissance writers, in
other words, may well be a matter of ideology. Even as an idea,
moreover, it has not been consistently at the centre of all esthetic
systems since the Renaissance. Older modes and ideas of literary
practice survived well into the age of print and private property.[19]
Classical esthetics in particular was not favorable to the notion of
auctorial originality and individuality. "We nourish ourselves on

[17] Illustrations of changes in the printed versions of poetry from one edition
to another have been brought together by A. F. Scott, *The Poet's Craft*, Cambridge, 1957. Among novels, obvious examples of texts that evolved considerably
are Flaubert's *Education sentimentale* and *Tentation de Saint Antoine*. Many
nineteenth century English novels also exist in several "texts," though this
problem has not attracted much critical attention (see Royal Gettman, *A
Victorian Publisher*, Cambridge, 1960, ch. 8). On the fluidity of the concept of
"text," see Lotman, p. 154.

[18] Hans Blumenberg, "Die essentielle Vieldeutigkeit des ästhetischen Gegen-
standes," *Actes du V*[e] *Colloque International d'"Esthétique* (Amsterdam 1964),
The Hague, 1968, pp. 64-70.

[19] On medieval conceptions of authorship, see E. P. Goldschmitt, *Medieval
Texts and their first Appearance in Print*, Oxford, 1943; also John Livingston
Lowes, *Convention and Revolt in Poetry*, Boston, 1922, Charles Lalo, *L'Art et la
vie sociale*, Paris, 1921, pp. 52-54, and Marshall McLuhan, *The Gutenburg
Galaxy*, Toronto, 1962.

the ancients and ingenious moderns," La Bruyère observed of the *Modernes* in the famous *Querelle*: "We squeeze, we draw from them as much as we can, we rifle their works, and when at last we become authors, and think we can walk alone and without help, we oppose our benefactors, and treat them like those children, who, grown pert and strong with the milk they have sucked, turn themselves against their nurses." [20]   On the fringes of high literature many writers were still willing to co-operate openly not only with the dead, but with the living too. The *Contes* attributed to Perrault, for instance, are an amazing conflation of folk materials and successive literary improvisations by various hands from the same coterie.[21] At the beginning of the eighteenth century, Lesage, d'Orneval and Fuzelier collaborated on a large number of plays in the commedia tradition for the Théâtre de la Foire. Diderot's contribution, half a century later, to the *Encylopédie,* to the *Correspondance littéraire* of Grimm and to Raynal's *Histoire des Indes* is hard to ascertain, and Diderot himself was not concerned to distinguish it.[22]

By the eighteenth century, to be sure, a different conception of literary property, of the literary product and of literary creation itself was already well established. But some writers who still remained close to older communal ways and ideas were acutely conscious of their passing. The conflict of two esthetics is reflected in Diderot's work, for instance, in the contrast between Rameau's nephew, the brilliant medium and improviser, and his rather colorless conversation partner Moi, who is nevertheless, as narrator of the tale in which they both figure as characters, the creator and writer of the enduring—and inexhaustibly signifying—text we still read today. A similar conflict runs through the celebrated correspondence with the sculptor Falconet. Diderot was himself troubled by the fear that he was "dissipating" his talents in co-operative works, in advice to friends, in talk. In a well known passage from his correspondence with Sophie Volland he likens his fellowtownsmen of Langres to weathercocks and adds somewhat ruefully: "As for me, I am a man of my home town; only residence in the

[20] "Des Ouvrages de l'esprit," in *Les Caractères.*

[21] See Marc Soriano, *Les Contes de Perrault: culture savante et traditions populaires,* Paris, 1968.

[22] See Michèle Duchet in *Revue d'Histoire Littéraire de la France,* 1960, 60: 531-56.

capital and assiduous application have corrected me a little." [23] It
is probably not indifferent that Diderot began his career with a
translation. " I read and reread him," he wrote at the beginning
of his translation of Shaftesbury's *Inquiry concerning Virtue and
Merit.* " I filled myself with his spirit; and I closed his book, so
to speak, at the moment that I took up my pen." [24] To some extent,
it could be argued, Diderot thought of all creation as translation.
As late as 1828 we can still set the words of Goethe to Eckermann
against Rousseau's ambition to cleanse his work of all otherness and
make it a pure embodiment of his own unique self: " The Germans
cannot cease to be Philistines. They are now squabbling about
some verses which are printed both in Schiller's work and in mine,
and fancy it is important to ascertain which really belong to
Schiller and which to me; as if anything could be gained by such
an investigation, as if the existence of such things were not enough.
. . . What matters the mine and the thine? One must be a thorough
Philistine, indeed, to attach the slightest importance to the solution
of such questions." [25]

Autonomy, originality, and self-expression, were thus fairly slow
to establish themselves either as a description of, or as a prescrip-
tion for, literary activity, and throughout the seventeenth and
eighteenth centuries, it seems fairly safe to assume, many writers
might have thought of themselves as artists in a way not too re-
motely unlike that in which the best singers of Russian *bylini* or
the Serbian epic singers studied by Lord were great artists in their
tradition. " In a game of tennis," Pascal remarked in a *pensée*
concerning style, " both partners play with the same ball, but one
of them returns it better." [26] In our own time Charles Dullin
once compared the classical playwrights to performers or producers,
interpreters like himself. "After all, what did Molière and
Corneille do all their lives but adapt? " [27]

It is worth recalling, moreover, that on their side the folklorists,

[23] Letter to Sophie Volland, 10 August, 1759.

[24] *Oeuvres*, ed. Assezat, vol. 1, p. 16.

[25] 16 December, 1828. The erosion of bourgeois individualism in recent times
has led to several attempts to get away from the bourgeois conception of
literary property. In his autobiographical sketch, *I myself*, under the year 1920,
Mayakovski notes: " Finished *150,000,000*. Published it without my name.
Wanted anyone who wished to continue and improve it."

[26] *Pensées*, ed. Brunschvicg, n° 22.

[27] Quoted by André Veinstein, *La Mise en scene théâtrale et sa condition
esthétique*, Paris, 1955, p. 297.

especially the Russian school, have come to emphasize the peculiar talents and styles of individual artists among the folk.[28] It is true that in most oral cultures gifted artists who have been heard to recount the same tale in different ways will deny ever changing a word or a line of the canon.[29] But they do so only because they do not think of the work as existing in their particular utterance of it. Fidelity to them means working within a given scheme and preserving both the scheme and the thematics, rather than repeating something word for word. The very notion "word for word"—which is surely closely linked to the written text—seems not to be meaningful to them. In all probability, it was only gradually, and in combination with a variety of historical circumstances, that the identification of works with individual graphically recorded utterances led to a conception of literary creation as absolutely original production, arising out of and in some way embodying a unique, substantial and autonomous self.

It seems, in short, that while there are real differences of literary practice between oral and literate poets, the conventions and values of his society, as well as the nature of oral composition itself, make the oral poet blind to whatever contribution he himself makes to the tradition, while different conventions and values and a different mode of existence of the written, and particularly of the printed, literary product encourage the literate poet—within a certain period of history at least—to deny that there is anything in his work that

---

[28] As early as 1873 Hilferding had begun to classify Russian folk material by author or singer rather than by genre, but the model for many folklorists has been Mark Azadowski's study of Vinokurova, the great Siberian *bylini* singer (*Eine sibirische Märchenerzählerin*, Helsinki, 1926, Folklore Fellows Communications, 68).

[29] Cf. Lord, *op. cit.*; Iurii Sokolov, *Russian Folklore*, transl. C. R. Smith, New York, 1950; J. H. Delargy, "The Gaelic Story-Teller," *Proceedings of the British Academy*, 1945, 31: 177-221; Linda Dégh, *Märchen, Erzähler und Erzählgemeinschaft*, Berlin, 1962; Ruth Finnegan, *Limba Stories and Story-Telling*, Oxford, 1967; see also Cecil Sharp, Introduction to *English Folk Songs from the Southern Appalachians*, 1917; Ruth Benedict, *Zuni Mythology*, New York, 1934; Geneviève Calame-Griaule, "Pour une étude ethnolinguistique des littératures orales africaines," *Langages*, 1970, 18: 22-47. In some cultures strict fidelity to tradition in more than fixed form types does, however, seem to obtain, according to some observers; cf. Mary M. Edel, "Stability in Tillamook Folklore," *Journal of American Folklore*, 1944, 57: 116-27, and Nora K. Chadwick and Viktor Zhirmunsky, *Oral Epics of Central Asia*, Cambridge, 1969, pp. 224-25, on the Turkmens of Central Asia. Nevertheless, the Chadwicks considered that strict memorizing was to be regarded as exceptional (H. Munro Chadwick and Nora K. Chadwick, *The Growth of Literature*, vol. III, Cambridge, 1940, pp. 867-69).

is *not* his own. Conceiving himself not as a vessel, through which
the tradition passes to be actualized for the community, but as an
isolated individual objectifying an individual discourse, he tries,
by establishing that it is his " property," to reappropriate that part
of him which he feels is objectified in his discourse and to which
he owes both an intense feeling of individual identity and a
sinking sense of alienation of that identity.

Even the fixity of the written work, which is usually contrasted
with the unstable oral tradition, cannot be simply taken for
granted. We have already alluded to the material instability of a
" text " which may exist in various manuscript and printed versions. But, the text itself—the permanent graphic imprint—is not
identical with the work. Let us imagine a text which exists,
apparently, in fragmentary or somehow unfinished form. (Pascal's
Pensées might serve as an example of such a text.) Whether we consider its fragmentariness to be the result of some mechanical defect
or accident, or part of the author's design, will make all the
difference to our idea of the work represented by this text. In order
to form a conception of the work, therefore, we have to go beyond
the text itself to the context—what we know of the author's intentions, for instance, or of the esthetics of the period.

In general, the relative material stability of the written or printed
text is complemented by an extremely mobile element which is as
indispensable to the realization of the literary work as the graphic
inscription itself. It is characteristic of all literary works, written
or oral—that is, of all works which we decide to consider as
literature—that unlike mere reporting, say, they are intended—or
we judge them worthy—to be heard or read more than once.[30]
Successive readings (or performances) of the same text, like successive performances of the same oral programme, will, however, be
different. This is easily accepted in the case of performances of oral
works, but it is also true of written or printed texts. Indeed it is
well known that against a background of identity—the same musical
score, for instance, performed on different occasions or by different
performers—differences are the more acutely perceived. Theatrical
performances of dramatic texts provide another illustration of this
principle. Erwin Piscator has commented interestingly on two productions of Schiller's *Die Räuber* which he directed, the first in

---

[30] This point is made vividly by C. S. Lewis, *An Experiment in Criticism*,
Cambridge, 1962, p. 2.

Berlin in 1926, and the second in Mannheim in 1957. In 1926, he tells, the political situation was revolutionary, and Schiller's play was presented as a call to sustain revolutionary activity. The play's dramatic elements were therefore foregrounded in the early production, while the cynical reflective monologues of Franz were allowed to retreat into the background. The 1957 production took place in the totally different political and social conditions of what Piscator calls a successful Restoration. Deeply grounded doubts that any revolutionary might harbor had risen to the surface, and Piscator therefore highlighted the monologues.[31] As Lotman put it, increasing the element of identity in two "readings" to the point of complete coincidence of the textual parts throws into relief the parts that do not coincide.[32]

One might imagine that such difficulties are overcome and complete identity achieved in cases where variation is reduced to zero by the absence of a live interpreter or executant, as in works of figurative art, movies, music on records or tape, and productions of literary art which are meant to be read silently, with the eyes. It is doubtful that this is so, however. The work of art is not exhausted in the text (the score in music, the material part of a figurative work) but resides rather in "a relation of textual and extra- or con-textual systems," to quote Lotman again.[33] Without taking into account the contextual situation—the absent text, for instance, to which a given text is opposed and which thus constitutes its context, the tradition of which it is part and which may be incorporated in it as a complex pattern of quotations, allusions and parodies, and in general the framework of beliefs and expectations in which it is or once was perceived—it is not even possible to determine what the structurally active and significant elements in the text are, or once were. The writer himself may point to the context he intends for his work. Lotman observes that even as he broke down the old rhythmic system of Russian poetry, Mayakovski was careful to keep the memory of it alive in the reader's aware-

---

[31] *World Theatre*, 1968, 17: 337-45. Cf. Gaston Baty's account of three versions of a scene from *Le Malade imaginaire* in *Théâtre*, ed. Paul Arnold, Paris, 1945, pp. 91-96.

[32] Lotman, *op. cit.*, p. 84.

[33] *Ibid.*, p. 85. The position is not an unfamiliar one. It is implied by C. S. Lewis, for instance, when he points out that *vers libre*, far from being simpler than metrical poetry, can be appreciated only by an ear well trained in metrical poetry (*op. cit.*, p. 103). Not surprisingly, Lewis defends literary history as an aid to appreciation (p. 121).

ness.[34] In time, however, we may lose sight of the author's context,
and one of the most important tasks of literary history, probably,
is to reconstruct it. Unless we view Wordsworth's prosody, for
instance, against the background of eighteenth-century verse, we
shall not know what to contemporaries was artistically effective in
it. Moreover, as Wordsworth's prosody came to constitute, in its
turn, the context of reader's expectations, the esthetic norm, his
poetry was perceived by a new generation of readers in a quite
different light from that in which it was perceived by his contemporaries. It may not be entirely fanciful to speak of two different
bodies of poetry. Similarly, a change in the contextual system may
alter the relation of the various language functions in a work
(expressive, communicative or denotative, poetic, conative), so
that a work of history, for instance, or an autobiography, or a
political pamphlet, in which the communicative or the conative
function was once prominent, may in course of time come to be
perceived in such a way that the poetic function dominates the
others.

Changes in the contextual system, in short, produce changes in
the degree of structural activity of the various elements making up
the complex ensemble of the work. And such changes in the contextual system occur both in the course of history and in the normal
life of the individual consciousness. Not everything that is present
in a work is revealed to every reader at a single moment in his life.
The self-identity of the written text is thus an abstraction, which is
arrived at only by amputating from the work the contextual system
without which it can have no meaning. The point was made
simply by T. S. Eliot in the well-known essay on *Tradition and
Individual Talent*: " No poet, no artist of any kind has complete
meaning alone. His significance, his appreciation is the appreciation of his relation to the dead poets and artists. You cannot
value him alone; you must set him, for contrast and comparison,
among the dead. I mean this as a principle of esthetic, not merely
historical criticism. . . . What happens when a new work of art is
created is something that happens simultaneously to all the works
of art which preceded it. The existing monuments form an ideal

---

[34] Lotman, *op. cit.*, p. 113. Cf. W. K. Wimsatt, *art. cit.*—" The escape from
models (in eighteenth century poetry—L. G.) was freedom, was expression, was
fun, only so long as the models were present as fields of reference for the
realization of new meanings. . . ."

order among themselves, which is modified by the introduction of the new (the really new) work of art among them." It is not preposterous, Eliot concludes, " that the past should be altered by the present as much as the present is guided by the past."

The written work of literature—" that strange spinning top," as Sartre calls it, " which exists only in movement " [35]—is thus, despite the—only relative—material stability of the text, no less dependent on performance of a kind than the oral one. It is always subject to variation according to the light that is projected upon it and the background against which it is viewed. The *Phèdre* that I hold in my hands in 1970 is not the work that was known to its first readers or even to the author himself. Nor can I hope to ressuscitate exactly the contextual structure of Racine's time, in relation to which the text was then perceived. It is not simply that to ressuscitate it I should have to know everything that Racine and his contemporaries knew (as a literary historian I may and must approach such a goal even though I cannot reach it) but that I should have to un-know many things which enter into the perceptual context of our own time and of which Racine was necessarily ignorant. There is, in sum, a sort of feedback effect from the user of literary texts to the texts themselves, and this effect, which makes for the polyvalence of the text—what Plato condemned as its uncertainty—also guarantees its longevity and its capacity, within limits prescribed by its objective structure, to impart different information to different users at different times, and even to the same users at different times, or to different users at the same time. Texts, in short, are a little like those medals which, according to the author of a " Discours sur les Maximes " appended to the 1665 edition of La Rochefoucauld's work, " represent the figure of a Saint and that of a Demon on the same face and by the same marks. Only the different positions of those looking at the medal change the object that they see. One sees the Saint, the other the Demon." [36] More dryly, Lotman observes that " in art . . . the sign, or the element discriminating its meaning, may be projected against many backgrounds, becoming in each case a bearer of different meanings.[37] It was this characteristic of works of art,

[35] *Qu'est-ce que la littérature?*, Paris, 1948, Collection " Idées," p. 52. See also some pertinent observations by Northrop Frye, " The Critical Path," *Daedalus*, 1970, 99: 268-342, on pp. 322-25.

[36] Edition of Paris, 1714, pp. 18-19.

[37] Lotman, *op. cit.*, p. 42. Cf. Felix Vodička, " The History of the Echo of Literary Works," in Paul Garvin, ed., *A Prague School Reader in Esthetics,*

perhaps, that Schiller tried to define, when he argued in the
Letters on the Aesthetic Education of Man that the work of art
combines freedom with law or limitation, its indeterminacy being
not an empty infinity ("leere Unendlichkeit") but rather a filled
infinity or all-inclusiveness ("erfüllte Unendlichkeit").

Performance thus appears essential to both written and oral
literature. But in different ways. The number of different performances in an oral culture is obviously infinite, but the range of
difference is fairly limited. All individuals do change, of course, if
only as they age, and one can imagine that a Russian recruiting
song, for example, might signify differently to a woman who had
seen a son or a husband drafted into the army and to one who
had no immediate experience of this tragedy. (In Czarist Russia
the period of service was something like twenty years!) Likewise,
many works of ritual and liturgical art change their meanings or
acquire new meanings in the course of the experience of a lifetime.
Nevertheless, even the scope of personal development is probably
restricted in oral cultures by the limited range of available experience. The homogeneity imposed by a relatively narrow range of
possible activities and experiences is consolidated, moreover, by
the strong mutual identification with each other of which the
members of oral communities seem unusually capable. Most importantly, oral literature is in large measure synchronic, like the
spoken language itself.[38] The entire tradition is immediately present and only immediately present. Nothing can be retrieved that
has slipped from memory; almost all the elements in the tradition
are thus fully intelligible in the light of present experience. There
can be few problems of interpretation, since the process of preserva-

Literary Structure and Style, Washington, D. C., 1964, pp. 71-78: "As soon as
the work is perceived on the basis of the integration into another context (a
changed linguistic state of affairs, other literary requirements, a changed
social structure, a new set of spiritual and practical values), then precisely
those qualities of the work can be perceived as esthetically effective which previously were not perceived as esthetically effective, so that a positive evaluation
may be based on entirely opposite reasons." (p. 79).

[38] Edward Stankiewicz contrasts poetry, which he considers a-synchronic, with
language, which *is* synchronic. "We return often to poetic traditions. Non-
poetic, ordinary language knows no returns; it is a progressive development in
time" (Sebeok, 1960, p. 430). Oral literature, however, *is* like language in this
sense, as Bogatyrev and Jakobson affirmed. On the synchronic character of oral
culture in general, see Jack Goody and Ian Watt, "The Consequences of
Literacy," in J. Goody, ed., *Literacy in Transitional Societies*, Cambridge, 1968,
pp. 27-68, especially pp. 30-31.

tion is at the same time a process of interpretation. Written literature, on the other hand, is a-synchronic, since texts from various periods, crystallisations of various moments in the literary tradition, are preserved graphically and are available to subsequent generations of readers and writers as well as to totally non-indigenous groups. Code and performance are separated, and interpretation becomes a central concern. The history of religion would doubtless offer telling illustrations of this passage from the synchronic to the a-synchronic. I shall use a simpler example.

Where proverbs are alive in an oral tradition, their meaning is never in doubt, even though it may vary with the context in which the proverb is used. " Every mickle maks a muckle," for instance, could be used positively as an encouragement to save or negatively as a warning against the cumulative effect of slight misdemeanors. But neither the user nor the listener will be in any doubt as to the appropriate meaning, and neither will distinguish between the form of the statement and its meaning. There will be no sense of *contradiction* between different usages. It is the collector of proverbs who becomes aware of them as structures distinct from their meanings and capable of generating meanings. Thus in England and France " rolling stones gather no moss " (" pierres qui roulent n'amassent pas mousse ") is universally taken to mean that if you wander about too much you will never settle down anywhere and build yourself a comfortable and enduring home. When I was a boy in Calvinist Scotland, however, I had no doubt, nor did any of my school-fellows or teachers, among whom it was popular, that it meant the opposite: if you don't keep moving and striving, you'll never amount to anything. You might have difficulty getting a user of proverbs to explicate the meaning of a particular proverb, but he will almost invariably be able to distinguish proper and improper usage. To someone who is not a user of proverbs, on the other hand—and I suspect the use of proverbs has been in decline since the last century—any proverb is problematic. I have asked several of my students at Johns Hopkins what they understand by " rolling stones gather no moss " and I find that many hesitate and will subsequently entertain both the meanings I proffer. Their hesitation, I am convinced,. has nothing to do with inability to explicate, but stems rather from lack of practice in using the proverb. To them, in short, it has become a *text*, like a passage from the Bible or from Shakespeare. Conversely, I would suspect, certain texts which have entered the popular culture to some extent—*Pilgrim's Progress* (until recently) or, in France, Hugo's *Les Misérables*—are not perceived as *texts,* but come, like oral materials, already fully clad in an interpretation that is part of a tradition.

The a-synchronic character of written literature radically alters the range of possible relations between artists and public and between both and the tradition. An oral culture need not, of course, be uniform. It may be made up of an infinite number of particular local, professional or even family traditions, but the point is that it is fully familiar to all those who are part of it and unknown to those who are not. It does not even offer itself to the outsider. The written tradition, on the other hand, is in principle open and universal. (It is no accident surely that universal religions are religions of scripture.) [39] Yet it is this very quality that makes it problematic. For while the texts are in principle universally available, the keys by which they can be deciphered are not. The very ability to read written characters was long the privilege of a few, and far from being a unifying force, writing was a divisive one. In a complex literate society the tradition may come to resemble a vast museum, filled with the discrete or only mysteriously interrelated relics and monuments of the past, to which a multiplicity of social classes and groups have widely varying access.

For the writer such a cultural environment may mean that the range of materials which he can draw upon in the creation of his own work in vastly enlarged and that his powers of selection and arrangement, as well as his personal responsibility, are enhanced. As Bogatyrev and Jakobson pointed out in their article, there is little or no variety of styles in individual folklore traditions, corresponding to different esthetic models or intentions. Variety is determined solely by the different folklore " genres " (saga, legend, anecdote, song, riddle, charm, etc.). Written literature, on the other hand, may embrace in a single period a number of schools of writers with independent or rival styles. Similarly, oral literature knows nothing of the revivals and renaissances which characterize written literature and which are due both to the physical preservation or recovery of past materials and to variations in the contexts of esthetic perception.

For the reader—and the artist is also a reader in so far as he too

[39] See on this Jack Goody, *op. cit.,* pp. 2-3, *et passim.*

must be a reader of others' works in order to produce his own—the passage from an oral to a written culture may mean an immense expansion of the scope of literature. Innumerable individual literary acts, performed at various moments in the course of the literary culture and graphically preserved as texts, are constantly available to be projected against a wide range of contexts, no single one of which, perhaps, need be considered the sole appropriate one. The feed-back from user to work, to which we alluded earlier, releases the text, potentially, from bondage to any particular context. The possibility that thus arises both of historically reconstructing the successive contexts in which a work has come alive and, in general, of multiplying the contexts in which we can view it by projecting on to it the light of our modern awareness and our modern disciplines—sociology, psychology, philosophy, etc.—enhances both the power of the text and the scope of our imaginative response to it. For each context will activate the potentialities of the text in a different way, by making different elements in it emerge as structurally significant. The effect we have in mind is similar to what is achieved in the theatre by the now familiar technique of shunting a text from one historical setting to another (performing Shakespeare in Victorian setting and dress, etc.). The historicity which characterizes the written work of literature is thus the condition of the active and creative relation in which the reader stands to it. Indeed, it seems that, far from fixing or controlling a work and its meanings, the written text allows them to be released and engendered. "To write," Barthes observes, "is to offer your word (*parole*) to others, that they may complete it." [40] As it becomes unmoored from its original source and context and floats out into history, the written text lays itself open, like that "most ambiguous object imaginable," which Valéry's Socrates found on the beach, to varied and fruitful encounters.[41] The oral work, on the other hand,

[40] Barthes, *art. cit.*, p. 17. In similar vein, Pierre Boulez, *Pensez la musique d'aujourd'hui*, 1963, quoted by H. Osborne, *Aesthetics and Art Theory*, London, 1967, p. 188: "It remains fundamental in my view to safeguard unknown potential which lies enclosed within a masterpiece of art. I am convinced that the author, however perspicacious he may be, cannot conceive the consequences—immediate or distant—of what he has written." All these comments recall Roman Ingarden's discussion of the determinate qualities and the indeterminate areas of the work of art. The possible or legitimate concretions of a work of art are negatively determined, according to Ingarden, but never completely determinate (*Das literarische Kunstwerk*, Halle, 1931).

[41] See *Eupalinos ou l'architecte*, in *Oeuvres*, vol. 1, Paris, 1931, pp. 133-42.

while it undergoes change, remains always, on any given occasion, undivided and fully present in its performance.

The reader's freedom, however, places on him the responsibility for selecting a context in which to situate the text and finding a key to decipher it with. In oral cultures, as I suggested, the tradition is internalized by all the members of the oral community and the same knowledge and culture may be said to be shared *mutatis mutandis* by all of them alike. It is thus easy to see why all the members of an oral community perceive a work in more or less the same way, and are also, on the whole, widely *capable* of perceiving it, even if there are differences of sensibility among them, as there are among human beings in any culture. As Paul Radin put it, summing up the views of many folklorists and anthropologists, "an audience in an aboriginal tribe is far better prepared to understand the implications of their literature than we are of our own. Every person there—parts of Africa and Polynesia-Micronesia excepted—has an all-embracing knowledge of his culture and participates in every aspect of it; every person has a complete knowledge of his language. There are no 'illiterate' or ignorant individuals." [42] In literate cultures, on the other hand, the tradition is not homogeneous or immediately present, and while this widens the range of possible contexts and thus of possible meanings of a text, it may also, in the case of the poorly prepared or inadequately educated reader, make the context completely problematic and the text, in consequence, opaque, inert, and meaningless. "The work exists," in Sartre's phrase, "only at the level of the reader's capacity." [43]

This is all the more likely to happen as works in the written tradition are characterized by a richness of implicit and explicit quotation from and reference to other texts, by a textual volume or density which makes great demands even on the cultivated reader. The text, in other words, may be not only hard to separate from, but well-nigh unintelligible outside of a complex pattern of intertextual references. Where the cultural development of the various groups and classes making up a society is seriously uneven or discontinuous, where there is no common language, and where literature, in consequence, has become a highly specialized activity, related to the language of a restricted and exclusive class, the freedom which the written tradition can introduce into the reader's

[42] "The Literature of Primitive People," *Diogenes*, 1955, 12: 1-28, on p. 3.
[43] *Quest-ce que la littérature?*, p. 59.

relation to works of literature will thus be at the same time a cause of bewilderment and estrangement to the many.

Historically, it may be, writing first divided the community only into those who had access to written culture and those who remained enclosed within the immediacy of oral culture. Both cultures, however, may have been relatively homogeneous at first. Though the revival of classical literature at the Renaissance implied the possibility of further revivals, the classical tradition was for a long time the only model for the modern literate writer; the canons and criteria of classical literature were experienced as in a sense present, because a-temporal, eternally true. On its side, the public too remained relatively homogeneous; it recognized immediately both the models to which the works of its writers referred and the models—often in the folk culture—to which they were opposed. Even in the seventeenth and eighteenth centuries the interplay of various rhetorical styles—Ciceronian eloquence and "style coupé," the style of the Ancients and the style of the Moderns—occurred within a single, generally accepted tradition. They were thought of as constituting the unchanging repertory of ornamental options available to the civilized writer as he set out to clothe his thought. The very idea of revivals and renaissances is probably linked to some such notion of a fixed repertory. Even the *Querelle des Anciens et des Modernes* had a model in Roman times, and those who took up the fight again in the late seventeenth and early eighteenth centuries might well have thought of themselves as reenacting an eternal scenario. This was, after all, the way in which the early Enlighteners and champions of "philosophie" thought of themselves. The illusion of universality, the absence of a sense of history, in our meaning of the term, from the literary consciousness of the classical period, from the Renaissance down to the eighteenth century, reflects both the relative homogeneity of the culture of this period and the relative slowness of objective social change. The range of contexts against which a text could be projected in order to be realized or concretized remained limited and fairly familiar to all citizens of the Republic of Letters.

In the course of the late eighteenth and early nineteenth centuries, however, a new esthetic situation seems to have arisen, doubtless as a consequence of altered historical conditions.

The educated bourgeoisie of the ancien régime occupied commanding positions of power and influence, but birth, even without letters, still remained a tangible value, and in a totally different and relatively autonomous sector of society, the old folk culture survived richly. In the nineteenth century the culture of the bourgeoisie, the symbolic counterpart of its economic and political power, had virtually ousted all other values. Acquisition of this culture, literacy and education, came to seem like stages on the road to power and prestige in a society that proclaimed itself "open to the talents." At the same time, commerce, industry and rapid urbanization broke up and transformed the rural communities, the erstwhile members of which, if they were ambitious, tried both to satisfy their own cultural needs and to improve their lot by the acquisition of the culture of the dominant class. In the end, the very success of the bourgeoisie in imposing its order and its values was at least one of the factors that contributed to overturn the long-established and relatively stable division of society into an illiterate folk reared in its traditional folkways, and a literate upper class trained in the classical and contemporary languages and literatures, and attuned to the texts which were the constant point of reference of its own writers. A multiplicity of publics of extremely uneven cultural backgrounds came into being and these finally undermined the political and, to some extent, the cultural hegemony of the old European *grande bourgeoisie*, that "great confederation," in Matthew Arnold's words, "whose members have, for their proper outfit, a knowledge of Greek, Roman and Eastern antiquities, and of one another." [44]

Released from direct relation to a collectivity, writers and artists achieved greater freedom than had probably ever been known, and this freedom with its attendant variety of traditions and styles emancipated literary language from any "natural" context and brought its specifically literary nature into view. The space between the language of ordinary use and literary language became a gulf, and literary language must have appeared to many something *sui generis,* narcissistic and mysterious. Thus at the very moment when literate culture became a universally desirable commodity, both as the only feasible answer to genuine cultural needs and as a symbol of power and position in society, the possibility of acquiring it seems, for the vast majority, to have receded ever further out of reach. While a small number of unusually well prepared readers

[44] *The Function of Criticism* in *Complete Works,* vol. 3, Ann Arbor, 1962, p. 284.

came to enjoy a freer, and yet narrower and more specialized, relation to works of literature than listeners in an oral culture could possibly enjoy, the vast majority found themselves virtually debarred from literary culture altogether, incapable of arriving at any adequate perception of literary works at all.[45] I. A. Richards' evidence in *Practical Criticism* indicates that a school-sized dose of literary education does not necessarily cure this ill.

* * * * *

It is to the difficulties and injustices of life in modern open societies that we should probably attribute the remarkable survival, from the Renaissance to the present day, of the topos of the lost closed community. In the history of literature and in literary criticism this topos appears in the form of nostalgia for a lost oral culture.[46] Nostalgia for the oral—as for the " organic community "—

[45] George Miller put the problem wittily at the Indiana University Conference on Style. Developing the theme of predictability/unpredictability, expectation/surprise, norm/variation, which ran through many of the discussions, he used the analogy of the relation of probability to surprise in a bridge hand to illuminate the importance, for the " surprise " concept, of *value* in the context of the game, and went on to ask what the rules of the literary game are. Perhaps great writers change them, he suggested, so that the critic's job is to discover the new rules. At any rate, in his view, skilful people know them, at some level, and they can be learned (Sebeok, 1960, pp. 394-95). The problem is precisely that a) most people no longer intuitively know the rules, b) in our own period they are constantly being changed or scrambled, and c) they are not taught to most people.

[46] Also, to some extent, in the persistent reluctance of many critics and amateurs of poetry to admit as proper to it what is not spoken or can only be perceived by the eye. It is true that, even unspoken physically, the sound of the poem is still present for most readers as a background against which the printed text is perceived. But the latter may have its own conventions. " Any thorough formalistic analysis of the structure of poetry and of its relation to the language in which it is written," John Hollander writes, " must deal with the written language as a system in itself, as well as with the spoken one " (*The Untuning of the Sky,* Princeton, 1961, p. 7). From the camp of the linguists Angus McIntosh points out that written signs carry two information loads—linguistic meaning, a direct reference to the code, and phonic meaning, information on how to speak the message should this be desired ("' Graphology ' and Meaning," in A. McIntosh and M. A. K. Halliday, *Patterns of Language,* Bloomington, 1967, pp. 98-110). Clearly the two can function independently, and interplay between them enhances the possibilities of the poem. So too, in some recent writing, do typography and layout, which may also be made to convey their own load of information; in a poem, however, as distinct from a drawing, these visual messages are always in an intimate relation to the visual and spoken aspects of the linguistic message.

Suspicion of the written text probably goes back to suspicion of language in general. The view that " mere " words betray the living thoughts of which they is understandable, at several levels, but its implications should be recognized. Frequently, as Raymond Williams demonstrated, it signifies ambiguously both rejection of the cultural and ultimately social inequality that has impoverished the lives of large numbers of mankind and compartmentalized the faculties and activities of the privileged themselves, and at the same time flight from the reality of cultural and social problems—and choices—into a realm of fanciful and subjectively satisfying solutions.[47] In the end, longing for a lost community is an idle and regressive, if poignant indulgence; and as long as we continue to store our cultural products, it is hard to see what other solution there can be to the problem of estrangement, than education. It may well be, as Sartre says, that works of the mind, like bananas, should be consumed on the spot; it is not likely, however, that Sartre would have us jettison all our stored rations—though, of course, this solution has been proposed. And most of us don't know how to eat these naturally; we have to learn. Neither access to nor utilization of the literary tradition can be regarded as automatic.

To argue for literary education, however, is not necessarily to argue for the present practice and values of literary education. As things are at present, literary education, while it appears to mark a recognition of the importance of teaching the codes by which artistic productions can be deciphered, merely perpetuates and in a way consecrates the cultural inequalities which in our society

are the images, and that written words, as images of images, are even less trustworthy, is a persistent one and pervades what has been called the folklinguistics of Western culture (cf. H. M. Hoenigswald, "A Proposal for the Study of Folk-Linguistics" in W. Bright, ed., Sociolinguistics, The Hague, 1966, pp. 16-21). Jack Goody (op. cit., Introduction) shows that the prejudice is by no means confined to the West. The prejudice in favor of the spoken has, in addition, an echo in an important debate in linguistics, some linguists (Hjelmslev, Uldall, McIntosh, etc.) maintaining stoutly that the system of language is independent of the substance (the stream of air or the stream of ink) in which it is expressed, so that the privilege of the spoken is unwarranted; see B. Siertsema, A Study of Glossematics, The Hague, 1965, pp. 111-13, for some pertinent quotations; also A. McIntosh, art. cit., p. 99.

[47] Raymond Williams, Culture and Society, 1780-1950, London, 1958. See also Richard Altick, The English Common Reader, Chicago, 1957, and various articles by Leo Lowenthal and his associates: "The Debate over Art and Popular Culture in Eighteenth Century England" (with Marjorie Fiske Lowenthal) in Literature, Popular Culture and Society, Englewood Cliffs, 1961, "The Debate on Cultural Standards in Nineteenth Century England" (with Ina Lawson), Social Research, 1963, 30: 417-33, "Der menschliche Dialog" (Lowenthal's own independent critique of the mass media), Kölner Zeitschrift für Soziologie und Sozialpsychologie, 1969, 21: 463-73.

correspond to social divisions and inequalities. There seems little doubt that where the early foundations of a cultural education have not been provided by the home, the family, the total social environment of the individual, the school will at best, in most cases, turn out persons of timid and routinized culture, whereas the highest ideal of our present culture is to be free—free, that is, precisely from school origins and school patterns. This free culture is in fact accessible, for the most part, only to those who have had the benefit of a large cultural formation outside of the school. What mass literary education does, therefore, is make a cultural distinction, which itself rests on social inequality, appear natural, grounded in inequalities of natural endowment and merit. "By symbolically shifting the essential of what sets them apart from other classes from the economic field to that of culture, or rather, by adding to strictly economic differences, namely those created by the simple possession of material wealth, differences created by the possession of material wealth, differences created by the possession of symbolic wealth, such as works of art, or by the pursuit of symbolic distinctions in the manner of using such wealth (economic or symbolic), . . . the privileged members of middle-class society replace the difference between two cultures, historic products of social conditions, by the essential difference between two natures, a naturally cultivated nature and a naturally natural nature." Almost all Pierre Bourdieu's work, from which the preceding sentence was quoted, has tended to show how literary and artistic "education" plays its part in the consecration of the social order, enabling educated men to believe in barbarism and persuading the barbarians of their barbarity. The mere existence of public museums, cheap books, schools and teachers, in short, does not guarantee that literary education will be democratic.

It is also possible that a thoroughly democratic society will alter both the present emphases of literary culture and the present position of literature in relation to other expressions of culture. As Raymond Williams has pointed out, it has been characteristic of generations of reformers and public educators concerned with culture from within the bourgeoisie, the English one at least, that they have tried to affect and improve the culture of society without

[48] Pierre Bourdieu, "Outline of a Sociological Theory of Art Perception," *International Social Science Journal*, 1968, 20: 589-612, on pp. 609-11. See also J. A. Bizet, "L'Action culturelle et les produits artistiques," *La Pensée*, March-April, 1970, pp. 84-92.

having to alter it in a larger and more fundamental sense. The aim has almost invariably been to entrust education to a clerisy, in one form or another. Probably this has something to do with a Romantic notion of the receiver or reader of genius, corresponding to the author of genius, and as distinct as he from the mass, in whose talents as readers no confidence could ever, in the very nature of things, be placed. It has been assumed, correspondingly, that what should be taught and transmitted is what, traditionally, in the existing society, has been " culture." Since possession of this culture serves as a justification for the privileges of the privileged, the culture itself was not open to question. Works in the literary canon were not only judged universal and eternal, they were conceived uniquely in terms of classification and appropriation (or appreciation). They had not to be criticized but to be acquired. The reader's task was to discover the universal validity of the texts in the canon or, more recently, to bring them " up to date " and make them " relevant." There was rarely any attempt to reveal their rootedness in an historical commitment, conscious or unconscious, which the presentday reader might wish to criticize and reject. In so far as literary education, like much modern literature itself, refuses to be the servant of the present social conditions, I am not sure that it can be content with a combination of historical criticism and creative criticism—what Michael Hancher calls the science of interpretation (explaining the works of the past in the light of their own context, trying to recover their " essence ") and the art of interpretation (reviving and interpreting them in the light of our present culture, making them usable, so to speak, by reactivating selected elements in them).[49] What makes me uneasy, from my present point of view, about such an easygoing combination is not only that it leaves deliberately unresolved the philosophical question of the essence of the literary work, but that it proposes no challenge to the existing culture, which is, indeed, characterized by its powers of accommodation. As Umberto Eco has suggested, the dynamics of rediscovery and revitalisation of past cultural products, which at the Renaissance was accompanied by a global restructuring of rhetorics and ideologies, occurs in our time at the surface of culture and leaves its basis relatively little affected.[50]

[49] Michael Hancher, " The Science of Interpretation and the Art of Interpretation," *MLN*, 1970, 85: 791-802.
[50] Umberto Eco, " Formes et communication," *Revue Internationale de Philosophie*, 1967, 21: 231-51.

It is not clear, as matters stand, how literary education can stop serving as a conservative ideological force. Perhaps a first step might be the adoption of a radically critical and alienating stance, from which the intimate relation of ideology and rhetoric could be explored and revealed, so that nothing in the literary tradition could any more seem innocent. In a moving passage at the end of *Writing Degree Zero*, Barthes summarizes the dilemma of modern literature, that is of literature which is acutely aware of its own literariness. " Literary writing," he says, " carries at the same time the alienation of History and the dream of History: as a Necessity, it testifies to the division of language which is inseparable from the division of classes; as Freedom, it is the consciousness of this division and the very effort which seeks to surmount it." Perhaps it should be a part of literary education to show the rootedness of all writing in a condition of language and ultimately of social and class relations. But it would be foolish, I think, to imagine that techniques of demystification will in themselves produce the conditions for democratic culture or democratic literary education. They may easily become only another cultural commodity to be appropriated and used as a sign and confirmation of privilege. It would be idle to speculate on the form literary culture will take in a possible democratic society or on the relation which such a society will entertain to the literary heritage as we envisage it in our society. As teachers of literature at the present time, we cannot much affect the place literature occupies in the social system of which we are ourselves, often unconsciously, the instruments. Indeed, that place may already be changing, as other symbolic values usurp the predominant place of literature, and to the extent that it is, so, we may be sure, is ours. As citizens, however, we may wish to work toward a society in which neither literature nor any other cultural product will function as a means of social and political exclusion and domination.

1971

NOTES ON THE CHARACTERIZATION OF A LITERARY TEXT ❦ BY EDWARD W. SAID ❦

> Thus it is true that the life of an author can teach us nothing and that—if we know how to interpret it—we can find everything in it, since it opens onto his work.
>
> Merleau-Ponty

I

In the 1968 survey he wrote of structuralism Jean Piaget broadly defined a structure as being a system of transformations, second, a totality, and third, capable of self-regulation (*autoréglage*).[1] These three characterizations of structure are obviously interconnected— and Piaget goes on to discuss their links—yet individually liable to different emphases within the various disciplines influenced by structuralist thought. To his analysis, however, Piaget brings his own formidable experience as a psychological empiricist and theoretician. For him the central problem in all structuralist theory is that of the connection between antecedence and constructivism, which raises the following series of questions: "les totalités par composition sont-elles composés de tout temps, mais comment ou par qui, ou ont-elles été d'abord (et sont-elles toujours?) en voie de composition?"[2] These issues have as much a bearing on Piaget's theses in genetic epistemology as they do, I think, on the theme of this essay. For despite recent tendencies in criticism (in, for example, the work of Roland Barthes) certain conventions, persisting perhaps from the late nineteenth century, have a strong hold upon the critical imagination. Thus we still have to deal with the nature of the author's *authority* over his text, with the origins and development of an author's work, with the location in time and in

[1] Jean Piaget, *Le Structuralisme* (Paris, 1968), pp. 5-16.
[2] *Ibid.*, p. 10.

society of a text, and with the sequential construction of a literary totality viewed as an ensemble of made relationships. Here is how Piaget phrases his own position:

> La genèse n'est jamais que le passage d'une structure à une autre, mais *un passage formateur qui conduit du plus faible au plus fort,* et la structure n'est jamais qu'un système de transformations, mais dont les racines sont opératoires et tiennent donc à une formation préalable des instruments adéquats . . . D'où cette conclusion, que la nature du sujet est de constituer un centre de fonctionement et non pas le siège *a priori* d'un édifice achevé; et si l'on remplace le sujet par une unité sociale, ou par l'espèce, ou la vie, ou même l'univers, il en sera encore ainsi.[3] (italics mine)

There are two important observations here: I shall consider them in reverse order, the second one first. Piaget makes a distinction between two possible conceptions of the subject (" la nature du sujet "), that is, the effective and centering motor principle in a structure. One is a conception of subject as pre-existing given, as a necessary *a priori* condition *for* the fully formed structure. The perspective accepted in this conception is wholly that of the completed structure, not as developing but as already developed. Opposed to this conception, with which Piaget is uneasy, is a view of the subject as a germinal principle whose force extends through, and therefore enables, a developing, constituting structure. Grossly dramatized then, the contrast is between a Platonic essence of priority, more formal and logically necessary than efficient, and a plastic, quasi-organic principle of growth, which goes from simple to more complex. At any rate the latter conception is central, whereas the former is practically marginal. I think it ought to be added that Piaget himself would be likely to consider this contrast as not exhausting our notions of " the subject," nor certainly of center, nor of genesis. The polarity he sets up is not only extreme but convenient, and this for reasons that have mostly to do with the type of experiments in psychological development he has been conducting for many years. For an example of the polemical uses to which the polarity might be put (but wouldn't be, I think, by Piaget himself) there are Lucien Goldmann's two essays on Piaget in *Recherches dialectiques.*[4] Then too there is the relevance of

[3] *Ibid.,* pp. 121-3.
[4] Lucien Goldmann, *Recherches dialectiques* (Paris, 1959), pp. 118-145.

Jacques Derrida's important variations on center, decentering and difference—themes whose urgency for the fundamentals of classification and opposition are particularly valuable—in *L'Écriture et la différence* and *De la grammatologie*.[5]

Now the clause I emphasized in quoting from Piaget above is crucial. *Passage formateur* implies graduation, conservation, and formation occurring together. The idea of a movement leading towards something (*qui conduit*) suggests purpose and direction. And *du plus faible au plus fort* requires, I believe, not only greater efficiency and strength in the structure thereby in the process of creation, but also an intensified concentration upon the achievement of completeness. In becoming " stronger " the structure realizes more of its latent powers of incorporation, and drops some of the freight that had hindered its encompassing movement hitherto. I am mixing metaphors a little, but I wish to avoid talking of developing force and form in organicist language. What I have in mind is a somewhat abstract scheme that allows me to describe a structure gathering force according to its own special laws, not according to those derived generally from nature. Coleridge, for whom the analogy of intellectual growth with natural growth was more or less habitual, brilliantly by-passes the recourse to organicism in the essay on " Method " (Number IV of *The Friend*) : what in Piaget's terms is " strength " in Coleridge's is "generality." Structure develops from mere specificity to impressive, over-mastering scope and generality. Thus another meaning for strength is wider incorporation and firmness of grasp. As Coleridge sums it up in Essay V in the same series: " all method supposes a principle of unity with progression." And since Piaget rightly speaks of structuralism as a method of thought the link between him and Coleridge is worth making. The two of them, however, remain open to C. S. Peirce's critique of synechism in " The Law of Mind,"

> that there is but one law of mind, namely, that ideas tend to spread continuously and to affect certain others which stand to them in a peculiar relation of affectability. In this spreading they lose intensity, and especially the power of affecting others, but gain generality and become welded with other ideas.[6]

[5] Jacques Derrida, *L'Ecriture et la différence* (Paris, 1967) ; *De la grammatologie* (Paris, 1967).

[6] *Philosophical Writings of Peirce*, ed. Justus Buchler (New York, 1955), p. 340.

Loss of intensity is the damaging point here, but one can admit that and still allow that a loss of one kind of intensity is replaced by gaining another kind: direct immediacy is replaced by a greater immediacy of continuity itself ("in this spreading they . . . became welded with other ideas").

All these dangerous abstractions will have been justified if a connection between them and the characterization of a literary text can be demonstrated. What is first of all necessary is that we situate our discussion as radically as possible; from that vantage point we view the text neither as the printed book, an object, nor very simply as a completed edifice of some sort. The ideology of most literary criticism today can be plainly described as permitting the confrontation of an inquiring critic with a resisting text, that is, between a flexible subject and a completed object. All the activity derives from the critic, to whose swoops and thrusts the text offers a resisting, but in the end a compliant, surface. Whether the critic seeks out depths (psychological, social, or otherwise) concealed in or by the texts so taken, whether he demonstrates formal relationships (between figures, parts, or otherwise) across the text, or whether he combines both approaches, his *pied-à-terre* is the text-as-completed-book. In the end, as Borges made the point cleverly in "Pierre Menard, Author of *The Quixote*," the text is enriched but it is still the same text with which the critic began. If ever the problem of identity were taken up—namely, the question of how an uninterpreted text differs from an interpreted text—we would find the prevailing ideology supporting a view that the interpreted text was more like the uninterpreted one than not. This is because the critic assumes, even imputes, problems to an uninterpreted text (what does it mean? what is its form? its significance?) and after solving them offers us an object *no longer in need of interpretation,* partially purged for his purposes of its problematics. The text is returned to a canon, or a tradition *more itself* than it had been before.

My earlier discussion of Piaget was designed to force upon us a different approach, the aim of which is to consider the text as a structure in the process of being composed, in the process of becoming a structure. In the criticism of the Geneva school, preeminently in the monumental studies of Georges Poulet, we have something resembling that approach, although it is necessary to keep in mind that any discussion of critical theory is a discussion as much about the *theory* as a conceiving matrix as it is about literature to which the theory is applied. Poulet tries first to locate a germinal point out of which the author's project develops, then he shows the project developing, and finally arriving at a point resembling the first. By that time the project is far more deeply and strongly understood. This method is not unlike Spitzer's circle of understanding, except that Poulet's claim is to have paralleled in his writing, and therefore duplicated, the author's own consciousness of totality. My difference from Poulet and others working in that tradition is that real allowances are made neither for the brute temporal sequence of an author's production nor for the author's shaping of the works into independent formal wholes. For the Genevans, text is an underlying plenitude of consciousness which, according to Poulet, is only existentially (but not ontologically) compromised by the individual work of art. Poulet's commentary is not metalanguage but primal language, which can also be characterized as purporting to be the language of unmediated consciousness. Its support of course is Poulet's marvelously penetrating, sympathetic consciousness. In the case of each writer studied, whether he be Pascal, Amiel, or Proust, Poulet's writing inhabits a privileged level of awareness that runs beneath or above or within (it does not matter which) the finished text-as-product.

The varied range of relationships possible between critic and text is more properly treated as a topic within the sociology of knowledge. Each historical moment produces its own characteristic forms of the critical act, its own arena in which critic and text challenge each other, and thereby its own depictions of what constitutes a literary text. Consequently I will not at all pretend that there is one notion of text that ought to be constant for all literary criticism. Nor can I deal here with the fascinating presuppositions employed by editors of literary texts: there is, however, an important job to be done in describing the philosophical prejudices that have operated, from antiquity to the present, when editors are "establishing a text." For there is a mythology that surrounds the notion of a *reliable text* as varied as it is often concealed, and the editor who takes the naively positivistic attitude that a text can be finally secured on the page does so in unwarrantable bad faith. (Incidentally, once one begins to examine the way in which critics today define their relation to a secure text a number of curious things emerge. The commonest metaphors used for the definition are spatial, physical or military: the critic is "close" or "far" from the text, one reads in "slow motion" in order to "get" the sense better, there are "defenses of reading," and prepositions like "within" and "inside" proliferate. It is rare to find an Anglo-American critic asking, however, where a text takes place, or how it takes place, or what it is, just as it is uncommon for him to consider writing—in its French sense of *écriture*—as anything more than the author's having to take a necessary step along the way to bringing out a book or a poem.)

In this essay I am arguing that the experience of certain major writers who aspire towards a highly specialized ideal of textual achievement must necessarily govern the *critic's* depiction of a text. What is constant for the critic is that there is always an authorial process of composition to be considered. And the exact nature of the process, in individual cases, can be grasped once the most notable patterns are identified. Yet we cannot be truly privy to an author's innermost struggles except, of course, through his own retrospective, and perhaps inaccurate, accounts. Thus our alternative is to take the author's career as wholly oriented towards the production of a text, especially if the author himself seemed obsessively concerned with just that metaphysic of craftsmanship. A further implication is that the author's career is a course whose record is his work, and whose goal is the integral text that adequately represents the efforts expended on its behalf. Therefore the text is a many dimensional structure. It is the source and the aim of a man's desire to be an author, it is the form of his attempts, it contains the elements of his coherence, and in a whole range of complex and differing ways it incarnates the pressures upon the writer of his psychology, his time, his society. The unity between career and text then is a unity between an intelligible pattern of events and for the most part their increasingly conscious transformation into writing.

If this formulation were left to stand it would be open to a major criticism. For underlying this view of the text as growing consciousness, regardless of how diverse the growth's expression, is an accepted *progress* and *development*. Yes, but what is of greater moment is the way in which the author's thought succeeds itself in time, and is therefore conscious of passing formatively (the phrase is Piaget's) from one stage to the next. The sheer weight of work done, for instance, influences the writer's thought by providing him with examples he need not repeat, or experiments he need not try again. Or if he repeats or retries he knows that he is doing just that. He is aware of what he has done: in that sense he is more generally conscious of what he can do even if, to take a common enough case, he unconsciously parodies himself some of the time. As I shall argue, although the text will be like a never-to-be-fulfilled ideal, a finality never attained, the author's asymptotic movement towards his goal gives him a greater sense of what he is doing all the time. Another more convenient way of settling in with a myth of progress here is to say that I shall be concerned with authors whose common trait is that they require from the critic a central thematic of development, organized around prominent levels of growth.

II

At certain moments in the history of literature and, to make the point more general, in the work of certain writers at other moments in history, to achieve a text—considered as an ideal goal for the writer—is extremely problematic. Why this is so is something I shall be speculating about a little later. I can now suggest that the difficulty for such writers or for such times as those is in being able to distinguish adequately between the author himself as a human being (however he characterizes himself), himself as a producing writer, and his production. It is those moments and those writers who ought to become a more prevalent theme of literary study, because it is their exemplary uncertainty that questions otherwise reified notions held about texts. Just as digressions in *Tristram Shandy* or *A Tale of a Tub* shed important light upon accepted notions of plot and narrative continuity, or just as irregular writers like Milton and Swift challenge and even modify the prevailing norms, so too these times and writers I have mentioned require a re-thinking of what it means to produce and complete a text. If, as Piaget says, structuralism in one of its negative aspects is a method " dirigée contre quelques tendances dominantes à l'époque " [7] then we can say that at certain times a writer's sense of the text he wishes to produce runs counter to the way in which the culture at large views a text.

With Piaget my notion is that these writers, like the contemporary

[7] Jean Piaget, " Le Structuralisme," *Cahiers internationaux de symbolisme*, 17-18 (1969), p. 76.

structuralists, view a text as the effort of an inclusive *career* commanded fully neither by public pressure (even though that plays a part) nor by the ordinary conventions that prescribe a literary vocation. On the contrary, the career is entirely original, hence its problems. To write for Grub Street is abhorrent, as is also the idea of writing a mere collection of works. The desired goal is a true whole, in which individual segments are subordinated to the totality of collective integration. Further, the career is even thought of as aberrant, not to say criminal. Thus whatever work gets produced suffers from radical uncertainty at the outset, is highly unconventional, possesses its own inner dynamic, is a constantly experienced but strangely ungraspable whole partially revealing itself in individual works, is haunted by antecedence and the future, and never finally accomplishes its ideal aims, at least in its author's opinion. Between the writer's life, his career, his text, we have a system of relations that passes *in real human time* from a weaker to a stronger (i. e. more marked, more individualized and exacerbated) form. And all this is something which gradually becomes the writer's all-encompassing subject. On a pragmatic level then, his text is his consciousness of the temporal course of his career, inscribed in language, riven through and through with precisely these matters.

Career is the important notion in what I have been saying so far about the writer. For any author, his writing life is what sets him off from the normal quotidian element. During the earlier European tradition great poets like Dante and Virgil were considered inspired by the poetic afflatus, which also shaped their poetic vocation and guaranteed special allowances for them as vatic seers. In the modern period I wish primarily to consider, the author's career is much less something impelled into course by " outside " agencies, whether they are called inspiration, Muses, or vision. I lose a great deal of specific accuracy by skipping over the periods of literary history until about the last quarter of the nineteenth century in England primarily, in order to remark that the idea of a poetic or authorial vocation as a common cultural myth underwent severe change. So thorough had been the subjectivization of approach, so detached from traditional practices had the writing enterprise become, and so individualistic a tone had the literary voice produced—at least among writers whose aspiration was to uncommon status—that the poetic *vocation* had come to be replaced by a poetic *career*. Whereas in the former there were memorial steps to be taken and a ritual progress to be imitated, in the latter not only did the writer need to *make* his art but also the very course of his writings. This had been a problem for the romantics certainly, as they vacillated between following classical models and, opposed to that, stubbornly hewing out their own ways.[8] But by the mid 70's in England, the self or, as Meredith called the self-centered person in his novel, the egoist had become one of the central themes in literature and indeed one of the author's main worries about himself.

We need to contrast a great popular institution like Dickens, whose career virtually included the public, with someone like Henry James, to make the change seem even more of a dramatic rupture between one generation and the next. James was not only a less accessible writer: his novels and his critical writings portrayed the lone figure surveying other writers or other individuals under the pressure of difficult choices in problems almost without precedent. This is especially true in the lives of characters in his novels. If we compare Pip in *Great Expectations* with Isabel Archer in *A Portrait of a Lady* we remark that the young man's ambitions are modelled after conventional patterns: to rise in the world, be a gentleman, have position, etc. Isabel's ambitions are vaguer, and her career is, she thinks egoistically, entirely of her own making.

Now very little of what I have been saying is more than a commonplace of literary history: that the writer, his form, his characters, his subjects, and his style became more private, less predictable. Still, there are unnoted consequences to be taken account of in the characterization of literary texts appearing in these newer conditions. The critic must hold that the poet's text became less ascertainable as the text's meaning became more obscure. In and of themselves words on a page become more and more *only* that, words on a page, and not as before, easily interchangeable with sense fixed for the reader in and by the words. Now the words gain meaning when juxtaposed with words from another work by the same author, and the whole " figure in the carpet " slowly emerges as the entire corpus is viewed in this comparative manner. In the end we see that there is an almost annoying closeness between an author's egoism and the character of his work. Or, to put it

[8] *Vide* W. J. Bate, *The Burden of the Past and the English Poet* (Cambridge, Mass., 1970).

differently, there is a practical and recognized coincidence between egocentricity and logocentricity.

Such a coincidence makes the author's role more the result of a performance (as Richard Poirier has recently shown) than the result of a special personality type. It is possible of course to say that this predominance of function over entelechy has always been true. All writers are in part performers, but in the modern period we are discussing the balance has shifted so much as to give the writer a role only when he is writing. He occupies no particular role once he no longer writes directly, as Dickens did, for a consuming public. Pushed back in on himself the writer experiences his vitality in the process of composition which, since it nourishes and depletes the writer's identity, is seen to be a system with ill-defined terminals, and boundaries always encroaching upon his intimate life. The writer becomes what Conrad called " the worker " in language, for whom the activity performed was " simply the conversion of nervous force into phrases." In writing there is no proper starting or stopping; there is only activity resumed or interrupted: and this because for the self there is no stopping or starting, but only a selfhood resumed or interrupted at some risk to the individual's security.

What are the ways in which we can now discuss these matters specifically? At the outset there is the problem of evidence. At one pole we have unmanageably large bodies of information to deal with, at the other, units so small as to take us into an infinite regress. For example, how can we begin to speak of a culture? Conversely, at what precise moment in a writer's life, at what stage in his private psychological development, can we locate his seminal insights? I propose a set of very gross, but I think useful, oppositions. As I conceive of them these oppositions are not abstractions that support a scheme, but rather practical exigencies faced by the author during his career. They might even be called the conditions of a writing career, those that make a career possible once the framework of a poetic vocation (in the earlier sense) is no longer available. They are conditions respected by the writer and by his critic, whose job by turn it is to re-distinguish the career's outlines in his writing. The oppositions therefore correspond to different phases of the career, yet even though they do follow each other their influence persists throughout the career. For example, Conrad's feeling that his career had no starting-point, a reflection obviously that had to do with his fragile sense of origins, was something his mind and temperament consistently reverted to. He writes Edward Garnett the following on June 19, 1896, after having already completed at least six important works:

> Other writers have some starting point. Something to catch hold of. They start from an anecdote—from a newspaper paragraph (a book may be suggested by a casual sentence in an old almanack). They lean on dialect—or on tradition—or on history—or on the prejudice or the fad of the hour; they trade upon some tie or some conviction of their time—or upon the absence of these things—which they can abuse or praise. But at any rate they know something to begin with—while I don't. I have had some impressions, some sensations of common things. And it's all faded—my very being seems faded and thin like the ghost of a blonde and sentimental woman, haunting romantic ruins pervaded by rats. I am exceedingly miserable. My task appears to me as sensible as lifting the world without that fulcrum which even that conceited ass, Archimedes, admitted to be necessary.

This sort of concern testifies ironically to Piaget's observation that " les racines sont opératoires. Even in his fiction Conrad's mind was attracted to reflections upon, scenes of, and feelings at *the beginning,* as for example in this famous passage from *Heart of Darkness*:

> " Going up the river was like traveling back to the earliest beginnings of the world, when vegetation rioted on the earth and the big trees were kings. An empty stream, a great silence, an impenetrable forest . . . We were wanderers on prehistoric earth, on n earth that wore the aspect of an unknown planet. We couʌa have fancied ourselves the first of men taking possession of an accursed inheritance to be subdued at the cost of profound anguish and of excessive toil . . . The steamer toiled along slowly on the edge of a black and incomprehensible frenzy. The prehistoric man was cursing us, praying to us, welcoming us—who could tell? We were cut off from the comprehension of our surroundings; we glided past like phantoms, wondering and secretly appalled, as sane men would be before an enthusiastic outbreak in a madhouse. We could not understand because we were too far and could not remember, because we were traveling in the night of first ages, of those ages that are gone, leaving hardly a sign—and no memories.

Although the oppositions (which I have yet to enumerate) follow each other then, they are all present potentially in every career and in every phase of the career. It is time and the sense of a course being passed through that reveals one or another of them more decisively. What is most important about them is that together they compose the author's career into a development that, from the point of view of his production, is the process that actively creates his text. Another qualification that needs to be made is that whereas I will be primarily discussing a period of about fifty years in British literary history—years that give rise to a radical re-thinking of what it means to create a text—there are examples from other periods to which some of the modern examples are relevant. All writers have the problems of the conflict between coherent development, let us say, and the mere dispersion of energy. All writers, certainly from the Renaissance on, have meditated in language upon the peculiarities of language. So while we can and do cite examples from many periods in history, it is the fifty years I have mentioned that provide us with a sustained examination of the issues, and in fact enable us to see more clearly the presence of these issues at other times. Such writers as Oscar Wilde, Gerard Manley Hopkins, James, Conrad, T. E. Lawrence in their works and lives completely transform the text from an object to be gained, into an unceasing struggle to be a writer, into what Lawrence called " the everlasting effort to write."

In these writers then we find attitudes to writing that judged by most standards are monstrously exaggerated. When Wilde adopted Axel's dictum that living was for servants, he might have been implying too that living, in the ordinary sense, wasn't for writers. As a project, being a writer took most of one's energy. Here is Conrad complaining to Garnett:

> . . . I seem to have lost all *sense* of style and yet I am haunted, mercilessly haunted by the *necessity* of style. And that story I can't write weaves itself into all I see, into all I speak, into all I think, into the lines of every book I try to read. I haven't read for days. You know how bad it is when one feels one's liver, or lungs. Well I feel my brain. I am distinctly conscious of the contents of my head. My story is there in a fluid—in an evading shape. I can't get hold of it. It is all there—to bursting, yet I can't get hold of it no more than you can grasp a handful of water.

The solitude of such experiences prompted the following outburst from Conrad to a French correspondent: " La solitude me gagne: elle m'absorbe. Je ne vois rien, je ne lis rien. C'est comme une éspèce de tombe, qui serait en meme temps un enfer, où il faut écrire, écrire, écrire." *Everything* was seen in the tormenting framework of the writing life. The result of so tyrannizing a domination was to turn even the writer's personal life, for the critic and for the writer himself, into matter for the writing project.

This is, I think, a significant critical point, since it has farreaching importance for the kind of literary study such writers entail. Beginning in about 1775, and after two generations of a community of writers like Joyce, Hopkins, Eliot, Conrad, Kafka, Mallarmé, etc., writers whose very energy was sapped by their efforts continually to experience and think their production into written life, it behooves the critic to consider everything by the writer (letters, notes, revisions, drafts, autobiography) as influencing the career. Once again therefore the critical notion of text comes to include a very wide network of relationships: between notes, for instance, and a "final" version, between letters and a tale, between revisions and early drafts, and so on. By the time most of the relationships are reconstructed by the critic the brute sequence of events in the writer's life has become quite modified. It has been decomposed into units that assemble sections of work into other significant wholes. Nevertheless, both the critic and the author militate against mere dispersion. Each has an interest in preventing the work from degenerating into a scattering of writings, governed successfully neither by personality nor by time. For the writer, as for the critic, the notion of career becomes the privileged one. The career allows for a sequence of intelligible development, not simply of accumulation. In husbanding his energies to shape his artistic life, the writer accepts the passage of time on his own terms: time is transvalued into a sequence of personal achievements connected by a dynamic of their own. The displacement of empirical time by artistic time is one of the happier results of the displacements of the normal human life by the writing career.

One or two qualifications remain to be made before we proceed to a descriptive listing of the seminal oppositions. In a paper of this length it is obviously impossible to write anything resembling a full literary history. The alternative then is to choose a number of figures who lift the period into a structural unity by virtue of two important qualities: one, their own systematic struggle with the difficulties of coherence, and two, the *strength* of their work, which compels the history of their period into forms and idioms they mold. This is especially paradoxical with the writers in question, for no writers could be more idiosyncratic—how then can they be considered exemplary of a period? Because the extremities to which their thought took them establish a pole from which all less tormented thought is measured. Thus although there was a rage of literary production contemporary with them, *they* abide as the major authors for whom production was always problematic. To them the text was above all the metaphor for an ideal resolution. Moreover the text was never simply completed, but was conceived in terms of something beyond even massive effort: and effort was what keynoted the continuing enterprise of their career. They never saw their text face to face. As T. E. Lawrence put it in *The Mint*: " Because when we write we are not happy: we only recollect it: and a recollection of the exceeding subtlety of happiness has something of the infect, unlawful: it being an overdraft on life."

III

The first opposition is the one that concerns us most directly when we discuss any writer: the conflict, constant in some cases, between an author's career as a productive writer, and either the beginning or the end of that career, i. e. the times when he has not yet begun to write, and when he has stopped writing entirely, or when he is concerned whether he can keep on writing. Sometimes the career is threatened with extinction during its progress. To the writer then what will matter pre-eminently is what matters to us as well: whether what he writes will appear on the page, in print, or in a book. Can he keep appearing? He may, as we shall see, endlessly bewail his inability to appear, and do his complaining in writing. Writing about his writing can be not writing at all from his point of view, just as appearing, as in Hopkins' case, is entirely sterile, without issue, almost as bad as not appearing at all.

The first opposition between career and non-career is capable of many modulations and gradations, yet all of them—we must require this—are fully evident to the writer himself. Thus he sees his life before he started his career as wholly different from the writing life. He worries whether he can continue to produce. He wonders what will make him stop. He examines the amount of time it takes him to write and the moment his immediate project is completed. In all cases, it is career versus non-career.

T. E. Lawrence, Conrad, Hopkins and Wilde are of paramount importance in exemplifying the kind of harrowing difficulty to which this opposition can put a writer. All of them were men to whom the writing life was literally secondary; that is, it followed and in most ways conflicted with another life. Conrad was a sailor, Hopkins a priest, Lawrence a man of action, Wilde a public personality. To none of them did writing come easily, and as a result each developed mannerisms of style and thought that make them seem endowed with what Hopkins called " a vice of queerness." Most of the mannerisms involved attempts to find suitable means for the expression in writing of experiences taken from their "other" life. In each case the interplay of forces between the writing career and the antecedent or, in the case of Wilde and Hopkins, concurrent form of life produced a specialization of literary technique. So specialized was it as to make the writing truly original, in the literal sense of that word. For Wilde's epigrammatic flair, to take one example, developed greater intensity and dazzlement the more he became known as a writer whose plays reflected the ethos of his outrageous non-literary life. By the time of *The Importance of Being Earnest* (1895) his manner had become so wilful that his characters in the play, through a remarkable brilliant series of moves, are able to originate themselves by the end of the work. I refer to the rituals of comic baptisms in the last act. Just as Wilde created himself—at what was later to be shown to be exorbitant expense—so too do his creations seem to be what Yeats called "self-born mockers" of ordinary middle-class life.

The public demands on Wilde made him pursue his vertiginous course to a conclusion that finally destroyed him as writer and as citizen. Yet in what Wilde considered a penitent work, *De Profundis,* we find him making of his career a shaped whole. If, he says to Douglas, I was formerly like the Marquis de Sade or Gilles de Retz, now, in prison, I am paying the price, but my new model is Christ. Wilde cannot help turning the brutal experiences of his life into a balanced *career* reflected in the juncture of his writing and public lives: the plays, epigrams, stories and fables of his demonic career are redeemed, balanced, naturalized by his horrible punishment, and his subsequent conversion. What we watch in *De Profundis* is Wilde's substitution of a fully shaped career made up of nice balances (sin, punishment, redemption: wit, jail, Christianity: writer-dandy, fall from favor, penitence) for any attempt psychologically, morally, or socially to understand what he was all about. The most he can say is that he understands the pattern of his life, which really means that like one of his plots, his career has triumphed, at least in his writing about himself.

The extent to which the formality of the writing career can oppose the threats of brute life is more startlingly shown in *The Seven Pillars of Wisdom*. Of this book and its author Malraux says perceptively: "The Arab epic became in his [Lawrence's] mind the medium for a grandiose expression of human emptiness." *Emptiness* properly refers to Lawrence's role in the Revolt. At first himself enthusiastically, then leader-initiator of the Revolt, then double-dealing British agent, then finally a man shocked at his hypocrisy, Lawrence turns himself into an author quite late in the book. Here is an important passage from Chapter 99:

> It was a hard task for me to straddle feeling and action. I had had one craving all my life—for the power of self-expression in some imaginative form—but had been too diffuse ever to acquire a technique. At last accident, with perverted humour, in casting me as a man of action had given me a place in the Arab Revolt, a theme ready and epic to a direct eye and hand, thus offering me an outlet in literature, the technique-less art. Whereupon I became excited only over mechanism.

By then the Revolt had gone its own way. Damascus was soon to be liberated, and all Lawrence could do was formally to reconstruct his role and his dubious achievement. There seemed to him no way to do that, and somehow to save himself, except by creating himself as historian-*manqué*, as author of epic mechanisms without conclusive meaning. Even when subsequently he did his own personality untold harm by trying to commit "mind-suicide" in the ranks of the RAF, he still sought for literary exoneration in *The Mint*, a precise and frank account of his conversion into common coin, which he rendered in the most "worked" prose he could manage.

The relation between a writing career and a life of risks in action was accompanied in Lawrence's case by what was no accident: an extraordinary solicitude for and, strangely, a constant series of losses of the actual manuscripts he produced. One of the most curious themes running through the literature and literary mythology of the period we are discussing is how very hard it was for the writer to make his works last, literally, in written form. The first manuscript of *The Seven Pillars* was destroyed, and Lawrence believed mysteriously in a plot behind the loss. Hopkins burnt his poems periodically. Wilde (comically it is true) averred how it took him half a day to put in a comma, then half a day to take it out. Mallarmé agonized over destroying the paper's blankness. Conrad's efforts physically to write were dogged with every known variety of psychologically caused illness like gout, arthritis, cramps, etc. Perhaps the most pitiless account of the writer's physical trouble in trying to make the text a printed object is to be found in George Gissing's novel of the period, *New Grub Street*. Every writer in the novel dies or loses his manuscript, so fearful are the dangers of print, so humanly destructive the conditions of its production. In all this we find a terrorism inflicted upon the writer for having dared transgress an apprehended, but generally unknowable, force, which his career in some way has offended.

Mysterious threats therefore necessitate the formulation of the authorial project on another level, where its ability to persist sinuously is rather devious. The writer's project, experienced within the special element of a career beset on all sides, achieved (if ever) in the solitary transcendance of a text always becoming, can be described in a unique language of effort and invisibility. It is a language grounded in negatives whose preponderance manages to stir the author's yearnings into expressions of almost unimaginable goals. I find all this described in the twenty-third of Rilke's *Sonnets to Orpheus,* Part I:

> O erst *dann,* wenn der Flug
> nicht mehr um seinetwillen
> wird in die Himmelsstillen
> steigen, sich selber genug,
>
> um in lichten Profilen,
> als das Gerät, das gelang,
> Liebling der Winde zu spielen,
> sicher schwenkend und schlank,—
>
> erst wenn ein reines Wohin
> wachsender Apparate
> Knabenstolz überwiegt,
>
> wir, überstürzt von Gewinn,
> jener den Fernen Genahte
> *sein,* was er einsam erfliegt.
>
> (O not till the time when flight

> no longer will mount for its own sake
> into the sky stillnesses,
> sufficient unto itself,
>
> that in luminous profiling
> as the tool that succeeded,
> it may play the winds' favorite,
> surely curving and slim,—
>
> not till a pure whither
> outweighs boyish pride
> of growing machines,
>
> will, headlong with winning,
> one who has neared the distances
> *be* his lone flight's attaining.)

And also in Merleau-Ponty's fascinated regard for Cézanne who, says Merleau-Ponty, saw his work as " only an essay, an approach to painting." The artist located his work in a hesitating place " at the beginning of the world." Thus located, the artist becomes " oriented toward the idea or the project of an infinite Logos." [9]

Thus the first opposition is the inaugural one for the writer, the radical question he must ask himself at the outset of his career. Linked with his ordeal by initiation is the second opposition, which wrings from the writer his sense of being in course, launched upon a career, and yet increasingly concerned whether he is on the right course. Ought he, for instance, to be producing one kind of sequence of works, or another? Does a given subject attract him for the right reasons, or for the wrong ones? A classic account of this set of issues, all of which derive from the opposition I mentioned, is Henry James's story " The Next Time." Ralph Limbert is a writer who vows, the next time, to write a book suited to the public. He never does, for " he had floated away into a grand indifference, into a reckless consciousness of art ": but James makes this occur shortly before Limbert's death. The career has run its course out of life entirely, although the right progess had been Limbert's most lively concern.

In the gradual development of a writer's career there occurs a

---

[9] Maurice Merleau-Ponty, *Sense and Non-Sense* (Evanston, 1964), pp. 9-19. See also Pierre Thévanez, " La Question du point de départ radical," in *L'homme et sa raison*, Volume I (Neuchatel, 1956). Also, Edward W. Said, " Beginnings," *Salmagundi*, Fall 1968.

time after which he becomes aware of certain idiomatic patterns in
the work. By awareness I do not necessarily mean that he is obsessively vigilant—although that is possible: there is the case of
Mallarmé—but that he can quote himself, refer to himself, be himself in ways that have become standardized because of the work
he has already done. What begins to be a concern for him is
the conflict between fidelity to his manner, to his already matured
idiom and, on the other hand, the desire to discover new formulations for himself. This then is the third opposition within the
career. Swift, for example, is an interesting figure because the
conflict I have identified is present almost continually in his writing.
So adept was he at impersonation that in each new piece, whether
it was *The Bickerstaff Papers, The Conduct of the Allies, The
Drapier's Letters,* or *Gulliver's Travels* a new voice emerged. And
yet there was no mistaking the Swiftian manner nor, more importantly, was there any mistaking Swift's devastating mimickry of
his enemies. Originality and habit in that case coexisted in a
truly productive tension. Browning, I think, is quite similar.
With Milton and Pope we feel that the gained manner has almost
overwhelmed the innovations, although in both writers the later
style (of *Paradise Lost* or *The Dunciad*) draws a variety of new
sounds and reaches from out of solidly formed reserves. At a ripe
moment in the career a writer like Yeats can even schematize the
earlier achievements in *A Vision* in order to vary his present and
later poems. When it happens, this moment is an entirely fortunate
phase in the career.

Hopkins, I think, perfectly understood the tension between innovation and repetition. In a set of notes made in 1873-4 entitled
" Poetry and Verse " he claimed for poetry the task of presenting the
"inscape" (or special distinguishing particularity, the inner structure) of speech.

(Poetry is in fact speech only employed to carry the inscape of
speech for the inscape's sake—and therefore the inscape must be
dwelt on. Now if this can be done without repeating it *once*
of the inscape will be enough for art and beauty and poetry but
then at least the inscape must be understood as so standing by
itself that it could be copied and repeated. If not / repetition,
oftening, over-and-overing, aftering of the inscape must take place
in order to detach it to the mind and in this light poetry is speech
which afters and oftens its inscape, speech couched in a repeating
figure and verse is spoken sound having a repeating figure.) . . .

Now there is speech which wholly or partially repeats the same figure of grammar and this may be framed to be heard for its own sake and interest over and above its interest of meaning. Poetry then may be couched in this, and therefore all poetry is not verse but all poetry is either verse or falls under this or some still further development of what verse is, speech wholly or partially repeating some kind of figure which is over and above meaning, at least the grammatical, historical and logical meaning.

" Oftening, over-and-overing, aftering " are effects that cannot be reduced to our habitual understanding. For they achieve the detachment of sense from the logic of discourse, and the delivery of sense into figures or patterns whose chief feature is a remarkable identity. Such figures, because marked and repeatable, enhance the language from which they have been fashioned: by exaggeration, they help us to perceive what is there but not readily perceptible. They take us over and over sounds, stressing them out of the ordinary into prominence. The dynamic of repetition (as Kierkegaard also saw) keeps one within reality even as a sort of new reality is being created. Hopkins used the technique in his own verse, thereby making a new idiom—that of sprung rhythm, heavily alliterated, with an entire vocabulary of powerful neologisms. His verse, he believed, was closely imitative of the fertile processes of nature, which while producing the essential rhythms of repeated events (spring, dawn, harvest) made them new each time.

A pronounced difference between the phase I have been discussing and the next one is that whereas formerly habitual patterns and originality intersect in the writer's consciousness, now *mere repetition* is viewed as one alternative of a pair, of which the opposite is the career's disruption by a failing impulse. Here too Hopkins' instance is instructive. In his later poems, the so-called " terrible " sonnets, one theme recurs with frightening insistence: how unproductive repetition is his lot. Tied to this is the certainty that what is being repeated is himself, sterile, uncreating, " widow of an insight." In the sounds of his verse, the alliteration now signifies dull repetition (a technique the more poignant because he had used alliteration earlier to signify diversity and exuberance) :

> birds build—but not I build; no but strain,
> Time's eunuch, and not breed one work that wakes.

In another poem he says:

> I am gall, I am heartburn. God's most deep decree
> Bitter would have me taste: my taste was me.

Hopkins' highly developed sense of self had in it a good deal of self-loathing. This is not true, for instance, of Wilde, who by the time he came to write *De Profundis,* repeated himself in the figure of Christ without realizing how familiar the locutions and the poses.

The fifth and final opposition, or axis of concern, is influential when the writer begins to view himself as at the end of his career, tempted with the idea of going on, and yet able to recognize that his writing has reached its conclusion. Works of recapitulation are common: Yeats's "The Circus Animals' Desertion," and Swift's "Verses on the Death of Dr. Swift" are perfect examples. In the latter poem, for instance, the poet not only projects his own death, but goes on to project the life he will lead in posterity. Swift's vision is to double the career by perpetuating it after his death. The main distinction of this phase is the artist's realization that his career has spent itself as a result of its own logic of continuity. The opposition is more accurately described as that between the subject of ending (in a work like *The Tempest*) on the one hand, and *writing* about ending on the other. The failing impulse produces suitably matching work with frequent references to an anti-poetic old age.

The principle that organizes the entire career, and knits together the five sets of oppositions, is the constantly entertained dilemma of whether the writing life conflicts with, runs parallel to, uniquely imitates, or finally stunts the human empiric life, the life that Wordsworth called "the still, sad music of humanity." Literary theorists from the romantics to I. A. Richards have often maintained that the writer is different from other men in degree, not kind, of experience; yet the more common sentiment is to be found in statements such as this one by Leopardi:

> To a sensitive and imaginative man, who lives as I have lived for a long time, constantly feeling and imagining, the world and its objects are, in a way, double. He sees with his eyes a tower, a landscape; he hears with his ears the sound of a bell; and at the same time his imagination sees *another* tower, *another* bell, and hears *another* sound. (italics mine)

To *another* we can add *alternative* in apposition. Conrad called himself *homo duplex,* since no one was more sensitive than he to the eccentricities of two lives in permanent conflict with each other. What is notable, however, is the way the modern writer has had of using his career to reconstruct, or re-make his private life over into a poetic career. Beyond the world of literature we find psychologists like Freud, philosophers like Nietzsche and Kierkegaard, anthropologists like Lévi-Strauss all defining the characteristically human in terms of what we might call the possibility of a second time. In all these cases language is excellent testimony to the manner by which a naive initial course gets itself transformed into a cultural second course, or recourse (I use the words course and recourse in Vico's sense).

A frequent metaphorical description of the recourse is that of the human family; the irony is in using a natural image to portray the highest version of artificiality. Elsewhere I have tried to show how narrative fiction in the nineteenth century was linked intimately with an attempt to reproduce in language the mysteries of human procreation.[10] Ibsen in the drama gives up his earlier style of exact realism in order to examine the enticements offered by art, which permits the artist to lead a life strikingly similar to biological life, yet without its limitations. In the later plays—*Hedda Gabler, The Master Builder, When We Dead Awaken*—Ibsen returns time and again to a depiction of the artist whose work is "his child," even though Ibsen can himself see a tragedy in the fates of the quasi-progenitors (Hedda and Lovborg, Kaya and Solness, Irene and Rubek). What they do not see is how they are doomed because of the illicitness of their alternative projects. The true symbolism of such visions is sexual of course, and it is in the poetry of Hopkins that we find a very pure performance of polysexuality, of an omnisexuality transferred from natural to literary life, underpinning the entire career and text.

I use Hopkins precisely because his sexual imagery plays itself out generally at the level of his writing project, and moves particularly at first in correspondence with his own consecrated celibacy. His poetry is launched in order to confirm, in repetition, a divine metaphysic of creation. Later his poetry will self-consciously feel itself a rival to the divine, so strongly has the authority of the poetic self become. Finally, the poetic project discovers itself imprisoned in the sterile vacancy of its isolation from the divine.

[10] Edward W. Said, "Narrative: Quest for Origins and Discovery of the Mausoleum," *Salmagundi*, Spring 1970.

By that time the completely poetic career has been divorced
(Hopkins' word is "widowed") from the divine thrust: the poet
exists as a eunuch on his own, his text a linguistic mutant that has
issued forth from an emasculated pen. This last discovery is made
out of a poetic history that begins with Hopkins perfecting a
technique intended to register as dramatically as possible the difference between stressed and unstressed phenomena. The poet's job
is to exaggerate the difference between stressed and unstressed since
by that difference reality itself is made intelligible. The poet and
his art then are the verbal equivalents of that difference, and out
of their rhythmic play springs (the word has a seminal value for
Hopkins) not only "the stress felt" but indeed the drama of
procreation by which the world can be understood. In *The Wreck
of the Deutschland,* his first major poem, Hopkins repeats the
articles of his submission to a divine "fire of stress" which, he says,
"hast bound bones and veins in me, fastened me flesh." Married
to the principle that made him, God's male authority, he then
becomes the re-creator of a sacrificial scene in which a courageous
nun receives God in a moment of extreme crisis. At that moment
Hopkins the poet joins the nun through his poetry, and together
they celebrate Christ's coming into her:

> But how shall I . . . make me room there:
> Reach me a . . . Fancy, come faster—
> Strike you the sight of it? look at it loom there,
> Thing that she . . . there then! the Master,
> *Ipse,* the only one, Christ, King, Head:
> He was to cure the extremity where he had cast her;
> Do, deal, lord it with living and dead;
> Let him ride, her pride, in his triumph, despatch and
>   have done with his doom there.

Thus the poet writes a scene in which the union between man
(or woman) and God has been enabled by an art miming the
rhythm of incarnation through impregnation.

As God is to man, so the poet to his poetry. Hopkins gives birth
to being by impregnations of fecund originality deriving from his
self-hood. Hence Hopkins' thoroughly distinctive art, which is at
once faithfully mimetic (feminine) of God's stress or impress upon
him, and creative (masculine) in a reproduced verbal utterance.
In the following lines, the abruptness of the language closely follows

the abruptness of the bursts of reality, as in writing the lines the poet himself follows God's fathering-forth:

> All things counter, original, spare, strange;
> Whatever is fickle, freckled (who knows how?)
> With swift, slow; sweet, sour; adazzle, dim;
> He fathers-forth whose beauty is past change:
>   Praise him.

As receptive woman, as creative man; as impregnated Christian impregnating the page; as stressed creature himself stressing language into weak and strong thrusts: in all these Hopkins plays a series of finely balanced roles especially atune to heaves, springs, darts, charges, rears, bursts, rises. He gives as he receives. Yet as creative poet, he begins to perceive that what he does is not only analogous to what God does, but something more.

Consider these lines which, after *The Wreck,* self-consciously formulate the poetic project:

> Í say móre: the just man justices;
> Keéps gráce: thát keeps all his going graces;
> Acts in God's eye what in God's eye he is—
> Christ—for Christ plays in ten thousand places,
> Lovely in limbs, and lovely in eyes not his
> To the Father through the features of men's faces.

This is the last part of a sonnet, hence " I say more " means primarily that the poet is adding to what he has already said. But second, the phrase draws attention to the poet's power to say more (Í say móre), over and above what is immediately perceptible evidence. The poet begins to launch his world. The poet's medium is language, as God's is natural reality, so that in the phrase that follows, the poet makes language produce more before our eyes and ears: he creates a new verb by pulling it forth out of an adjective—just→justices. Not only in issuing forth does the poet's power lie, but also in conserving through repetition, the opposite of playing out. The last four lines turn around the relationship between the verbs " is " and " plays," which together unite issuing forth (plays) and conserving (is). There is an entire series of startling identifications forged by Hopkins: between man and Christ, between Christ the one and Christ the many (he " plays in thousand places "), between Christ who is readily identifiable and Christ who takes on other forms ("lovely in eyes not his"). All

these identifications together are a sort of seductive dance to
entrance God (and we are to remember the " fickleness " of reality) :
they play *to* the Father who is their progenitor and, since the poet
has himself pointed them out, even created them in language, God
is literally their prospective mate also. What we are left with at
the end is a unity resembling marriage. Limbs and eyes are given
to the Father.

A great deal depends on the poet's generative power and, of
course, on his memory of his and God's past accomplishments. It
is when during his fully progressing career he realizes that this is
so, he recognizes his power to take life away as well as to endow it.
Hence the late sonnet " Carrion Comfort." God begins to with-
draw, so strong is the poet's selfhood and presence, attested to in the
body of work he has hitherto produced. Whereas formerly there
had been a balance between the poetic enterprise and the divine,
now Hopkins incorporates both roles within himself. In the following poem of imprisonment, the pronouns " we " and " you " all
refer to himself, now unnaturally performing more than one part:

> I wake and feel the fell of dark, not day.
> What hours, O what black hours we have spent
> This night! what sights you, heart, saw; ways you went!
> And more must, in yet longer light's delay.
>   With witness I speak this. But where I say
> Hours I mean years, mean life. And my lament
> Is cries countless, cries like dead letters sent
> To dearest him that lives alas! away.
>   I am gall, I am heartburn. God's most deep decree
> Bitter would have me taste: my taste was me;
> Bones built in me, flesh filled, blood brimmed the curse.
>   Selfyeast of spirit a dull dough sours. I see
> The lost are like this, and their scourge to be
> As I am mine, their sweating selves; but worse.

Soon this omnicompetent, but transgressing self will become
" Time's eunuch," unable to fecundate itself, even as its language
turns into mere repetition. In the most remarkable of his last
poems, " To R. B.," the tragedy of a poet whose career is completed,
yet whose sterility knows no relief, is mourned. The dominating
idea is that of the poet's mind bereft of its male thrust. Wears,
bears, cares—the alliteration conveys the stale sameness of a poet
missing rapture, although able to live on with " hand at work."

Instead of "the roll, the rise, the carol, the creation" (elements of poetic creation), there is only an explanation:

> The fine delight that fathers thought; the strong
> Spur, live and lancing like the blow pipe flame,
> Breathes once and, quenched faster than it came,
> Leaves yet the mind a mother of immortal song.
> Nine months she then, nay years, nine years she long
> Within her wears, bears, cares and combs the same:
> The widow of an insight lost she lives, with aim
> Now known and hand at work now never wrong.
> Sweet fire the sire of muse, my soul needs this;
> I want the one rapture of an inspiration.
> O then if in my lagging lines you miss
> The roll, the rise, the carol, the creation,
> My winter world, that scarcely breathes that bliss
> Now, yields you, with some sighs, our explanation.

The last yielding, which is cruelly opposed to fathering-forth, delivers an explanation, which is the poorest substitute for a poetic text. The career has matured to a winter in which no blossom can live. And this kind of finale is true for most of the authors I have mentioned. Their production moves conclusively to a terrible self-indictment. The words do not inhabit a creative text, but are rather the verbal dead remnants of a course that has turned aimlessly back to its origins in the poet's self-hood. Therefore we have a literature proclaiming itself not literature, although the personal relic so despondently described at least proves the presence of a disconsolate human voice. Yet it is this human voice, detached from any text, that will be swallowed up in the work of subsequent generations of writers. The text gives way to a lone voice, which thereafter gives way—in books like those contrapuntal encyclopedias by Joyce (*Ulysses* and *Finnegans Wake*), Huxley (*Point Counterpoint*), Borges (*Ficciones*), Orwell (*1984*)—to a super-formalization of the mechanism of writing. If previously the poet like Hopkins was left only with his highly developed authority, then later language will exist without an author or authority or a human subject. Structuralism commemorates the loss even as its methods of analysis permit it glimpses of a text proceeding to disappear. For all of which the modern poetic career we have examined is the human evidence.

1970

THE STYLISTIC INTERPRETATION OF LITERARY TEXTS ✁ AMADO ALONSO

In order to avoid useless polemic, let us begin by granting that every study which contributes to the better comprehension and interpretation of a literary work is legitimate. Every kind of study is welcome if it adds to our knowledge of a literary work or if it permits us to feel and enjoy it better.

The traditional study of literature has dealt with many important aspects such as the ideologic, historic, folkloric, linguistic, biographic, social, religious; the only thing which had been neglected by traditional criticism is the specifically *poetic* values. Criticism has decided whether a work is of great, average, or scant literary value. But in most instances such evaluation amounts to no more than a faint underlining in a vague system of academic classifications, and, in the best of cases, our great philologians give us rapid, isolated glimpses of the *true* poetic content of the work, without submitting this aspect to a systematic study.

In every poetic production, however (and, of course, I call poetic production not only verse compositions but also every artistically valuable literary creation) the only thing essential—as a poetic production—is its poetic kernel. In the *Quijote* there are represented thoughts, ideas, cultural European currents of the time, national forces and ambitions, a profound personal vision of life; all this could very well have been set forth in the form of a treatise, intellectually ordered and justified—but then it would not constitute a poetic creation. There is also in the *Quijote* a critical portrayal of social life, common wisdom, geographic references, and literary criticism; and all of this could have been presented as topics of information—but then the work would not constitute a poetic creation. And one may go further: it will be readily admitted that if Cervantes had intended primarily to inform us concerning the geography of Spain he would have given us facts in greater quantity, and more precise and better integrated than they appear in the *Quijote*; if he had intended to write a treatise on the cultural ideas which interested him, he would have developed such ideas in greater detail and would have shown us explicitly his own point of view; if he had wished to record the customs and social forces of his time, he would have provided us with more detailed and exact information than is to be found in his work. In short, each one of the aspects of the literary work except the poetic would, if considered as a subject in itself, have turned out better if treated by itself, systematically, and according to its own exigencies. And yet, in this piecemeal, unsystematic and partial form in which these subjects appear in literary master works, their power to vitalize the human heart is incomparably greater. And this is because the power they possess belongs to the poetic architecture in which the social or historic or ideologic themes (the so-called contents) enter as materials of construction. That architecture is of a specific type which *in lato sensu* we call 'artistic' and, in reference to literature, 'poetic'—and the character of which, as such, is revealed in the aesthetic pleasure which is produced in us. Traditional philological criticism methodically studies contents and the value thereof; but is it not also the duty of literary history and of literary criticism to attempt the *methodical* understanding of the poetic in literary works? My two-fold proposition is, first, that the poetical represents not only one but the basic aspect for studies of literary criticism, and, secondly, that it is incumbent upon the new philological discipline, usually called stylistics, to seek out, to appraise, and to rectify the methods suitable for a systematic and rigorous analysis of this aspect of literary works.

Stylistics is style-study. As regards 'style,' this is generally understood to mean an author's particular use of language, his idiomatic mastery and virtuosity, as representing an *additional part* of the literary construction; there have been a number of doctoral dissertations which have attacked the question of style from this point of view. I grant the occasional desirability of such a conception of style; I grant likewise the usefulness of some of these theses as contributions to the study of the style of the authors in question. But the term 'style' has another meaning which is more suitable to the purposes of stylistics: *style is the expressive system of a work, of an author, of an epoch.*

According to this definition stylistics must study the literary work as a poetic structure, taking into account the *two* essential aspects: the manner in which it is constructed, both as a whole and in its elements, and the sort of aesthetic delight which it produces,

in other words the work must be considered both as a created
product and as a creating force—as ἔργον and as ἐνέργεια. Whether
the work in question be a small poem, a novel, or a tragedy, the
investigator of style seeks to perceive the *modus operandi* of the
psychic forces which form the composition of the work, and to
penetrate deeper into the aesthetic pleasure which derives from the
experience and contemplation of the poetic structure. After that,
and only after that, each one of the elements is studied and viewed
in its structural rôle within the poetic creation: what does this
diminutive express or suggest? How is the rhythm achieved, what
does it reveal concerning the act of poetic creation, and what
aesthetic effects does it produce? What are the special characteristics
of the metaphors, of which elements are they made, and what are
the particular procedures of artistic condensation employed by the
author?

Stylistics is concerned, then, with the expressive system of a work,
an author, or a group of related authors. An expressive system
embraces everything from the internal constitution of the work to
the suggestive power of the words and the aesthetic efficacy of
rhythmical interplay. And by 'internal constitution' I am referring to that world which, in his poem, in his tragedy, or in his
novel, the poet shapes out of his sentiments and his thoughts. What
is essentially poetic consists precisely of this created structure or
architecture; this does not mean, however, that the so-called contents
lose their importance for study—indeed these have a qualitative
interplay in the form or construction itself. For it is impossible to
think of the very same form with different contents; the contents,
with their characteristic nature, are formative in themselves.

To clarify this point I should like to adduce an example from
another art. In a painting the form or artistic construction is made
up of lines and colors and the counterbalance of the two. But these
are not the only compositional elements: the construction is made
up also of the very materials represented. The wise distribution of
cloth, stone, human flesh, vegetable life, sky and water, produces
in the painting a harmony of the sensations that are evoked. Notice
the formative rôle played by the white and rose-colored tints of
feminine flesh against the red and violet velvets; should the pieces of
cloth be replaced by other materials of the same color—by stone, for
example, or by vegetation—the composition itself would be thereby
altered; that is, the 'form' would change. It is well-known that a

painting provokes in us not only visual sensations but, particularly, those which are tactile and thermal—as well as various associations of all degrees. These tactile and thermal sensations, these associations, are provoked by the materials depicted (by the contents); thus the contents, with their characteristic material quality, are elements of form. If in a painting an apple is replaced by a clay ball, there will be produced a profound alteration in the harmony of sensations, in the form, even though the clay ball be of the same size, the same form and the same color as the apple. Every work of art is essentially the creation of a structure, of a form; but it is always a structure made up of *something*, a form extracted from *something*. Considered in this way, complementary concepts of matter and form are subordinated to the one all-important concept of form. Our poet likewise creates first and foremost, with his sentiments and his thoughts, a *form*. The thoughts play a rôle in the poetic structure by virtue of their specific qualities; this is why stylistics must study thoughts and ideas as well as feelings. But the former should not be studied *in and for themselves*, as a system rationally justified, but only as expressive elements, as an indirect expression of a deeper 'thought' of a poetic nature: an intuitional vision of the world and of life, felt, lived, and objectified in the poetic creation.

The great critics of past generations have often dealt with the *Weltanschauung* of a poet whenever the poet (a Dante, a Sophocles, a Cervantes) has been thought to have a world outlook of his own, and his works to possess a philosophical, religious, social or moral content. Knowledge of this sort is a precondition for stylistic studies, but the particular characteristic of stylistic treatment consists in considering the poet's vision of the world also as a *poetic creation*, as a construction basically aesthetic. It was not Cervantes' main concern in the *Quijote* to depict the world wherein he had lived, as an ordinary citizen in real life; in his work of art, the vision of the world which is the basis of the life of the citizen Cervantes has been evaluated, sifted and purified; certain tendencies have been emphasized, others subordinated; his own clear vision has given form to the significance of this world; it has become organized, reduced to artistic forms, to an ideal pattern. This reduction to form belongs to poetic creation. Stylistics, then, interests itself in this creative character of an author's vision of the world, but only with the aesthetico-poetic consequences of this vision—not with its philosophico-rational aspects *in se*. This can be seen most easily in the case of lyrical poems, in which the vision of the world is ordered according not to rational knowledge but to a personal vision of factual elements which have been adapted to the emotional unity of the moment.

Although feeling and sentiment are present in every literary creation they acquire their highest constituent importance in lyric poetry. The emotional attitude which is crystallized in a lyric poem may be derived from real events in the poet's life, as, for example, in the *Coplas por la muerte de su padre* of Jorge Manrique or in the love ballads of Lope de Vega; again, as in the serene poetry of Fray Luis de León, this attitude may be 'achieved' by the poet, as a refuge from the disquieting anxieties with which the world torments him; there may even be a question of a dramatization of sentimental attitudes, as in Espronceda's *Canción del pirata* or the *Romancero gitano* of García Lorca. In all cases, even when an autobiographical basis is present, the poet has shaped and adjusted his sentiment, in the same manner that he has crystallized his vision of the world. The emotion which the poet has experienced in real life may perhaps have been trivial and vulgar; but when his spirit acquires that privileged creative tension which we call inspiration, then there appear in his work of art splendors and forces by which the raw material has been qualitatively transformed and given the universal value of an ideal pattern. And it is with this transfigured sentiment, not with the raw material of emotion, with which stylistics deals; the poem should not be treated as a biographical document nor as a monument of a moral attitude which may have been underlying the original experience.

And here we arrive at the capital point of our subject: since sentiment and personal *Weltanschauung* are communicated in poetry not directly but only by means of the suggestive, evocative procedures employed by the poet, the task of stylistics must be to study the *expressive system* of an author. Thus everything that has an efficacious value for suggestion must be studied and this not by dissection but by evoking the 'biological' forces at work in the poem. We must seek to discover how the poem developed as an objective construction, i. e., how the 'form' of the poem developed, and how the original reality has been especially prepared to serve as the expression of the sentimental substance intuited by the poet. Stylistics must also study rational thoughts insofar as these have been transformed into poetry; the particular manner in which fantasy operates in its own inventions; the secret order of the poem underlying its apparent whimsicality; the poet's exploitation of the possibilities of his idiom; the expressive intentions with which he has filled out and renewed common syntactical formulae, the expressive procedure to which he has subjected the meaning of words and phrases. Finally the rhythm must be considered: that is, the aesthetico-suggestive construction to which the poet has subjected the phonetic material, the organic activity developed in actualizing the sounds, the aesthetical organization of the given language.

Of course in every literary creation the essential is always that which the poet has succeeded in creating—not what he may have attempted, and failed, to create; we can interpret only what is contained in the poem before us. This, however, does not mean that it is possible completely to exclude the poet: what meaning could a poem have if one were to pretend that it has not come forth from the spirit of a poet? Every poem is an intentional construction and thus may be understood and enjoyed only if the reader grasps the intention around which the poem has been organized. It is precisely what is objectivized in the poem that allows us to discern this prime intention; by the same token, the reader should not consider any intention which he may know to have existed in the poet's mind but which has not been objectively realized.

The only way to perceive the meaning of a poem is to accept it, and recreate it, word by word, verse by verse, in accordance with its rhythmic imagery: to imagine it, I might say, as the work must have developed, shaped by the intention of a concrete human being. And I am not simply recommending this as one way of reading a poem; I maintain that this is the *only* way possible. Each new reading of a poem carries us, willy-nilly, to the moment of the poetic creation which has been perpetuated in the poem. The expressive system of an author can be understood only as a living functioning process, as an efficacious manifestation of that privileged activity which is called poetic creation. This expressive system of a poem, of an author, of an epoch can be the object of systematic study; and it is this alone which is deserving of stylistic treatment.

Let us then remove the existing taboo against studying the poetic in poetry; for this last is nothing recondite or *ineffabile*. The poets who have made excursions into criticism (Goethe, Lessing, Coleridge, Sidney, Wordsworth, Juan Ramón Jiménez, T. S. Eliot) have all raised problems which were *poetic*; indeed it has been the poetic aspect of literary works, even when these were dedicated primarily to other ends, with which the great body of English critics has constantly and lovingly dealt; in our own time, there are critics like John Middleton Murry and I. A. Richards who, each in his own way, are seeking and finding the poetic values of literature. This is likewise the way of Croce, Dilthey, Simmel, Santayana and Ortega y Gasset who often couple their historical and philosophical interests with elucidations of the poetic side of literary works.

We philologists, too, and we philologists especially, must cooperate in this search for poetic understanding, but we must do so in our own way: carrying out our studies with a method capable of improvement and progress. We can and we must shape a discipline, a tradition of research, by ever anew rectifying and extending our poetico-literary knowledge, which knowledge will pass to successive investigators. The method which we can develop must be based on our particular professional competence, that is, on our professional knowledge of linguistic phenomena and their values. Our point of departure must be the recognition that, just as each idiomatic expression has a meaning fixed by language, so it has also a complex of suggestive powers, likewise, but not as firmly, fixed by language. The meaning of a word is better established by tradition than is the suggestion emanating from the word, although both are *somewhat* fixed (neither completely so; and both are fixed in a particular manner in each language). To use the phenomenological terminology of Edmund Husserl, an expression is the sign of the object signified and an indication (or 'connotation') of all that is implicitly meant by the expression—especially of the complex psychic reality from which this expression is derived. There are, then, two types of contents for words and phrases: signified or denoted, and indicated or connoted. The possibility of stylistic studies is based on the fact that the indicated or connoted content, though not so firmly fixed as is the signified content, is, nevertheless, far from arbitrary: at least it is oriented in a certain direction by linguistic, and at times by literary and historical, tradition. We already possess some brilliant studies of this aspect of language; the Geneva professor, Charles Bally, is a pioneer in this type of study. The idea of starting from the idiomatic peculiarities of an author in order to make a short-cut to his soul has been set forth, clarified and magnificently exemplified in the works of Karl Vossler, who has been followed by Leo Spitzer, Dámaso Alonso, Ernst Robert Curtius and others; with Albert Thibaudet, too, who excels in literary criticism, the method occasionally follows the same trend: from the external linguistic traits of an author toward his interior being. The philological training of such writers assures the most solid basis for a scholarly handling of the discipline of stylistics.

1942

THE TWO CRITICISMS ✌ ROLAND BARTHES

✌ We have at present in France two parallel types of literary criticism: on the one hand a criticism we shall call for the sake of simplicity *academic* [*universitaire*], which uses a basically positivistic method inherited from Lanson; and on the other hand an interpretive criticism, the representatives of which (very different among themselves, since they include J.-P. Sartre, Gaston Bachelard, Lucien Goldmann, Georges Poulet, Jean Starobinski, J.-P. Weber, René Girard, and J.-P. Richard) have in common an approach to the literary work which can be associated, more or less, but in any case consciously, with one of the great current ideologies—existentialism, Marxism, psychoanalysis, phenomenology—so that this criticism could also be called *ideological*, in opposition to the first which, for its part, refuses any ideology and claims only an objectivity of method. There exist, of course, links between these two forms of criticism: for one thing, ideological criticism is practiced for the most part by professors, for in France, of course, for traditional and professional reasons intellectual status is readily confused with university status; and further, the University does sometimes recognize interpretive criticism, certain works of which are doctoral theses (apparently sanctioned more freely, it is true, by boards in philosophy than by boards in literature). There is however, if not conflict, real separation between the two types of criticism.

If academic criticism were nothing other than its announced program, which is the rigorous establishment of biographical or literary facts, it would be hard to see why it would foster the least tension toward ideological criticism. The achievements of positivism, its demands even, are irreversible—no one today, whatever his philosophy, would dream of challenging the necessity for scholarship, the value of historical accuracy, the advantages of a close analysis of the literary " circumstances," and if the importance

This essay has been translated from the French by Catherine and Richard Macksey.

attributed to the problem of sources by academic criticism already implies a certain concept of the literary work (we shall come back to this), there can at least be no objection to treating this problem with rigor, once the decision is made to pose it. At first glance, then, there is nothing to keep the two criticisms from recognizing each other and from collaborating; positivistic criticism would establish and discover the " facts " (since this is what it demands) and would leave the other criticism free to interpret them, or more precisely, to "give them meaning" [*les "faire signifier"*] with reference to an announced ideological system. If this conciliatory point of view is, however, utopian, that is because, in reality, between academic criticism and interpretive criticism there is no division of labor, no simple difference between a method and a philosophy, but an actual rivalry between two ideologies. As Mannheim has demonstrated, positivism itself is in effect an ideology like any other (an observation which in no way detracts from its usefulness). And when it becomes the inspiration of literary criticism, positivism reveals its ideological nature on at least two points (to concentrate on the essentials).

First of all, in deliberately limiting its investigations to the "circumstances" of the work (even if inner circumstances are involved), positivistic criticism is already using a quite biased concept of literature; for to refuse to inquire into the being of literature is to subscribe thereby to the idea that this being is eternal, or, if you like, natural; in short, that literature *can be taken for granted* [*va de soi*]. And yet, what is literature? Why does one write? Did Racine write for the same reasons as Proust? Not to ask these questions is to answer them, for one is adopting the traditional common-sense concept (which is not necessarily historical sense), to wit, that the writer simply writes *to express himself* and that the being of literature is in the " translation " of sensibility and of the passions. Unfortunately, as soon as one touches on human intentionality (and how can one speak of literature without doing so?), positivistic psychology no longer suffices, not only because it is oversimple but also because it involves a deterministic philosophy which is completely out of date. The paradox is that historical criticism is here rejecting history. History tells us that there is no external essence of literature, but that under the name of literature (which itself, for that matter, is recent) there is rather a gradual development [*un devenir*] of forms, of functions, of institutions, of reasons,

of quite diverse projects, the relativity of which it is, precisely, the
historian's job to show us; otherwise he condemns himself to an
inability to explain the "facts"—by refraining from telling us
why Racine wrote (what literature might represent for a man of
his period), criticism prevents itself from discovering why at a
certain point (after *Phèdre*) Racine stopped writing. Everything
is connected—the most minute of literary problems, even anecdotal,
may find its key in the mental or intellectual framework of a period,
and this framework is not our own. The critic must admit that it is
his very object, literature, in its most general form, which resists
him and escapes him, and not the biographical "secret" of its
author.

The second point on which academic criticism clearly shows its
ideological involvement is what might be called the analogy postulate. We know that the main work of academic criticism consists in
searching for "sources"; it is always concerned with relating the
work under consideration to something *other*, to something *elsewhere* in literature. This *elsewhere* may be another (antecedent)
work, a biographical circumstance, or a "passion" actually experienced by the author which he is "expressing" (*expression* is
always the term) in his work (Orestes is Racine at twenty-six, in
love and jealous, etc.). Moreover, the second term of the relationship, which is always *analogical*, is much less important than its
nature, which is constant in all objective criticism; it implies the
conviction that writing is never anything more than *reproducing,
copying, being inspired by*, etc. The differences that exist between
model and work (which it would be hard to deny) are always
attributed to "genius," a concept before which the boldest, most
opinionated critic suddenly gives up his right to speak and the
most cautious rationalist is transformed into a credulous psycholo-
gist, respectful of the mysterious alchemy of creation, at the precise
point at which the analogy can no longer be seen. The *resemblances* of the work, then, are held answerable to a rigorous positivism; its *differences*, to magic. Now this is a postulate. It can
be maintained with equal justice that the literary work begins
precisely at the point at which it deforms its model (or, to be
more cautious, its point of departure). Bachelard has demonstrated magnificently that the poetic imagination consists not in the
formation of images but on the contrary in their *deformation*; and
in psychology, which is the privileged domain of analogical ex-

plications (a written passion must always, it seems, derive from an experienced passion), we now know that the phenomena of *denial* are at least as important as the phenomena of conformity. A desire, a passion, a frustration can very well produce *exactly* opposite representations. A real motivation can reverse itself in an alibi which belies it. A work can be the very fantasy which compensates for the negative in life—Orestes in love with Hermione is perhaps Racine secretly tired of Duparc. Similarity is by no means the sole relationship between creation and reality. *Imitation* (taking the word in the very broad sense Marthe Robert has just given it in her admirable essay, " The Old and the New " [1]), follows devious paths; whether it is defined in Hegelian or psychoanalytical or existential terms, a powerful dialectic is continually wrenching the model away from the work, submitting it to powers of enchantment, compensation, derision, aggression, the value of which—that is to say, the *meaning-for* [*valant-pour*]—must be established not in terms of the model itself but in terms of their place in the general organization of the work. Here we are touching on one of the most serious responsibilities of academic criticism—concentrating on the genesis of the literary detail it runs the risk of missing the functional meaning of the detail, which is its truth. To inquire with ingenuity, rigor, and dogged perseverance into the question of whether Orestes was Racine or whether the Baron de Charlus was the Comte de Montesquiou is to deny that Orestes and Charlus are essentially the *terms* of a functional network of figures, a network whose articulation can be apprehended only from within the work in itself, not in its roots. The homologue of Orestes is not Racine but Pyrrhus (according to an obviously differential approach); the homologue of Charlus is not Montesquiou but the Narrator, precisely insofar as the Narrator *is not* Proust. In short, the work is its own model; its truth is to be sought not in depth but in breadth, and if there is a relationship between the author and his work (who would deny it? the work does not descend from Heaven; only positivistic criticism still believes in the Muse), it is not a pointillist relationship which would accumulate piecemeal, discontinuous, and " profound " points of resemblance, but quite to the contrary a relationship between the author

---

[1] *L'Ancien et le Nouveau* (Paris: Grasset, 1963).

as a *whole* and the work as a *whole*, a relationship of relationships, a homological rather than an analogical correspondence.

Here we seem to be approaching the heart of the matter. For if we examine now the implicit refusal with which academic criticism opposes the other type of criticism, if we try to find the reasons for it, we see at once that this refusal is in no way the banal fear of newness. Academic criticism is neither retrograde nor out of fashion (a little behind the times, perhaps); it knows perfectly well how to adapt. Thus, while having practiced for years a conformist psychology of the normal man (inherited from Théodule Ribot, Lanson's contemporary), it has just "recognized" psychoanalysis by sanctioning through a very well received doctorate the remarkable criticism of Charles Mauron, strictly Freudian in its discipline. But in this very recognition it is the line of resistance in academic criticism which is exposed, for psychoanalytic criticism is *still* a psychology which postulates an *elsewhere* removed from the work (the childhood of the author), a secret of the author's, a problem to decipher which is still the human soul, even though a new vocabulary may have to be accepted. Better a psychopathology of the writer than no psychology at all. By relating the details of a work to the details of a life, psychoanalytic criticism continues to practice an aesthetic of motivations founded entirely on an external relationship. It is because Racine himself was an orphan that there are so many Fathers in his theater. The supremacy of the biography is safe; there are, there always will be, authors' lives to be excavated. In sum, what academic criticism is disposed to admit (little by little, and after successive efforts at resistance) is paradoxically the very principle of an interpretive criticism, or if you like (although the word is still frightening), an ideological criticism; but what it rejects is that this interpretation and this ideology may decide to work within an area purely internal to the work. In short, what is refused is *immanent analysis*; anything is acceptable so long as the work can be related to *something other* than itself, to something other than literature. History (even Marxist history), psychology (even psychoanalytical psychology) — these *elsewheres* will be admitted little by little; what will not be admitted is a procedure which situates itself *within* the work and establishes the latter's relationship with the world only after having completely described it from within, in its functions, or, as we now say, in its structure. What is rejected then is, broadly speaking, phenomenological criticism (which instead of *explicating* the work *makes it explicit*), thematic criticism (which reconstitutes the internal metaphors of a work), and structural criticism (which considers the work a system of functions).

Why this rejection of immanence (whose principle, moreover, is often misunderstood)? Only contingent answers can be given for the moment. Perhaps it is through stubborn obedience to the ideology of determinism, which insists that the work is the " product " of a " cause " and that external causes are more " causes " than others; perhaps it is also because moving from a criticism of determinations to a criticism of functions and significations would imply a profound conversion of the norms of knowledge and thus of the technique and of the very profession of the academic. We must not forget that, since research is not yet separated from teaching, the Academy labors but it also grants degrees; so it has to have an ideology based on a technique sufficiently difficult to constitute an instrument of selection. Positivism provides it with the demand for vast, difficult, patient knowledge; immanent criticism—or so it seems at least to the University—demands, before the literary work, only a capacity for *astonishment*, difficult to measure or quantify. One can understand why the University would hesitate to alter its requirements.

The original French text appeared in MLN *78 (1963).*

CRITICAL REFLECTIONS ON LITERARY STUDIES ✌ RENÉ GIRARD ✌

We hesitate to bring up the quarrel M. Picard is waging against the *nouvelle critique*. It has to be done, though, since *MLN* is somewhat involved in the affair. It was in these very pages, it will be remembered, that the article appeared (before it figured in the *Essais critiques*) which drew M. Picard's wrath against M. Barthes.[1] On a page of *Le Monde*, which I do not have in front of me, M. Picard accused M. Barthes of craftily slipping his anti-Sorbonnic propaganda into the place where it was most likely to be believed: foreign journals with "ill informed" readers. I cannot guarantee the literal exactness of his other assertions, but I was struck by that "ill informed," and I believe I make no mistake in attributing it to M. Picard.[2]

We were the accomplices, albeit involuntary, of a vast, encircling conspiracy threatening M. Picard and the Sorbonne which he embodies. We were cat's paws without knowing it. Fortunately there was M. Picard to enlighten us. The news was reaching us. It remained only for us to make honorable amends to the professor himself and to the Sorbonne, who had been jointly "defamed" (the word is there—I am not inventing it) by M. Barthes's article.

Let M. Picard be reassured; we have not been used. Roland Barthes has not taken advantage of our good faith. He has not forced our hand. However ill informed we may be, neither M. Barthes nor M. Picard himself was altogether unknown to us when we asked M. Barthes to give us his "Deux Critiques."

It seemed superfluous to us at the time to review the facts. Since then M. Picard has renewed and broadened his attacks against M.

This essay has been translated from the French by Catherine and Richard Macksey.

[1] "Les Deux Critiques," which first appeared in *MLN*, LXX, 6 (1963), pp. 447-52, was reprinted in *Essais critiques* (Paris; Editions du Seuil, 1964), pp. 246-51. An English translation appears in this volume.

[2] *Le Monde*, March 14, 1964.

Barthes and other critics in a pamphlet which is attracting a certain amount of attention: *Nouvelle Critique, nouvelle imposture.*[3]

Controversy is not always bad. On both sides of the Atlantic we need some stimulation. But, still, the debate should have a real object. The plots M. Picard sees surrounding him have only the most remote connection with current intellectual life. On the one hand there is the reasonable, docile criticism of sensible people the principles of which seem so natural that it needs no definition. And on the other hand there is the subversive, perverse, one is tempted to say *deviationist* criticism, the very existence of which *defames* the Sorbonne and all decent people.

In this system, M. Jean-Paul Weber represents and perhaps even embodies psychoanalysis, just as M. Picard embodies the Sorbonne. Sartre would speak here of a universe of essences. I would have thought M. Weber as different, say, from the Lacanians as M. Picard himself is different from M. Weber. In the same way, between the criticism which sees in the work the emanation of a subjectivity always identical with itself, always susceptible of apprehension in an immediate intuition, the criticism of M. Poulet for example—between this and the criticism which at the heart of the work and in our relationships with it gives the place of primary importance to intersubjective relationships, I would have believed the distance to be as great as between M. Picard and the *Treatise on the Sublime.* Such fine nuances doubtless carry no weight in the face of the almost planetary encirclement now threatening the Sorbonne.

The most ill informed of our readers or editors would, I believe, recognize within criticism differences which are strangely man-handled if not even obliterated in M. Picard's critical Western. The *nouvelle critique* has its weaknesses and even its ridiculous points. It is contradictory, tumultuous, sometimes unfair. It is wide open to contemporary thought, to all sorts of influences. It is, in a word, alive. That is hard to forgive.

In a hundred years ours will probably look like the period of a metamorphosis in the very concept of literature, a revolution comparable, in a sense, to that of Mme. de Staël and her time. Mme. de Staël did not simply add to the discourse on literature the *theme* of history. She was the first to grasp *all* themes historically. Her

---

[3] Paris: Jean-Jacques Pauvert, 1965.

theory of history was perhaps inadequate; her ideas doubtless lacked originality. Her importance lies elsewhere. For since Mme. de Staël, one can no longer speak of literature in the same way as before; or rather, one may, but anything one may say about it without taking her into account is marked by sterility.

Today it is not a question of history, at least not in its nine-teenth-century sense, but perhaps of *anthropology*, in a sense as yet not easy to define. One can reject this or that critic on the basis of his particular options, but this is an evasion of the main issue. The *nouvelle critique* is no more existentialist than it is Freudian or Marxist or structuralist. It must, however, take into account Hegel, Marx, Sartre, Freud, and, today, Lévi-Strauss and Lacan. The "sciences of man" besiege us. Despite appearances, despite differences M. Picard seems not to suspect, this broadening of the context does not contradict but rather confirms the concern with the creative experience which is also characteristic of the twentieth century.

Mme. de Staël and her group were accused of a dreadful abuse of jargon. They too quoted at every turn rebarbative thinkers. They seemed sometimes more at ease in a misty, romantic Germany than in classical, reasonable France. Every revolution takes place in con-fusion and disorder and leaves behind much dross. Depriving men of their habitual points of reference, it seems to them to be destroy-ing what in fact it is transforming.

The revolution in criticism is already accomplished. One might say that M. Picard's pamphlet confirms it, to the very degree that its author embodies—this is important to him and must be true—an authority and a continuity necessarily opposed, in the intel-lectual order, to freedom and to life. Without going back to Rabelais and Port-Royal (a little heavy for all our shoulders), one can fit M. Picard into an already venerable tradition, that of Brunetière excommunicating naturalism. We should note that it was for literature itself that the academic dogmatism of yesteryear saved its thunderbolts—already a bit damp. The fact that they are brandished today against a criticism which is constantly open-ing out affords one more argument for those who call ours an essentially hermeneutic period and see as its task "an inventory of significations." More than ever before, the best of our writers are critics. It is they, and not the recipients of showy literary prizes, who today are the stewards of our literary heritage; it is they who are renewing it. M. Picard may embody the Sorbonne, but Roland Barthes is creating the literary works of our age.

One may wonder, moreover, whether the Sorbonne's opposition, not to mention its approval, can any longer confirm anything whatsoever. But who gives a thought to the Sorbonne nowadays? Not a single idea of this half-century is associated with it in even a negative way. One could not call the Sorbonne hostile; it does not recognize contemporary thought and is not recognized *by* it. Not that the Sorbonne cannot claim eminent men, as it always has, but their presence there is always exceptional. One is astonished to find them there and always forgets that they *are* there as soon as they get involved in the real issues of their day. Even in academic circles in France it is no longer toward the Sorbonne that the intellectual community turns its attention. It is always elsewhere, it seems, that *things are happening*.

The revolution in criticism is accomplished; it even dates back to the beginning of the postwar period. But one could hardly say that it has triumphed; it remains strangely marginal. It might yet even prove abortive. We were already aware of this; the fact is now confirmed by the truly extraordinary delight occasioned by M. Picard in quarters at times quite opposed to his real values. M. Picard is a true historian. One can disagree with him on many points without showing any lack of respect for the scope of his work, for the thoroughness of his documentation, for the discretion of his focus on this or that detail. M. Picard believes today that he is serving the cause of literary history. He is mistaken. He is encouraging a phenomenon which is particularly widespread in our day and which we must call by name: academic anti-intellectualism, flourishing everywhere but taking on different forms in different places. What is the ubiquitous obstacle to living thought, in the United States as in France? Mme. de Staël had only Napoleon to contend with. Our tyranny is better disguised but universal; it is identical with the bureaucratic organization of literary studies.

The vertiginous growth of literary studies has its good side, of course, for which we are ever grateful, but it sometimes resembles a malignant proliferation. Our libraries, ever more numerous, buy an ever growing number of books published by more and more university presses. Our system of publications functions as a closed circuit. No longer does any external sanction control our intellectual life. We have become our own signifying totality, and it is perhaps time to ask ourselves what indeed it signifies. Who will distinguish in our studies on the one hand what springs from a true desire for knowledge, from free intellectual activity, and on the other what exists only as a function of the insatiable bureaucratic machine, demanding servile conformity to its requirements, having no other aim than to insure its own indefinite expansion? The more neutral, colorless, and repetitious the results of our sacrosanct *research*, the better they answer our administrative demands. This situation would seem to call for extreme vigilance, and yet the *nouvelle critique* alone provokes any anxiety in us. Could it be that anti-intellectualism has already triumphed in places claiming to be impregnable fortresses of intelligence and culture?

The so-called *nouvelle critique*, however aberrant at times, and perhaps in its very aberrations, is always implicitly calling into question the very system that produces it. It is always the protestation of an individual. In its best proponents it is more, but if it were never more than that it would still deserve our sympathy. The so-called *nouvelle critique* stubbornly insists on seeing in art, in thought, in literature, something more than one of the cogs (and one of the least) in the machinery of the academy. It is unorthodox criticism, criticism which defies administrative pigeonholes, tiring and pretentious criticism, criticism which demands " interdisciplinary " training. It is the spoilsport of the academic publication game.

One can understand that Picard would be welcomed as a savior. The most " Picardian " among us are not always the most learned. Between genuine literary history and living criticism there should be no quarrel. In its truly dynamic period literary history did not claim to be an end in itself. It saw itself as the basis and the instrument for a richer and deeper interpretation. If certain works are as *definitive* as we are told, we must not be asked to redo them. The greatest homage one can render to literary history is not to repeat its work indefinitely but to use its results.

Living thought is always more dynamic than ready-made thought; it asserts itself, believes in itself, it is dogmatic and has an obligation to be so. To pretend that this dogmatism is *dangerous*, that it is a threat to our intellectual freedom, is a joke. This freedom cannot be exercised without the clash of contradictory beliefs. Today there is no conflict, no debate, no dialogue, no real life outside of the *nouvelle critique.*

We have in America a dominant aesthetic. It claims to be eclectic, devoted to beauty, infinitely broad-minded. Its antidogmatism sometimes reaches the point of intolerance vis-à-vis living thought. What is the derivation of this aesthetic? It curiously combines somewhat emasculated fragments of the New Criticism with European academic conformism. It proclaims the autonomy of art in order to defend the autonomy of departments of literature, ever threatened by the conquering disciplines, the " truly scientific " disciplines. An essentially bureaucratic credo, art for art's sake tempered by bibliography is also a defeatist credo. The scientism which challenges our rôle is not itself challenged. Feeling incapable of impugning it, we impugn philosophy in general. But we become so suspicious, so narrow, that we can no longer see the difference between the " social sciences" and the " sciences of man." In the latter we see a new enemy, and not the opportunity they offer to renew literary studies, to emerge finally from the crisis which engulfs us.

Our slogans—all defensive and negative—are aimed at preserving the insularity of a discipline which grows day by day more desiccated. They can all be related to a holy horror of what is called reductive or even reductionist criticism. Barthes uses the language of psychoanalysis and is therefore reductionist. Actually he is not, and he explains himself on this point with great clarity, but to no avail. The only reduction to which psychoanalysis leads is, obviously, a reduction to the author himself, to the psyche of this author. Now this author in Barthes's *Sur Racine* is hardly mentioned. And that is precisely the surprising point; that is what we should talk about. On the first page of the introduction, anyone may read:

> The language is somewhat psychoanalytical, but the treatment is hardly so. . . . The analysis here presented does not concern Racine at all, but only the Racinian hero: it avoids inferring anything about the author from the work or about the work from the author. It is a deliberately circumscribed analysis.[4]

If we are correcting the error of which Barthes is the victim, it is not because we, too, feel the enormity of the crime of which he

[4] *Sur Racine* (Paris: Editions, du Seuil, 1963), p. 9.

stands accused; it is because this error appears to us to be symptomatic in its absurdity. It is enough simply to utter the word reductionist to strike us dumb. Our critical faculties abandon us,
and it does not even occur to us to ask the simplest of questions:
" He is reductionist, and why shouldn't he be? "

Any vigorous thought is sooner or later bound to arrive at its
own bases; it will end, then, in reduction. We can of course remain
ignorant of our first principles, believing ourselves to be alone in
having none, even glorying in this vacuum; but none of this does
credit to our thought.

The word " reductionist " is, in fact, rather tiresome. It is surprising to find it used so much by those who claim a devotion to
beauty. The truth is that the word reeks of punitive bureaucracy
from a mile away. It plays the same role in our ever-so-slightly
sclerotic universe as " Trotskyite " did in Stalinist Russia. It tells
more about those who brandish it on every occasion than about
those whose instant damnation it proclaims, in a perpetual verbal
exorcism.

It is not the fact of reduction that matters to the critic, but what
precedes it. The Hegel of the *Phenomenology* reduces everything
to mind. So we are spared the trouble of reading him. A pity.
What a formidable reduction might we not witness, from *Antigone*
to *Rameau's Nephew*, if we were to moderate slightly our dogmatic antidogmatism. The reductive thought of Hegel embraces a
prodigious amount of material; the least reductive criticism imaginable might very well embrace nothing at all, might never overcome
a pathetic emptiness.

The reduction phobia threatens to emasculate all critical thought.
There are those who reject contemporary criticism *in toto*, on the
pretext that it is " philosophical." There is, in our period as in
any other, philosophical criticism, but it is not always the criticism
which appears philosophical. The Cartesianism, or the positivism,
of traditional criticism is not recognized as philosophical by our
antiphilosophers. The criticism that offends them, on the contrary,
is the criticism which is so much more wary of philosophy than
ever before that it can speak *all* the languages of philosophy. One
cannot say that it reduces art to philosophy without by the same
token saying that it reduces philosophy to art. A clever and
shrewd aestheticism like Valéry's could " reduce " to pure aesthetics
any will to systematize. Sartre affirms that every work of art con-

tains a latent philosophy, but one can turn his proposition around: a philosophical system is an unconscious work of art. The philosophical, in the traditional meaning of the term, enjoys no privileges in contemporary criticism.

It would take only a little humor, perhaps, and a little true faith in literature to apply Valéry's reduction-in-reverse to structuralism. In Lévi-Strauss there is at least as much literature as in many a place where it is today being sought feverishly. The concept of *model*, put forward by structuralism and extended by it to cultural phenomena, is perhaps only a metaphor rich enough and accurate enough to be systematized, a metaphor with multiple dimensions, whose existence, moreover, poses many problems. The recourse to models has diverse implications but, from an admittedly schematic point of view, it represents, with regard to the science of the past, something analogous to preciosity in the literary order. Instead of appealing, for the description of an object, to conflicting and multiple metaphors, to fugitive images whose choice depends on no conscious system, one adopts a single metaphor, as all-inclusive as possible and pushes it to its furthest limits, prolonging its usage even beyond previously tolerated limits, beyond a now dated "good taste." That was the way preciosity proceeded. And it is precisely an impression of preciosity that Lévi-Strauss first makes on new readers. To say this is not to attack either science or literature but rather to observe their closeness. Literary preciosity fails, doubtless, from an inability to communicate intuitions which are essential but too subtle for the sloth and vulgarity of its readers; despairing, then, it falls into paradox and pure vanity. Structuralism, however, may succeed precisely because of its will to systematize; because of the scientific precisions to which it resorts, the rigorous methods with which it arms itself in order to formulate, to preserve, and to transcend intuitions which are at times quite analogous, at least fundamentally, to those of the past.

Those who cannot penetrate structuralism, those who remain closed in a more general way to all dialectical thought, see in the contemporary effort only a will to paradox, a desire to surprise, a gratuitous attack on common sense. And yet, thought which intends to be thought about literature cannot be based on common sense. It cannot reject structuralism, among other things, without rejecting a mode of knowledge which is much closer to the best literature than the positivism of yesteryear. Structuralism brings out, between the parts and the whole and between the whole and the parts, homologous relationships whose existence is affirmed by an aesthetic criticism which can neither reveal nor demonstrate them. Far from being hostile to authentic aesthetic understanding, structuralist knowledge is perhaps only its extension and development. This is perhaps why structuralism cannot recognize aesthetics as a separate domain, any more than the truly religious can see any distinction between the sacred and the profane.

We ought to claim structuralism as being naturally our own. It would permit us to join the contemporary desire for cultural interpretation without betraying (as did the old sociologism and psychologism) the privileged place which we accord and which must always be accorded to the great works. The criticism which thus draws close to the sciences of man, in the broadening of its interpretive function, is not the least *literary* in the best sense of that word. But it probably should not answer to the name of " literary criticism," which is too limited by its traditional usage and too liable to misunderstandings. This broadened interpretation may constitute, alongside literary history, a true academic discipline. This discipline, it will be said, does not exist. That is exactly what we mean; we must create it.

There are today hundreds, perhaps thousands of us devoting ourselves to literary studies. We are not giving away any secret if we affirm that our books and journals are not always very, very original or essential to knowledge. When veritable armies are competing as laborers in the same literary vineyard, duplications are inevitable. Perhaps it is better to republish the same books than to publish nothing at all. It is perhaps inevitable that these repetitious works should almost always receive favorable reviews. But we must not exceed certain limits. We must not erect this system into a standard of the human spirit. We do just that when we show our claws only before the great talent of a Goldmann or a Barthes and pull them in, predictably, before the imitative and the banal. We do just that when we deplore the time " wasted " in examining the malaise in literary studies. We do just that when we send our colleagues back to urgent but ill defined tasks which await them, it seems, from time immemorial. Whatever the pretext, let us not exhort each other to maintain the status quo.

To what urgent tasks, then, should our young people address themselves? Would we like to see them publish the new, nth version of *Tartempion, His Life and Works* in 133 beautifully printed pages with large typeface? M. Prud'homme is not of course always wrong, and we do sometimes lose our way by leaving the beaten path. But who is talking about paths? On the vast and monotonous superhighways of academic criticism the traffic is so heavy that any defection ought to be hailed with shouts of joy, or at the very least with sighs of relief. Even if nothing good were ever to come of it, anything which does not completely usurp the qualifier " new " deserves to be encouraged, even if only to relieve the congestion in the mainstream.

The kingdom of orthodoxy, as far as I know, is not about to fall to the distaff side. Conformism is alive and well. An ever growing number of guides offer to direct our first steps in the work of Tartempion. No famine threatens in the area of *Tartempion, His Life and Art*. Initiations into the fraternity of Tartempionians succeed each other with accelerating rhythm. The *Tartempion revisited* has not yet been parcelled out. We must of course persevere in this rich vein, but it is not in such pressing need that we should channel toward it the enthusiasm of a whole new generation or discourage the least impulse toward a new direction.

Must we really, faced with any work of some difficulty, call the author back to the demands of clarity and nontechnicality imposed on him, it seems, by his role as intermediary between the work and that now mythical creature, the "common reader?" These perpetual recalls to an order which is no more (and perhaps never was) hide from us the real conditions of our academic pursuits. Sainte-Beuve, we all agree, was addressing himself to nonspecialists. But there was only one Sainte-Beuve and he had an audience. The Modern Language Association numbers more than 20,000 Sainte-Beuves and no audience whatsoever. This is no catastrophe; far from it; we talk to each other and we are, all by ourselves, more numerous than the audience of Sainte-Beuve, of Molière, or of Shakespeare. We provide our own audience, and that should be enough. The myth of the enlightened common reader has not the least foundation in our intellectual and sociological situation. We can be and we must be as technical and as philosophical as the actual level of our academic audience will allow. Our intellectual autarchy presents certain dangers but also some advantages. Nobody, absolutely nobody, is asking us for a new introduction to the work of Tartemption.

If the *common reader* should someday present himself to one of us, confessing a desire to be enlightened, in terms not too abstruse, on the subject of Tartempion, we can always guide him to the dozen or the half-dozen recent books which answer his needs perfectly and which, as yet free of dust and untouched by human hands, await him and him alone in our library.

The common reader proves singularly ungrateful. He does not want us, it seems, to condescend to his level. Our solicitude leaves him cold. The only criticism that interests him at all is that of Goldmann and Barthes, the unreadable *nouvelle critique*.

The " urgent " tasks can wait. What we need is truth. We owe it to ourselves and to the prodigious system of higher education with which America has provided itself. Everything demands of us a real leap forward. The " publish or perish " system is no less destructive of the research it claims to honor than of teaching. It creates a "mediocracy" of researchers desperately attached to stock ideas. Genuine talent gets lost in a mob dominated by a timorous ultra conservatism. A system as vast as ours is necessarily conservative. We aren't asking it to be revolutionary. What worries us is its feeble capacity to respond to new ideas, the time it takes to assimilate recent acquisitions. It is a bit demagogical to suggest to our flocks that aside from these black sheep, the " new critics," all is for the best in the best of all possible academies.

The intellectual enlargement that the times demand is no easy feat. We must face up to the problem. In trying to avoid it we must not—even with the Sorbonne's approval—construct a critical dogma all the more narrow and intolerant as it claims to be liberating. This dogma always comes down to the absolute and insurmountable separation of, on the one hand, the aesthetic (elusive, ineffable, nebulous, misty, exquisite, reassuring) and, on the other hand, intelligence (tedious, systematic, forbidding, destructive of all beauty). If we examine this distinction thoroughly, we still find the basic defeatism which we demonstrate vis-à-vis the exact sciences, a defeatism which today has no further reason to exist.

We must be initiated into complex thought, into difficult methods we have been taught to neglect. But our universities, precisely, dispose of resources which would make it possible to make up for lost time. If the spirit of bureaucracy does not triumph, we shall certainly undertake, and on a grand scale, thanks to postdoctoral fellowships, thanks to the literally staggering means to which we all have access, what certain groups are already trying to do at the Ecole des Hautes Etudes. The crisis of the "humanities," the student problem, all of this is linked to our intellectual timidity and calls for an effort on our part to rethink all of our themes with today's intellectual resources.

Literary studies are in crisis; no one, I think, would dream of denying it. In Lanson's day everyone could believe he was playing his little role in the vast workshop of advancing knowledge. Knowledge, founded thenceforward on truth itself, had only to pursue its imperturbable march forward. No one believes this any more. At the end of the war the crisis could still be seen as transitory. Peace would bring back the old order. This hope is gone. The atomic age is not a return to the *belle époque.*

To observe this is not to kneel before some historical idol. It is rather to draw the consequences from the impasse in which traditional criticism finds itself. To escape this impasse we are more and more avoiding the great problems. In Lanson's day no subject was taboo. Lanson himself tells us that he wants to *explicate* works. He fears neither the psychological nor the sociological. His concept of "influences," moreover, is not so simplistic as the one attributed to him. Henri Peyre points this out, with justice, in his introduction to the *Essais,* which he had the happy idea of republishing.[5] Lanson anticipates many contemporary themes. He is at times closer to those who attack him than to those who claim to carry on his work.

The divergences are no less real for this. At the beginning of the century we still dreamed of being able to define once and for all the great terms of literary history—classicism, romanticism, realism, etc. A segment of literary reality was to come and take its place under each of these words. It was always a question of cutting out this segment with *exactness.* The idea of scientific precision with Lanson does not refer solely to the establishment of facts—the domain in which it is still intact today—but remains linked to the principle of a division of the literary substance around certain key words, certain chapter headings. This is what we no longer believe in. The undertaking demands a concept of language which is no longer ours.

Then we sought the frontiers of classicism or romanticism, in

---

[5] Gustave Lanson, *Essais de méthode, de critique et d'histoire litteraire,* ed. Henri Peyre (Paris: Hachette, 1965).

the way a Bismarck or the diplomats of Versailles sought natural
frontiers on ordnance survey maps. We believed that words had
a real substratum which we tried to determine. Words, it seemed,
were like watertight receptacles, placed in literature for all eternity;
they were jars, duly labeled, awaiting their definitive contents. At
that period, to repose the grand problems meant to propose a new
distribution of the literary jam among these eternal jars. The more
time passed, the more the shifts from one jar to another multiplied
and accelerated. Some thought to stop this interminable shuffling
by adding new jars. Jars of all sizes and shapes jostled each other
in growing confusion.

The honor of having upset all these jars goes to our Professor
Lovejoy of Hopkins. He showed that the word romanticism, for
example, had a multiplicity of meanings, sometimes contradictory.
So the jars were not watertight; in fact they were full of holes. That
is all fine and good, but where will this criticism stop? Does romanticism mean nothing, or does it on the contrary mean too
much? If we give up this word, why should we trust the rest? Historians of literature are certainly not the only ones to play the role
of the fabled knight trying to fill the enchanted, unfillable keg.
What becomes of literature itself, that mistress of ambiguity, if we
reject equivocal terms?

This criticism of language leads straight to logical positivism
and its sequellae. We shall next try to base all knowledge on a
verbal reduction in which things adhere to words. But literature
enjoys no privileged status here. And so we stand convicted of
radical *irrelevance*. Contemporary aestheticism does not answer
this criticism but embraces it, submits to it body and soul, and
thereby renounces our claim to a share of truth.

This criticism is nonetheless necessary. The categories of our
literary history depend on certain words and on their history. Classicism, for example, makes a very late entrance, at first more acri-
monious than majestic. Littré puts a wary little cross beside this
word rejected by the French Academy. A neologism, it designates
a literary ideology, invented after the fact, in the period of ideologies, to correspond to romanticism [*à " romantisme," ou même
à " romanticisme "*]. A veritable abyss separates this modern classicism from the old *classicus* from which it derives and which it
imbues with its ideological effluvia. Classic will henceforth be
opposed to romantic, and it is within a system of oppositions that
all these terms signify. With its three sibilants and its two shrill

i's, rising from the false gravity of the *a*, classicism [*class-si-cisme*], at the beginning of the nineteenth century, has the very sound of a controversy growing sharper.

Current criticism, we should point out here, is continually reproached for looking at the past through twentieth-century glasses. But this is no worse, perhaps, than looking at it through nineteenth-century glasses. Boileau does not talk about existentialism or about structuralism. But he does not talk about classicism either. I fail to see why classicism should survive if we must banish jargon.

In the middle of the nineteenth century the opposition between classicism and romanticism is blurred. The past appears thenceforth as a national treasure to be catalogued. The concepts which existed shortly before only in their reciprocal opposition are now to be added together. Perhaps that is what Lanson means when he affirms that criticism divides and literary history unifies. This latter verb is not quite exact. True unity is not a sum but a dialectic totality. The very idea of totality is foreign to literary history. That is precisely its weakness; today we have to choose between an outmoded positivism and one form or another of dialectical thought. Literary history does not unify; it can only add up. And what it adds is not really addible. The sum has no stability. Every modification of detail echoes throughout the system. It is not a matter of correcting a detail here or there, as they tell us, of tightening some bolt, of replacing a worn-out part with a new one. A whole *world vision* is in question, as Lucien Goldman would say. The learning of 1900 today reflects the world of 1900 no less than the *Mémoires d'Outre-Tombe* reflect the first quarter of the nineteenth century, the spiritual universe of Chateaubriand, Mme. de Staël, Benjamin Constant; with the difference that Benjamin Constant, Chateaubriand, and Mme. de Staël, much more than the petits-bourgeois professors of the triumphant Third Republic, are aware of *being immersed in* a particular historical period. They seem in many ways closer to our own cosmopolitan values.

The vision which fifty years ago sustained the overall plan of our literary history has vanished. If Nerval is entitled to only a footnote in Lanson's manual—a footnote shared, moreover, with Maurice and Eugénie de Gúerin—it is not because of an easily rectifiable error. Nerval cannot figure in the French romantic school as called for by this overall plan. This romantic school must be the counterpart of classicism as it is then conceived, just as Second Empire sculpture is made for the Classical Paris that surrounds it. Nerval does not measure up. He lacks a certain elegant stance, a monumental quality, a classicism-of-the-romantics to balance the romanticism-of-the classics. Indeed, that is just why we like him so much today. He rises among the ruins of a certain handbook romanticism. That Romanticism served as a buttress to the vaulting of Classicism. Everything has crumbled at once. Classicism survives, but within a new opposition to a newcomer: the baroque, whose presence upsets all previous designations.

One must control systems of opposition and not be controlled by them. Lanson, it will be said, foresaw the dialectical nature of certain oppositions. His formulas always have subtle shadings. He affirms, for example, that a certain author is influenced by another *although* he differs from him on numerous points. He will show us that romanticism and realism, *in spite of* their antagonism, have many common traits. Lanson demonstrates great *flexibility*. Frequently, he sees clearly even against his own principles; he rides roughshod over obstacles which ought to stop him. It is when he gives in to his intuitions that he interests us. And his scientific pretentions surprise us more and more; they are at best barely visible outside his methodological writings. Does this mean we must give up all rigor, all intellectual rules in literary studies? That would be to give up knowledge itself. Of course it is absurd to criticize the scientism of Lanson. But neither, perhaps, should we justify Lanson in the name of an intuitionism and an impressionism which lead nowhere. We must recover the demand for rigor and surpass it. If we look closely, we find that these nuances and this flexibility we admire so much in Lanson have no character of ineffability. These intuitions can be systematized. It is because realism and romanticism share the same literary project that they can be opposed to each other. Every opposition rests on a ground of identity. One may say of Lanson what Proust says of M. de Norpois, the diplomat of *A la Recherche*: his *althoughs* and *notwithstandings* are *becauses* unrecognized as such. But we have to recognize that oppositions and " influences " are dialectically linked, that the positive and the negative are inseparable the one from the other. In literary history one can proceed neither by positivist addition, nor by those absolute and quickly outmoded negations that living literature needs in order to survive. Whether we like it or not, the problem of dialectical thought presents itself, and even on the most technical level, before any ideology.

We cannot ignore the controversies surrounding language. The renaissance of dialectics is quite significant for us. For we are devoured by a secret scorn for our own language, forever irreducible to that of the exact sciences. Merleau-Ponty, structural linguists, and yet other thinkers show us that any language which is not equivocal ceases to have meaning. If there is any privileged language, it is not the poorest but the richest in ambiguities, in associations and resonances, both convergent and divergent. Ought we not examine the bodies of thought which claim to be able to restore literary studies to their full dignity?

As professionals in the field of language we must look squarely at the sickness afflicting language. There are those among us who are ready to believe, along with society as a whole, that nonquantifiable speech is essentially vain and empty speech, tolerable only if recognized as pure gratuity or simple diversion. Our faith in the object of our study has weakened. Perhaps this faith cannot be reconciled with a serene adherence to the values of contemporary society. But this adherence appears today as all the more appealing since, by a curious ricochet effect, we profit from the very thing that demeans our endeavors in the eyes of the world: the idea that there is no knowledge, in the strict sense of the word, except in the exact sciences and in tangible results—preferably explosive.

To reject without examination the kinds of thought that run counter to the dogma from which we are suffocating is to push intellectual paralysis to the point of a death wish. Are we to scorn minds that restore to us both our literature and our discourse on literature?

Are we to scorn those minds that restore to us Lanson himself? Lanson is rigorous within the limits of the language that determines him, but he is still more poetic than true, for that language is no longer ours. We must rediscover Lanson, integrate him into our literature, in other words, justify the love he inspires in us. How could we not love Lanson, that remote god who hovered ever and anon over our adolescence?

We did not approach him directly, but he quenched our thirst. Lanson, that surging but invisible spring which rained manuals and outlines on our lycées, which nourished the least of our professors. It is no wonder that we know him badly, that we oversimplify him: he came to us simplified and deformed. Well into the twentieth century this apostle of positivism reached us only by dint of becoming a legend. And, at the completion of this metamorphosis, what an admirable and irreplaceable mnemo-technic device is provided by that classicism and that romanticism, always as perfectly opposed and symmetrical as the Old and New Covenants in medieval sculpture. As in earlier centuries, French youth of our century were ignorant of the Bible but they had Lanson, who more or less replaced it, for he lacked neither prophets, major and minor, nor fathers, nor martyrs, always in equal numbers, always highly symbolical. The four great figures of Romanticism, all " lyric," all " picturesque," carry on an eternal dialogue in our memory with the four great figures of Classicism, always *reasonable*, invincible champions of " human nature." We had our tables and our concordances, our canonical and deutero-canonical books. It is only a matter of time before that Lanson will in our memory join a Péguy, who found him quite formidable and who would have loved him himself if he had known him at the right moment.

Our Lanson, we repeat, is not the real one. As reinterpreted by somewhat naïve exegetes and allegorists, his work filled all the better its role of Holy Scripture. And who knows whether the betrayal of which he was the victim did not provide in the long run a deeper truth? If we abuse a more or less imaginary " Lan-sonism," if Lanson makes us snicker foolishly, it is because he recalls our childhood for us and it is against our childhood that—perverse old children—we never stop rebelling. Positivism was not essential to Lanson, for in a simpler form, perhaps, this same perversity was already whispering to that excellent man that, from the elevation of his brand new scientific perch, he dominated the whole of literature and that he was in possession of that system of Judeo-Christian symbols—a symbolism the essential nature of which escaped him, not because it was alien to him but, on the contrary, because he was, like so many others, without being aware of it, still cosily berthed inside it. That symbolism, we must admit, is far more ample than the encyclopedism of the nineteenth century and far more important, even for the understanding of works allegedly beyond its range. If contemporary thought can just discover this truth, without regard to any philosophical or theological *parti pris,* it will not have proved unworthy of literary studies.

The original French text appeared in MLN *81 (1966).*

GENETIC STRUCTURALISM AND THE HISTORY OF LITERATURE ⁊ LUCIEN GOLDMANN ⁊

Genetic-structuralist analysis in the history of literature is only the application in this particular area of a general method which we believe to be the only valid method in the Sciences of Man. That is to say that we consider cultural creation a sector which is, while privileged, nonetheless of the same nature as all other sectors of human conduct and, as such, subject to the same laws and presenting to scientific inquiry difficulties which, if not identical, are at least analogous.

In the present article we shall try to bring out some of the fundamental principles of genetic structuralism as applied to the Sciences of Man in general and to literary criticism in particular, as well as some reflections concerning the analogy and the opposition between the two great complementary schools of literary criticism associated with this method: Marxism and psychoanalysis.

Genetic structuralism begins with the hypothesis that every instance of human conduct is an attempt to give a *significant response* to a particular situation and tends thereby to create an equilibrium between the acting subject and the object upon which the action turns, the ambient world of the agent. This tendency toward equilibration, however, always retains a fluid and provisional character insofar as any more or less satisfactory equilibrium between the mental structures of the subject and the external world leads to a situation within which the behavior of men transforms the world, this transformation rendering the former equilibrium unsatisfactory and engendering a tendency toward a new equilibration which will in its turn be superceded.

Thus human realities present themselves as two-sided processes: *destructuration* of old structures and *structuration* of new totalities capable of creating equilibria with the possibility of satisfying the new exigencies of the social groups producing them.

This essay has been translated from the French by Catherine and Richard Macksey.

In this perspective, the scientific study of human deeds, economic, social, political, or cultural, involves the attempt to bring to light these processes by revealing both the equilibria they break down and the new equilibria toward which they are oriented. This said, we have only to undertake a concrete investigation in order to encounter a whole series of problems, the most important of which we shall sketch here.

In the first place, there is the problem of knowing who is, in reality, the *subject* of the thought and of the action. Three types of response are possible, and they involve radically different attitudes. One can in fact (and this is the case of the empiricist, rationalist, and, recently, phenomenological positions) see the subject as the individual; one can also (and this is the case of Romantic thought) reduce the *individual* to a simple epiphenomenon and see the *collectivity* as the only real and authentic subject; or, finally, one can (and this is the case of dialectical thought, Hegelian and, above all, Marxist) admit, along with Romanticism, that the *collectivity* is the real subject, but without forgetting that this collectivity is nothing more than a complex network of individual interrelationships and that one must always define with precision the structure of this network and the particular place in it occupied by the individuals who manifestly appear to be the subjects (if not the final subjects, at the least the immediate subjects) of the behavior under consideration.

If we leave aside the Romantic position, oriented as it is toward mysticism and denying any reality or autonomy to the individual, insofar as the individual is perforce integrally identified with the group, we may seriously ask why in the first place the work of literature should be related to the social group and not to the individual who wrote it. For if the dialectical point of view does not deny the importance of the individual, neither do the rationalist, empiricist, and phenomenological positions deny the reality of the social milieu on the condition that it be seen only as external conditioning, as a reality acting on the individual in a causal way.[1]

The answer is simple: in trying to grasp the work in its specifically cultural characteristics (literary, philosophical, or artistic), the study which relates it solely or principally to its author can,

[1] In this perspective a sociological study can, at most, help to explain the genesis of a work, but in no way aid in its understanding.

within the present capabilities of empirical research, in the best of cases account for its internal unity and for the relationship between the whole and its parts; but such a study could never in any case establish positively the *same type* of relationship between the work and the man who created it. On this level, if one takes the individual as subject, the greater part of the work under consideration remains accidental, and it is impossible to get beyond the stage of more or less intelligent and ingenious reflections.

For as we have said elsewhere, the psychological structure of the individual is too complex a reality to be analyzed in the light of this or that collection of testimony about an individual who is no longer living, or an author one does not know directly, or even on the basis of intuitive or empirical knowledge of a person to whom one is more or less closely bound by friendship.

In short, no psychological study could account for the fact that Racine wrote exactly the body of dramas and plays that he wrote or explain why he could never have written the plays of Corneille or those of Molière.[2] Now however curious it may seem in connection with the study of great cultural works, sociology manages to discover more easily the necessary links in associating them with collective unities the structures of which are much more easily revealed.

These unities are doubtless only complex networks of interpersonal relationships, but the complexity of the psychology of individuals derives from the fact that each of them belongs to a greater or smaller number of different groups (family, profession, nation, friendships, social class, etc.) and that each of these groups affects his consciousness, thus contributing to the birth of a unique, complex, and relatively incoherent structure; whereas, inversely, as soon as we study a sufficiently large number of individuals *belonging to one, identical social group,* the action of the other different social groups to which each of them belongs, and the psychological effects due to this belonging, cancel each other out and we find

---

[2] However, if it is impossible to integrate into the biographical structure the content and the form—in short, the truly literary, philosophical, or artistic structure—of great cultural works, a school of psychology of the genetic-structuralist type, psychoanalysis, does succeed to a certain degree in identifying, alongside this *specific cultural essence,* a structure and an *individual* significance of these works which it believes it can fit into the biographical development. At the end of this article, we shall explain briefly the possibilities and the limits of this procedure.

ourselves considering a much simpler and more coherent structure.[3]

In this perspective, the relations between the truly important work and the social group, which—with the creator as intermediary —is found to be in the last analysis the true subject of the creation, are of the same order as the relations between the elements of the work and its ensemble. In the one case as in the other. we are considering the relation between the elements of a comprehensive structure and its totality, a relationship which is at once comprehensive and explicative in kind. This is why, if it is not absolutely absurd to imagine that had the individual Racine received a different education or lived in a different milieu, he might have written plays like those of Molière, it is, on the other hand, absolutely inconceivable to imagine the noblesse de robe of the seventeenth century developing an epicurean or radically optimistic ideology.

This is to say that, insofar as science is an effort to identify necessary relationships between phenomena, efforts to relate cultural works to social groups as their creating subjects prove—at the current level of our knowledge—much more fruitful than any attempt to consider the individual as the real subject of the creation.

Once this position is accepted, however, two problems arise. The first is that of determining the order of relationships existing between the group and the work; the second, that of determining which works and which groups can be so related.

On the first point, genetic structuralism (and more specifically the work of Georg Lukács) represents a real turning point in the sociology of literature. All other schools of literary sociology, old and new, try in effect to establish relationships between the content of literary work and that of the collective consciousness. This procedure, although it can sometimes produce results where similar transpositions really exist, does present two major drawbacks:

---

[3] Empirical statistics arrives at analogous conclusions: it is practically impossible to predict without a great margin of error whether Peter, Jack, or John will marry, will have an automobile accident, or will die in the coming year, but it is not difficult, on the contrary, to predict with a very small margin of error the number of marriages, accidents, and deaths which will take place in France in such and such a week. Even admitting this, and although related phenomena are involved, there are considerable differences between these statistical predictions concerning a reality the structures of which have not been defined and a genetic-structuralist analysis.

a) The writer's use of elements of content from the collective consciousness, or more simply, of the immediate empirical aspect of the social reality surrounding him, is almost never systematic or general and is found only at certain points in his work. To the degree, then, that the sociological method is exclusively or principally directed toward the search for correspondences of *content*, it fails to grasp the unity of the work, which is to say, its *specifically literary* character.

b) The reproduction of the immediate aspect of social reality and of the collective consciousness in a work is, generally speaking, most frequent when the writer is least creative and is content to describe or relate his personal experience without transposition.

This is why a sociology of literature oriented toward *content* often shows an anecdotal character and proves fruitful and efficient when it studies undistinguished works or *literary trends* but progressively loses validity as it approaches works of greatness.

On this point genetic structuralism has represented a complete change in orientation. Its fundamental hypothesis is precisely that the collective character of literary creation derives from the fact that the *structures* of the universe of the work are homologous to the mental *structures* of certain social groups, or in an intelligible relationship with them, whereas on the level of content, that is, of the creation of the imaginary universes governed by these structures, the author enjoys complete freedom. The utilization of the immediate aspect of his individual experience in the creation of these imaginary universes is no doubt possible and frequent but by no means essential, and the illumination of the process constitutes a useful but secondary task in literary analysis.

In reality, the relationship between the creative group and the work presents itself most often on the following model: the group constitutes a process of structuration which develops, in the consciousness of its members, affective, intellectual, and practical tendencies toward a coherent response to the problems posed by their relationships with nature and their interpersonal relationships. With few exceptions these tendencies still fall far short of effective coherence. They are, as we have noted, thwarted in the consciousness of individuals since each of them belongs to numerous other social groups.

Thus mental categories exist within the group only in the form of tendencies more or less advanced toward a coherence which we have called a *world vision*, a vision which the group, then, does not create, but the constitutive elements of which it develops (and the group alone can develop them) along with the energy necessary to bring them together. The great writer is precisely the exceptional individual who succeeds in creating in a certain field, that of the literary (or pictorial, or conceptual, or musical, etc.) work, an imaginary, coherent—almost rigorously coherent—universe whose structure corresponds to that toward which the whole of the group is tending. As for the work, it is, alongside other works, of inferior or superior quality according to its departure from or its adherence to rigorous coherence.

We can see the considerable difference which separates content sociology from structuralist sociology. The first sees in the work a *reflection* of the collective consciousness; the second sees in it on the contrary *one* of the most important *constitutive elements* of that consciousness, the element which permits the members of the group to become aware of what they were already thinking, feeling, and doing without having any objective knowledge of its signification. One can understand why content sociology proves more efficacious where mediocre works are concerned, whereas, inversely, genetic-structuralist literary sociology proves more fruitful where one is studying the masterpieces of world literature.

And yet an epistemological problem must be raised: even if *all* human groups act on the consciousness, the affectivity, and the behavior of their members, only the action of certain particular and specific groups is of such a nature as to favor cultural creation. So it is particularly important for concrete research to identify such groups in order to know in what direction to orient its investigations. The very nature of great cultural works indicates what the characteristics of these groups must be. These works in fact represent, as we have already said, the expression of world visions, that is, slices of imaginary or conceptual reality structured in such a way that, without having to complete their essential structure, one can develop them into all-inclusive totalities or universes. This structuration, then, can be related only to groups *whose consciousness tends toward an all-inclusive [globale] vision of man.*

From the point of view of empirical research, it is certain that for a very long time social classes have been the only groups of this kind—although we may still ask whether this assertion is valid for non-European societies, for Graeco-Roman antiquity and the periods that precede it, and perhaps even for certain sectors of contemporary society; but once again we must emphasize the point that this is a problem for positive empirical research and not a question of the ideological sympathies or antipathies we find at the root of all too many sociological theories.

However this may be, the assertion of the existence of a link between great cultural works and social groups oriented toward a global restructuration of society or toward its conservation eliminates at a stroke any attempt to link these works to a certain number of other social groups, notably to the nation, to the generation, to the province, to the family (to cite only the most important). Not that these groups do not act upon the consciousness of their members and, by the same token, upon that of the writer, but they can explain only certain peripheral elements of the work and not its essential structure.[4]

The empirical data, moreover, corroborate this affirmation; the fact of belonging to French society in the seventeenth century can neither explain nor make comprehensible the work of Pascal, Descartes, and Gassendi, or that of Racine, Corneille, and Molière, in that these works express different and even opposed world visions, even though their authors all belonged to seventeenth-century French society. On the other hand, this common membership may account for certain formal elements common to the three thinkers and the three writers.

After these preliminary considerations, we come to the most important problem for any research of the genetic-structuralist type: that of the delineation [*découpage*] of its object. Where the sociology of economic, social, or political life is concerned, this problem is particularly difficult and absolutely basic; in effect, one cannot study structures until one has designated in a fairly rigorous way the ensemble of immediate, empirical data that belong to them, and inversely, one can designate these empirical data only insofar as one has already a more or less well-developed hypothesis concerning the structure which constitutes their unity.

From the point of view of formal logic, this methodological circle may seem insoluble, but in practice it is easily resolved, like all such circles, by a series of successive approximations.

---

[4] Sociological work of this kind is of the same order as content sociology, which likewise can account for only certain secondary and peripheral elements of literary works.

Beginning with the hypothesis that one can bring a certain number of facts together in a structural unity, one tries to establish among these facts the maximum number of comprehensive and explicative relationships, trying at the same time to take in other facts which seem alien to it. One thus comes to eliminate some of the original facts, to add others, and to modify the initial hypothesis. One repeats this operation through successive approximations until one arrives at the point (the ideal point, more or less realizable according to the case) of a structural hypothesis able to account for a perfectly coherent ensemble of facts.[5]

When one studies cultural creation, it is true that one finds oneself in a privileged situation with regard to the initial hypothesis. It is in fact probable that the great works of literature, art, or philosophy constitute coherent, significant structures, so that the first delineation of the object of study is a given. And yet one must be on guard against the temptation to trust this presupposition too absolutely. It does in fact happen that the work may contain heterogeneous elements which must be distinguished from its essential unity. Further, if the hypothesis of the unity of a work has great credibility for the truly important works considered in isolation, this credibility diminishes considerably when we consider *the body of work of a single author*. This is why, in concrete research, we must begin with the analysis of each one of the author's works, studying them in the chronological order of their composition insofar as it can be established.

This study will permit us to form provisional groupings of his writings, on the basis of which we will seek in the intellectual, political, social, and economic life of the period structured social

---

[5] By way of example, one might begin with the hypothesis of the existence of a meaningful structure of dictatorship. One would then group together an ensemble of phenomena such as, for example, political regimes in which the government enjoys absolute power. But if one tries with a single structural hypothesis to account for the genesis of all such regimes, one quickly realizes that dictatorship is not a significant structure and that one must distinguish groups of dictatorships of different natures and significations; whereas, for example, the concepts of revolutionary dictatorship or of post-revolutionary Bonapartist dictatorship seem to constitute workable concepts.

In the same way, every attempt at a unitary interpretation of the writings of Pascal (and they have been numerous) fails before the fact that the two most important works, *Les Provinciales* and *Les Pensées*, express essentially different perspectives. To understand them, one must consider them as expressions of two structures, distinct, though in certain aspects related.

groupings into which we can integrate, as partial elements, the works being studied, establishing between them and the whole intelligible relationships and, in the most favorable cases, homologies.

The progress of a genetic-structuralist analysis consists in the delineation of the groups of empirical data which are set up as structures, as relative totalities,[6] and in their subsequent inclusion as elements in other, vaster structures of the same nature, and so on.

This method presents, among others, the double advantage of first conceiving the *ensemble* of human accomplishments in a unitary way and, second, of being simultaneously *comprehensive* and *explicative*, for the illumination of a significant structure constitutes a process of *comprehension*, while its insertion into a vaster structure is a process of *explication*. For example: to reveal the tragic structure of the *Pensées* of Pascal and of the theatre of Racine is a process of comprehension; to integrate them into extremist Jansenism while bringing out the structure of the latter is a process of comprehension with regard to Jansenism, but a process of explication with regard to the writings of Pascal and Racine; to integrate extremist Jansenism into the overall history of Jansenism is to explicate the first and comprehend the second. To integrate Jansenism, as a movement of ideological expression, into the history of the seventeenth-century *noblesse de robe* is to explicate Jansenism and comprehend the *noblesse de robe*. To integrate the history of the *noblesse de robe* into the overall history of French society is to explicate the former while comprehending the latter, and so forth. Explication and comprehension, then, are not two different intellectual processes but one and the same process related to two frames of reference.

Let us emphasize, finally, that in this perspective—in which the passage from the appearance to the essence, from the partial, ab-

---

[6] In this procedure, especially in cultural sociology, it is well to use an external and quantitative safeguard. When the interpretation of a piece of writing is concerned, it goes without saying that one can have a certain number of different interpretations which each account for from sixty to seventy percent of the text. This is why such a result must not be taken as scientific confirmation. On the other hand, it is rare to find more than one interpretation that integrates eighty to ninety percent of the text, and the hypothesis is quite likely to be valid. This probability increases greatly if one succeeds in utilizing it efficaciously in the explication of other texts one had not considered, and especially if (as was the case in our study of seventeenth-century tragedy) one succeeds in illuminating and even in predicting a certain number of facts unknown to specialists and historians.

stract empirical datum to its concrete and objective signification, is accomplished by integration into relative, structured, and significant totalities—every human accomplishment can and even must possess a certain number of concrete significations, differing according to the number of structures into which it can be integrated in a positive, feasible way. Thus, for example, Jansenism has to be integrated through the means already indicated into seventeenth-century French society, where it represents a retrograde and reactionary ideological current in opposition to the progressivist historical forces embodied primarily in the bourgeoisie and the monarchy and, on the ideological plane, in Cartesian rationalism. It is, however, every bit as legitimate and necessary to integrate Jansenism into the overall structure of occidental society as it has developed down to our own time, a perspective in which Jansenism becomes a progressivist ideology inasmuch as it constitutes one of the first steps in the direction of going beyond Cartesian rationalism toward dialectical thought. These two significations are of course neither mutually exclusive nor contradictory.

In this same order of ideas we would like finally to focus our attention on two problems of particular importance in the present state of literary criticism: (1) the problem of integrating literary works into two real and complementary totalities which can furnish elements of comprehension and of explication, to wit: the individual and the group, and (2) from this point on, the problem of the function of cultural creation in the lives of men.

On the first point, we have today two scientific schools of the genetic-structuralist type that correspond to the attempt to integrate works on the one hand into collective structures and on the other hand into individual biographies: Marxism and psychoanalysis.

Passing over the already acknowledged difficulties of bringing out individual structures, let us begin by considering the two schools at the level of methodology. Each proposes to comprehend and to explicate human achievements by integrating them into structured totalities, that of collective life in the one case and that of the individual biography in the other. Thus they constitute related and complementary methods, and the results of each of them ought to reinforce and complete those of the other.

Unfortunately, as genetic structuralism, psychoanalysis (at least as elaborated by Freud [7]) is not sufficiently consistent and is much too marked by the scientism that dominated university life at the end of the nineteenth century and the beginning of the twentieth. This is obvious on two capital points.

First, in Freudian explications the temporal dimension of the future is completely and radically missing. Under the influence of the deterministic scientism of his day, Freud entirely neglects the positive forces of equilibration that operate within any human structure, individual or collective. Explication means, for him, a return to childhood experiences, to instinctive forces repressed or suppressed. He neglects completely the potential positive function of consciousness and of relationship with reality.[8] Second, the individual, for Freud, is an absolute subject for whom other people can be only *objects* of satisfaction or of frustration. This perhaps accounts for the absence of future we have just noted.

It would no doubt be wrong to reduce the Freudian libido too strictly to the sexual domain. It is nonetheless always *individual*, and in the Freudian view of humanity the collective subject, and the satisfaction afforded the individual by a collective action, are entirely lacking.

One could develop at length, with the help of numerous concrete examples, the distortions caused by these perspectives in Freudian analyses of cultural and historical phenomena. From this point of view Marxism seems to us to be incomparably more advanced, in that it takes into account not only the future as an explicative factor but also the individual signification of human achievements along with their collective signification.

Finally, on the level that interests us here, that of cultural works, and literary works in particular, it seems incontrovertible that the latter can be validly integrated into significant structures of both

[7] We know too little of its subsequent developments to speak with any assurance.

[8] One would doubtless be tempted to explain this characteristic of Freud's work by the fact that he was a doctor and studied primarily sick persons, that is, beings in whom the power of the past and mental blocks predominated over the positive forces oriented toward equilibration and toward the future. Unfortunately, the criticism we have just formulated is equally valid for the philosophical and sociological studies of Freud.

The word "future" is found in the title of only one of his writings and—typical of the whole body of his work—it is called *The Future of an Illusion*, and its content proves that this future is nonexistent.

the individual and the collective type. It goes without saying that
the real and valid significations which these two types of integration
can bring out are at the same time different and complementary.
The integration of literary works into the biography of the individual can reveal only their individual signification and their relationship with the biographical and psychic problems of the author:
that is to say, whatever may be the validity and the scientific rigor
of this kind of research, it must of necessity situate the work outside
of its strictly cultural and aesthetic context and place it on the
same level as all other individual symptoms of this or that patient
in psychoanalysis.

Even assuming—without granting—that one could, on the individual level, validly relate Pascal's writings to his relationship with
his sister, or Kleist's writings to his relationships with his sister and
his father, *one would have shown one affective signification of these
works, but without touching on or even approaching their philosophical or literary signification.* Thousands and tens of thousands
of individuals have surely had analogous relationships with the
members of their families, and we fail to see how a psychoanalytical study of these symptoms could account in the slightest degree
for the difference in kind between the writings of any madman
and *Les Pensées* or *Prinz Friedrich von Homburg.*

The sole—and rather limited—service that psychological and
psychoanalytical analyses can render literary criticism seems to be
that of explaining why, in a given concrete situation in which a
given social group has developed a certain world vision, such and
such an individual, thanks to his individual biography, was particularly qualified to create a conceptual or imaginary universe to
the extent that he could find therein among others a satisfaction
derived from or sublimating his own unconscious aspirations.[9]
Thus it is only on the basis of a historico-sociological analysis that
the philosophical signification of *Les Pensées,* the literary and
aesthetic signification of Kleist's theatre, and the genesis of both
can *be understood as cultural facts.*

As for psychological studies, they can at best help us to under-

---

[9] Inversely, sociological study can furnish no information on the individual
biographical signification of literary works and can offer psychoanalysts only
relatively secondary information on the forms of real or imaginary satisfaction
of individual aspirations favored or imposed by collective structures at a given
period and in a given society.

stand why, among hundreds of Jansenists, Racine and Pascal were precisely the ones able to express the tragic vision on the literary and philosophical planes; but without offering us any information (beyond secondary and irrelevant detail) concerning the nature, the content, and the signification of the expression.

Finally, there remains the task of dealing schematically with a particularly important problem: that of the individual function (games, dreams, morbid symptoms, sublimations) and the collective function (literary, cultural, and artistic values) of the imaginary with regard to significant human structures, all of which present the common characteristics of the dynamic and structural relationships existing between a subject, collective or individual, and an ambient milieu.

The problem is complex and neglected. In closing this article we can only formulate a vague and tentative hypothesis. It seems to us, in effect, that on the psychic level, the action of the subject always presents itself as an ensemble of aspirations, tendencies, and desires the complete satisfaction of which is blocked by reality.

Marx and Lukács on the collective level and Piaget on the individual level have studied closely the modifications introduced into the very nature of these desires and aspirations by the difficulties and the obstacles presented by their object. Freud has shown that, on the individual level, desires, even modified, cannot be content with partial satisfaction and cannot be repressed without problems. His great merit lies in having discovered that a rational relationship with reality demands as its complement an imaginary satisfaction capable of taking on the most diverse forms, ranging from the well-adjusted structures of the *lapsus* and the dream to the maladjusted structures of alienation and madness.

It may be that the function of culture is analogous, in spite of all the differences. (We do not believe, for example, in a collective unconscious.) Human groups may act rationally upon reality and adapt themselves to the frustrations and partial satisfactions imposed by this action and the obstacles it encounters only to the degree that this rational and transforming action is accompanied by complete satisfactions on the level of conceptual or imaginary creation.

We must add, however, that if on the individual level repressed instincts subsist *in the unconscious* and tend toward a symbolic satisfaction which is always *possession*, collective tendencies, often implicit but not unconscious, tend not toward the *possession of an object* but toward the *realization of a coherence.*

Cultural creation thus compensates for the mélange, the compromises, the inconsistencies imposed on subjects by reality and facilitates their integration into reality, which is perhaps the psychological basis of catharsis.

A hypothesis of this kind, which would easily combine the valid aspects of Freudian analysis with those of Marxist studies of art and cultural creation, might account for both the kinship so often detected by theoreticians and the difference in nature (which remains no less real) between, on the one hand, the game, the dream, and even certain morbid forms of imagination and, on the other, the great literary, artistic, and even philosophical creations.

The original French text appeared in MLN *79 (1964).*

Beyond Formalism

GEOFFREY HARTMAN

Five years ago, on this campus, F. W. Bateson attacked what he called "Yale formalism." His main targets seem to have been Cleanth Brooks, René Wellek and W. K. Wimsatt, and he has recently added Yale's "pseudo-gothic Harkness Tower" to this distinguished list. Bateson defined formalism as a tendency to isolate the aesthetic fact from its human content, but I will here define it simply as a method: that of revealing the human content of art by a study of its formal properties. This definition does not say that form and content are separable, nor does it infer that the human and the formal could not be caught and exposited as one thing by a great interpreter. It does suggest that the literary scholar establishes a priority which has procedural significance, and which engages him mediately and dialectically with the formal properties of the work of art. I do not know whether the mind can ever free itself genuinely of these procedural restraints—whether it can get beyond formalism without going through the study of forms. I am sure, though, that the faults of those whom Bateson calls formalists are due not to their formalism as such but rather to their not being formalistic enough; and that, conversely, those who have tried to ignore or transcend formalism tend often to arrive at results more abstract and categorical than what they object to. My argument on these points will develop in a twofold way: I want first to take up an interpretation by Mr. Brooks, and a comparable one by Mr. Bateson, to suggest that their faults are alike (that neither critic is enough of a formalist); and will then consider an essay by an avowed anti-formalist, Georges Poulet, to suggest that he is more formalistic than he thinks, and that where he is less so his work may fail to situate the writer. My conclusion is a sceptical one, or else critical in the Kantian sense: to go beyond formalism is as yet too hard for us; and may even be, unless we are Hegelians believing in absolute spirit, against the nature of understanding.

I

In " Irony as a Principle of Structure " (1949) , Mr. Brooks interprets two of Wordsworth's lyrics on Lucy: " She dwelt among the untrodden ways " and " A slumber did my spirit seal." The essay is well-known, and I can limit myself to recalling what it says about Wordsworth. Mr. Brooks is anxious to show that irony is a general aesthetic structure, that it is found variously in the poetry of every school or period. Wordsworth, as in the Lucy poems, is a challenge to his thesis: common feeling as well as common verbal usage prevent us from thinking of such poetry as " ironic." Yet Mr. Brooks' armed vision, examining poems as clear as water, reveals to us new animalcules of structure. The following comment on the second stanza of " She dwelt among the untrodden ways " is representative of his argument for the presence in the Lucy poems of something comparable to witty contrast:

> The violet and the star . . . balance each other and between themselves define the situation: Lucy was from the viewpoint of the great world, unnoticed, shy, modest, and half hidden from the eye, but from the standpoint of her lover, she is the single star, completely dominating that world. . . . The implicit contrast is that so often developed ironically by John Donne in his poems where the lovers, who amount to nothing in the eyes of the world, become, in their own eyes, each the other's world—as in " The Good Morrow " . . . or as in " The Canonization," where the lovers drive into the mirrors of each other's eyes the " towns, countries, courts "—which make up the great world; and thus find that world in themselves. It is easy to imagine how Donne would have exploited the contrast between the violet and the star, accentuating it, developing the irony, showing how the violet was really like its antithesis, the star, etc.

To this let me add a quotation from Mr. Bateson's analysis of what he calls the dreamlike or unreal quality of the same poem:

> Wordsworth's method here is to combine positive and negative ideas so that they cancel each other out. . . . A simple example of the method is the paradox propounded by the last two words

of the poem's first lines. How can *ways* be *untrodden*? . . . There are two similar verbal contradictions in lines 3-4 and 9-10. . . . If it is possible to use language so loosely that *untrodden* need not mean 'not trodden,' that *love* cannot connote *praise*, and that *unknown* obtains a positive sense ('known to a few'), *and yet be completely intelligible*, the neighbouring oppositions and collocations of grammar and logic also tend to become discredited. Both the private and the public worlds retreat into a common unreality for the reader, who emerges with the impression that the boundaries between them are less absolute and perhaps less important than the surface meaning of these three sentences had suggested.

The same structure of "contradictions" is said to appear in the antithetic yet merging images of violet and star.[1]

The two interpretations have a problem in common. Both puzzle over a style that is felt to be, in some sense, a *no style*. Bateson recalls Matthew Arnold's comment that nature itself seemed to have written Wordsworth's poems for him. Yet Bateson interprets this as involving an attack on language as such. "In order to get at meaning behind language he has had to discredit and break down the ordinary apparatus of language." Hence those subversive qualifications. Yet to Wordsworth himself it surely seemed as if he were returning to, not breaking down, ordinary language: poetic diction is discarded for a natural diction. Unless "She dwelt among the untrodden ways" is a special case in Wordsworth's canon, Mr. Bateson's view is non-historical in that his understanding of the poet does not harmonize easily with the poet's understanding of himself.

Mr. Brooks' view is also non-historical in that no effort is made to relate the new and subdued style to the more overt style it replaced. Mr. Brooks suggests that there are at least two poetic modes centering on the art of contrast, and that Wordsworth's art differs from that of Donne or Marvell in favoring "simple juxta-position with no underscoring of the ironical contrasts." But he

---

[1] *Wordsworth: A Re-Interpretation* (London, 2nd ed., 1956), pp. 31-33. As a curiosity I might add that the first person to draw attention to the contrast implicit in the violet-star image was Mary Shelley in *The Last Man* (1826). "[Wordsworth's] lines," her narrator says, "always appeared to me rather a contrast than a similitude." He goes on to compare two women, Perdita "a violet . . . cowering from observation" and Idris "the star, set in single splendor, ready to enlighten and delight the subject world."

does not connect these modes, or read one of them out of court
by means of an Act of Uniformity. Thus we are left with two
essentially unhistorical descriptions of Wordsworth's style. Mr.
Bateson's is perhaps less formalistic, and more historical, in going
directly from a formal feature to a generalization about the engagement of the poet in his society and in the language moulded by it.
But we cannot check whether it goes genuinely from the one to the
other. The only kind of ideal or " objective " interpretation is that
in which we can cross-check our terms (rather than particular
exegeses or conclusions) by relating them to the poet's own or to
those prevalent in the poet's milieu. Interpretation is bringing the
poem forward into the present, which is acknowledging its historicity, which is grounding our terms in history. To do this we
must go beyond both Bateson and Brooks and describe as historically as possible the difference between the Wordsworthian 'no
style' and the stylish style it challenged.

Wordsworth's subtler mode serves to free the lyric from the
tyranny of *point*. To recover what the pointed style implied is to
review a considerable segment of literary history. The pointed style
as it developed in seventeenth-century England is witty and antithetical: everything in it is sharp, nervy, *à pic*, and overtly so like
a hedgehog. Metaphysical poetry, on which Brooks' poetics is ultimately based, although he has extended its range with the help
of Coleridgean theses, is a particular development of the pointed
style: indeed, its freest and richest efflorescence, even in prosody
where " point " and " roughness " unusually combine. Neoclassicism
pruned the hedgehog and smoothened the prosody. But both metaphysical and neoclassical style are essentially epigrammatic, and
each mediates between two recognized, divergent traditions of the
epigram. Scaliger had classified these as *mel* and *fel*; and tradition
varied these terms as *sweet* and *sour*, *sugar* and *salt*, *naive* and
pointed.[2] Short epigrams, writes Robert Haydn in his *Quodlibets*
(1628)

---

[2] See J. C. Scaliger, *Poetices Libri Septem* (Lyons, 1561), p. 171, Appendix
pro Epigrammate. Scaliger associates the " honey " type of epigram with Catullus,
and lists no less than four anti-types characterized by the terms " gall," " vine-
gar," " salt," and one that is outlawed " in qua foeditas est." He seems to
distinguish, further, between a continuously pointed epigram (" consertam,
densam, multiplicem ") and a finer, more naturally developed kind (" species
quaedam nobilis ac generosa . . . aequabilitate plena . . . ut sit venustas cum
gravitate, & acumen cum lenitate "). For echoes of Scaliger, or further evidence

> Short epigrams relish both sweet and sour,
> Like fritters of sour apples and sweet flour.

This may also, of course, reflect the Horatian *utile dulci*. Yet the condiments were not always so deliciously mixed. Because the sonnet had become identified with petrarquising poetry, or the sweet and honeyed mode, epigram was often contrasted with sonnet, as specialized in gall and the sour. Sir John Harrington, in his *Elegant and Witty Epigrams* (1618), sees it this way:

> Once by mishap two poets fell a-squaring,
> The sonnet and our epigram comparing,
> And Faustus, having long demurred upon it,
> Yet at the last gave sentence for the sonnet.
> Now for such censure this his chief defence is,
> Their sugared taste best likes his lick'rous senses.
> Well, though I grant sugar may please the taste,
> Yet let my verse have salt to make it last.

Those final lines, of course, are supposedly pointed and salty, like the concluding couplets in Shakespeare's sonnets—sonnets which, though essentially "sugared,"[3] attempted to marinate the style of love. By a natural development, since epigram and sonnet were not all that distinct, the pointed style often became the honeyed style raised to a further power, to preciousness. A new opposition is consequently found, not between sugared and salty but between pointed (precious, overwritten) and plain. Samuel Rowland gives us a bumbling sketch of that opposition at the turn of the century, when he describes an English *précieux ridicule* ordering his servant to fetch him his cloak:

> He utters speech exceeding quaint and coy:
> Diminutive, and my defective slave,
> Reach my corps couverture immediately.

of the prevalence of these categories, see Ben Jonson, *Epigrams* (1616), II and XLIX; also John Peter, *Complaint and Satire in Early English Literature* (Oxford, 1956), p. 297, and the valuable introductions in James Hutton, *The Greek Anthology in Italy* (Ithaca, 1935) and *The Greek Anthology in France and in the Latin Writers of the Netherlands* (Ithaca, 1946).

[3] "The sweete wittie soule of Ovid lives in mellifluous and hony-tongued Shakespeare, witnes his *Venus* and *Adonis*, his *Lucrece*, his sugred Sonnets among his private friends, &c." Francis Meres, reprinted by G. G. Smith, ed., *Elizabethan Critical Essays* (Oxford, 1904), II, 317.

> My pleasure's pleasure is the same to have,
> T'ensconce my person from frigidity.
> His man believes all's Welsh his master spoke,
> Till he rails English, Rogue, go fetch my cloak! [4]

Wordsworth redeems the mother tongue from such precious and foreign artifice—but without railing. The Lucy poems, Lucy herself, are directed against something non-English: Lucy is no German-Gothic spook or French coquette. The style of the poems is a new and gentle plain style. Following Ben Jonson's example English poetry had tried to marry plain style to the sinew and maleness of point. The poems of Herbert, and especially those of Marvell, are an exceptionally successful blend of the naive and the pointed epigram.[5] Ben himself had chosen plainness as most appropriate for the epitaph, where things were to be expressed at once pithily and simply. Yet precisely the epitaph succumbed most often to the tyranny of point. Eighteenth century elegiac verse at best is smooth antithesis and elegant turn: at worst, striving for the simplicity of pathos, as in the verses on the Lady who passed away at Bath (" She bowed to the wave, and died ") the expectation of point leads to splendid instances of the art of sinking. Lyttleton's epitaph on his wife illustrates the usual and perverse smoothness of eighteenth century elegiac lyricism. Here is Lyttleton's Lucy:

> Made to engage all hearts, and charm all eyes,
> Though meek, magnanimous; though witty, wise;
> Polite, as all her life in Courts had been;
> Yet good, as she the world had never seen. . . .[6]

And here is Wordsworth's:

> A Maid whom there were none to praise
> And very few to love

[4] *Letting of Humor's Blood* (1600). See the highly instructive section on Epigrams in J. W. Hebel and H. H. Hudson, *Poetry of the English Renaissance 1509-1660.*

[5] I have tried to broach the question of Marvell's epigrammatic style in *ELH*, XXXI (1964), 185 ff.

[6] See also Wordsworth's *Essay on Epitaphs*, where this poem is quoted. For Dr. Johnson, on the road to Romantic sensibility, elegy and epigram came to stand in opposition. His *Dictionary* (1st ed., 1755) defines elegy, inter alia, as " A short poem without points or affected elegancies," where point is defined as " A sting of an epigram; a sentence terminated with some remarkable turn of words or thought."

> Fair as a star, when only one
> Is shining in the sky
> She lived unknown, and few could know
> When Lucy ceased to be. . . .

Is this not a tender parody of Lyttleton's pointed inanities? Instead of a *catalogue raisonné* of mutually qualifying and even alliterative antitheses, Wordsworth's statements are almost tautological, or with a second clause so simple as not to qualify the first in any calculating (plus or minus) fashion. Lucy is in her grave, subtract one: but the difference, as Wordsworth says, is incalculable. His verbal style purifies the mannered lyric and particularly the elegiac epigram.

In the light of this abbreviated history of lyric style, what Brooks calls irony or paradox is not an independent structural principle but is mediated by literary traditions developing in contradistinction to each other. The sharper epigram, often satirical, but not inevitably so, prided itself on a continuous fireworks of pointed sentiments and phrases, while the honeyed epigram had to justify itself by parallel yet finer devices. These devices, when they are truly fine and not merely dainty, are hard to describe because they grow naturally out of language or thought. To define them by terms drawn from the rhetoric of the copious style is futile, since we have to do with relatively brief and intensely personal verses—with lyric poetry. The only historical procedure open to us is to see how the modern lyric liberates itself from the tyranny of the witty style. The quarrel of the epigrammatists is especially intense at the beginning of the seventeenth century, when the vernacular art-lyric is freeing itself from its subordination to music, emerging as an independent genre, and so finding its own resources, both of the mellifluous and the pointed kind. The initial dominance of that pointed style we are accustomed to call metaphysical is probably due to this war of independence, since point, combined with roughness of versification, was at farthest remove from the musicality of music. Both Sidney's and Shakespeare's sonnet series participated in this battle of sugar and salt. The battle did not cease with the independence of the lyric: the two modalities remained, now mixing, now antagonistic. We begin to recover in this way the historical terms that validate Brooks' description of Wordsworth's style as " juxtaposition without an underscoring of the ironical contrasts,"

and Bateson's more specialized observation on the subversive antitheses in " She dwelt among the untrodden ways."

Our conclusion was reached, however, by a ' formalistic' exercise
in literary history. While existential issues are not excluded they
remain closely associated with literary technique. Whatever ideas
a composer may have must be translated by a set of equivalences
into musical phrase: so it is here with human concerns that express
themselves as modifications of style. I would not be so naive as to
equate formalism with an understanding of the history of style,
but I do not see, whatever else may be added, that it can do without
this understanding. And only now, I feel, are we in position to ask
the kind of question that might indeed lead beyond a primary
concern with style or form or even poetry. The history of style
itself seems to urge us beyond formalism by asking: what is the
point of *point*? Conversely, what is achieved by Wordsworth's creation of so pointless, so apparently simple a style?

The question may serve to clarify the modern and recurrent
aspiration towards a ' natural' style. It can be charged that neoclassical poetry, or lyricism Old Style, was a didactic and digital
poetry, calculating, pointing, computing too much by fingers and
feet. It knew its weakness, certainly; and much of the theory of
the time cautions against false wit and excessive *pointe*. (Marjorie Nicolson has written about " The Breaking of the Circle ";
it is also useful to consider " The Breaking of the Point.") Perhaps
Wordsworth comes to reveal rather than teach, and so to free poetry
of that palpable design which Keats still charged him with. All
truth, said Coleridge, is a species of revelation.

Revelation of what? The question cannot be answered without
a certain kind of pointing, as if truth were here or there, as if life
could be localized, as if revelation were a property. Yet Wordsworth's concepts of nature, of natural education and of poetry, are
all opposed to this reduction. Who knows, Wordsworth asks in
The Prelude,

> . . . the individual hour in which
> His habits were first sown, even as a seed?
> Who that shall point as with a wand and say
> ' This portion of the river of my mind
> Came from yon fountain? '

The error in such pointing is not only intellectual, due to that "false secondary power . . . by which we multiply distinctions"; it is also spiritual. Pointing is to encapsule something: strength, mind, life. It is to overobjectify, to overformalize. It implies that there is a fixed locus of revelation or a reified idolatrous content.

Yet pointing in this larger sense cannot be avoided: it seems inextricably tied to the referential nature of signs or the intentional character of thought. All Wordsworth can do is to emancipate the direction of the reference. The Lucy poems, taken as a sequence, remove the mimetic dependence of imagination on reality, or on any fixed order of ' this then that.' We cannot tell whether the poet is reacting to an imaginary thought or to an actual death, or which of the two came first. Lucy's death is reflective rather than reflected; it is, in fact, so strongly linked to the awakening consciousness as to be coterminous with the latter.[7] Lucy is a fiction integral to the mind: did she not exist she would have to be invented. Her mode of being, therefore, cannot be reduced to the imagined or the real by a temporal principle of anteriority or an ontological one of priority. Between the imagined and the real there is, in Merleau-Ponty's words, a "modulation of coexistence." Reflection becomes revelation and alters so radically the relation of consciousness to itself that Wordsworth sometimes denies primacy to his point of departure. Thought "hath no beginning." This is something Georges Poulet, to whom we now turn, and who loves beginnings, should interpret.

II

If it is hard to be a thorough formalist, it is equally hard to be a genuine anti-formalist. Georges Poulet's work may help to illustrate this. What I say is critical of him, but I take it for granted that his work is sufficiently esteemed to withstand my barbs.

Poulet has not written on Wordsworth, though a long essay on Romanticism refers to him as well as including a section on Coleridge. I prefer to choose for analysis his essay on Henry James in *Les Métamorphoses du Cercle* (1961). Poulet's method is to place himself in a writer's consciousness. He can do this by ignoring all

[7] To interpret this link as expressive of the primacy of consciousness is to reintroduce the (now causal) notion of ' this then that' and with it the magical view that Wordsworth's thought is symbolically killing Lucy off. See Bateson's thesis in *Wordsworth: A Re-Interpretation*.

formal distinctions, as between part and whole, or preface, novel, journalistic comment, *obiter dicta*. He may be sacrificing lesser forms to greater, but this would have to be proved, not assumed. Chronological distinctions are also ignored: the method, in truth, approaches that of the synoptic reading of the gospels. In the case of the gospels there is of course a central event, a common mythos responsible for the clustering of the original stories and which outweighs their divergencies. It is not surprising that something similar to this center is assumed by Poulet as common to the biblia of the individual writers. This center is the artist's ' cogito,' a continuously generated relation linking thought to the world, the *I think* to the *I am*. This is the crux relation, as it were. It precedes or constitutes all other relations of time, space, imagery, action.

Henry James' cogito is defined in the following terms. " To become conscious of oneself and the world is to be conscious of a double expanse whose borders are impossible to reach and whose parts cannot be separated out. Everything is connected, continuous and growing, everything stretches out as an illimitably growing web. We search in vain to discover something that might be isolated." The problematics of the Jamesian consciousness derive from this situation in which form is impossible except as a self-constituted and always illusory act. In James the formalization of consciousness is the very center of the literary activity, and there are no forms to be transcended except those imposed by the individual consciousness on itself.

Poulet aims at nothing less than the rewriting of literary history as a history of human consciousness. (Of masters he acknowledges, among others, Marcel Raymond, Paul Hazard, the Abbé Bremond, and Gaston Bachelard.) But are there not as many consciousnesses or cogitos as there are individuals? Poulet admits the difficulty and proposes a solution. The only way to emerge from this infinity of individuals, and to gain something that can be called history, is to postulate a period consciousness in which contemporaries participate.[8] The problem faced is similar to that of Dilthey who also wishes to respect the uniqueness of the individual and was obliged to postulate a typology of world-views which subsumed, as a genus does its species, types of great men. In the absence of an explicit

[8] Cf. J. Hillis Miller, " The Literary Criticism of Georges Poulet," *MLN* 78 (1963) , 471-488.

comment by Poulet it is difficult to decide whether his period consciousness is a heuristic device, or whether it is grounded in a Hegelian view of the development of the human spirit.

Poulet's predominantly thematic method helps him to periodize
the cogito of each writer. The themes chosen by him are well-
known: space, time, center-and-circle. It is less obvious, perhaps,
that these themes play the same role in the periodization of consciousness as Lovejoy's unit-ideas in the history of ideas. Lovejoy
sees the history of ideas developing as the continuous attempt to
reconcile an original paradox or antinomy in the idea of God.
Time and space yield similar paradoxes for Poulet who traces the
reconciling strategies of individual writers. His work illustrates and
enriches rather than revises the accepted historical outlines; and
his history remains a history of ideas with expanded materials and
a finer method. I do not mean to suggest that a critic must rewrite
literary history, but it is a curious anti-formalism which strains at
the gnat of genre distinctions and is obliged to swallow the camel
of periodization. I am not sure that Poulet gives us more than a
subtle and expanded Great Chain of Inner Being. A considerable
achievement, certainly; but is it what Poulet intended?

The need to periodize, which I take as a residual formalism, can
seriously and detrimentally influence Poulet's studies. Many observations on James, acute and interesting as they are, would be
more adequate to someone else; to Butor, or Virginia Woolf, or
Valéry. They rarely reach to the quick of James' consciousness, to
that which makes him unmistakably Jamesian. Take this remark,
for instance, on the passage of time: " Time," says Poulet, " is
realized by substitution, not of one moment for another but of one
place for another. It is as ' localized ' a time as possible. James'
novel becomes a succession of changes of locale." This is certainly
true, and Butor in *La Modification* may only exploit the technique,
yet the remark omits something more primitive and essential in
James, his refinedly superstitious response to spirit of place. The
fact is that there are few neutral places in the world of his novels:
place is always impregnate with spirit, and spirit is characterized
by intentionality. The displacement of a person, as from America
to Europe, is the start of a spiritual adventure involving a gothic
traversing of unknown areas of influence, not necessarily forbidden
rooms, recesses and gardens, yet analogous to these. Place has
presence or is an extension of a presence: and if people fall under

the spell of others, it is because they cannot escape an intentionality that extends to place and haunts imagination like a ghost.

If Poulet loses by the formalism he must retain, does he gain by what he rejects? It is part of his antiformalism to make no distinction between Coleridge's primary and secondary imaginations. The I AM implicit in every act of consciousness is also the I AM revealed by art. In art as elsewhere consciousness feels out or I-am-izes the world; and the relation, in the original cogito, of "I think *therefore* I am," is shown to be phenomenological rather than logical. All knowledge is personal knowledge, a construction putting us in relation to the world and to ourselves. It is as if Cartesianism were the trauma or primal scene of the history of consciousness which the individual mind progressively repeats. The structure of this repetition is what concerns Poulet, but he does not link it explicitly to the manifest form of the work of art. This omission, however fatal, gives him a certain initial advantage over the formalist critic. By looking *through* form, as Blake claims to look through rather than with the eye, Poulet gains his unusually intimate access to the writer's mind. It does not matter to him whether he enters that mind by door or window or through the chimney: he tells us what he finds inside without telling us how he got in. Yet one thing he cannot properly describe—the essential latency of what he finds, the quality of art's resistance to intimacy. Art, says Wallace Stevens, *almost* resists the intelligence. In Poulet the differential relation of form to consciousness is lost. Yet form represents the Other to the practising artist; it is form he must I-am-ize. And the stronger his concern with form the more difficult his task: here, if anywhere, is "the seriousness, the suffering, the patience, and the labor of the Negative."

The essay on James shows how interesting yet unsatisfactory Poulet can be on the subject of form. We have already noted his remark that since, in James, life gives no single or definitive clue for its organization the artist himself must cut the tangle and find a limiting view. Thus "point-of-view" is not a technique to achieve interiority but a way of limiting introspection in order to make character and plot possible. Consciousness as such appears to be no problem; the only problem is how to represent it.

A difficulty of *representation*, however, is not yet a difficulty of *being*. Poulet either assumes or does not make the connection. He writes as if everything were a procedural rather than substantive matter; and he is probably misled by James' casual style of self-commentary. It is admirable that James should talk in such objective if engaged fashion about his art, but this will deceive no one truly respectful of his realized art: of verbal style, plot as story, plot as pressure of story leading to discoveries, and thematic structure. Of these Poulet respects only one kind of thematic repetition, the imagery of point and circle, and there he misses the fact that "point" is by no means divested of sting, and wavers between its neutral and its wounding sense. Things come to a "point" with difficulty in James because that point is knowledge and knowledge is still under its old curse: it is an originative wound, a seeing of the evil mixed in with the good. Consciousness is the place at which being reveals itself as wounded. James' problem is not that of facing as a writer the plenitude of things and having arbitrarily to limit it: his problem is not to be able to think of consciousness as disinterested, as a free and innocent appetite. Its appetitiveness is what is curbed by the self-imposed convention of point-of-view, though the momentum of James' novels erodes all such curbs.

That the difficulty is one of being rather than of representation is reflected by everything so naturally excluded from Poulet's essay. He does not mention the central importance of marriage, and a Jamesian marriage, or an analogous contract, is what principally generates, as well as imposes form on, consciousness. If we respect the simplest themes and structural features of James' novels, we must describe his cogito as follows. In the beginning the mind is conscious of a plot or secret marriage of some kind. Eventually, the mind is conscious of itself—of its own complicity or 'secret marriage.' Consciousness, in other words, is not at all free or disinterested. It is knowingly or unknowingly the result of a contract, as in *Faust*, of a conspiracy, as in the Fall, or of a covenant like the crucifixion. Such *liaisons dangereuses* implicate us, make us historical, and create in us a new and powerful awareness. From this perspective each novel is seen to be a story that exacts from its hero and often from the story-teller himself a contractual quid pro quo. Consciousness must be paid for, and the usual wages are sacrifice and death. Thus whatever stands greatly against consciousness is drawn into a plot whose acquisitive and inquisitive purposes blend; the plot tests, until it destroys, the illusion that there is innocence or disinterestedness. I find no way to reconcile this view with Poulet's benevolent conclusion: "The astounding peripheric

activity of multiple consciousnesses has, in James, the effect of in-
flating reality by charging it with all the possibilities it implies.
Truth is a center surrounded by a luminous halo of both infinite
and finite possibilities." No wonder that Bachelard commended
phenomenology as "une école de naïveté"! This is the expanse,
not the expense, of vision. Consciousness here is purely a good,
and its triumph a matter of mental technology. The shadow-side
of James is elided.

It is not that Poulet cannot respect this side of a writer (see, for
example, his important study of Pascal).[9] Perhaps his error might
have been avoided by considering the form of the novels and of
their sequence, yet I doubt it is directly caused by the absence of
this check. The flaw seems to reside in too optimistic a view of the
Progress of Consciousness. Poulet is certainly too optimistic regarding James. By unperplexing James' "consciousness of consciousness," or substituting a perplexity of representation for one
of being, he harmonizes James with a stage in the history of consciousness that might have been reached. As long as the artist,
moreover, is in phase with a supposed historical progress, the problem of evaluation need not arise, and Poulet prefers it that way.
His view of history is too formal, and his understanding of the
writer not formal enough. He has not been able to situate James
either in history or in the realm of values.

III

I conclude with the following observation. The case against
formalism was stated eloquently forty years ago in Trotsky's *Literature and Revolution*. "Having counted the adjectives," says Trotsky
of the formalist, " and weighed the lines, and measured the rhythms,
a Formalist either stops silent with the expression of a man who
does not know what to do with himself, or throws out an unexpected
generalization which contains five per cent Formalism and ninety-
five per cent of the most uncritical intuition." Our modern formalist is more sophisticated than this literary quasi-scientist but the
remedy would seem to be the same. What is needed for literary
study is a hundred per cent of formalism and a hundred per cent
of critical intuition. Like all counsels of perfection this one sets
an impossible ideal. But I do not see why the study of forms

[9] *Études sur le temps Humain* (1949), ch. 3.

should distract from genuine critical intuition, or why there should be competition between virtues. There are many ways to transcend formalism, but the worst is not to study forms. Even multiplying distinctions in the manner of Northrop Frye helps to free literary study because it frees the mind vis-a-vis literature. Categories and forms are man-made before they are authenticated by tradition, and if we think Frye proposes too many terms and Brooks too few, we may have to rethink the whole question of terminology in an arduous, perhaps philosophical way—in fact to examine the *term* aspect of terms.

Lest these comments seem too unobjectionable, I should add that there is good reason why many in this country, as well as in Europe, have voiced a suspicion of " Anglo-Saxon formalism." The dominion of Exegesis is great: she is our Whore of Babylon, sitting robed in Academic black on the great dragon of Criticism, and dispensing a repetitive and soporific balm from her pedantic cup. If our neo-scriptural activity of explication were as daring and conscious as it used to be when Bible texts had to be harmonized with strange or contrary experience: i. e., with history, no one could level this charge of puerility. Yet our present explication-centered criticism *is* puerile, or at most pedagogic: we forget its merely preparatory function, that it stands to a mature criticism as pastoral to epic. Explication is the end of criticism only if we succumb to what Trotsky called the formalist's "superstition of the word." To redeem the word from the superstition of the word is to humanize it, to make it participate once more in a living concert of voices, and to raise exegesis to its former state by confronting art with experience as searchingly as if art were scripture.

1966

Symbolic Criticism ✤ by Ezio Raimondi ✤

To my friend
Charles S. Singleton

Discussing contemporary criticism with that amiable empiricism which still seems the secret of the English, especially in polemical exchanges, Graham Hough, who is a reader with a diligent and, one might say, rationalistic historical bent, as comfortable with the last, *fin de siècle* Romantics as with the poetic universe of a Lawrence, has written that if we take as a point of reference the concrete exercise of interpretation we can currently distinguish two types of reading and of criticism—the one positivistic, the other symbolic. The first recognizes as its proper aim the illumination of the linguistic and cultural facts which constitute the evidence, the individuality of a text. The second postulates that a literary work contains a hidden or implicit sense and that it is the strategy of the reader to bring to light this profound significance, immanent in the construction, in the internal form of a text.

This dichotomy is not new in Anglo-Saxon culture: it can be found, just for example, in the lucid little book of Helen Gardner, *The Business of Criticism*, or in the sound lectures of Ronald S. Crane, *The Languages of Criticism and the Structures of Poetry;* and it corresponds (as these authors state) to the old exegetical opposition between literal meaning and spiritual meaning, an opposition which has been posed anew in completely different ways by the poetry of the last two centuries as a conflict between predication and suggestion. This comparison with medieval hermeneutics implies, in the eyes of those who make it, an irreducible reservation; but this does not alter the fact that the symbolic attitude is in accord with certain aspects of modern sensibility and may represent one of its primary (perhaps even distinctive) characteristics. With good reason Roland Barthes, when taking a programmatic stand on the

This essay has been translated from the Italian by Catherine and Richard Macksey.

nouvelle critique, as the French call it, and on its bases, has maintained that what separates it from traditional interpretations is its awareness of that second language—profound, vast, symbolical—of which the work of art is made. As soon as we have agreed to consider the work of art in itself, from the point of view of its own constitution, it becomes impossible, Barthes continues, not to affirm that certain texts demand a symbolical reading, the principle of which is that of the plurality, of the verticality of meanings—of *polysemia,* to use a Dantesque term.

There is a question here not, of course, of deciding who is right but only of noting the success and the breadth of a cultural attitude, supported moreover by the most diverse investigations, in a framework of perspectives and relationships which it is rather difficult to bring together, especially when one remains within the confines of a single linguistic tradition, ignorant, as is so often the case, of the parallel experiences of neighboring traditions. Even though the roots of the phenomenon are to be found, certainly, in postsymbolist literature, with the great experiments of a Yeats, an Eliot, a Joyce, a Claudel, a Rilke, a Proust, a Broch, we must not forget, on the level of theoretical reflection, the contributions of philosophers like Ernst Cassirer, Susanne Langer, Philip Wheelwright, Paul Ricoeur, and Gaston Bachelard, who have helped to make the symbol a focal concept of contemporary culture, in support of a new phenomenology, adopted by the linguists, of the metaphor, of the image, of poetic ambiguity. On the other hand, it is impossible to be unaware of the role of psychoanalysis and the penetration of its interpretive models, whether we assume the theses of Freud, of Jones, of Szondi, or of Lacan, not to mention Melanie Klein, or accede to the revisionism of a Jung or a Fromm, or accept the psycho-existentialist thematics of a Binswanger, in the version of a Foucault for instance. And finally there remains, as another decisive presence, the lesson of anthropology, with its research concerning the structures of myth and analogico-ritual thought, launched by Frazer's *The Golden Bough* (not to go so far back as the great Romantics) and leading up to the explorations of a Malinowski or a Campbell, the structuralism of a Lévi-Strauss, or, in a Jungian context, the archeology of an Eliade or a Kerényi. But it is also true that with respect to literature these interests and orientations tend to change places, to overlap, to be confused. The fact that the Eliot of *The Waste Land* uses Frazer or Weston and that the Mann of *Joseph and his Brothers* consults Kerényi indicates precisely a fluid and open connection, within which it is inevitable that the problems posed for an attentive reader should become so intertwined that one can no longer distinguish them clearly, so natural is the passage from one to another. As one acute observer of contemporary literary culture has said, the problem of metaphor and of poetic imagery automatically involves us in the problems—bound together by semantics—of myth and indirect language.

Only after a monitory introduction of this kind, with the approximate values of our classification defined in advance, can we agree to recognize within symbolic criticism, or " semantic " criticism, as some prefer to call it, three lines of development corresponding to the three fundamental nuclei we have already indicated. Thus there is a first, metaphoric-ontological form; a second, thematic-psychoanalytical one; and a third, mythico-ritualistic one. In order to examine them more closely, we must make a selection—because of the superabundance of material—and this makes it necessary to proceed by examples according to a scheme which must be somewhat arbitrary and yet instructive. If we exclude at the outset Dante criticism (within which, however, one ought by now to grant to the *dantista* Pascoli a position of prominence in Europe precisely for his metaphorical reading), the area in which the interpretive logic of symbolic ontologism has been exercised with greatest perseverence seems to be that of Shakespeare studies, where we can speak of a real tradition in the proper sense. In saying this we are not referring so much to the experiment of Caroline Spurgeon's *Shakespeare's Imagery and What It Tells Us* (with its very serious limitations due to the psycho-biographical fallacy) as to the great studies of G. Wilson Knight, to the readings of L. C. Knights, of Robert Heilman, of Harold Goddard, of Derek Traversi, and even of F. R. Leavis or Wolfgang H. Clemen. These critics share more or less in the conviction that the concepts of character and of dramatic action do not get at the deep structure of the text, but rather obfuscate its inventive resonances, its imaginative dynamics; that the time has come to substitute, for a positivism of naturalistic bent, a symbolic reading, cleaving to all the expressive tensions of poetic language, to the drama which is kindled within every metaphor and is communicated as it proliferates to the different levels of the imagery. The text, the brilliant Peter Brook would agree, becomes an organism, a mystery to be sounded with a stethoscope.

In one of his most representative books, *The Wheel of Fire,* appropriately prefaced by T. S. Eliot, Wilson Knight envisages in almost these terms what is to be considered a truly interpretive reading. Every drama, he informs us, is to be understood as a visionary unity, summoned to obey only its own internal laws. To arrive at this, the reader must identify the spatial and temporal elements of the text with which he enters into a dialog, correlating every speech and every event both with the temporal sequence of the "story" and with the special, imaginative and ideological atmosphere which envelops the work. Consciousness of these new elements no longer leads to a search for the old verisimilitude but to the idea that a drama represents a great metaphor, by means of which the original vision is projected in a system of forms appropriate to the demands of its own nature. The coherence of the story, therefore, is to be measured on the basis of the whole stylistic organism in the movement of a symbolic language the events of which cannot conform to the processes of quotidian realism. And here one must attend especially to the secondary images, in which Shakespeare is abundantly rich, because if certain images constantly recur in the same associative context and this power of association proves to be of some intensity, each of these images, even in isolation, implies the presence of this common value with its emotive and conceptual background.

Knight has been reproached, however, with the charge that a criticism like his runs the risk of reducing itself to a series of general oppositions, of the life-death, love-hate, order-chaos, light-darkness type, lacking any discriminating grasp when confronted with individual texts. And, in effect, his visionary-metaphysical penchant almost always goes beyond the thematic horizon of a work, to the verge of a neo-romantic fantasmagoria. Knight's position appears decidedly more balanced and less arbitrary when, in the retrospective pages of his *Some Shakespearian Themes* (1959), he specifies that the meanings underlying the level of story and characters take the form of a living structure, and that if this structure of meanings is closely connected with certain recurring and interrelated images, the mind of the reader is obliged to turn back on itself, to reexamine its vision of the before-and-after, to seize the totality in its parts, to infer from the interplay of the

parts a living whole. Therefore only in relation to this more vast
and complex meaning, defined by the literal sense and by its
undertones, by the dramatic situation and the progress of the
action, by the symbols and by the interaction of the various attitudes
realized in the characters, can the system of the imagery assume its
proper fullness of meaning as a sort of armature, a magnetic axis
around which gathers the energy of the poetic language. Thus, for
example, a term such as " justice," implicit or explicit, runs through
the whole text of *King Lear* and, in a dialectical relationship with
other key words, conveys a mobile image of life. Each of these
words, precisely because of its evocative charge, creates a sphere of
ambiguity, a constellation of complementary and sometimes contrasting meanings, within a space which expands in the unexpected-
ness of the metaphor.

The notion of the "complex word," to which Knight refers,
recapitulates the subtle semantic experimentation of Empson, on
the model of *Seven Types of Ambiguity* and *The Structure of
Complex Words,* and in a certain sense marks the passage to a
criticism of a more traditionally stylistic type—midway between the
" New Criticism " [1] and Spitzerian philology—which concerns itself
with the metaphorical universe of a writer. Within this newly
delineated group some figures must be mentioned at the outset:
the scholarly Stephen Ullman of *Style in the French Novel* and
The Image in the Modern French Novel, with its chapters on the
symbol of the sea in *Le Grand Meaulnes,* on the metaphorical
texture of Proust's *Recherche,* on Gide's imagery; or even, changing
our scope a bit, Pierre Guiraud's lexicographical research and
his theory of the stylistic field, which calls for a vertical reading in
a dynamic system of expressive values and sublinguistic patterns,
and picks up again, moreover, the symbolism of Gaston Bachelard
with its fertile phenomenology of material imagery, of archetypes,
and of cosmic-oneiric complexes. But perhaps, for one who follows
the work of the *nouvelle critique,* to mention the fascinating and
at the same time ingenuous Bachelard (of *L'Eau et les rêves, La
Terre et les rêveries du repos, La Terre et les rêveries de la volonté,
L'Air et les songes*) is to invoke inevitably the name of Jean-Pierre
Richard, even if his thematic method cannot be said to derive

---

[1] For discussions of the "New Critics," see entries in the bibliography under
Krieger and Stallman [Ed.].

uniquely from the *imagination poétique* and welcomes with optimistic openness many other leads, from existentialism to structuralism, from Poulet to Barthes or Ricoeur.

As we read in *L'Univers imaginaire de Mallarmé*, the work in which Richard's criticism unfolds in all the richness of its subtle textures in search of a poetry which is an adventure of being, a *theme* is a concrete principle of organization, a scheme or an object around which, through the reverberation of analogy, of secret but insistent resonances, a world tends to constitute and develop itself. If it is true, as Mallarmé said, that the essence of poetry is inherent in the " motifs which compose a logic, out of our very fibers," then the intervention of the critic must propose to extract these motifs from the " fibers " of the text, that is, from its verbal texture and its imaginative substance, concentrating on the favorite materials of Mallarmé's poetic landscape (which will be crystal, fire, veils, creams, mists, foam, clouds, limpid waters . . .), on the privileged forms of his scenarios (for example, fountains, hills, fingernails, corollas, peninsulas), on the objects which are transformed into fetiches (mirrors, fans, diamonds, dancers, butterflies, snowflakes, chandeliers), on the harmony of sounds and rays of light which adumbrate a mysteriously emblematic reality. And it is clear the while that this museum of the concrete imagination cannot be recovered unless one penetrates beneath the surfaces, into the deeper levels of the work, into the subterranean labyrinth of a language which is exceedingly sinuous in its semantic movement. What is finally important, then, is to uncover an internal syntax, a mysterious armature, as Mallarmé would have said, which helps the reader enter into the dynamics of a system without arresting the fluidity, the mobility, of its themes.

How this model system functions critically Richard himself makes clear, and it could hardly be better put:

> The themes within this active system will have the tendency to organize themselves, as in all living structures, combining into flexible wholes governed by the law of isomorphism and by the search for the best possible equilibrium. This notion of equilibrium (coming originally from the physical sciences, but important for sociology and psychology as Lévi-Strauss and Piaget have shown) seems potentially most useful for comprehending the realm of the imagination. In effect, we observe that themes arrange themselves in antithetical pairs, or, in a more complex

manner, in multiple, balanced systems. In his aspiration toward
the idea, for example, Mallarmé oscillates, it would seem, between a desire for openness (the idea dispersed, *vaporized* into
suggestion or into silence) and a need for closure (the idea
summed up, reduced to an outline and a definition). The enclosed and the open, the precise and the elusive, the mediated
and the immediate, are among the mental pairs in which we
believe we have revealed, at quite different levels, the presence of
the Mallarméan experience. It is important, then, to observe
how these oppositions are resolved, how their tensions are ap-
peased, either in new notions of synthesis or in concrete forms
which realize satisfying equilibria. The opposition between the
closed and the open leads thus to certain beneficent figures,
within which these two contradictory needs are both satisfied,
either simultaneously or in sequence: for example, the *fan*, the
book, the *dancer*. . . . The essence will succeed in simultaneously
condensing and diffusing itself in a synthetic phenomenon:
music. At other times the equilibrium will assume a static form,
through a play of forces precisely imbricated among themselves,
whose total balance produces the euphoria of "suspense." Thus,
as we know, does Mallarmé conceive the internal reality of the
poem and the ideal architecture of the objects which the poem
must reorder within itself: grotto, diamond, spider web, rose
window, kiosk, sea shell—images which reveal the desire for a
total correlation of nature with itself, for a perfect equation of
things. The mind, then, is envisioned as the keystone of this
architecture, the absolute center through which everything communicates, balances, is cancelled out.[2]

Although Richard's reading moves vertically into the depths of
the inventive consciousness, to the point of unveiling the chain of
symbols and of analogical relationships from which the " sense "
of a work emanates, it is apparent that psychoanalytical theories
condition it in only a marginal way and only through the mediating
filter of Bachelard's systems of imagery. In reality, those who wish
to familiarize themselves with symbolic criticism of Freudian inspiration should turn rather to the Wilson of *The Wound and the
Bow* and to the Sartre of the essay on Baudelaire, not to mention
the now classic pages of Otto Rank on *Der Mythus von der Geburt
des Helden*, of Marie Bonaparte on Poe, of Ernest Jones on *Hamlet*

---

2 J.-P. Richard, *L'Univers imaginaire de Mallarmé* (Paris: Editions du Seuil,
1961) , pp. 26-27 [Ed.].

and Oedipus, or the contributions, as brilliant as they are hermetic, of Jacques Lacan on analytic symbolism. But with the exception of Lacan, whose rigor of imperiously systematic thought must be acknowledged, many of these applications to literature of the key of psychoanalytical exegesis remain episodes, personal experiments, from which generally can be derived no critical formula which is objectively conscious of the connections and the distinctions made necessary by the tenet that a work is not only a consequence of the past already lived but also a future inventing itself, an original act concluded within itself. And as for symbolism, we must at the outset distinguish, as the linguist Benveniste teaches us, between the symbolism of the Freudian unconscious and the symbolism of language itself: the first, in fact, has the character of universality, and the rapport between the symbols and the referents is defined through the richness of the signifiers and the unicity of the signified; the second, on the other hand, always realized in a particular language, is linked with things and to each individual's experience of them, and the rapport between these symbols and the things they stand for can be accertained only a posteriori, in a plurality of profoundly dissimilar signs combined into extremely diverse formal systems.

Among the scholars who have sought to derive from psychoanalysis a coherent method of reading, without betraying the structural autonomy of the literary fact, we should immediately cite Charles Mauron and Jean-Paul Weber, who also figure among the protagonists in the French debate surrounding the *nouvelle critique:* we are thinking particularly of Mauron's *Des Métaphores obsédantes au mythe personnel* and of Weber's dyptich, *Genèse de l'oeuvre poétique* and *Domaines thématiques.* According to Mauron —to begin with the scholar who aspires to be the more scientific and the more faithful to Freudian theses—the psychocritical analysis, as he calls it, must attempt to bring to light, from beneath the deliberate structures of the text, the involuntary associations of ideas and the probable expressions of unconscious processes. To do just this it is necessary to superimpose the texts of a writer, to make them interact with each other, so as to isolate certain obsessive groups of images common to all. Then the terms are established in which these structures or associative networks recur and are transformed within a work; and there results a " musical " study of the various themes in their regroupings and their metamorphoses,

which finally leads to the underlying image of a "personal myth,"
to be understood in connection with the unconscious of the writer
and its dynamics and to be then submitted to verification in a
confrontation with his biography. The personal myth of a work
of art has a genesis, a complex history, a lived duration; born of
the obsession of certain memories, inscribed in dramatic scenes
where action and characters emerge as typical (like Valéry's
sleeper or Mallarmé's dancer), the myth manifests itself as a richness of analogical equivalences, as movement, magical disposition of desire, since "the external object becomes internalized,"
persona within the persona, and "groups of internal images,
charged with love or fear" project themselves onto reality. The
"interior universe" of a poem is illuminated by this flow, by these
prodigious exchanges.

Jean-Paul Weber, too, speaks of themes, but with a value different from that of Mauron, whom he expressly opposes in refuting
a rigid Freudian context and a questionable scientific assuredness.
In his perspective, which calls however for other reservations, the
theme is, broadly speaking, identified with an infantile event or
situation, susceptible of manifesting itself in a work or in a cycle
of works, either symbolically or openly, with personal or metapersonal characters. The personal theme, like the metapersonal,
must be distinguished from the Freudian complex inasmuch as
the theme is situated on this side of the orthodox inventory of
psychoanalysis and defines a different stratum of implicit meanings, to which correspond an unlimited number of structures and
intermediate forms. Thus, as every writer has a personal theme
which he seeks unconsciously to attack by means of the most diverse
symbols, every esthetic dominant in which he expresses his relationship with the world implies a metapersonal theme which links it
indissolubly and physically to a certain horizon, to a variable from
childhood and its universe; so that one can conclude that every
work of art emerges as the function of two variables, metapersonal
and personal, both deriving from the domain of infancy. And if
it is true that a text always implies an omnipresent thematic recollection, it follows that the theme is submitted to a modulation,
to an orchestration of symbols and analogies, which establish precisely the *domaine modulateur*, the profound level of a work.

After isolating clear and distinct memories common to a whole
system of texts and deducing from them a symbolic meaning,
it will then be the job of thematic analysis to delineate the

ensemble of the linguistic and stylistic obsessions, in the light of a certain or probable fact of memory, and to try finally to bring back the universe of a writer to the fundamental unity of a theme, without excluding, as Weber added more recently, the possibility of a bi-thematic dialectic and new forms of combination. From a phenomenological point of view, then, the theme which informs a work and provides the key to it, even in a plurality of images and of secondary cycles, may present itself as an object (the clock of Vigny or of Poe), or as a legend which explains a print (Hugo's tower of the rats), or as an aggregate of reminiscences which inform a childhood gesture (Mallarmé's bird, fallen and killed), or more generally as the reflection of a very particular memory, unique or multiple. One could indeed repeat with Blanchot that a symbol is composed of events, gestures, imperceptible acts (a smile, a hand being raised, plaster flaking off a wall), but at the same time it announces something which transcends each of these particulars and even negates itself in the mythical dimension of a global meaning which coincides with that of the world and human existence.

The answers Mauron and Weber give to the problem of the symbolic imagination may suggest a mythology, but they ignore the anthropological aspect of myth, immanent in language, which certainly has not lacked prominence in French culture since the memorable works of Dumézil or Lévi-Strauss and the new structural investigations of Greimas. It would suffice to recall, along with Georges Gusdorf's *Mythe et métaphysique*, Gilbert Durand's *Structures anthropologiques de l'imaginaire* and, even more important, his *Décor mythique de la Chartreuse de Parme*, the heuristic thesis of which postulates, again on the literary level, that a work always separates into two halves, on the one hand semiological expressions and on the other a metalinguistic and constitutive semantic base, which are connected by the universal models and symbols of a mythical thought. But if, following the turn of the discussion, one really wishes to get acquainted with criticism of the anthropological-mythical type, one should leave the French and return to the Anglo-American cultural scene, where the technical lesson of Frazer, Harrison, and Cornford combined with the Freudian or Jungian perspective and the symbolic patterns of Cassirer or Langer shows great influence on a criticism which is by tradition sensitive to the semantic levels of metaphor. This is a tradition marked by lively agreements and controversies which favors experiments and more comprehensive reflections. Since, on the other hand, the field before

us is so vast, we must limit ourselves to establishing the essentials
and refer the reader, for a closer view of the historical context, to
the volume of Richard Chase, *Quest for Myth*, and to the no less
valuable collection, prepared by a linguist of the stature of Thomas
A. Sebeok, *Myth: A Symposium.*

Meanwhile, as there come quickly to mind the Shakespeare pages
of John Holloway, of J. I. M. Stewart, or Francis Fergusson's *The
Idea of a Theater*, all suggestive examples of semantic analyses on
a mythico-ritualistic key, one's attention cannot fail to be arrested
by the works of Philip Wheelwright, *The Burning Fountain* and
Metaphor and Reality, in that they elaborate a rigorously semantic
interpretation of literature based on the metalogical concept of
the ground common to poetry, myth, religion, and metaphysics.
Rite and myth indicate a way of acting and a way of seeing, which
assume the existence of a hidden reality and introduce into every
metaphorical process an ontological tension, regulated on the cyclic
rhythm of nature. As a complex of stories, true or invented, which
seek to unveil the inner value of man and of existence, myth
expresses the profound meaning of things, through the telling of
a story in the form of a dramatic action, a vital part of which is
the play of images, the presence of archetypes and imaginative
emblems with all of the paradoxes and the metamorphoses which
spring from their encounters. This may be the case in the fourth
sermon of Buddha, in the *Oresteia* of Aeschylus, in Eliot's *Four
Quartets*. And yet Wheelwright's metaphysics seems vague when
juxtaposed—and the comparison comes naturally—with the apocalyptic encyclopedism of Northrop Frye, to whom we owe, however
controversial it may be, the more complex idea of mythico-symbolic
criticism, based as it is on the premise that the structural principles of literature have with mythology and comparative religion
a connection no less close than that between painting and geometry.[3]

A discussion of Frye should always take as its point of departure
his " summa," *The Anatomy of Criticism*, and bear in mind not
only the great book on Blake, *Fearful Symmetry*, but also the
elegantly instructive chapters of *The Educated Imagination*, of *The
Well-tempered Critic*, and of *A Natural Perspective*. But since we
must limit ourselves to an abbreviated treatment, it is more appropriate to concentrate attention here on the essay in *Fables of Identity*

[3] For the English Institute colloquium on Northrop Frye, see the bibliography
entry under Krieger, ed. [Ed.].

dealing with the archetypes of literature, which has the advantage, among others, of presenting fairly simple patterns, still in outline form. Here again we begin with the concept of rite and find in it the origin of the tale, the rite being a temporal sequence of acts with a hidden meaning; whereas the structures of images are fragments of meaning, of oracular origin, deriving from an epiphanic instant and having no direct connection with time. Myth is the central force which assigns archetypal meaning to the rite and an archetypal tale to the oracle; thus it is equivalent to archetype, even though strictly speaking myth refers to tale and archetype to meaning. Thus, in the solar cycle of the day, in the seasonal cycle of the year, and in the organic cycle of life, we find a single pattern of meaning out of which myth constructs a central story around a figure which is sometimes the sun, sometimes the principle of vegetative fertility, sometimes a god or a hero. Since this solar myth divides itself into four phases, one can easily derive from it a fundamental four-part scheme. The first phase, which corresponds to dawn, to springtime, and to birth, includes the myths of the birth of the hero, of resurrection, and of victory over the forces of darkness, winter, and death; its secondary characters are the father and mother, and it constitutes the archetype of the romance. The second phase, which is the moment of the zenith, of summer, and of matrimony, with its myths of apotheosis, of sacred nuptials, and of entry into paradise, and with its secondary figures of friend and spouse, defines the archetype of comedy, of pastoral, and of the idyll. The third, archetype of tragedy and elegy, is related to sunset, to autumn, and to death, and involves the myths of downfall, of violent death, of sacrifice and isolation, with their subordinate characters, the traitor and the siren. Finally, the fourth phase is the archetype of satire as the moment of darkness, of winter, and of dissolution, accompanied by the myths of the flood, of the return to chaos and defeat, underlined by the presence of the ogre and the sorceress.

In Frye's judgment, the tendency of rite and epiphany in the direction of the encyclopedic solution is fully actualized in the definitive subject matter of myth, which shapes all of the sacred texts of the religious tradition, beginning of course with the Bible, which is where the literary critic must always begin, referring to this exemplary " literature " in order to move then legitimately from archetypes to types, and to see above all how drama emerges from the ritual aspect of myth and the lyric from the epiphanic aspect, in contrast with the epic, which instead tries to continue an encyclopedic construction. In the last analysis the primary myth of literature coincides, in its narrative aspects, with the myth of the search, the "quest," while if we talk in terms of meaning, it becomes the vision of collective force, of the innocent world of desires satisfied, of free human society. Such a vision can by turns be comedy or tragedy, according to whether the search rises to a redeemed universe or follows the path of nature's own cycle. And in connection with this vision we can draw up a second scheme of five sections arranged in the hierarchic framework of the "great chain of being." In the comic vision the human world is a community or a hero who represents the self-realization of the reader, with its archetypal images of the banquet, of communion, of order, of friendship, of love; in the tragic vision there is anarchy, tyranny, or a man alone, the hero abandoned and betrayed. As for the animal realm, the comic vision incorporates a community of domestic animals (sheep or doves), archetypes of pastoral images, in contrast to the tragic vision, where animals of prey predominate —wolves, vultures, serpents, dragons. The flora of the comic vision is represented by a garden, a park, a tree of life, a rose, as archetypes of arcadian images; while in the tragic vision there is a sinister forest, a wilderness, a moor, a tree of death. The mineral order is for the comic vision a city, an edifice, a temple, a precious stone, archetypes of geometrical images; whereas in the tragic it presents itself as desert, ruin, rock, or in sinister geometric images such as that of the cross. And finally we come to the world of the formless, which in the comic vision is a river, whereas in the tragic it is transformed into a sea, just as the narrative myth of dissolution often becomes the myth of the deluge, and the combination of sea and images of violence produces the leviathan or other monsters of the deep.

As anyone who has read the *Anatomy of Criticism* well knows, archetypal criticism as theory of myth, presented only in broadest outline in the *Fables of Identity* chapter, is subsequently integrated with a historical criticism of modes, an ethical criticism of symbols, and a rhetorical criticism of genres. But even in this wider context it occupies a prominent position, since only out of its logic can come the unity of a system within which all the traditional procedures of literary analysis can finally find their raison d'être and by virtue of which literature can become again a unique, majestic organism endowed with constant laws and forms.

Like an enchanted forest in the hands of an extraordinarily clever magician who never tires of discovering analogies, mysterious figures, surprising derivations and oppositions, Frye's criticism may appear from time to time to be a sort of embryology in the manner of Blake or Spengler, a gnostic odyssey, a taxonomy of the imagination, an apocalypse of Kierkegaardian " repetition," an Aristotelian utopia transplanted into symbolism, for which the last chapter of *Finnegans Wake* might serve as emblem. And it is understandable that Frye's ecumenism encompasses, in the purest state of cultural sublimation, probably all of the promises and the limitations of symbolic criticism. In perhaps no other work does the necessity of mythology, paradoxically combined with the principles of mathematics and of science, reveal such a profound diffidence toward history (Eliade would call it fear) which is characteristic of any cyclic vision and its symbolic metamorphoses. Myth, as Eliot says à propos of Joyce, is a way of controlling, of ordering, of giving form and meaning to the immense panorama of futility and anarchy which is contemporary history. But when literature becomes a myth, a universal apocalypse of man, history withdraws from the stage and time dissolves into epiphany, into rediscovery and permanence of common archetypes.

It remains to be asked—and the question is unavoidable for those who continue to believe, as philologists, that a text is a structure of verbal signs—whether this search for symbols does not make criticism give up distinguishing, identifying what is different and unpredictable, what confers on a book the inimitable features of a unique event. Many an exercise in mythico-symbolic reading, lacking the commitment of a Frye or an Auden, has fed this suspicion—even to the point of Robert Weimann's Marxist severity in *New Criticism und die Entwicklung bürgerlicher Literaturwissenschaft*. But even scepticism may be dangerous, if it leads to the rejection of an experiment only because the dialog introduces a new dialectic. Perhaps it is better to agree with Wilhelm Emrich, a German student of the symbolism in *Faust*, when he observes in his essay *Symbolinterpretation und Mythologie* that literary scholarship cannot stop at the affinity between the poetic symbol and the mythical symbol but must always bring to light, in the case of the former, its distinctive historico-lyrical character and its new semantic content; and this is possible only when the variable of history, rather than being discounted, is used as the reagent of individuation, whose elements include the empirical world, psychological conflicts, the tensions of an epoch, political events, and personal resonances. If provincial prejudice does not cloud our judgment—and we must give some credit, following the felicitous example of Debenedetti (or of a Sanguineti), to the Avalle of the *Orecchini of Montale*, to the Bàrberi Squarotti of *Symbol and Structure in the poetry of Pascoli*, to the Galimberti of *Dino Campana*, to the Giachery of *Verga and D'Annunzio*, to the Tagliaferri of *Beckett and literary over-determination*, to the Jesi of *Literature and Myth*, to the Biasin of *The Smile of the Gods*—we could say that new Italian criticism, in diverse modes and temperaments, has chosen as the way to symbols the high road of history. The problem is now not to stop, as Althusser admonishes, at the empiricist ideology of historicism.

The original Italian text appeared in MLN *84 (1969).*

BIBLIOGRAPHIC NOTE

The following bibliographic citations may be of some assistance to the reader of Professor Raimondi's essay.—Ed.

Althusser, Louis. *Pour Marx*. Paris, 1965.
Auden, W. H. *The Enchafèd Flood*. New York, 1950.
———. *The Dyer's Hand*. New York, 1962.
———. *Forewords & Afterwords*. Edited by E. Mendelson. New York, 1973.
Avalle, D'A. S. *"Gli orecchini" di Montale*. Milan, 1965.
Bachelard, Gaston. *La Psychanalyse du feu*. Paris, 1938.
———. *L'Eau et les rêves*. Paris, 1942.
———. *L'Air et les songes*. Paris, 1944.
———. *La Terre et les rêveries de la volonté*. Paris, 1948.
———. *La Terre et les rêveries du repos*. Paris, 1948.
———. *La Poétique de l'espace*. Paris, 1957.
———. *La Poétique de la rêverie*. Paris, 1960.
———. *La Flame d'une chandelle*. Paris, 1962.
Barthes, Roland. *Critique et Vérité*. Paris, 1966.
Benveniste, E. *Problèmes de la linguistique générale*. Paris, 1966.
Biasin, G.-P. *The Smile of the Gods: A Thematic Study of Cesare Pavese's Works*. Ithaca, 1968.
Binswanger, Ludwig. *Grundformen und Erkenntnis Menschlichen Daseins*. Zurich, 1953.

————. *Being-in-the-World.* New York, 1963.

Bonaparte, Marie. *Edgar Poe, étude psychanalytique.* Paris, 1933.

Brook, Peter. *The Empty Space.* New York, 1968.

Burke, Kenneth. *Language as Symbolic Action.* Berkeley and Los Angeles, 1966.

————. *The Philosophy of Literary Form: Studies in Symbolic Action.* 2nd ed. New York, 1957.

————. *A Grammar of Motives and a Rhetoric of Motives.* Cleveland, 1962.

Campbell, Joseph. *The Hero with the Thousand Faces.* New York, 1949.

————. *The Masks of God.* 4 vols. New York, 1959-68.

Cassirer, Ernst. *Die Philosophie der symbolischen Formen.* 3 vols. Berlin, 1923, 1925, 1929. English translation: New Haven, 1955, 1957, 1959.

————. *Wesen und Wirkung des Symbolbegriffs.* Darmstadt, 1956.

Chase, Richard. *Quest for Myth.* Baton Rouge, 1949.

Clemen, Wolfgang H. *Shakespeares Bilder. . . .* Bonn, 1936. English translation (*The Development of Shakespeare's Imagery*) : Cambridge, Mass., 1951.

Cornford, F. M. *From Religion to Philosophy.* Cambridge, 1912.

————. *The Origins of Attic Comedy.* Cambridge, 1914.

————. *Principium Sapientiae.* Cambridge, 1952.

Crane, Ronald S. *The Languages of Criticism and The Structure of Poetry.* Toronto, 1953.

Dumézil, Georges. *Mythe et épopée: L'Idéologie des trois fonctions dans les épopées indo-européens.* Paris, 1968.

————. *Heur et malheur du guerrier.* Paris, 1969.

————. *Mythe et épopée II: Trois types épiques indo-européens.* Paris, 1971.

Durand, Gilbert. *Le Décor mythique de " la Charteuse de Parme ".* Paris, 1961.

————. *Les Structures anthropologiques de l'imaginaire.* 2nd ed. Paris, 1963.

Eliade, M. *Le Myth de l'Eternel Retour.* Paris, 1949. English translation: New York, 1955.

————. *Mythes rêves et mystères.* Paris, 1957. English translation: New York, 1960.

————. *Le Sacré et le profane.* Paris, 1959. English translation: New York, 1959.

————. *Images et symboles.* Paris, 1962. English translation: New York, 1961.

————. *Aspects du mythe.* Paris, 1963. English translation: New York, 1963.

————. *Méphistophélès et l'androgyne.* Paris, 1963.

————. *Naissances Mystiques.* Paris, 1965. English translation: New York, 1965.

Empson, William. *Seven Types of Ambiguity.* London, 1930.

————. *The Structure of Complex Words.* New York, 1951.

Emrich, Wilhelm. " Symbolinterpretation und Mythenforschung," in *Protest und Verheissung, Studien zur Klassischen und modernen Dichtung.* Frankfort am Main-Bonn, 1960.

Fergusson, Francis. *Idea of a Theater.* Princeton, 1949.

Foucault, Michel. *Maladie mentale et psychologie.* Paris, 1961.

————. *Folie et déraison: Histoire de la folie à l'âge classique.* Paris, 1961.

————. *Naissance de la clinique.* Paris, 1963.

————. *Raymond Roussel.* Paris, 1963.

————. *Les Mots et les choses.* Paris, 1966.

————. *L'Archéologie du savoir.* Paris, 1969.

————. *L'Ordre du discours.* Paris, 1971.

Frazer, J. G. *The Golden Bough.* 3rd ed. London, 1911-15.

Freud, Sigmund. *The Complete Psychological Works of Sigmund Freud (Standard Edition).* Edited by James Strachey. 23 vols. London, 1953-66.

Fromm, Erich. *The Forgotten Language.* New York, 1951.

Frye, Northrop. *Fearful Symmetry: A Study of William Blake.* Princeton, 1947.

————. *Anatomy of Criticism.* Princeton, 1957.

————. *Fables of Identity: Studies in Poetic Mythology.* New York, 1963.

————. *The Well-Tempered Critic.* Bloomington, 1963.

————. *Romanticism Reconsidered.* New York and London, 1963.

————. *The Educated Imagination.* Bloomington, 1964.

————. *A Natural Perspective: The Development of Shakespearean Comedy and Romance.* New York, 1965.

————. *The Return of Eden: Five Essays on Milton's Epics.* Toronto, 1965.

————. *Fools of Time.* Toronto, 1967.

————. *The Stubborn Structure.* Ithaca, 1970.

————. *The Critical Path.* Bloomington, 1971.

Galimberti, C. *Dino Campana.* Milan, 1967.

Gardner, Helen. *The Business of Criticism.* 2nd ed. London, 1963.

Giachery, E. *Verga e d'Annunzio.* Milan, 1968.

Goddard, Harold. *The Meaning of Shakespeare.* Chicago, 1951. ·

Greimas, A. J. *Sémantique structurale.* Paris, 1964.

Guiraud, Pierre. *Style et littérature.* The Hague, 1962.

————. *Le Jargon de Villon ou le Gai savoir de la Coquille.* Paris, 1968.

Gusdorf, Georges. *Mythe et métaphysique.* Paris, 1953.

Harrison, Jane. *Prolegomena to the Study of Greek Religion.* Cambridge, 1903.

———. *Themis.* Cambridge, 1912.

———. *Epilegomena.* Cambridge, 1921.

Heilman, Robert B. *This Great Stage: Image and Structure in "King Lear."* Baton Rouge, 1948.

———. *Magic on the Web: Action and Language in "Othello."* Lexington, 1956.

Holloway, John. *The Story of Night: Studies in Shakespeare's Major Tragedies.* London, 1961.

Hough, Graham. *An Essay on Criticism.* New York, 1966.

Jesi, F. *Letteratura e mito.* Turin, 1968.

Jones, Ernest. *Hamlet and Oedipus.* Garden City, N. Y., 1954.

Jung, C. G. *The Collected Works of C. G. Jung.* 19 vols. New York and Princeton, 1953-.

Kerényi, K. *Umgang mit Götlichem.* 2nd ed. Göttingen, 1961.

———, and Mann, Thomas. *Romandichtung und Mythologie. Ein Briefwechsel.* Zurich, 1945.

Klein, Melanie. *Contributions to Psychoanalysis.* London, 1950.

———. *Developments in Psychoanalysis.* London, 1952.

Knight, G. Wilson. *The Wheel of Fire.* 4th ed. London, 1949.

———. *The Olive and the Sword.* London, 1944.

———. *The Crown of Life.* London, 1947.

———. *Principles of Shakespearean Production.* 2nd ed. London, 1949.

———. *The Imperial Theme.* 3rd ed. London, 1951.

———. *The Shakespearean Tempest.* London, 1953.

———. *The Mutual Flame.* 3rd ed. London, 1955.

———. *The Sovereign Flower.* London, 1958.

Knights, L. C. *Explorations.* London, 1946.

———. *Some Shakespearean Themes.* London, 1959.

———. *An Approach to "Hamlet."* London, 1960.

———. *Further Explorations.* London, 1965.

Krieger, Murray. *The New Apologists for Poetry.* Minneapolis, 1957.

———, ed. *Northrop Frye in Modern Criticism.* New York, 1966.

Lacan, Jacques. *Ecrits.* Paris, 1966.

———. *The Language of the Self.* Edited by Anthony Wilden. Baltimore, 1968.

Langer, Susanne K. *Philosophy in a New Key: A Study of the Symbolism of Reason, Rite, and Art.* Cambridge, Mass., 1942.

———. *Feeling and Form.* New York, 1953.

———. *Philosophical Sketches,* New York, 1962

———. *Mind. A nEssay on Human Feeling.* I and II. Baltimore, 1967 and 1972.

Leavis, F. R. "Imagery and Movement." In *Scrutiny,* XIII (1945).

————. *The Great Tradition*. London, 1948.

————. *The Common Pursuit*. London, 1952.

Lévi-Strauss, C. *Les Structures élémentaires de la parenté*. Paris, 1949.

————. *Race et Histoire*. Paris, 1952.

————. *Tristes Tropiques*. Paris, 1955.

————. *Anthropologie structurale*. Paris, 1958.

————. *Le Totémisme aujourd'hui*. Paris, 1962.

————. *La Pensée sauvage*. Paris, 1962.

————. *Mythologiques I: Le Cru et le cuit*. Paris, 1964.

————. *Mythologiques II: Du miel au cendres*. Paris, 1966.

————. *Mythologiques III: L'Origine des manières de table*. Paris, 1968.

————. *Mythologiques IV: L'Homme nu*. Paris, 1971.

Malinowski, B. *Argonauts of the Western Pacific*. New York, 1922.

————. *Crime and Custom in Savage Society*. London, 1926.

————. *Sex and Repression in Savage Society*. London, 1927.

————. *A Scientific Theory of Culture*. Chapel Hill, 1944.

————. *Sex, Culture and Myth*. New York, 1962.

Mauron, Charles. *Introduction à la psychanalyse de Mallarmé*. Neuchâtel, 1950.

————. *L'Inconscient dans l'oeuvre et la vie de Racine*. Gap, 1957.

————. *Des métaphores obsédantes au mythe personnel*. Paris, 1963.

————. *Psychocritique du genre comique*. Paris, 1964.

Murray, Gilbert. *Hamlet and Orestes*. London, 1914.

Murray, Henry A., ed. *Myth and Mythmaking*. New York, 1960.

Neumann, Erich. *Ursprungsgeschichte des Bewusstseins*. Zurich, 1949. English translation: New York, 1962.

————. "The Structure of the Archetype," in *The Great Mother*. London, 1955.

Rank, Otto. *The Birth of the Hero and Other Essays*. New York, 1959.

Richard, Jean-Pierre. *Littérature et Sensation*. Paris, 1954.

————. *Poésie et profondeur*. Paris, 1955.

————. *L'Univers imaginaire de Mallarmé*. Paris, 1961.

————. *Onze études sur la poésie moderne*. Paris, 1964.

————. *Paysage de Chateaubriand*. Paris, 1967.

Ricoeur, Paul. *Finitude et culpabilité: I: La Symbolique du mal*. Paris, 1960.

————. *De l'interprétation*. Paris, 1965. English translation: New Haven, 1970.

————. *Le Conflit des interprétations*. Paris, 1969.

Sartre, Jean-Paul. *Baudelaire*. Paris, 1947.

————. *Saint Genet, comédien et martyr*. Paris, 1952.

————. *L'Idiot de la famille*. 3 vols. Paris, 1971-72.

Sebeok, Thomas A., ed. *Myth: A Symposium*. Bloomington, 1958.

Spitzer, Leo. *Stilstudien.* 2 vols. 2nd ed. Darmstadt, 1961.

―――. *Meisterwerke der Romanischen Sprachwissenschaft.* 2 vols. Munich, 1929-30.

―――. *Romanische Stil- und Literaturstudien.* 2 vols. Marburg, 1931.

―――. *Essays in Historical Semantics.* New York, 1948.

―――. *Linguistics and Literary History.* Princeton, 1948.

―――. *A Method for Interpreting Literature.* Northampton, 1949.

―――. *Romanische Literaturstudien, 1936-1956.* Tübingen, 1959.

―――. *Essays on English and American Literature.* Princeton, 1962.

―――. *Classical and Christian Ideas of World Harmony.* Baltimore, 1963.

Spurgeon, Caroline. *Shakespeare's Imagery and What it Tells Us.* Cambridge, 1935.

Squarotti, G. Bàrberi. *Simboli e strutture della poesia del Pascoli.* Messina-Florence, 1966.

Stallman, R. W. "The New Critics." In *Critiques and Essays in Criticism 1920-1948,* edited by R. W. Stallman. New York, 1949.

Stewart, J. I. M. *Character and Motive in Shakespeare.* London, 1949.

Szondi, Lipot. *Schicksalanalyse.* Basel, 1944.

Tagliaferri, A. *Beckett e l'iperdeterminazione letteraria.* Milan, 1967.

Traversi, Derek A. *An Approach to Shakespeare.* 2nd ed. New York, 1956.

―――. *Shakespeare: The Last Phase.* New York, 1953.

―――. *Shakespeare: From "Richard II" to "Henry V."* Stanford, 1957.

―――. *Shakespeare: The Roman Plays.* London, 1963.

Ullman, Stephen. *Style in the French Novel.* Cambridge, 1957.

―――. *The Image in the Modern French Novel.* Cambridge, 1960.

Weber, Jean-Paul. *La Psychologie de l'art.* Paris, 1958.

―――. *Genèse de l'oeuvre poétique.* Paris, 1958.

―――. *Domaines thématiques.* Paris, 1963.

Weimann, Robert. *New Criticism und die Entwicklung bürgerlicher Literaturwissenschaft.* Halle, 1962.

―――. *Shakespeare und die Tradition des Volkstheaters.* Berlin, 1967.

Weston, Jesse L. *From Ritual to Romance.* Cambridge, 1923.

Wheelwright, Philip. *The Burning Fountain: A Study in the Language of Symbolism.* Bloomington, 1954.

―――. "Poetry, Myth, and Reality." In *The Language of Poetry,* edited by A. Tate. Princeton, 1942, pp. 3-33.

―――. *Metaphor and Reality.* Bloomington, 1962.

Wilson, Edmund. *The Wound and the Bow.* New York, 1941.

THE ANTITHESES OF CRITICISM: REFLECTIONS ON THE YALE COLLOQUIUM *

J. HILLIS MILLER

This Colloquium testifies to an important shift of focus in American literary criticism. The temper of the conference can be accounted for partly by the topics chosen for papers and partly by the fact that so many of the participants are European-trained or teach in departments of romance language or of comparative literature. Even so, the new orientations of the Colloquium have significance for American criticism generally. A few years ago one would have expected an American colloquium on literary criticism to be a dialogue between our native formalism and other approaches. Quite recently, for example, Professor Murray Krieger described present-day literary criticism in America in terms of a conflict between a fading " new criticism " and the archetypal approach. The latter is, for Krieger, the most viable alternative. At the Yale Colloquium, however, neither the new criticism nor archetypal criticism figured centrally, in spite of the fact that there was a paper on the work of Northrop Frye. There was hostility to neither, but a sense that their lessons can be taken for granted. For most of the participants part of the impetus for the next advances in literary study will come from one form or another of European criticism. Assimilating the best recent continental criticism, American scholars may come to develop new forms of criticism growing out of American culture as well as out of the encounter with European thought.

This article was written to comment on papers given at the Yale Colloquium on Criticism and was published in *MLN* 81 (December 1966).

The Yale Colloquium suggests that this is in fact already taking place.

Tensions between antithetical approaches are fundamental to the critical enterprise. The Colloquium brought a number of the most important of these into the open where their variety and complexity could be seen. Sometimes these tensions were present in the mind of a single participant. Sometimes they emerged in the clash of the discussions, or from the juxtaposition of two papers. In any case, they governed our thinking.

Among the antitheses were the following: the nominalization of literature versus its periodization; reification versus totalization; the notion that an authentic image in poetry is unique versus investigation of literature in terms of *topoi*, archetypes, or other fixed forms transcending the particular; novelty versus tradition; relativity or historicism versus some form of absolutism; the end of history (or history transformed into an "eternal Platonic state") versus endless history; temporal form versus spatial form; hermeneutic, polyrhythmic, dialectical, or discontinuous time versus linear, organic, "natural," or continuous time; structure versus form; the notion that literature is autonomous versus the notion that it should be studied in terms of some context, biographical, social, metaphysical, or religious; microscopism versus the panoramic view; poetry as an end versus poetry as a means; yielding to the work as an experience or meaning which is its own justification versus the attempt to do something with the work for oneself, to assimilate it into the critic's own patterns of meaning; subjectivity versus reality; metaphysics versus science; poetry versus the novel; angelism versus original sin; alienation versus authenticity; disengagement, objectivity, or detachment versus engagement, commitment, or involvement; ontology versus intersubjectivity; dualism versus monism (a conviction that observer and observed are two or a conviction that they are one); criticism as interpretation versus criticism as the means of developing a theory of literature; criticism as a form of literature versus criticism as the science of interpretation or as the practice of a certain methodology.

It will be seen that some groups of these pairs interpenetrate and overlap bewilderingly, while some pairs seem to stand by themselves or to be related only distantly to the others. The opposition between the notion that literature and ontology may be one and the notion that literature deals with the relation between several minds is related, for example, to the opposition between poetry and the novel. The critic interested in the way literature may express truths about ultmate being will find more to his taste in Stevens or Keats than in Thackeray or even in Proust. On the other hand, the acceptance or denial of original sin seems to have little to do with the opposition between time and space, though there may in fact be secret connections between the two antinomies. In any case, the presence of these oppositions is visible everywhere in the papers of the Colloquium. In fact they cover the whole field of critical theory, if not in themselves, certainly in their implications, as contour lines do not touch every square foot of a mountain, but taken together outline its complex surface. The work of a particular critic tends to be defined by where he stands on the mountain, by his perspective, explicit or implicit, on the issues raised by the oppositions I have listed. This placing is often so taken for granted that it is never recognized for what it is—the foundation of a critical method.

Though the antitheses of criticism overlap, they do not form a neat continuum. There are breaks and contradictions between any one opposition and some of the others. They cut the field of criticism in different and often incompatible ways. To borrow a word from Gerard Manley Hopkins, the oppositions might better be thought of as so many topographical "cleaves" of the landscape of criticism, rather than as logically connected pairs. Nor are the antitheses dialectical. It is not possible to proceed from their opposition to some grand synthesis transcending the problems of criticism in a comprehensive system—with all the critics clasping hands and singing a final chorus. Ours is a fallen world, and literary critics, like everyone else, must endure the *malconfort* of a pull between opposing tendencies of the spirit. In the case of literary criticism, it is the peculiarity of these tensions that to ignore the attraction in one direction and yield without reservation to the lure of the other is to court disaster.

I shall now try to follow several of the lines suggested by the antitheses I have named. To do this will show how the oppositions melt into one another, how it is possible to move from one to another within the space of criticism, and how various methods of criticism can be placed according to coordinates within that space.

II

A constant source of quarrels among critics is disagreement about the context in which a work of literature should be studied. The oppositions within an important set of the antitheses of criticism are implicit in these quarrels.

Perhaps the poem should be studied by itself. Each poem has a unique meaning, and this meaning is generated solely by the words of the poem. Poetic language is self-contained or self-referential. Whatever meanings it has are there on the page, shining forth from the words themselves, and not to be found in other works by the author or in books read by the author. Perhaps the location of uniqueness in literature is the image, and the critic should, like Gaston Bachelard, detach each authentic image from its surrounding words. These blur the freshness and generative integrity of the image. The image is poetry at its source, and therefore each should be studied in isolation. Only in this way can its psychic dynamism, its intrinsic originating power, be identified.[1]

Such microscopism is opposed by all those theories of literature which argue that a word or image in a poem is of little meaning in itself. It gets its meaning from its context. Words, after all, have a complicated cultural history. The notion of intrinsic meaning is not incompatible with the idea that each image draws into itself all those connections it has with its various contexts. The critic must identify those connections, not for their own sake, but in order to show what is really there in the words of the work. He must show how a certain text draws its life from similar passages in other works by the author, or from books read by the author, or from the social and historical milieu in which it came into existence, or from the tradition to which it belongs. A work of literature is defined by what is around it. Literary criticism must therefore take a wide view and see both the work and all its environments.

But where does the context of a poem stop? Its relations to its surroundings radiate outward like concentric circles from a stone dropped in water. These circles multiply indefinitely until the scholar must give up in despair the attempt to make a complete inventory of them. Worse yet, as he proceeds in his endless quest,

---

[1] See especially the introductory chapter of Bachelard's *La poétique de la rêverie* (Paris, 1960).

the poem, which once filled the whole span of his attention, gradually fades into the multitude of its associations. Finally it becomes no more than a point of focus for the impersonal ideas, images, and motifs which enter into it. Instead of being a self-sufficient entity, it is only a symptom of ideas or images current in the culture which generated it.

If the critic avoids this penchant of literary study and returns to the poem itself, another danger awaits him. The more completely he cuts the poem off from its mesh of defining circumstances, the less he can allow himself to say about it. The poem means only itself, and any commentary falsifies it by turning it into something other than itself. Fearing the heresies of paraphrase and explanation, he is reduced to silence, or to repeating the poem itself as its only adequate commentary.[2]

Literary criticism disappears at either extreme, and any valid criticism must stand somewhere between. The choice of a place to stand plays a large role in determining the procedure of any critic. Bachelard sees a dichotomy between the image and its contexts, and can say, " Entre le concept et l'image, pas de synthèse." [3] Many other critics feel that the context of an image, far from being a conceptual abstraction, is its latent meaning and inheres in its being. For Georges Poulet or Jean-Pierre Richard, Albert Béguin or Marcel Raymond, the essential context of any passage is everything else its author wrote. The meaning of a text can be defined only in terms of the system of relations which ties it to the patterns of an *œuvre*. Psychological criticism does not have that respect for the manifest meaning of a text which Poulet, for example, shares with Bachelard. Nevertheless, it is like the criticism of the " école de Genève " in assuming that the proper context for literary interpretation is the coherence of one man's life. For the Freudian, Sartrean, or Lacanian critic, however, the meaning of a passage is latent. A given paragraph can only be deciphered when it is understood to be the disguised expression of the author's governing com-

---

[2] Jean Starobinski has eloquently described this paradox of criticism in *L'œil vivant* (Paris, 1961), pp. 24-27. A few sentences here and in another place in my essay are taken from a paper I have written for a volume sponsored by the Modern Language Association on the relations of literary study and various other disciplines.

[3] *La poétique de la rêverie*, p. 45.

plex or project, or of the occult chain of meanings whch rules his life.[4]

Other critics assume that the proper context for criticism is social or cultural. Sociological, Marxist, structuralist, or anthropological criticism received much attention at the Yale Colloquium, as did the idea of "structure." This word is often used today to describe a notion of context in which the element to be studied participates in its environment rather than being surrounded by it or being determined by it from the outside. "Structure" may be used in opposition to the idea of "form" to suggest a many-layered system of meanings made up of dynamic interchanges rather than being fixed in a static pattern. (Many formalists would reply that if structure means this, they have been structuralists all along.) Or "structure" may suggest the notion of a system in which any element is meaningless except in its relation to the others. A word in a sentence, an image in a poem, a gesture, action, or speech performed by a person, a Sioux among the Sioux or a Parisian in Paris—each of these is a center of exchange for meanings, but is without meaning in isolation. The notion of structure is similar in all these contexts (as is suggested by the influence of structural linguistics on anthropological structuralism), but it makes a great difference for literary criticism which context is taken as most important.

The critics who choose the context of society as the essential one for literature would deny that the *œuvre* of a writer is any more self-sufficient than a single poem by that writer. Both are parts of a social or cultural system and are irradiated with social meanings. If critics who choose smaller contexts are often most interested in poetry, sociological critics often choose ficton. The novel, they argue, is the genre developed to explore the relation of the individual and society. The social system in which a man lives determines the form of his subjective life, and even poetry, which often seems exclusively concerned with epistemological or ontological problems, will reflect the class-structure or the economic structure of its author's society. For a critic like Georg Lukács or Lucien Goldmann a man is so pervaded by the structures of the society surrounding him that these seize him and force him to express them,

---

[4] A recent example of such criticism, in this case influenced by the work of Jacques Lacan, is Jean Laplanche, *Hölderlin et la question du père* (Paris, 1961).

wittingly or unwittingly. There is no simple notion of determinism here. A man is free to respond slavishly, rebelliously, or creatively to his society, but however he responds his work will be testimony to the nature of his society. The great realists are those who mirror their societies without distortion. This often means that their work as dramatic expression is truer to the facts than their conscious beliefs or than the meanings they thought they were putting into their work.

Most of the kinds of criticism I have discussed so far, with the notable exception of the *école de Genève*, are in one way or another "scientific" or "objective," conceiving the language of literature as being "out there," and as forming objective systems of meaning which inhere in other larger objective systems. These structures can be studied in a way which will make literary study part of the collective body of research to which we give the name of science. Structural linguistics, Russian formalism, the American new criticism, Lacan, Lukács, Lévi-Strauss—all in one way or another consider language and literature in this way. Another important group of critics agree that the study of literature should be objective and scholarly, but disagree with most forms of criticism so far mentioned in their conception of the nature of literature. For them literature tends to be thought of as a self-enclosed spiritual sphere. This sphere is inhabited by all the good writers and forms a sealed tradition with an evolution of its own which can be studied in isolation. Such critics often cut literature off from the structures which seem all-important to a Lukács or a Lévi-Strauss, but on the other hand they see Western literature as forming a system of its own in which the meaning of a writer's work is determined by its relation to the whole. An individual image is authentic not because it represents the absolute novelty Bachelard finds in it, but because it repeats or embodies some *topos*, archetype, or other fixed form of the culture to which it belongs. This culture is imaged as a spatial panorama in which each new valid image finds a place determined by its relations to the other images already there. In such critics the same idea of structure may be found as is present in structural linguistics or in the thought of Lévi-Strauss, but the reality seen as so structured is very different.

T. S. Eliot was a critic of this sort. He expounds in "Tradition and the Individual Talent" a view of history which sees the literature of Europe from Homer to the present as forming a harmonious whole. If this is the case, then the addition of an authentic new work will alter the meanings of all the other works back to *The Iliad*, and the meaning of the new work will lie in its relations to the others, its conformity to them. But what of the work which does not conform? In a sense such a work will not exist at all, as, in Christian theology, evil has only a negative existence. The consequences for analysis and judgment of this view of literature are expressed in *After Strange Gods*, Eliot's most intransigent polemic. Hardy, Lawrence, and Yeats receive the harshest criticism. Because they thought for themselves, or dared, as Yeats said of himself, to make a new religion " of poetic tradition, of a fardel of stories," [5] they are heretics all. They dwell outside the closed community of European letters and must be condemned for whoring after strange gods.

If Eliot's book expresses the extreme consequences of a certain notion of tradition, this notion nevertheless has great strength among critics. It is represented in different versions by three of the critics discussed in the Colloquium: Frye, Auerbach, and Curtius. The papers at the Colloquium showed the complex forms this kind of criticism takes in the work of these men: the eternal archetypes of Frye in their spatialized fixity mirrored in the cyclic evolutions of literature; the nostalgia for a unified European culture in Curtius' admirable gathering of *topoi* in *Europäische Literatur und lateinisches Mittelalter*; the tension in Auerbach's thought between an idealism seeing history as an eternal Platonic state and a historism seeing literature as responding to social forces almost as much as it does for Lukács.

From the microscopism of Bachelard, with its call for an exclusive focus on a single image, to the varied forms of panoramic criticism in Lukács, Curtius, or Auerbach the antithesis between no context and an ever-widening context may be followed as one of those topographical guide-lines crossing the landscape of criticism. My own position is near the middle. In my reading of literature the single poem or novel is never enough. It can never be made fully transparent or fully comprehensible if it is kept in isolation. On the other hand, I become uneasy when the work is placed in the context of a whole period or culture. The qualities and themes which Matthew Arnold or Wallace Stevens share with their ages

[5] *The Autobiography of William Butler Yeats* (New York, 1953), p. 70.

seem often the least important aspects of their work, and I fear the dissolution of their uniqueness in the gray dusk of historical or para-historical generalizations. When I read an author I have the conviction that my experience is most like that of encountering another human being, a mediated encounter it is true, and unsatisfactory for that reason, and yet in another way giving deeper and more intimate knowledge than I have even of those persons I am closest to in the "real world." Though the people I know are fully present in each gesture or phrase, nevertheless this presence of the whole in the part can never be understood without knowledge of the whole, without prolonged acquaintance with the person in various situations, so that what is most personal and characteristic of him may be detected as the constant presence in the variety of his behavior. In the same way, a single novel or poem can be understood only if it is read in the context of the other work by that author. Only then will what Proust called the "novel and unique beauty" of the author become visible.

III

My discussion of the problem of context has touched on many of the other antitheses of criticism. One of these is of great importance at the moment: the opposition between monism and dualism. The assumption that existence is divided into subject and object, mind and things, is deeply a part of our culture. It is present in many forms: in the philosophical traditions stemming from Descartes and Locke; in romanticism in poetry, with its preoccupation with epistemological themes; in the habitual technique of fiction, with its dependence on "point of view" as a generative structural principle; in the methodology of science, with its setting of the knowing mind against knowable things.

Much modern criticism inherits this dualism. This is to be expected, since modern criticism is the child of its culture, and in particular the child of romanticism, though often the ungrateful and rebellious child. The presence of dualistic assumptions is especially evident in the quarrels between those who want to make criticism a science, or who want to judge literature by its correct "mirroring" of reality, and their opponents, whom they accuse of "subjectivizing" literature. On the one hand, Curtius and Eliot tend to think of European culture as a self-contained spiritual whole, and a critic like Georges Poulet describes criticism as consciousness of consciousnesses. Poulet's dependence on the dualism descending from Descartes is apparent in the way he seeks in each writer for the *Cogito*, a unique version of the act of coming to self-consciousness in which what persists through all the experiences of the self is revealed. From this "point de départ" all the spiritual adventure of the writer is generated. If this adventure participates in anything outside itself, it shares in the collective consciousness of the age. This again is something subjective, and can be described in the same terms as individual consciousnesses. Poulet attempts to do this in the chapters on the Renaissance, baroque, the eighteenth-century, and romanticism in *Les métamorphoses du cercle*.

On the other hand, a critic like Lukács also assumes a dualism of subject and object, though he uses it in an opposing way. Nineteenth- and twentieth-century "bourgeois" thought, in his view, is undermined by subjectivism, which he defines as a withdrawal into an unreal never-never-land of the mind. This detachment from reality is a symptom of the decadence of the bourgeois intellectual. Opposed to subjectivistic writers like Kafka, Beckett, or Joyce are the true realists like Thomas Mann, Conrad, or Shaw. The latter mirror modern social and economic reality accurately rather than inhabiting a non-existent domain of the mind. Lukács's dependence on a rather simple version of dualism is especially apparent in this metaphor of the mirror. The figure is of course traditional, and goes back in particular to nineteenth-century theories of realism in fiction. Just as Stendhal defines the novel as "un miroir promené par les grands chemins," and just as George Eliot, in a famous chapter in *Adam Bede*, says that her aim is "to give a faithful account of men and things as they have mirrored themselves in my mind,"[6] so Lukács praises Mann for being "an extreme type of the writer whose greatness lies in being a 'mirror of the world.'"[7]

Georges Blin has shown how paradoxical is the concept of realism in fiction.[8] His analysis is based on one version of that monism which is as characteristic of twentieth-century thought as the persistence of dualism. This unification of existence is not, in its most persuasive forms, attained by the dialectical transcendence of

[6] The passage is in Chapter xvii.
[7] *Essays on Thomas Mann*, trans. Stanley Mitchell (London, 1964), p. 16.
[8] See "Liminaire," *Stendhal et les problèmes du roman* (Paris, 1960), pp. 5-16.

dualism. If the latter is accepted as a starting point it is impossible to think or feel one's way out of it. At best one can experience, as some English romantic poets do, a momentary coalescence of subject and object, followed by a fall back into the normal bifurcation of existence. Many important twentieth-century writers and artists have avoided this situation by assuming that a union of subject and object is the primordial situation, the "given." Dualism is a derived state, perhaps cultural in origin, perhaps an almost irresistible illusion.

There is a tradition for this monism, too, though it is usually of an idealist cast. Blake, like Smart and Macpherson, expresses in his poetry a visionary or apocalyptic unity of subject and object, and Shelley holds that mind and world are one realm which has been artificially divided in our experience of them. T. S. Eliot in his dissertation picks out as central in F. H. Bradley's thought the notion that dualism is an inevitable illusion following upon the breaking apart of the original unity of "immediate experience." Since that unity is what "really is," any system of thought which begins with the assumption that either subject or object is primary will be led into contradiction.[9]

The most appealing twentieth-century versions of monism, however, are neither idealist nor materialist. This opposition, a contemporary monist would say, is itself a product of dualist thought. In spite of the continued strength of dualistic thinking, and in spite of the resistance of thinkers like A. O. Lovejoy,[10] the new monism has strengthened and has appeared more or less spontaneously in widely different areas. Its most elaborated philosophical form is in the phenomenology of Husserl, Heidegger, and Merleau-Ponty, but it is present too in the linguistic philosophy of Wittgenstein's *Philosophical Investigations*, or in the insistence that a work of art means itself, rather than "representing" anything, of the American abstract expressionists, or in the transcendence of dualism in the later work of Wallace Stevens, or in the affirmation that "anywhere is everywhere" of William Carlos Williams.

The new way of thinking has important implications for literary criticism. An understanding of dualistic thought is essential to the

[9] See *Knowledge and Experience in the philosophy of F. H. Bradley* (London, 1964).
[10] See *The Revolt against Dualism* (New York, 1930).

interpretation of those works which embody it, and even a monist would see a derived truth in dualistic experience. Nevertheless, it is possible to distort novels and poems in the direction of a dualism which they do not in fact express. The form of nineteenth-century English fiction, for example, is determined by dualistic thinking. Even so, George Eliot, Trollope, Meredith, or Hardy often present with admirable concreteness the inherence of a man's mind in his body and in his physical and social surroundings. Fiction was taking for its province an exploration of the nuances of intersubjectivity long before this category became important for twentieth-century philosophy. To the degree that the insights of twentieth-century monism are compelling they can usefully determine the procedures of criticism—the questions it asks and the range of its assumptions. This has in fact already happened, as in the influence of phenomenology, in various ways, on the criticism of Sartre, Poulet, or the later Bachelard, or in the monism implicit in the various forms of structuralism.

IV

One of the areas where the opposition between dualism and monism has especial force in contemporary criticism is that named by another antithesis of criticism, the one between temporal form and spatial form. This opposition is nearly the same as that between linear, organic, natural, or continuous time and hermeneutic, polyrhythmic, dialectical, or discontinuous time. Linear time is spatialized time, whereas for Heidegger space is a modification of existential time. One of the accomplishments of the Yale Colloquium was to bring this opposition to the surface, most explicitly in the admirable paper of Paul de Man, but less overtly at other times in the papers and discussions.

There is some evidence that a tendency to think either in spatial, visual terms or in dynamic, temporal terms may be innate in individuals. Each of us may be born either a little Platonist, with a penchant for thinking in terms of visual figures, optical space, and geometrical diagrams, or a little Aristotelean, with a penchant for thinking in terms of interacting energies in movement. Nevertheless, many qualities of our culture, and in particular those associated with dualistic assumptions, work to make spatialized thinking easy for us. The domination of eyesight over the other senses follows naturally from an assumption that man is subjective mind opposed to a physical world spread out before him. The passivity, detachment, and abstraction of a book culture may reinforce this, as does our habit of assuming that man's proper business is the reduction of the world to abstractions, numbers, patterns, maps, charts, and diagrams. Time, according to this way of thinking, becomes a fourth dimension of space, something open to linear representation. The charts of dates in history books, for example, suggest that time is a line stretching backward through the French Revolution to the Norman Conquest, then to the birth of Christ, with other events at measured intervals between, and in many forms of applied mathematics there is a coordinate showing time as a line.

Much modern literary criticism is permeated by spatial thinking. This may be seen in the diagrammatic patterns of Northrop Frye's *Anatomy of Criticism*,[11] or in some of the habitual metaphors of the "new criticism," or in discussions of fiction in terms of the "curve of the plot," or in the insistence, in Joseph Frank's celebrated essay, that modern literature has a "spatial form," or in the spatialized model of literary history in T. S. Eliot's "Tradition and the Individual Talent." There is a tension in Georges Poulet's criticism, to give another example, between an interest in time and a habit of dialectical thought, on the one hand, and the attraction to spatial form evident in the key image of *Les métamorphoses du cercle* and in *L'espace proustien*. Even the concept of structure, which is often explicitly opposed to that of form in a dichotomy between dynamic movement and fixed design, has a tendency to become geometrical pattern after all. Lévi-Strauss offers his spatial diagrams of exogamy and other forms of social relationship, and in the work of Jacques Lacan there is an interesting conflict between the use of diagrams and the employment of non-spatial mathematical models to express chains or transformations of meaning.

The tradition in modern thought and art which rebels against dualism would also claim that spatial thinking is an abstraction from the concrete richness of experience. Human existence is funda-

[11] Another good example of Frye's use of spatial metaphors is his essay, "Myth, Fiction, and Displacement." "We are," says Frye of our reading of a novel, "continually, if often unconsciously, attempting to construct a larger pattern of simultaneous significance out of what we have so far read. . . . We expect a certain point near the end at which linear suspense is resolved and the unifying shape of the whole design becomes conceptually visible" (*Fables of Identity* [New York, 1963], p. 25).

mentally temporal, and even our experience of space is falsified if it is described in terms of geometrical abstraction. Among those forms which are falsified by spatialization, such thinkers would say, is literature. Literature is a temporal, not a spatial art, and should be described as such, in vocabulary proper to its temporality.

Bergson of course is an important innovator in this twentieth-century reaction against spatialization, but Paul de Man properly pointed to Bachelard's *La dialectique de la durée* and to Heidegger's *Sein und Zeit* as important parts of this tradition. In the latter there are provocative comments on the way spatial metaphors are native to our language and natural to our thinking, and Heidegger provides a classic analysis of time as the basic dimension of human existence. Once again, however, there are parallels between modern philosophy and modern literature, parallels which are not a matter of influence but of simultaneous manifestations of similar tendencies of thought. Much modern poetry, for example, is poetry of the moment. It often describes the moment as an evanescent flowing, each instant appearing out of nowhere and reaching toward a goal which transcends it, so that it vanishes in the reaching. An example of such poetry is the late work of Wallace Stevens, as in the fluid improvisations of " An Ordinary Evening in New Haven " or of " A Primitive Like an Orb." William Carlos Williams, ·to give another example, expresses his denial of dualism by an avoidance of abstract visual images and by an emphasis on the more intimate senses, hearing, tasting, touching, and that kinesthetic mimesis whereby we internalize the world with our muscles and nerves. The verbal forms appropriate to these senses cooperate, in poems like " To All Gentleness," Book Five of *Paterson*, or " Asphodel, That Greeny Flower," to take the reader into a region of immanence, where space is the expansive movement of the instant in its flowing.

The affirmation of the unity of subject and object and a replacement of space by time as the basic dimension of existence are two salient characteristics of twentieth-century thought. Literary criticism has developed modes of interpretation which match the new attitudes, but in many areas this development is not complete. No one yet, for example, has done full justice to the complexity of temporal structure in fiction or to the subtle variation in grasp of interpersonal relations from one novelist to another. These are not a matter of the curve of the action, or of the design of the whole,

or of the patterns of imagery, but are concretely present from paragraph to paragraph in the language of the novel as it opens temporal perspectives and relates minds to one another in ever-changing
ways. It is extremely difficult to honor in criticism the flow of our
experience as we read the words of *Middlemarch* or *To the Lighthouse*. In the interpretation of fiction, more perhaps than with any
other literary form, it is hard for the critic to remain in touch with
the immediate quality of the work. It is easier to create a structure
of one's own than to identify the living structures of the novel in
question. The Yale Colloquium in its discussion of the masters of
recent criticism recognized our necessary dependence on their work,
but the papers and especially the discussions were also oriented
toward the criticism that has not yet been written. The antitheses
of criticism will remain, but perhaps in the years to come some
of the most important criticism will be done on the basis of the
swing to monism and temporality in twentieth-century thought.
It is by their fruits that you will know them. No critical method,
no presuppositions about man and the world, will guarantee the
writing of good critical studies. New perspectives may sometimes,
however, reveal aspects of works of literature which have so far
remained hidden.

1966

OF STRUCTURALISM AND LITERATURE [1] ࣳ EUGENIO DONATO ࣳ

Structuralism is in fashion, and its situation presents some similarities with that of existentialism in 1945. It has ardent defenders and dedicated enemies. Like existentialism it is beginning to gain academic respectability, entire issues of magazines are devoted to it and some who lack the intellectual passion required to embrace or fight an idea are beginning to search for its origins and trace its possible history— a most effective means of by-passing an intellectual movement and reducing its relevance. Yet we may still ask ourselves whether this structuralism that is brandished around on the intellectual scene really exists or whether—again similar to the situation of existentialism after the war—what we have are structuralists having perhaps a certain sympathy for each other's work yet each working along his own lines quite independently of any concern for a common ideology. If for some time one could have been led to believe that the works of Jakobson, Lévi-Strauss and Lacan, to mention the most important names, had a general common direction, today such a view is rather questionable and the future will perhaps accentuate the differences rather than emphasize the similarities.

For our present purpose we shall not avoid the term structuralism in spite of the deformation and over-simplification that it implies. We shall, in the hope of not remaining completely tangent to our subject, isolate a few common concerns and attempt to see the different treatments that they get. If such an enterprise

[1] This text was given as a lecture at the Seminar fur Allgemeine und Vergleichende Literaturwissenschaft of the Freie Universitat Berlin on the 27th of May 1967.

does not do justice to the richness and importance of the work of
thinkers like Lacan and Lévi-Strauss it might hopefully suggest
some of the preoccupations which are central to their individual
developments.

If one were to ask a well-informed person to trace the development of structuralism his answer might possibly run something
along the following lines: the originator of structuralism was
Saussure; after him came the linguistic circle of Prague which developed a highly accurate description of the phonetic laws that
govern all languages; and then came Lévi-Strauss who transposed
the phonological models to anthropology. After Lévi-Strauss' work
the validity of the linguistic model became recognized to such a
point that other disciplines attempted the transposition and very
slowly a body of knowledge emerged—sometimes referred to as
" sciences de l'homme "—where without giving up the individual
concrete problems of each discipline, all came to recognize a common nucleus which is most easily discernible or most easily attain-
able through linguistics, since language gives us a most complete
and comprehensive model for all human activities. Yet, such a
panoramic view would remain inaccurate, besides being oversimplified, in implying a methodological continuity.

Let us begin with Saussure. Saussure's contribution is not a
unified theory but presents operational levels which if hierarchically
ordered are not necessarily interdependent. The best known innovation of Saussure is, of course, his treatment of the linguistic
sign. If today we can take it for granted that the linguistic sign is a
complex entity consisting of two distinct elements, a signifier, a signified and a functional relationship binding them together, we hardly
appreciate the revolution that such a notion introduced.[2] The

[2] Saussure's definitions run as follows:
" Le signe linguistique unit non une chose et un nom, mais un concept et
une image acoustique."
" Nous appelons *signe* la combinaison du concept et de l'image acoustique."
" Nous proposons de conserver le mot *signe* pour désigner le total, et de
remplacer concept et *image acoustique* respectivement par *signifié* et *signifiant*."
" Le lieu unissant le signifiant au signifié est arbitraire, ou encore, puisque
nous entendons par signe le total résultant de l'association d'un signifiant à
un signifié, nous pourrons dire plus simplement: *le signe linguistique est
arbitraire*."
(This is often represented by S/s where S stands for the *signifiant* and
s for the *signifié*).
F. de Saussure. *Cours de Linguistique Générale*, Paris 1964, pp. 98-100.

treatment of the signifier independently of the signified permitted the development of modern phonology—which to this day remains one of the greatest methodological successes of structuralism—whose models were later carried over to the study of nonlinguistic domains. However, when the Saussurian formula is transposed to a non-linguistic domain the question of whether what one is transposing is a fundamentally linguistic model or whether one is using what I shall call in this context an epistemological operator—namely, the decomposition of certain given cultural phenomena into correlated aspects governed by two independent orders which in turn are connected to each other by a set of functions—still remains open. The ambiguity of this problem can be traced back to Saussure himself, for if Saussure was attempting to lay the foundations of linguistics he made these very foundations dependent upon another science which he called semiology and which was to be a study of signs—linguistic and non-linguistic—in their utmost generality. This science-to-be which remains at the barely embryonic stage (in the works of Saussure) will have within the structuralist movement a rather independent history. If for a moment we jump half a century and look at the works of Barthes with the hope of resolving the ambiguity that was present in Saussure we shall find it still present but in a modified version.

Barthes, in an attempt to get such a young science on its feet, postulated that since semiology was to be a science of all signs and since of all the systems of signs the linguistic ones were those that had been most systematically treated, semiology at its beginnings should take the patterns of linguistics and apply them to other domains.[3] Barthes' original project has shown itself to be extremely fruitful. One need only mention his essays on the rhetoric of the

On this issue see also, E. Benveniste, *Problèmes de Linguistique Générale*, Paris 1967, pp. 49-55.

These distinctions were not, of course, new to Saussure, Saussure's privileged position lies in the fact that the later developments of linguistics introduced, through their influence a new epistemological space which gave to his considerations their revolutionary qualities.

[3] See R. Barthes, "Elements de Sémiologie" in *Communications* no. 4, pp. 91-144.

This ambiguity can be traced back to Saussure for if he says: " La linguistique n'est qu'une partie de cette science générale, les lois que découvrira la semiologie seront applicables à la linguistique . . ." *op. cit.*, p. 33.

He also goes on to say: " la linguistique peut devenir le patron general de toute sémiologie, bien que la langue ne soit qu'un système particulier." *op. cit.*, p. 101.

image [4] and more recently his brilliant study of fashion; yet the original ambiguity as to whether the categories that are involved in the articulation of each system of signs remains. It is still impossible in the present state of affairs to determine whether the major categories articulating each system of signs have an independent existence or whether, basically they are linguistic categories which one rediscovers by reducing each system of signs to a fundamental linguistic model.

The question is actually two-fold: On the one hand can a system of signs admit a set of organizing patterns independently of the linguistic ones which have been used to study them, and on the other hand how far does the success of such semiological studies depend on a primary translation of the original systems of signs into a linguistic equivalent? Such a procedure is sometimes explicitly stated as, for example, in Barthes' study of fashion [5] where he studies the language of fashion and not fashion *per se*.

The question as to whether systems of signs which cannot find an immediate linguistic equivalent, such as painting or music, can be treated by semiology, has theoretical consequences that are further reaching than the purely methodological preoccupation. They bring into question the nature of the linguistic sign and more particularly the nature of the relationship that binds the signifier to the signified.

For Saussure this relationship was arbitrary, but necessary. Arbitrary since there is no natural relationship between them, necessary in as much as every community has to agree on a set of cultural, hence conventional relations which permit signs to become a means of communication. Such a solution describes more than defines the relationship in question and tends to reduce the linguistic sign to a mere means of communication. Over-simplifying, we can say that such a position carried to its logical conclusion reduces linguistics to a general theory of communication. The question of the nature of the relationship between signifier and the signified could, of course, be clarified by what might be the nature of the signifier or the signified independent of the function that they acquire when bound together in the linguistic sign. This question is dependent upon another question: can the signifier exist independently of the signified and vice-versa? Of course, linguists tend to consider this

[4] R. Barthes, "Rhétorique de l'image" in *Communications* no. 4, pp. 33-39.
[5] R. Barthes, *Système de la Mode*, Paris, 1967.

question irrelevant and reduce the issue to whether the order governing the signifier is at all connected with the semantic content of the global sign or whether language at its operational level is simply dependent on its phonetic order.

Rosolato and Leclaire, two psychoanalysts, are the only ones to the best of our knowledge who have attempted the description and analysis of language truncated of one of its essential dimensions. They have shown that such an extreme phenomena exists in some types of demential speech and schizophrenic speech in particular,[6] such deviant states being the only cases which permit one to speak of the existence of signifiers unconnected to any signified and vice-versa signifieds not represented by any signifier.

This digression was in part to suggest that the functions that relate the signifier to the signified are perhaps not simple and certainly cannot be taken for granted. For besides being related to language as a tool of communication the psychiatrist's considerations lead us to suspect that the relationship which binds the signifier to the signified is intimately related to the relation of the individual to his language. The linguists have avoided the question. Indeed some linguists have gone as far as to postulate the existence of something which they call a " fluent speaker " to be used as a criterion of whether a linguistic statement is acceptable or not. But we can see that this category of the fluent speaker is precisely there to avoid some of the broader questions that the linguistic sign, as expressed in the Saussurian formula, originally raised for us.

Before going back to the general view of the development of structuralism sketched above we may note that although there is at present a highly precise phonetic description, the attempt to build structural semantics on the same model, has been a total failure. Between the first phonetic developments and the recent semantic attempts we find the anthropological works of Lévi-Strauss and the psychoanalytical works of Lacan which might suggest that it is perhaps in their works that we shall find an answer to the question that linguistics raised but left unanswered.

It is a common view that Lévi-Strauss' work stems from the application of linguistic patterns which he had come to know through his long friendship with Roman Jakobson, to the study of kinship systems and South American myths. Lévi-Strauss has done a great

---

[6] G. Rosolato, " Sémantique et altérations du langage " and S. Leclaire, " A la recherche d'une psychothérapie des psychoses " both in *L'Evolution Psychiatrique.*

deal through his early articles to perpetuate such a view,[7] yet the close reader of the *Structures Elémentaires de la Parenté* could well ask himself whether a knowledge of linguistics is at all necessary to appreciate his enterprise and his immense contribution to the subject. As a matter of fact it is striking when reading the Anglo-Saxon anthropological commentaries on Lévi-Strauss' work to find a good appreciation of his work by anthropologists whose tradition is Radcliffe-Brownian and who have little if any interest in linguistics. There is no doubt, of course, that in his own thinking, Lévi-Strauss was influenced by the work of his linguist friends; yet, the linguistic categories, after having gone through the sieve of anthropological material, come out changed to the point of being almost unrecognizable. Lévi-Strauss himself has pointed out that in studying kinship systems, one cannot simply transpose the phonetic model, since there was nothing equivalent to a phoneme in his anthropological material. What he carries over is a general approach which has guided him in the organization and treatment of his material. In this way, Lévi-Strauss' attempt is different from the Barthian attempt at creating a general semiology.

In Lévi-Strauss' treatment of kinship systems, there are two things which we should point out. First, there exists something roughly equivalent to the Saussurian division between signifier and signified. The signifier corresponds to an individual kinship term taken as an element in a set of functions defined by the combinatorial properties through which the terms enter in relationship with the other terms of the system, and which for a particular society are defined by the nomenclature it uses and the positive or negative rules which it stipulates. The signified, on the other hand, would roughly correspond to the psychological characteristics with which each individual invests each particular function and element. In so doing, Lévi-Strauss breaks radically with the Radcliffe-Brownian tradition, for he precisely eliminates from the domain of scientific consideration all the attitudes and feelings, and so forth, which enter into the way the individual conceives of the function that he fulfills in a society.[8] Lévi-Strauss has shown that in kinship systems the terms combine according to a rigorous logic and a precise economy; thus, all the individual classificatory systems correspond to an organization

---

[7] See for example "L'analyse structurale en linguistique et en anthropologie" in *Word*, vol. 1, no. 2, pp. 1-12, now in *Anthropologie Structurale*, Paris, 1958.

[8] On this issue see Lévi-Strauss' chapter on the mother's brother and the father's sister in *Anthropologie Structurale*, Paris, 1958.

of the general pattern in which the group A gives a woman to a group B which in turn gives a woman to a group C and so on, until the end group gives a woman to the group A. We can see that the system functions like a precise mechanism in which the individual's feelings or attitudes have no place. Each group A, B, C, D, and so forth, remains absolutely identical to itself at the end of the cycle yet something has happened. A certain sign, in this particular case a woman, has been exchanged among groups and this particular movement of a sign defines what Lévi-Strauss calls the law of exchange of women which is a universal order governing all kinship systems independently of the particular modalities that a particular society might use to implement it.

Our purpose here is not to enter into an extended discussion of kinship systems. It should, however, be already apparent that one of the major contributions of Lévi-Strauss to structuralism has been to enable the treatment of the subject of a given human activity as one of the elements of a highly and systematically organized set of functions dependent on a general Law, and the possibility of treating this subject independently of the consciousness, awareness, emotions or affective attitudes that he may have of or towards himself as subject. It should also be apparent even from these few remarks that in Lévi-Strauss' treatment, the Saussurian bar that stands between the signifier and signified is treated methodologically as an absolute division in which the two orders of the signifier and the signified can be treated completely independently from each other. If I spoke of the *Structures Elémentaires de la Parenté*, it is because often and especially in literary circles a great deal of importance is given to Lévi-Strauss' treatment of myth, disregarding completely his early works which in many ways contain the key to his future development. In *La Pensée Sauvage*, Lévi-Strauss generalizes the problem to classification and taxonomy, and shows that at least within a certain type of society, the different terms used to describe nature, the individual, time and space, are highly organized among themselves into closed coherent patterns. These patterns in turn will be the code which will be required to decode the myths to show their fundamental organization. One should bear in mind that the demonstration of Lévi-Strauss holds only for a certain type of society and the general closed order that governs *La Pensée Sauvage* holds true only for them. Whether this is also true for our occidental historical society is a question which is left open, and a simple transposition of the conclusions of *La Pensée Sauvage* and *Le Cru et le Cuit* should not be taken for granted.

As we said, in the *Structures Elémentaires de la Parenté* we can observe that the subject is not only submitted to a rigorously designed set of functions but the set of functions define him as subject. This point is worthy of elaboration. Traditional philosophy had left us as its legacy what we may call a full subject, and consciousness was what constituted the individual as subject. If on the French scene we were to take Sartre as the last tenant of such a position, we can best see how such a fashion of thinking the problem of the subject reached an impasse, for no philosopher has probably ever searched or desired a greater lucidity for the consciousness of the individual, yet, at the same time, found his behavior so opaque to himself. The structuralist subject is empty, uninhabited by consciousness, emotion, affectivity, and so forth. It is only a term within a general set of functions which in fact constitutes him as subject and these functions take precedence over the elements they articulate.

This radical change is only a reflection of a more basic change, namely, the relation of each discipline to its object of study. Traditionally, it was the different objects of study that conditioned the specificity of each discipline. Instead of the traditional view which gave a primacy to the object and postulated its primacy—sociology is the study of societies, ethnology, the study of primitive societies, literary criticism, the study of literature, and so on—we could conceive of each discipline as being defined by the different functions that it articulates and the specific subject that emerges from this set of relationships.

Anthropologists use the term *ego* to denote the individual in terms of whom the whole terminology of kinship system is deployed. For it is the one term that is not named in them, and their whole terminology—mother, father, brother, father's brother, and so forth—is there to denote a set of functions that bind him to the member of the community and constitute him as subject of the kinship systems; but as much as he is the subject, he cannot be named.

Lévi-Strauss, in the *Structures Elémentaires de la Parenté*, has seen that this *ego* is absolutely empty, or at least that all his reality is circumscribed by all the functions which define the relationships in which he enters. This term of kinship systems which the anthropologist defines by *ego* presents some very striking resemblances to those linguistic entities called shifters. Shifters are those parts of speech through which the individual accedes to language, the two best examples of this being proper nouns and personal pronouns. There is very little in linguistics on proper nouns. Jakobson's redundant definition: ". . . la signification générale d'un nom propre ne peut se définir en dehors d'un renvoi au code. Dans le code de l'anglais, ' Jerry ' signifie une personne nommée Jerry. La circularité est évidente: le nom désigne quiconque porte ce nom," [9] is almost equivalent to the linguist's admission of defeat in front of this mysterious entity constituted by proper nouns. As for personal pronouns, we have a classical article of Benveniste, in which he shows that the personal pronoun " I " cannot be defined outside of the linguistic reality in which it manifests itself. Besides, every time the present pronoun " I " is used it implies on the part of its user a *dédoublement*. To quote again from Benveniste: " *Je* ne peut être défini qu'en termes de ' locution,' non en termes d'objets, comme l'est un signe nominal. *Je signifie* ' la personne qui énonce la présente instance de discours contenant *je*.' Instance unique per définition, et valable seulement dans son unicité. . . . Mais, parallèlement, c'est aussi en tant qu'instance de forme *je* qu'il doit être pris; la forme *je* n'a d'existence linguistique que dans l'acte de parole qui la profère. Il y a donc, dans ce procès, une double instance conjuguée: instance de *je* comme référent, et instance de discours contenant *je*, comme référé. La definition peut alors être précisée ainsi: *je* est l' ' individu qui énonce la présente instance de discours contenant l'instance linguistique *je*.' " [10]

But at this point, the linguist is at a loss, for he is unable in purely linguistic terms to define the relationship between the " I " that speaks and the " I " that is spoken of. Curiously enough, the interest of linguists for shifters has come much later than the ethnologist's interest for kinship systems or proper nouns. Lévi-Strauss has spoken extensively of proper nouns in *La Pensée Sauvage*, there again to show that in certain particular societies the proper noun defines the individual as a function of the rest of the social group in which he is included. But of course in these societies, the main preoccupation is always with the individual as function. The individual is what he is because of the various functions that bind him to the rest of the community within the

[9] R. Jakobson, *Essais de Linguistique Générale*, Paris, 1966, p. 177.
[10] E. Benveniste, *Problemes de Linguistique Générale*, Paris, 1966, p. 252.

total economy of the system. This, however, is not true for our occidental society. For if we had to characterize our society, its most striking feature would be an absence of distinction between the individual as subject and the consciousness or affective attitudes which inhabit the subject. As Rosolato will say, if in our society we introduce ourselves by our proper names it is to prevent having to give or to define the content of the name we exhibit. In the case of the personal pronoun " I," what interests Lévi-Strauss is, of course, the " I " that is spoken of and not the " I " that speaks. If a kinship system were to be compared to language (but this is only a metaphor) *ego* is spoken by system but *ego* does not speak the system. The necessity of methodologically treating the human phenomenon in terms of functions rather than in terms of discrete elements, and the whole new problematic about the subject which this necessity introduces, constitutes for us the most fundamental novelty of structuralism and that which gives it today its fundamental philosophical status. It is this which has made Lévi-Strauss and Lacan thinkers in their own right independently of their specific fields and professional preoccupations. The linguistic structuralism which preceded contemporary anthropological and psychoanalytical structuralism ought to be regarded as a preparation—perhaps a necessary one—to what comes to full fruition later on. The methodology of the linguist, fruitful as it may have been, could in no respect have had a philosophical status to permit it, at least within the French scene, to displace the predominant importance of Sartre and Merleau-Ponty.

Before we go any further, two remarks may not be out of place. This order which governs the human phenomena, or to be more precise, this set of functions which governs the relationship between a given set of terms and invests with meaning one empty term, mainly the subject, should not be thought of or conceived in terms of a spatial metaphor. It should not be seen as something hidden behind or lying underneath and outside manifestation. As we have already said, this order exists at the level of the signifier; this order is the most exterior, the most apparent, and perhaps for this very reason the most difficult to see. If anything structuralism has taught us to apprehend the surface and has shown us that in the past for wanting to see too much in depth, we neglected the appearance—an appearance which structures our reality, or rather which transforms reality into the real and beyond which there is literally nothing. As for the subject which it brings into question, in spite of the temptations, we must not be led to think of it as the traditional philosophical subject, as the subject of the consciousness, or as a psychological subject.

Returning then to our original consideration we can say that in relationship to linguistic theory Lévi-Strauss has used the Saussurian formula to be able to isolate a certain domain which in turn he shows to be rigorously ordered. To maintain our linguistic terminology we can say that for Lévi-Strauss there exists an order governing the signifier which is independent from that of the signified. If we continue our transposition of terms we can say that for Lévi-Strauss, also, the question of whether there can exist an order of the signifier independently of the signified is irrelevant. In Lévi-Strauss' terms, the signified without signifier would correspond to the status of man before culture—that is a domain closed to human understanding—and signified without signifier is also excluded by the presence of human societies, having all a cultural dimension.

Therefore, with Lévi-Strauss we have gained a greater precision in the methodological requirements for treating the order of the signifier and if this had led us to a new problematic of the subject, we are still unable to clarify what the relationship between signifier and signified is. We can now see, however, that this question is fundamental with regard to whether structuralism is merely a methodology or whether this methodology implies a particular epistemology.

In order to answer the question, we shall turn to Lacan. However, we shall have to do so obliquely and approach the problem with a new consideration of the linguistic sign, for the latter is, perhaps, not as simple as the linguists have led us to believe.

Language, for the linguist, is primarily a means of communication and as a means of communication it not only involves a signifier and a signified but also a rather simple and unequivocal relation between them. We know, however, that language is not only a means of conveying messages, that on the one hand there exist discourses such as pathological speech in which the communication aspect of language is completely subordinated to the problem of the relation of the subject to his discourse. On the other hand, we also know that language does much more than simply convey messages since—and literature is the best possible example of this— the semantic possibilities of language are all the richer when it is furthest from its mere quality as a tool of communication.

Already with Levi-Strauss it was possible to see that the use of a linguistic terminology was not the easiest or most precise way of denoting his treatment of kinship terms. One could, as well, have said that, given kinship systems, what Lévi-Strauss had found was an order which henceforth we shall call the symbolic order [11] which governs their global articulation independently of the particular terms to which it applies. And in as much as this order is constituted by a set of functions, it is possible to isolate them and to treat them independently.

The linguists preoccupied perhaps with the inevitable semantic aspects of language did not point out the presence of such an order in language. It is the psychoanalysists who have circumscribed it as far as language is concerned. In Rosolato's words: " Le *symbole* est ce signe transmué qui comprend un *réseau* de relations entre *signifiants* et *signifiés*, eux-mêmes, par ce fait, plurivalents. Ceci entraîne comme conséquence, que le symbolique ne rende pas compte ' de quelque chose,' ne représente pas non plus. . . . Le *symbolique* apparaît comme catégorie dès que le signe acquiert la dimension supplémentaire du symbole; le symbolique assure, aussi, l'accession à un *état* (un stade) de compréhension ouvert à la pensée qui se pense, à la *relation* qui saille, le sujet s'y insérant ou en ayant tenu compte." [12]

It should be apparent to us that the symbolic order is independent of the linguistic sign and not located within it as a too hasty application of the linguistic model could have led us to believe, even though, of course, the symbolic order cannot exist without language as a system of signs, just as a function cannot be isolated from the domains that it maps.

It is this symbolic order that again is going to constitute for us a subject. It will do so, however, by relating to each other elements taken from the domain of the signifier independently of the signified attached to them. For here again—and the example of kinship systems should help us understand this—the signified is only a

[11] The expression " ordre symbolique " has been mostly used by Lacan and the French psychoanalysts. The reader should be careful not to confuse the expression "symbolique" with the more common notion of "symbol" that is an arbitrary signifier associated by convention with a given signified. For this common type of symbolism Rosolato uses the expression " allegorical." For a more precise definition of these terms see G. Rosolato, " Le Symbolique " in *La Psychanalyse*, no. 5.

[12] G. Rosolato, " Le Symbolique " in *La Psychanalyse*, no. 5, pp. 224-226.

semantic charge attached to the signifier but remains independent of the order that governs it.

To come back to the symbolic order. It is not enough to say that the signifiers can combine with each other to produce among themselves an independent order. One still has to specify which functions are at play to produce the mapping of the domain of the signifier upon itself. Lacan has pin-pointed these functions in two specific mechanisms which he calls metaphor and metonomy. Metaphor is the substitution of one signifier for another, whereas metonomy is the displacement of one signifier by another.

Metaphor and metonomy of course, correspond exactly to what Freud had called condensation and displacement, and indeed Lacan has been instrumental in bringing in a new awareness to the whole linguistic considerations that are implicit in the work of Freud, and which, especially under the influence of American psychoanalysis, one has tended to forget. For Lacan not only was Freud an accomplished linguist but in his treatment of dreams he anticipated the development of future linguistics.

The unconscious speaks and like every speech brings into question the subject of the enunciation, a subject which cannot be treated independently of the particular symbolic order that governs it. For to quote Lacan: " Notre définition du signifiant (il n'y en a pas d'autre) est: un signifiant, c'est ce qui représente le sujet pour un autre signifiant." Hence the signifier of the subject " sera donc le signifiant pour quoi tous les autres signifiants représentent le sujet: c'est à dire que faute de ce signifiant, tous les autres ne représenteraient rien, puisque rien n'est représenté que pour. Or la batterie des signifiants, en tant qu'elle est, étant par là même complète, ce signifiant ne peut être qu'un trait qui se trace de son cercle sans pouvoir y être compté." [13]

We can see here that we have gone a step beyond what the linguist had to say about the subject of the enunciation for if the linguist is capable, by using the shifters, of showing that the speaker and the subject of the enunciation do not coincide, he is unable to say anything more about the subject of the enunciation which remains necessarily an undefined category since the order that constitutes it escapes the considerations that remain at the level of the linguistic sign. Furthermore, if shifters point to the subject of the enunciation they are not adequate to it since even a state-

[13] J. Lacan, *Ecrits*, Paris, 1966, p. 819.

ment not containing the shifter implies the subject of the enunciation without having a specific term to represent it. To quote Lacan, " On peut ici tenter, dans un souci de méthode, de partir de la définition strictement linguistique du Je comme signifiant: où il n'est rien que le *shifter* ou indicatif qui dans le sujet de l'énoncé désigne le sujet en tant qu'il parle actuellement. C'est dire qu'il désigne le sujet de l'énonciation, mais qu'il ne le signifie pas. Comme il est évident au fait que tout signifiant du sujet de l'énonciation peut manquer dans l'énoncé, outre qu'il y en a qui diffèrent du Je, et pas seulement ce qu'on appelle insuffisamment les cas de la première personne du singulier." [14]

Let us note that the shifter " I " and the subject of the enunciation never coincide. The " I " is what only sometimes represents the subject for the speaker who in this sense is two stages away from the subject of his discourse.

It is impossible for us to go in detail into the complexities of Lacan's theoretical elaboration. Let us, however, briefly and purely suggestively quote Lacan again on the relationship of the individual's consciousness to the subject of the symbolic order. " Si l'homme vient à penser l'ordre symbolique, c'est qu'il y est d'abord pris dans son être. L'illusion qu'il l'ait formé par sa conscience, provient de ce que c'est par la voie d'une béance spécifique de sa relation imaginaire à son semblable, qu'il a pu entrer dans cet ordre comme sujet. Mais il n'a pu faire cette entrée que par le défilé radical de la parole, soit le même dont nous avons reconnu dans le jeu de l'enfant un moment génétique, mais qui, dans sa forme complète, se reproduit chaque fois que le sujet s'adresse à l'Autre comme absolu, c'est-à-dire comme l'Autre qui peut l'annuler lui-même, de la même façon qu'il peut en agir avec lui, c'est-à-dire en se faisant objet pour le tromper. Cette dialectique de l'intersubjectivité, s'appuie volontiers du schéma suivant:

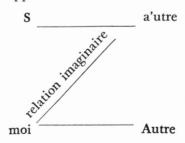

[14] *Idem*, p. 800.

désormais familier à nos élèves et où les deux termes moyens représentent le couple de réciproque objectivation imaginaire que nous avons dégagé dans la *stade du miroir*." [15]

Leaving aside the problems raised by A which need not concern us here we can see that at this point a, where the individual becomes aware of himself through a set of imaginary identifications he remains cut off from the symbolic order and can only reach it through a process that takes him through an imaginary dimension, which itself goes through the other (a') as the other is given to him in his daily intercourse and who acts as a mirror for the way in which the individual sees himself.

Without going into a great deal of elaboration we can see how the disciples of Lacan have come to locate the relationship between the order of the signifier and the signified precisely along this imaginary axis. In other terms, the problem of the bar that in Saussure's formula was left undefined and which in Lévi-Strauss was taken as an absolute break, here for the first time acquires a meaning. The relationship of the signifier to the signified runs along the imaginary axis; in other words, all semantic considerations are dependent upon the individual's perception of himself, and although this may be affected by an alteration in the symbolic order, they do not in any way govern it. This may also clarify the reason for which language, as a tool of communication, rests at one level on a social convention since the semantic content of the sign has to be readily decodable by any member of the linguistic community; hence, it has to rest on the way each individual perceives himself in relation to his surrounding social and natural reality.

From this perspective we can also see the rigour of Lévi-Strauss' methodology, for in articulating the symbolic order he has developed a methodology to permit him to speak of the symbolic order without having to make any reference to the imaginary axis or to the problem of how the individual is aware of himself as living the symbolic order.

Here an objection could be raised, mainly that in Lévi-Strauss' work the patterns that he discovers are universal whereas the patterns that psychoanalysis links up are individual and vary with each case. Let us here, however, be a bit more careful. The kinship system of Lévi-Strauss consists precisely in pointing

[15] *Idem*, p. 53, see also pp. 548-549.

out the fundamental mechanisms by which his symbolic order is constituted; the mechanism can function in more than one way by producing the various systems that the ethnologist observes around the globe. We must also note that Lévis-Strauss' work has been in those domains, kinship systems, taxonomy and myth where, so to speak, the function of the awareness that the native has of himself is practically irrelevant; whether the methodology can be completely extended is still an open question. We must finally also remark that the very fact that such studies are possible with certain societies and not with others, points to the existence of a radical difference between the two, which in this case we may briefly summarize as the following: in those societies which practice " La Pensée Sauvage " the individual is conceived as being separate from his function, which explains the rigorous kinship laws, the very ritualized proper names and the very systematic taxonomy that they use to describe both the individual and the nature that surrounds him, whereas in our western historical society the individual and function are hopelessly intermingled, and it is perhaps in this intermixing of function and individual that we have to search for the historical dimension of our own society.

It has often been said that structuralism is anti-historical or a-historical. This remark deserves some qualification. Indeed, as far as the constitution of the subject goes, structuralism does not give a primacy to history, but this does not mean that from a structuralist point of view one cannot raise the problem of history. Lévi-Strauss distinguishes between two types of societies, those that he calls " cold " society and those that he calls " hot " society. Needless to say, ethnologist though he is, his preoccupation is with cold societies—that is those societies that, in spite of changes, tend to maintain the social organization always identical to itself and independent of the vicisitudes of time.

Lévi-Strauss has shown how indeed in their organization, these societies deploy mechanisms which, so to speak, abolish their temporal dimension to produce institutions which will be able to maintain themselves. In such cases it would be more precise to talk of a specific temporality that goes with a certain type of organization, and even though this remains yet to be proven, one can suspect that the very possibility of producing such temporality is not independent of the fact that in such societies individual and function remain separate from each other. The problem of history becomes acute in historical societies and most particularly in our occidental one. But then, perhaps, the historical dimension of our society is a function of a specific temporality which itself is dependent upon the intermixing of the individual and the functions that govern him. Within those societies that practice " La Pensée Sauvage " an individual can always answer the question " what am I? " Whereas in our society it is the question that always remains open. Lacan has defined the unconscious as that part of one's speech which one lacks to establish the continuity of one's discourse, and perhaps history is nothing more than the result of a temporality which stems from the need of the individual to define " what I was " in order to rationalize " what I am."

Such a brief survey of structuralism cannot do it justice. We have perhaps said too much and too little. We wanted, however, to suggest that structuralism cannot be simply identified to the concrete applications through which it has come to be known but that its fundamental problematic hinges on the order that governs human phenomena and the kind of logical subject that is requisite to carrying on such a task. In its development structuralism points in two distinct directions: at the general rules that govern any process in which a certain structure is evident, and at a hermeneutical reading of any constituted structure. Structuralism in its treatment of the individual has replaced the old existentialist categories of inter-subjectivity by something else which we may call an inter-alterity which attempts to elucidate the relationship between the subject and the structures through which he is constituted. This last consideration is at the heart of all epistemological considerations of the relationship of the observer to the structures that he studies. If we did not elaborate on this last point it is because it is implicitly obvious in the case of Lacan and psychoanalysis, while Lévi-Strauss has given an elucidation of how it applies to his anthropological work in *Tristes Tropiques.*

Language is the stuff of literature and one would have expected that an intellectual current which took so much of its inspiration from linguistics would have turned to literature as a privileged domain. On the whole, however, the applications of structuralism to literary criticism have been rather disappointing. As a matter of fact one could almost say that with the exception of Barthes there has hardly been any attempt to systematically transpose the categories developed by other disciplines to a literary domain. Curiously enough if one had to draw a balance sheet, it is in the works of Lévi-Strauss and more especially in the works of Lacan that one would find a great deal of references to literature. Interesting, however, as these references may be, they do present for the critic a very special problem, for if Lévi-Strauss has written on Rousseau, or if Lacan has done extended studies on Poe, Gide, Sade and Goethe, and if the latter's works contain innumerable literary allusions the authors have, in all of these cases, used literature more as a tool than as an end, and even though for the literary critic they offer very powerful intuitions or show the possibility of new perspectives on a given author, they fall short of providing a systematic methodology with which to look at literature.

If attempts at transposing linguistic categories to literature are not numerous they do, however, exist. Here, we must distinguish between the various ways critics have gone about carrying on such an enterprise for their results differ considerably and according to the way in which they have approached the problem.

Let us leave aside the early attempts of the Russian formalists who for literature attempted a course parallel to that which the School of Prague took for phonetics (but with less success), to concentrate on the contemporary French scene. In recent years there has been a renewed interest in these early precursors but this return to the origins is strongly mediated by Lévi-Strauss' works on myth and as we shall see later this mediation is not without raising serious problems.

Without over simplifying too much we can say that the attempt at transposing the linguistic patterns to literature has been tried in one of two ways. First by a direct transposition of either phonetic models or the categories developed by phonetical linguistics, or else in a slightly more general fashion, the application of the patterns that govern the greatest linguistic unit that is the sentence to a given literary work. Second, the search in a given literary work for what might correspond to the universals of language.

As examples of the first attempt let us mention either the study of Lévi-Strauss and Jakobson of *Les Chats* [16] of Baudelaire or the

[16] C. Lévi-Strauss, and R. Jakobson, " Les Chats de Charles Baudelaire " in *L'Homme*, vol. II, no. 1, 1952.

attempts of Todorov to study the formal structure of the novel. Of Lévi-Strauss' and Jakobson's study let us just say that they quite successfully succeeded in isolating a phonological layer and studying its organization. The material which they use in this particular article is a single poem. One can see that for such a task there exists a lower limit to what the critic has to take into consideration. The criterion for this lower limit is empirical. There exists a threshold below which one would not be able to find all the elements that enter into the constitution of the system. The upper limit is more open for if the method in this particular study is applied to one poem of Baudelaire there is no reason why it could not be generalized to say the complete poetical corpus of Baudelaire and, for periods where the literary output is reasonably uniform, to greater units of poetry.

What is striking in this approach is the fact that the layer that is brought forth by the analysis constitutes a very limited part of the text with which one is faced.

Todorov's work is different, and this diversity could be seen as dictated by the very different object with which he is concerned. If what Lévi-Strauss and Jakobson have done is readily applied to a poetical corpus or at the limit, say, to a play by Racine, it would seem almost impossible to transpose it to a novel. In the case of the novel what Todorov has done is to attempt to break down its formal pattern into a small number of narrative units, and given these narrative units he then attempts to detect a rule by which they combine with each other. He proceeds as if there existed what one might call a generative narrative grammar, which would govern the formal construction of any narrative literary work. Todorov has tried to illustrate this approach by studying *Les Liaisons Dangereuses*.[17] Here again the work lends itself to such a treatment but whether the same techniques could be applied, say, to Proust, remains doubtful, and whether it could be generalized to include the narrative in its most generic aspect is even more so.

The two enterprises we mentioned are based simply on an analogy between language as the object of linguistics and literature as the object of a literary criticism. The second attempt might look similar to the first for transposing the universals of discourse,

[17] T. Todorov, "Les catégories du récit littéraire" in Communications, no. 8, 1966, pp. 125-151. "Choderlos de Laclos et la theorie du récit" in *Tel Quel*, pp. 17-28, no. 27.

problems of shifterization, time relationships or the problem of voices and not seem very different from applying phonetic patterns or general formal grammatical relationships to the understanding of literature. Here also we might be dealing with simple analogy. In fact the similarity between the two is rather deceiving.

This second approach has been exclusively attempted by Barthes.[18] Barthes begins by stating that his work is based on a fundamental homology between grammar and discourse in general. Beginning with this hypothesis in the first moment he develops what he calls a rhetoric of discourse, and in this lies his profound originality. The categories that he uses to elaborate this rhetoric are not the individual phonetics or grammatical patterns but the universals of language. The universals of language represent at the level of language, some general relationships of the speaker or writer to his discourse and thus bring into question the problem of the subject. Personal pronouns, as we already said, denote the relationship of the speaker to the subject of his enunciation. The time relationships reflect a temporality as constituted by the narrator's present to the time sequence of his verbs.[19] Voices reflect the relationship of the speaker to the action of the verb. At any rate Barthes, having isolated these universal categories that govern the relationship of any speaker to his own speech, goes on questioning how each individual author fulfils, in his own different way, this inevitable requirement of language. So far Barthes' work has consisted of analysing how historical writing from Herodotus to Michelet has faced these problems. There is no reason why the method cannot be generalized and in terms of pure methodology this seems to us one of the most pregnant approaches and one of which we will hear more of in the future.

Within the broader context of a semiology that would take into account anthropology as well as linguistics there would be one set of considerations regarding the movements of certain privileged " signs " within a given cultural context, which could readily find an application to literature but which so far have not been exploited. A given body of literature, such as the works of a writer

[18] Unfortunately the results of Barthes recent work along these lines which has constituted the heart of his teaching at the Hautes Etudes for the past three years has not yet been published.

[19] On these three issues see E. Benveniste, *op. cit.*, pp. 168-175, 225-236, 237-250, 251-258, 258-266.

or the work of a given group of writers, let us say the Jansenists for example, can be considered as a sign that circulates between two groups, the producers and the consumers, the givers and the receivers. Methodologically speaking literature could be compared to the circulation of women in the kinship systems studied by Lévi-Strauss. It is obvious that the sign circulates mostly for the value of the signifier yet the very circuit in which it is caught invests it with a semantic value which affects the very structure of the order that governs its signifiers. Let us give a concrete example to illustrate this point. Goldmann has shown that the *Pensées* of Pascal and the plays of Racine are both latently invested with a Jansenist world view.[20] What Goldmann, however, would be unable to explain is precisely the difference between the *Pensées* of Pascal and the plays of Racine.

If one accepts the fact that the plays of Racine were written to be consumed by Versailles whereas the *Pensées* of Pascal were not, one would more easily be able to define what originally constitutes that difference, besides eliminating all the problems concerning the author's awareness of the implicit content of his work that Goldmann's presentation brings about. How was it that the court did not recognize the ideology implicit in the plays or, and this is more important, how was it that Racine who was expounding a Jansenist world view was doing this through the theatre, that is through a form that is condemned by the very ideology that he was exposing? If, on the other hand, we replace the plays of Racine in the circuit through which they move, we understand better the particular contradiction expounded in them, that is how to be oneself, yet how to live in the world if the world is corruption and if there is no escape from this world. We also understand better the cultural groups through which the text circulates, mainly the dilemma of Jansenism which condemned the world yet had to proclaim its condemnation of the world to the very world that it condemned, and also the nature of Versailles' dilemma in front of the Jansenists, since their very action within the world excluded them and put them outside the world.

Such considerations have to be preceded by a knowledge of the two groups. To this end one can study the signs in their static moment rather than in their dynamic moment, in other words, all

[20] L. Goldmann, *Le Dieu Caché*, Paris, 1956.

one has to do is study a certain literature as defining a certain group.

Let us now go back for a moment to kinship systems. The very kinship system defines clans, groups, and so on, yet it is the very kinship systems which determine the matrimonial alliances, that is the circulation of women which constitute the very clans and groups with which we started. In other words the static aspect and the dynamic aspect cannot be separated from each other since they literally refer to each other as their founding element. If I mentioned this possibility of applying semiology to literature it is partly because it is in this direction that structuralism could recuperate the thought of traditional historical criticism and at the same time correct its onesidedness.

All applications of general semiology tend, of course, by their very nature to completely dissolve the individuality of the literary works as literary works, and minimize its creative aspects and practically abolish the relationship that exists between the writer and his work. For such an approach would be equivalent to studying literature as a sub-set of the general means of communication which a group uses to bind and, at the same time, define its various constitutive elements, and here an anecdotical remark might not be out of place. If in France it is Roland Barthes who has done a great deal for semiology it should at first be surprising that he never thought of applying it to literature, all the more so since literature is one of his main concerns. But on the other hand we can see why Barthes, the critic, is too involved with, and too aware of, the very act of writing and the dilemmas of the writer, to use a method which would dissolve what from another perspective constitutes the very uniqueness of the creative aspects of the literary act.

So far all the possible applications of structuralism to literary criticism that we have described deny in many ways the specificity of literature. This could have been predicted in the first place since what we have said so far applies to literature only in as much as literature is a system of signs among others, and in no way privileged in relationship to them. Saussure had made a distinction, within the general domain of linguistic reality, between *langue* and *parole*. *Langue* is that part of the linguistic phenomenon which is independent of any one individual utterance but which defines the general conditions which make them possible. *Langue*, as such, transcends any individual speech and is not a function of the speaking subject. For Saussure in particular, and the linguists in general, there is no doubt that *langue* is valorized in relationship to *parole*. But as we suggested earlier the evolution of structuralism has consisted in giving a greater and greater emphasis to *parole* at the expense of *langue*. The whole problematic of the subject, as a matter of fact, hinges on the articulation between *langue* and *parole*. Let us, therefore, now turn to literature to consider it within this second aspect.

An author writes; the result of his act can be compared to an utterance. As with most utterances it would seem that the writer's purpose is to communicate a message and statements, "to say something." He tells a story, describes a situation, relates an event, yet, as we know, language communicates only because of a certain number of fundamental properties which make communication possible. Communication is not at the heart of the linguistic act but only an epiphenomenon, the infant that symbolizes his world through the *Fort/Da* uses language in, so to speak, a stronger way than when we use it to vehiculate all the possible messages in the world. And so with literature, if literature tells a story, if the author has to always use a reference, it is simply a consequence of the fact that he is manipulating a linguistic sign. As a first approximation we can, therefore, say that the main function of the writer is to articulate the signifier in a certain fashion so as to constitute an order which will define the subject of the utterance; and here we find our earlier dilemma. The subject of the enunciation is not identical with that which designates the subject of the enunciation, nor is it identical with the speaker as subject. The relationship between the three is dialectical and none of them can be isolated from the other two. Faced with this configuration the task of the critic is either to elucidate for a given author the particular relationships established between the subjects involved, or else to study purely the configuration of the signifying chain and deal only with the subject of the enunciation that is the subject of the symbolic order. It is in this context that Barthes has defined literary criticism as "l'art de remplir le Je de l'enonciation."

The first of these instances has already a tradition behind it. Sartre looked upon literature as that which establishes a particular intersubjective attitude of the writer to the world. But the very treatment of intersubjectivity as Sartre developed it is insufficient.

The individual is not caught in a deadly and unresolvable war with the other, but instead has to cope with the Sartrian other through his very own otherness which reflects to him a mirror image of his double. At this level it will be true that the author is always his work—Flaubert's *Madame Bovary c'est moi*—yet, always remains distinct from it. We can also see why a certain historic criticism unable to recognize the real subject of the literary utterance, but unable nevertheless to escape the dilemma of the subject as such, has attempted to get around the problem by filling in the author—considered the subject of his literary utterance—with all sorts of extra-literary historical or sociological material.

Let us add that such an elucidation of the relationship of the author to the subject of his work—exemplified for instance by Jean Delay's work on Gide [21]—is particularly suited and fruitful in the case of a psychotic writer. For within a psychotic structure the individual self tends to disappear in front of a subject that speaks through him. The psychotic literally does not speak but is spoken. Let us mention, as an example of such a case, Laplanche's study of Hölderlin.[22] This would in a way, explain why madness is the horizon of literature and why so many poets have felt it as a limit that exerted a particular fascination on them and the greatness of those who like Hölderlin were able to live their poetical experience to a point of self-annihilation.

Much has been said of Lévi-Strauss' analysis of myth and its application to literary criticism, what we have just said should prove the futility of such an enterprise. As Lévi-Strauss says, and who should know better than him, a myth can be characterized by the fact that it is a linguistic utterance that does not have a subject —a myth " speaks itself." Myths, therefore, can be considered within the spectrum of various modes of linguistic speech as that which is furthest and most different from a literary one.

Let us go back for a moment to the second possibility that we envisaged. In other words for the critic to deal purely with the subject of the enunciation, independently of the relationship of the latter to the author. For such a critic, in spite of all the constraints that the work imposes on him, in spite of the obligations for him of accounting for the totality of all the elements present

[21] J. Delay, *La Jeunesse d'André Gide*, 2v. Paris, 1956, 1957, on this work see the comments of Lacan in *Ecrits*, pp. 739-764.

[22] J. Laplanche, *Holderlin et la question du Père*, Paris, 1961.

in it and describing the symbolic configuration that governs it, having to reinstate this order in language his own verbalization becomes independent, and in front of the text of the critic the author runs the danger of being relegated to a pre-text. It is at this point perhaps that criticism turns itself into literature and recognizes itself similar to the literary work, the child and the servant of language.

All these considerations are based on an assumed identity between the act of speaking and the act of writing, for structuralism has been concerned with the individual as subject of his speech. It should, perhaps, be our task as literary critics to attempt the description of the individual as subject of the written word in the hope of better delineating the literary phenomenon. Whether man the writer will be able to exist independently of man the speaker or whether he will be subordinated to him, is a question that only the future will be able to decide. Within the present epistemological horizon literary criticism like all the other disciplines which have come to be called " sciences humaines " have to recognize the primacy of ethnology and psychoanalysis, for as Michel Foucault says: ". . . psychanalyse et l'ethnologie ne sont pas tellement des sciences humaines à côté des autres, mais qu'elles en parcourent le domaine entier, qu'elles l'animent sur toute sa surface, qu'elles répandent partout leurs concepts, qu'elles peuvent proposer en tous lieux leurs méthodes de déchiffrement et leurs interpretations. Nulle science humaine ne peut s'assurer d'être quitte avec elles, ni tout à fait independante de ce qu'elles ont pu decouvrir, ni certaine de ne pas relever d'elles d'une manière ou d'une autre." [23]

And yet, as the poetic act revealed itself to be less and less free, the poet discovered himself to be not the creator of words but he who had to live their servitude and thus the poem precipitated with vertigenous velocity towards the white page of Mallarmé. This did not go without compensation for if the poet stopped being a creator it was because he had to live the experience of language like the ethnologist and the psychoanalyst have to live an experience that fashions them as subject. With the disappearance of the creative act the critical experience began to emerge but this critical act accepts the knowledge it expounds only as a secondary by-

[23] M. Foucault, *Les Mots et les Choses*, Paris, 1966, p. 390.

product—to express itself it is obliged to search in language its poetic dimension, the only one capable of moulding it into the subject, hence an unexpected reversal. It is the ethnologist and the psychoanalysist who begin again the old quests for a pristine language. The old passionate search of the poet for a Word adequate to its Truth has become nowadays in the works of a Barthes, Lévi-Strauss or Lacan that of a critical idiom adequate to its subject. In this resides perhaps the revenge of language on those who tried to steal its secrets.

1967

THE STRUCTURES OF FICTION ✌ BY FRANK KERMODE

✌ The question is whether there is a chance that some mode of structural analysis can satisfy the requirements of criticism, if we take those to be: first, that there should be available for any work we take to be worthy of preservation and of public interest some fairly systematic account which is itself acceptable to an informed public; and secondly that this account should try to tell the truth and know how much of the truth it can tell.

There is no doubt that we are in and will for some time remain in a period of which the preferred instruments for the description of novels and their truth are those of structural analysis, and I confess to a strong feeling that novels are extremely resistant to these instruments, whatever may be said of other kinds of fiction. To substantiate the feeling I should have to demonstrate that all such methods fail with all novels, but I do not know all the methods, let alone all the novels; and new varieties are always being devised. The best I can hope to do is to make it seem unlikely that they will work.

In what follows I have recounted three fictions which are not novels and examined three different ways of determining structure and meaning. Then I discuss a novel and its resistance to this *kind* of analysis. The first two analyses are by methods which derive largely from linguistics, the second of them being not merely structural but structuralist. The third belongs to an older type, but one that is still in general critical use. The example I use comes from New Testament criticism, but can stand for other kind of typological analysis of structures. The novel I have chosen to end the discussion happens to be a fairly complicated one, but that seems reasonable if you reflect that nobody needs sophisticated analyses of simple ones. Better still, of course, would be a large number of difficult texts, but that is not possible in the present situation.

Obviously I am offering nothing more than an hypothesis but at least it exposes itself for reasoned rejection. Having made these

prior explanations I shall now simply tell the stories. In all
probability the first alone is unfamiliar.

This is a Clackamas Chinook story, called 'The "wife" who
"goes out" like a man,' or 'Seal and her younger brother dwelt
there.'[1]

I. They lived there, Seal, her daughter, her younger brother,
I do not know when it was, but now a woman got to Seal's
younger brother.

They lived there. They would go outside in the evening. The
girl would say, she would tell her mother: "Mother! There is
something different about my uncle's wife. It sounds like a
man when she 'goes out!'" "Don't say that! (She is) your
uncle's wife!"

"They lived there like that for a long time. They would 'go
out' in the evening. And then she would tell her: 'Mother!
There is something different about my uncle's wife. When she
'goes out,' it sounds like a man." "Don't say that!" Her uncle
and his wife would 'lie together' in bed. Some time afterwards
the two of them 'lay' close to the fire, they 'lay' close besides
each other. I do not know what time of night it was, but something dripped on her face. She shook her mother. She told her:
"Mother! Something dripped on my face." "Don't say that!
Your uncle and his wife are 'going.'"

Presently then again she heard something dripping down.
She told her: "Mother! Something is dripping, I hear something." "Don't say that. Your uncle (and his wife) are 'going.'"

The girl got up, she fixed the fire, she lit pitch, she looked
where the two were lying. Oh! oh! She raised her light to it.
In his bed her uncle's neck was cut. He was dead. She screamed.

She told her mother: "I told you something was dripping.
You told me: "Don't say that. They are 'going.'" I had told
you there was something different about my uncle's wife. When
she 'goes out,' it sounds like a man. . . . You told me: "Don't
say that!" She wept.

Seal said: "Younger brother! My younger brother! They (his
house posts) are valuable standing here. My younger brother!"
She kept saying that.

But the girl herself wept. She said: "I tried in vain to tell
you. My uncle's wife sounds like a man when she urinates, not

[1] Dell H. Hymes, "The 'wife' who 'goes out' like a man: Reinterpretation
of a Clackamas Chinook Myth," *Social Science Information* 7 (3) (1967), pp.
173-199.

like a woman. You told me: 'Don't say that!' Oh! Oh! my uncle!" The girl wept.

Now I only remember that far.

II. The second story is more familiar.

King Laius and Queen Jocasta, who rule over Thebes, have a son called Oedipus. Because of a prophecy that the son would kill the father Oedipus is exposed on a mountain, but survives, and kills Loius in a brawl at a crossroads. When Thebes is threatened by a monster, the Sphinx, Oedipus solves its riddle, so causing its death, and winning the hand of Jocasta in marriage. Oedipus becomes king of Thebes; but when it is discovered that he has been married to his mother and killed his father he blinds himself, and his mother-wife commits suicide.

III. Here is the third story, so familiar that you can forgive its being told only in part, and divided into two discontinuous sections.

Part I. And being in Bethany in the house of Simon the leper, as he sat at meat, there came a woman having an alabaster box of spikenard very precious; and she brake the box and poured it on his head. And there were some that had indignation within themselves, and said, Why was this waste of the ointment made? For it might have been sold for more than three hundred pence, and have been given to the poor. And they murmured against her. And Jesus said, Let her alone; why trouble ye her? she hath wrought a good work on me . . . she has come aforehand to anoint my body to the burying. And as they did eat, Jesus took bread, and blessed, and brake it, and gave to them, and said, Take, eat, this is my body. And he took the cup, and when he had given thanks, he gave it to them: and they all drank of it. . . . And Jesus said unto them, All ye shall be offended because of this night. . . . But after that I am risen, I will go before you into Galilee. . . . And he cometh, and findeth them sleeping, and saith unto Peter, Simon, sleepest thou? couldest thou not watch one hour? . . . And when he returned, he found them asleep again. . . . And he cometh the third time, and saith unto them, Sleep on now, and take your rest; it is enough, the hour is come; behold the Son of man is betrayed into the hands of sinners. . . . And they all forsook him and fled. And there followed him a certain young man, having a linen cloth about his naked body, and the young men laid hold on him: And he left the linen cloth, and fled from them naked. . . .

Part II. . . . Joseph of Arimathaea, an honourable counsellor,

which also waited for the kingdom of God, came, and went boldly
unto Pilate, and craved the body of Jesus. . . . And he brought
fine linen, and took him down, and wrapped him in the linen,
and laid him in a sepulchre. . . . And when the sabbath was
past, Mary Magdalene, and Mary the mother of James, and
Salome, had brought sweet spices, that they might come and
anoint him. . . . And entering the sepulchre, they saw a young
man sitting on the right, clothed in a long white garment; and
they were affrighted. And he saith unto them, Be not affrighted:
Ye seek Jesus of Nazareth, which was crucified: he is risen: he
is not here: behold the place where they laid him. But go your
way, tell his disciples and Peter that he goeth before you into
Galilee . . . And they went out quickly and fled from the
sepulchre; for they trembled and were amazed: neither said they
any thing to any man; for they were afraid.

IV. The fourth is the novel: A young man of moderate and
conservative opinions, in the disturbed Russia of the late nineteenth century, asks only a successful career, but is suddenly and
against his will involved in an assassination plot. The assassin,
a fellow student, had wrongly supposed that the hero's habitual
silence indicated approval of extreme radical views, and so
sought shelter from the police in his room. The young man
betrays his friend to the police, and is thereafter employed by
them in counterespionage. He arrives in Geneva and becomes an
associate of a group of political exiles, including the assassin's
mother and sister. He is regarded by them as a brave comrade, the
equal of the martyred revolutionary, but he is troubled by memories of the night of the betrayal, and finally, without apparent
provocation, admits his guilt. Made deaf by blows on the ears
which destroy his eardrums, he is knocked down by a street-car,
and crippled.

I. The Chinook story happens to be of a kind to which most of
us would grant, to use a vague formulation, literary merit, and the
analysis I shall discuss, which is by the anthropologist Dell M.
Hymes, by no means neglects this aspect of it; so we see at once that
this is not a Lévi-Straussian analysis. Hymes first summarises an
approach he intends to reject: it is psychoanalytic in character,
stressing the theme of transvestism, the apparent horror of homo-
sexuality, the tense quality of the feeling concerning females. This
interpretation makes two important assumptions, first that the
murder was committed by the 'wife' in revenge for the aspersions
cast by the girl upon her method of urinating and upon her

sexuality; secondly that the story, being of revenge, is incomplete, since an account of the family's revenge on the 'wife' would normally follow. Also in this view, the principal character of the story is the 'wife.'

Hymes in general objects to this because of a methodological assumption it makes, which is that "a purportedly universal theory, be it psychoanalytical (as in the present case), dialectical, or whatever, can go straight to the heart of a myth before having considered its place in a genre structurally defined and functionally integrated in ways perhaps particular to the culture in question." The application of such a theory disturbs the story and makes for forced interpretation. Thus there is no indication whatever in the story that the 'wife' overhears what the girl says to her mother, but this version assumes that she did. It follows that to call the story one of revenge is to distort it, and it also follows that the incompletion hypothesis is redundant. More knowledge of the society's myths would have also told against the suggestion that a story named as this one is, and told as this one is, could have had as its principal character a person who never speaks, has only a secondary place in the action, which is primarily concerned with mother and daughter, and is not even mentioned in the title.

Mr. Hymes now produces his own analysis, which assumes that there will be for such stories a *native system,* as proper to the culture as its systems of kinship, diagnosis, wedding ceremonies, and so forth. The structural characteristics of the story will therefore be ethnographic ('within an individual culture') rather than ethnological ('cross-cultural'), so that what needs to be studied is the native system and not cross-cultural resemblances. The assumption is the important one that among people growing up in a particular community there will normally be an early-acquired grasp not only of the overt formal features ('surface structure') of the story, but of its underlying relations ('deep structure'). This is not quite the bold Chomskyan analogy recently proposed by Roland Barthes,[2] and at present interesting other critics also, that we have an innate literary faculty comparable to the linguistic, that we can form a set of rules, arrange the transformations necessary to lift our deep-structural fable elements to the surface, recognise the meaning of stories previously unheard, accept the narrative equivalent of grammaticality and detect tabulatory deviance.

[2] *Critique et Vérité,* Paris, 1966, p. 57.

Hymes is explicit that he is not telling us about the structure of the mind or claiming to discover specific universals analogous to those postulated of grammatical structure; he seeks a descriptively adequate account of the rules within a limited society, and thinks that this is all that can be had.

This is an important limitation, since modern structural analysts are on the whole inclined to seek universal validity. The only people who will have implicit knowledge of the structure of this myth are competent natives of the culture. The rules sought are therefore culture-specific. The analysis will not work at some hypothetical deep level where may be found either relational structures for expressing culture-nature antinomies, of some universal *fonction fabulatrice*. But of course the claim is that this more modest approach is the one that gets the structure right.

The analysis may be summarised thus. The title tells us that Seal is the principal character and it is her mistake and not her daughter's that concerns us most. In fact that girl is guilty of nothing; what is wrong is Seal's inappropriate, and in the issue tragic, regard for propriety. The murder is not motivated by revenge or anything else; murders in Clackamas myths do not have to have motives. Generically the ' wife ' is a Trickster, not a transvestite or homosexual, as may be inferred from other stories of the society. So the analyst arrives at the conclusion that the culpable Seal forms, with her brother and daughter, a familiar Clackamas consanguineal trio, mentioned in functional order, in the first sentence of the myth: " They lived there, Seal, her daughter, her younger brother," that is, culpable actor, advising actor, victim; and the trio is placed in a situation where, on the advent of the " wife," a conflict develops between social norms and the empirical situation. Seal observes the norms (' don't talk like that about your uncle's wife ') and the girl observes the empirical situation. With regard to these two terms, Clackamas myth can be represented thus:

	1	2	3	4
SOCIAL NORM	+	+	−	−
EMPIRICAL SITUATION	+	−	+	−

where SN + means Norm upheld, SN − Norm violated, ES + means adequate response to the empirical situation, and ES − inadequate response to it. The present story belongs to the second type, which is common, and corresponds in some ways to what we call tragedy. Type 1 is rare (it would be comic, and represents the continuance of a good society), Type 4 is like farce or possible *sparagmos,* Type 3 Hymes describes as 'mixed' and it seems to correspond to nothing. Anyway, the story of Seal's foolish observation of the norms fits neatly into this 'grammar' of the society's stories.

Or, the whole story can be represented by representing the 'dialectics of actors' in a diagram adopted from those in which Lévi-Strauss shows a myth as a progression from an initial proposition through a succession of mediating terms. Here the initial (kinship) proposition represents the title of the myth, the second row represents the first sentence, and so on through the story's progress.

$$
\begin{array}{cccc}
\text{El Si} & \text{El Si}\,|\,\text{Mo} & \text{Mo} & \text{Mo} \\
\downarrow\;\longrightarrow & \text{Da}\,|\,\text{Si Da}\;\longrightarrow & \text{dripping}\;\longrightarrow & \text{death} \\
\text{Yo Bro} & \text{Yo Bro}\,|\,\text{Mo Bro}\;\;\text{Da} & & \text{Da}
\end{array}
$$

I can't do justice to Hymes here, but it does emerge that these successive mediations do rather more than simply stress the social point of the story. The third row represents the " wife " who made water like a man, the fourth the dripping of another liquid, not resulting, as Seal presumably supposes from copulation, but from murder; and the fifth and last remembers these significant liquids when it contrasts the drily mourning mother, repeating her empty lament for her brother, and the weeping girl, who alone had been alive to what her senses told her about the liquid sounds heard earlier. (As Hymes remarks, it is also the girl who provides the light—the whole story hitherto having taken place in darkness—which allows full appreciation of the empirical situation, and also provides a contrast with the darkness not unlike that between the minds of mother and daughter.) Mr. Hymes thinks it proper that a structural analysis should attend to imagery, expressive detail, and even, I think, to plot and coherence, formal considerations which at least confirm the sociological interpretation of structure.

Naturally he takes the myth to be complete as it stands, and regards the interpretations which say it is not complete as vitiated in this and other ways by a 'sociopsychological perspective' which

neglects important elements, not all of them, I would add, peculiar
to the culture concerned, in order to seek some hypothetically
universal latent content.

Mr. Hymes is an anthropologist and his ultimate interest in
the myth is functionalist. He does allow the possibility of plural
interpretations, but it is clear that he believes one must see the
structure not in relation to some universal psychoanalytical or
other hypothesis, but in relation to the known 'grammar' of the
society and of its narrative genres. He would probably not deny
that when one has done this and so got the story right (for instance,
abandoned the erroneous position that it is an unfinished narrative
of revenge) one can say other kinds of thing about it, for instance
one can discuss the imagery of urine, blood and tears, or speak of
the climax and resolution of the plot, and that these ways of speaking are borrowed from a more 'universalist' in fact from European
literary-critical approaches to narrative. However, his priority is
clear; the structure of the myth is not occult, and the determination
of it can proceed only from a knowledge of 'natively valid rules.'

II. The second narrative is the Oedipus myth, analysed as
follows by Claude Lévi-Strauss:

Cadmos seeks
his sister
Europa,
ravished by
Zeus

Cadmos kills
the dragon

The Spartoi kill
one another

Labdacos (Laius'
father) = lame (?)
Oedipus kills   Laius (Oedipus' father)
his father,   = left-sided (?)
Laius

Oedipus kills
the Sphinx
Oedipus = swollen-foot (?)

Oedipus marries
his mother,
Jocasta

	Eteocles kills his brother, Polynices
Antigone buries her brother, Polynices, despite prohibition	

This now celebrated analysis [3] will stand, in the present context, as characteristic of Lévi-Strauss's analytic method. He splits the myth-narrative into constituent elements, sometimes called, on a linguistic analogy, *mythemes*; the foregoing table does not contain all the mythemes of the Oedipus myth, but the claim is that all others would fall under the same classification or be dismissible as ' noise.' The ' horizontal ' reading of the myth—the story as we know it—is accordingly subsumed to a vertical structure represented by the four columns; we are concerned, as it were, not with the melody, which is a secondary elaboration of the basic sense of the myth, but with the harmony, the vertical reading which tells us its hidden structure. Just as, on the structuralist view, one has to repudiate experience to understand reality, so one has to repudiate narrative to understand the structure of myths. The diachronic, for example history, has to be destroyed before one can get down to the essential business, the synchronic structure.

Contemplating the verticals in the diagram above, one perceives that the first column contains situations all of which are character-ised by an *overvaluation of kinship* (incidentally an attractive way of talking about incest). The second column features, in that it deals in parricide and fratricide, an *undervaluation of kinship*. In the third monsters are killed by heroes, and in the fourth the heroes are all deformed, i. e., they are monsters; this is because they are autochthonous and so, in accordance with what Lévi-Strauss de-scribes as a universal belief, walk clumsily. The overcoming of the monsters represents, in the third column, *a denial of the auto-chthonous origin of man,* and the monstrousness of the family in the final column stands for the *assertion of the autochthonous origin of man.* Although Oedipus was known to have been born of

[3] *Structural Anthropology*, translated by Claire Jacobson and Brooke Grundfest Schoepf, London, 1968, pp. 214 ff.

Jocasta, his family limp continues to associates him with autochthony. So the relationship of the four columns may be expressed
thus:

$$I \; : \; II \; :: \; III \; : \; IV$$

The overvaluation is to the undervaluation of kinship as the denial
is to the assertion of the autochthonous origin of man. The
religion of the Greeks maintained autochthony, but the Greeks
knew very well how children were born, so that there was a discrepancy between empirically observed natural fact and the claims of
a cultural institution. The myth conceals a way of putting this
problem, and so becomes an instrument of what some sociologists
call 'universe-maintenance' and what Lévi-Strauss designates a
'logical tool' of the kind that everybody, everywhere and always,
employs for the purpose, whether savage or civilised. Using different materials, we come up with artefacts that look different but
are structurally analogous to this one.

Lévi-Strauss works on a corpus of myth, and his method would
not serve were myth not 'translatable,' that is to say, if many
variants could not be studied at once. And he sees that this makes
it different from poetry (or novels) which ordinarily do not have
variants. But in principle he must believe that structures of this
kind are there, whether or not they can be analysed, and that any
attempt to analyse them would attend to the verticals at the expense of the horizontal movement of the plot, which is all a matter
of secondary elaboration, even if it happens to be manipulated by
the interests of Sophocles—who must be admitted, whatever he
made of the myth, to have been ignorant of its true structure. It
follows that Lévi-Strauss is in no way concerned with any notion of
'competence'—with any 'knowledge' of rules, of the kind Hymes
has in mind when he speaks of the deep structure of stories as the
native knows it. The Lévi-Strauss interpretation is universalist and
unconcerned with the 'horizontal' relationships of the mythemes.
In short, the myth has for him not a culture-specific grammar but a
species-specific algebra. Story makes the structure socially viable, but
in doing so obscures the true structure, which is always occult, and
which requires the arcane equipment devised by *l'homme structural*
for its divination. It may be important to add that the claim is to
scientific verifiability and also to exclusivness. If I were able to
show that *Macbeth* has to do with a relationship of greetings to

deaths, and of animals and parts of animals to spirits, I should be claiming that your reading of *Macbeth,* which perhaps concerns itself with murder, conscience, hallucinated language, plot and imagery, was appropriate only to the *bricolage* employed, to the materials the society happened to have handy. There is as yet little literary analysis on these lines, but obviously there will be more.

III. The gospel story, as my extracts already suggest, may also be segmented for analytical purposes, though of a different kind. The following table may be helpful:

3	anointing of Jesus	embalming of Jesus' body (3)
1	the sacred body (in (1) the Last Supper)	Joseph wraps the body / in linen (2)
5	' I will go into Galilee '	youth in white stole in sepulchre (4)
4	abandonment in garden	' He goeth before you into (5) Galilee'
2, 4	desertion by youth in white lien	The women flee (2, 4)

The events in the left column preceded, those in the right succeeded, the Crucifixion. The numerals suggest only a few of the connections between these events.

This example is borrowed from the late Austin Farrer's studies in St. Mark. In his first treatment of the subject, in *The Glass of Vision* (1949) Dr. Farrer argued one case that the true conclusion of the gospel is xvi.8; that nothing was lost which the spurious remainder of the chapter which we now have in our bibles has replaced. He returned to this problem in *A Study of St. Mark* (1951), and my account need not attempt to distinguish between the two treatments. In yet another work, *St. Matthew and St. Mark* (1954, second ed. 1966) Farrer retracts part of his original thesis, changes his view of the ending, and gives up a large part of the typological argument developed in the earlier books. Again, for my purposes, I can ignore this last work, having explained that Farrer used it to modify his position; what is needed here is a full-blown argument about typological structure.

Once we have taken the general point that the segments isolated in the diagram are typologically interrelated, and before we understand these interrelations in detail, the first question likely to arise concerns the place in the story of the young man in the white linen cloak, who left it in the hands of his assailants and escaped naked. He occurs in no other gospel, though he might presumably still be a person who happened to be around, and the episode something that simply occurred, and struck an eyewitness. This does not mean that it could not be caught up into the pattern that St. Mark developed, for, as Farrer says (*A Study in St. Mark*, p. 88) "he begins, of course, from fact, from the tradition of Christ's mighty works; but . . . in the building up of his Gospel the facts fall into such a pattern that, like true works of God, they become expressive." In this instance the young man is not to be taken simply as an interesting bit of history; he must first be related to the saying of Christ, "When ye see the abomination stand where he ought not, then let them that are in Judaea flee to the mountains, and let not him that is in the field turn back to fetch his coat" (Mark, 13.14).

Thus the young man's abandonment of his cloak was predestined. Nor is that by any means the whole significance of it. The punishment of a temple watcher who fell asleep on duty was to be beaten and stripped of his linen stole; so the cloak is associated with the breach of a sacred duty, and not only on the part of the youth, but on that of the disciples also, who failed to watch with Jesus. Furthermore, Joseph wraps the body of Christ in linen to honour it (the same unusual word is used for cloak and shroud) ; and then the youth in the white stole appears in the sepulchre (the same word for 'youth,' and St. Mark does not use it elsewhere). The youth in the cloak is caught up into a very complicated pattern.

Other elements of the pattern may be more simply represented as narrative ironies, and Dr. Farrer did try this. The point is (*Glass of Vision*, p. 139) that men do not know what to do with the divine when it falls into their hands. "A woman tries to anoint the Lord for glory, only to learn that she has fore-anointed him for burial. The apostles attempt heroics in defence of Christ, but when it comes to it they forsake him and flee, that he may remain and die for them. . . . The Arimathaean carefully buries him whom no sepulchre can hold, and the women, not understanding why his fore-anointing for burial with that festal nard had been providential, bring funeral myrrh to embalm the already risen God." But this does not by any means do full justice to the pattern. Consider the two columns of our schema. (I) A woman anoints Jesus (II) women come to anoint him. (I) Jesus says he will precede his disciples in Galilee (II) the angel recalls the saying. (I) Jesus gives the disciples his sacramental body, which they used. (II) They vainly wall up his physical body. (I) and (II) end in flight, by followers as unprepared for joy as for disaster.

There are more refined parallelisms. A Joseph begs the body of Christ from Pilate, as a Joseph begged Pharaoh to allow him to bury Jacob in Canaan. That Joseph, fleeing Potiphar, left his garment behind; and when left for dead by his brethren appeared again to them dressed in a robe of glory. The typological merges with philological argument when we consider that the last words of Mark xvi.8—*ephobunto gar*, for they were afraid—echo those of Gen. xlv.3—*etarachthesan gar*, for they were troubled—in the Septuagint translation which Mark knew. The philological argument of Lightfoot—that there is no impossiblity in the use of *gar* at the end of the work—is now supported by Farrer's argument that this makes a satisfactory ending for positive literary reasons, vv. 1-8 being "a strong complex refrain answering to all the ends of previous sections in the Gospel to which we might expect it to answer," (*Study*, p. 174) as well as to the parallel passages we have already discussed.

We observe that the analyst is here, like Hymes earlier, arguing that a true appreciation of the structure of the work renders redundant all hypotheses of incompletion; it enables one to understand that the work has a satisfying end. And this is one respect in which Farrer and Hymes join in differing from Lévi-Strauss, to whom endings are of no interest whatever. Nevertheless, it is clear that there are important differences between Hymes and Farrer. In Farrer's St. Mark, although I think he would have contested the expression, incidents and arrangements of incidents are typologically generated; that the author of the work imitated Jewish intertestamentary writing, and that without falsifying historical fact he used such patterning as would " supplement logical connection " (*St. Matthew and St. Mark*, p. 115), Farrer himself says. In Hymes there is a typology of incident, of course, but it is not in the same way generated; it is not consciously put there, it is merely observed. Perhaps (I am still speaking of Farrer's earlier views on the ending) perhaps verses 9-20 were added by people who missed the sense of a full close at 16.8, just as those who call the Chinook story incomplete have misunderstood its structure. In any case both predicate narrative structures with significant endings, in a sense of which this could not be said of the Lévi-Strauss analysis. It is interesting that here we are dealing, for the first time, with an historical narrative, and that it has nevertheless an occult structure.

It doesn't matter much, for my purposes, whether all the patterns in Farrer's reading are acceptable; many scholars do not think so; but it was certainly not wrong in principle to seek them, for there are typological phenomena of this kind in the New Testament, whose authors did, under the pressure of their convictions and their sense of an impending end, arrange conformities with Old Testament types, and possibly arithmological patterns too. The presumption was, that much that had never been within the domain of human understanding was now intelligible, had now been brought into sense. The story was moving to its end, and parts of it could be seen to be relevant to this end. There had been incomplete figurations, and now there was a tremendous actuality; why should those figures not inhere in the account of the facts? The young man was *there,* as the ointment was spikenard and the box alabaster; as Peter warmed himself at the fire, for it was a cold night of early spring; as Simon, who carried the cross, happened to be the father of Alexander and Rufus. Jesus, who comments on the symbolism of the costly ointment, says nothing about the symbolism of the boy deserting him, nor does the narrator. But, it might be argued, at such a moment, in such a story, nothing is merely *historisch,* all is *geschichtlich.* And typological understanding of it permits its transfer from the one to the other by establishing silent communication with a significant past, or concordances within a wholly meaningful text (the white stole, the winding sheet, the saying of Jesus about the coat). On the other hand it may be, and has been argued, that the study of the gospel by this method disastrously reduces the historical actuality and the immediacy which most Christians seek in it: so Professor Helen Gardner in her remarks on Farrer (*The Business of Criticism,* Oxford, 1956, pp. 26 ff.). We shall come back to this issue in another form.

I have now to work out some conclusions from these first three instances. Hymes seeks native rules, a culture-specific grammar; the end of his story is a true end, and interpretation can in part be evaluated in terms of whether or not they accept it. Lévi-Strauss is universalist and uses a species-specific algebra. To him it makes no difference where you end the story, or even how it ends. Farrer, though of course protesting the universal importance of the literal truth of his story, finds in it types and relations which are sect-specific, and which play a role in the organisation of the historical detail; the author, that is, arranges the story in accordance with schemata known only to like-minded persons, among whom we presumably cannot count St. Matthew, or the author of the additional material in Chapter xvi. To Farrer the end of the story is of crucial importance, and much of what he says is based on the argument that the *proper* expectations of the reader are satisfied by the ending at xvi.8. The resemblance and dissimilarities existing between Hymes and Farrer I have already touched on, but one more should be added: Farrer's text is the only one where the personality and mental habits of the narrator become important, and the only one that is in a recognisable way historical. If Farrer is to be believed, a narrative which we should regard as of the highest historical importance merely as a plain account of what happened, is yet at the same time very elaborately structured. The mere fact that such narratives are held to exist is of some importance to critics of fiction.

Let us observe, finally, that each of these methods of analysis has a certain affinity with the material it works on. Thus, although Lévi-Strauss's method would in theory work for the other cases, it has most propriety where the material is exiguous and lacking in redundancies.[4] Hymes's method requires intimate social knowledge; it also requires, in both teller and analyst, an interest in story. Farrer's method assumes the intervention of a learned and inventive mind in both story and analysis. The role of the teller is slightly different in each case: unimportant to Lévi-Strauss, important to Hymes because skill was needed, and because either sex could tell the tale differently; extremely important to Farrer, not only because the truth or falsity of the story is a matter of life or death, but because only a certain kind of teller could have given the material such idiosyncratic shapes.

IV. This is the kind of account you might get in some dictionary of literature of the plot of Conrad's novel, *Under Western Eyes*. You recall that it is, essentially, if that word doesn't beg the question, the story of a young man who betrays his revolutionary fellow-student, is drawn into counter-espionage, **and finally, out of** conscience, abandons his perfectly secure cover and accepts the punishment visited upon him by the exiled revolutionaries with whom he has been associating.

---

[4] For the argument that Lévi-Strauss's whole method is affected by or founded on the poverty of the societies he studies, see Henri Lefebvre, *Le langage et la société*, Paris, 1966, pp. 194 ff.

Only someone who had never read the novel could accept this, or the fuller account I gave at the beginning, as having very much to do with what Conrad wrote. For anybody who had would start at once, and in one way or another, to say that in leaving out confusions and ambiguities, even in the behaviour and demeanour of the young man Razumov, I have grossly falsified a work of which the ethics and politics are extremely complex and which has other dimensions too.

Again, one could hardly give any intelligible account of the Chinook story without mentioning all the characters that occur in it, whereas we habitually do this in discussing novels; I missed out not only the Haldins, mother and daughter, not only Mikulin, whose question "Where to?" constitutes one of the most famous narrative climaxes in Conrad, not only the highly individualised revolutionaries, but also the language teacher who tells the story.

And here we are in deep waters. In the other stories the narrator was not himself characterised, and except in the last his identity was of no interest. In all three we assume that the purpose of the narrator is to communicate without unnecessary ambiguity, and we assume that he has an authoritative grasp of the story. But the story of Razumov is told by a language teacher who has no such authority. He is not even a Russian, being merely a chance acquaintance of the family into whose Geneva circle Razumov insinuates himself after betraying the young man, brother to Natalie and son to Mme. Haldin. This language teacher constantly emphasizes the degree to which his foreignness incapacitates his understanding of the situation, adding that he cannot supplement this deficiency by the exercise of imaginative power, because in that respect he is also very deficient. He further draws attention to the need of using words, which he thinks poor vessels of truth, indeed he calls them "the great enemies of reality." Perhaps his skill as 'a student of many grammars' gives him some insight into the idiom of Russian behavior; perhaps that disordered lexical profusion reflects the discontinuities and vaguenesses of Russian conduct; but he despairs of knowing enough to make Eastern habits and reactions sympathetic in Western eyes.

Now although it may appear oversimple to say so, Conrad had Eastern eyes and did not require to entrust the narrative task to a person less perfectly qualified to discuss Russians than he was. And he has deliberately chosen for his story a grammar which is

not native. Why? He believed, as we know, that the only good
reason for writing novels was to tell the truth, and claimed that in
Under Western Eyes he was stating his " honest convictions " as to
the moral complexion of certain facts. We know from his discursive writings on the subject what these convictions were; yet the
narrator chosen is by education and nationality capable of expressing them only very imperfectly.

One example will make the situation plain. *Under Western
Eyes* goes on a little longer than my synopsis suggests: Razumov,
deaf and crippled, returns to Russia, where he is nursed by Tekla,
formerly of the Geneva group and cherished by the revolutionists,
including Sophia Antonovna. All this is bewildering to the old man,
who knows what reason these people had to detest Razumov. In
the conversation which ends the book the language teacher talks
with Sophia about Peter Ivanovitch, a Bakunin-like figure who had
been dominant in the Geneva circle. The language teacher had,
with some reason, treated this character with dislike and contempt,
as an exploiter of women and a poseur. He had hoped for a large
legacy from his putative mistress, Mme de S—; but on failing to
get it he returned to Russia where he married a peasant girl and
lived with her in circumstances of great danger. And this the
narrator learns from the aging revolutionist Sophia Antonovna.
But why, he asks, should Peter Ivanovitch take such a risk? " He
just simply adores her," says Sophia. " Does he? Well, then, I hope
she won't hesitate to beat him," answers the language teacher. But
Sophia, ignoring these words, ends the conversation, and, more
remarkably, the novel, by declaring in a firm voice, " Peter Ivanovitch is an inspired man."

Why should the book end thus? Sophia is not a central character,
and the man she is speaking of is not a central character, and
her opinion of him, expressed in defiance of the narrator's own,
seems an odd way to end. The reason must be that the true ending
is not the fate of Razumov, but rather a demonstration of the
fallibility of the narrator, of his inability to see the point of any
Russian character or act. The only alternative is to dismiss the
whole thing as yet another and by now wholly superfluous example,
of the impenetrability of the Russian character. That would be
a weak ending indeed. No, what the end states strongly is the
fallibility of the novel's own way of stating things. Why choose
this fallible way? Because the truth is so difficult, all modes of

enquiry so falsifying, that the novel must be an image of the difficulties both of truth and communication, must mirror the deceptions inherent in enquiry itself? Whatever we say about that, it is clear enough that the novel is going to present serious obstacles to methods of analysis which assume the authority of narrator and the truth of reports. Nor can the degree of distortion here introduced be offset in the calculation, since it is not invariant. It appears that by this narrative device alone it is possible for the novel to declare itself to be of indeterminate structure and thus out of bounds to structural analysis. Conrad emphasizes this when he talks about the language difficulty. There is no way of discerning such a deep structure as Hymes seeks in his myth, nor of establishing a relation between types and truth of the kind Farrer proposes.

This indeterminacy can be demonstrated in many different ways, of which I will mention only one or two. We may speak of a novel's tendency to emit what might, on a straight theory of communication, be regarded as noise. Whatever information *Under Western Eyes* may impart concerning "the moral complexion" of certain political facts, is complicated by signals which at least seem to blur that information. Russia, though terrible in its anarchies, is nevertheless associated with life; this is "the irremediable life of the earth as it is," and has a grim complexion, but it *is* life and even spiritual life. Switzerland, however, is contrasted with this life; it is not only clear as against Russia's mistiness, ordered as against Russia's anarchy, quadrangular in its shapes as against the vast Russian formlessness, but dead as against Russia's life. So too with England; a country which is as Miss Haldin twice remarks, out of contention with life, having "made a bargain with fate," and obtained "so much liberty for so much hard cash." Form and order, it appears, are for the bourgeois. Miss Haldin thinks the world is "inconceivable to the strict logic of ideas," but the English narrator (despite his failure at the end of his story) thinks it "a thing of form." The revolutionary Haldin actually speaks of Razumov as a kind of Englishman, but when Razumov tried to make a bargain with fate it doesn't work; he is Russian, and is swept into spiritual experiences, hallucinations, the darkness of the soul. He fills in the terrible time before midnight and Haldin's betrayal by scrawling two-dimensional images of impossible simple orders, but Haldin slips down a three-dimensional spiral staircase to his fate, and Razumov takes his Russian soul to Geneva.

This matter of the Russian soul becomes one of the most important of the book's many 'redundant' plots. The Russian soul is in exile in the obvious Swiss air. Near the bandstand which is to be the meeting place of Miss Haldin and Razumov sit a solitary Swiss couple, their fate " made secure from the cradle to the grave by the perfected mechanism of democratic institutions. . . . The man, colourlessly uncouth, was drinking beer out of a glittering glass, the woman, rustic and placid, leaning back in the rough chair gazed idly around." Not only are the man and woman, in an obvious sense, redundant to the story; so are the hard shine of the beer-glass, the palpable roughness of the chair, the vacant hard-edged soulless scene, ordered, visible, dead, like the postcard hills and islands. In the revolutionists' headquarters Russian mess is trailed across Swiss order. Razumov sits on the neat pointless islet writing, under the statue of Rousseau, reports for the Russian secret police, who are somehow, it seems, part of the image of irremediable life as the philosopher of the social contract is not, and have more to do with soul and spirit (not that this is ever *said*) .

This interest in soul and spirit penetrates the language of the book, usually in apparently casual or accidental ways. It is Haldin who first institutes a division of body and soul (" My spirit shall go on warring in some Russian body ") and this evanescent figure acquires a kind of substance when Razumov sees Haldin's phantom body in the snow. To say that Razumov is haunted by the phantom of Haldin is a cliché; but Conrad caught it up and made it work for him, so that it takes on great profuseness and a complexity at first concealed by the ordinary quality of our expectations. Into the ordinary continuities which effect in a novel a guarantee that the kind of life exhibited is the familiar kind, an affair of clocks and stairs, there intrudes a different kind of life, which we must explain and relate to the other as best we may, a life which has exceptional use for the words ' phantom,' ' ghost,' ' apparition,' ' soul,' 'ghoul,' ' spectre.' They are not merely a part of Razumov's fevered private language; they occur at large, they have as it were leaked, and stained the texture of the narrative. Certainly they contribute to the peculiar dialect of Razumov's guilt, as when he says to Mikulin, " If he were lying here on the floor I could walk over his breast,"— where, as Milkulin's misty aposiopeses simulate the vague and sinister Russian landscape, we suddenly see Haldin's body in the midst. But they can occur in the speech of others who know no-

thing of Razumov's guilt or these private images. There is Miss
Haldin, describing her visit to Peter Ivanovitch, and her encounter
with Tekla. The hall of the château was empty, there was "nothing, nobody, not a soul." Again an ordinary colloquialism with
only a shade of over-emphasis. But she adds, "I stayed where I
was—and I did see a soul. Such a strange soul." Now although
one says of a room, that there's not a soul in it, one does not say,
there *is* a soul in it. The deviation from normal usage is therefore
significant, but of what? As part of a kind of soul-plot which it is
hard to relate more than tenuously to the ostensible themes of the
novel. When Miss Haldin meets Razumov he materialises before
her, like an apparition. When Sophia tells him, "You have begun
well, but you must wait until you have trodden down every particle
of yourself under your feet," she is borrowing from Razumov's
wholly private language. It is Haldin's phantom he has trodden on.
The remainder of that conversation is haunted by ghosts, even the
ghost of tea.

The question arises, in this secret plot, as to how ghosts and
apparitions are seen. In the flashback on Razumov's departure from
Russia he sees an apparition of Haldin on his bed, and calls the
figure 'ghoul' and 'phantom.' His leaving the country involves,
among other things, a visit to an oculist; the question of what you
can see, including the question of seeing the dead and 'falsehood-
breeding spectres,' grows urgent. Razumov sees the phantom and
also the phantom's mother, so described, and white as a ghost.
Miss Haldin appears, "as unforeseen as the apparition of her
brother," and continues to haunt him, as she has done ever since
she "suddenly appeared" in the garden of the villa. Finally,
reaching the end of his endurance, he finds himself in a shadowless
Swiss box of a room still seeing the phantoms. Miss Haldin speaks
of a vision of the future, but Razumov argues that only the blind
see such visions, which are not visible to his clear eyes, which do
however perceive "strange things and unexpected apparitions."
The old lady, we learn, expects, in the extremity of her grief, to see
her dead son; Natalie thinks she will. And again they speak of
spirits and phantoms. Miss Haldin, known for her "trustful eyes,"
drops her veil to the floor. When Razumov confesses the mother sits
looking at a phantom head in her lap, and the veil lies, "intensely
black in the white crudity of the light," at Razumov's feet. He picks
it up and presses it to his face. At this point Razumov seems, to

the narrator, to vanish; astonishment has perhaps "dimmed his eyes." But then "the slamming of the outer door restored my sight." Razumov has departed, taking Natalie's veil. Her eyes have changed; now they contain shadows, not, as before, the clear steady flame of her soul. Razumov, deaf from the blows to his ears, is blinded by lightning and walks into "a phantom world." Switzerland has transformed itself from its usual brightly lit obviousness, its banal visibility, into a place of mist; Razumov is struck down by a substantial streetcar he can neither see nor hear.

I have set down some, by no means all, of the strange plot of phantoms, mist, seeing, etc., that takes shape within *Under Western Eyes,* quite inexplicitly, and, in a context of language ostensibly devoted to the explanation or elucidation of the 'moral complexion' of certain facts. It is clearly not explanatory, nor in any obvious sense logically related to the remainder of the book. Some theory of irony might make it fit, might, so to speak 'justify' it. But the fact remains that a redundant plot of a bewildering kind is instituted and maintained by a wide range of devices, some narrative (the oculist, the storm) some lexical (the phantom—apparition complex) some imagistic (the veil) some simply, and for short, magical (Sophia using the language of Razumov's private obsession). These irrelevances, if so they are held to be, are bred out of the very body of the novelist's creation. How shall we study their structures?

At first blush there must seem to be some comparison between the activity of Conrad and that of St. Mark, as Farrer describes it. For the evangelist took a narrative and, as he developed his account of it, allowed it to suggest many figurations of event, image and word which, on the view of some critics and believers, are in one sense redundant, though Farrer and others may see them as redundant in the sense used by communication theory—and so as fortifying the concordance of the book. He even allowed his ending to be determined, not by a crude criterion of narrative completeness—there being no more to say—but by the completion of certain unobvious typological relations. Conrad, as we have seen, performs certain parallel operations. He makes a great number of occult figurations coexist with the record—essentially continuous, though for various reasons not continuously presented—of quotidian occurrences, with clocks and stairs, with what is needed to indicate continuities of life and personality. But whereas the most adventurous

Christian interpreter of the gospel will feel obliged, as Farrer does, to assert the primacy and unequivocal veracity of the surface narrative, Conrad does nothing of the kind, but rather allows the verisimilitude of the simple narrative to support, and in the end be put to question by, complexities of figuration which are always threatening to contradict the simple tale, or to fly off into irrelevance. Only a novelist and his interpreters may argue as this novel does, that "a train of thought is never false," or that "there may be truth in every manner of speaking." To put the difference another way, St. Mark was a revolutionist, and in Conrad's opinion revolutionists hate irony; but novelists do not, and *Under Western Eyes* employs it right to the last word. Irony, the indeterminable degrees of irrelevance in the figuration of minor plots, permanently distinguish novel from gospel; the kind of authority claimed is in the end utterly different; and Farrer's typology assumes kinds of authority which can never be thought of in relation to novels. Thus an analysis of typological structure which depends upon certain assumptions as to the *kerygma* is wholly inappropriate to novels because of its assumption that there is a basic determined structure, and that the structures of episode and subplot are logically related to it.

The profusion of plots, and the fundamental indeterminacy of the basic situation, are also indications that the 'structuralist' methods of analysis will fail to say anything very relevant or interesting. *Under Western Eyes* depends for many of its effects on the rendering of temporal complexities, with which such modes of analysis are ill equipped to deal. Furthermore, the form of the novel, as Conrad says, involves, in its "intellectual aspect," an "exact understanding of the limits traced by the reality of his [the novelist's] time to the play of his invention."[5] The play of this understanding produces what is usually a large and noisy object of great complexity, which bids for our attention in many competing ways, all of which in the end undermines any hope that there is some central determined structure we can isolate as fundamental; the form of the novel and the ambition and habit of the novelist conspire against such confidence. According to Lévi-Straussian myth-analysis the redundancies detectable in a cluster of variant versions of the same myth are keys to the structure, since the apparently chance repetition of some elements affords statistical

[5] *A Personal Record*, p. 95.

assurance that they are part of what is being communicated; whereas the presence of others which, however striking in themselves as part of a narrative, do not fall significantly into patterns of thematic or mythemic repetition, is merely evidence that there is a medium of noise in which information is formed. But this analogy is not, as I have already said, helpful to the analyst of fiction. There are no variants, and no criteria for distinguishing information from noise. Finally the structuralist method fails for much the same reason as the typological: each assumes something about the nature of the structure sought which is not properly to be assumed of the structures of novels.

As to the first kind of interpretation, one looks at it more hospitably because it brings to the job of functionalist interpretation traditional instruments of literary criticism: the dynamic understanding of plot, and of the plot-functions of narrative, image and lexical patterns. Furthermore the notion of a narrative grammar, whether specific to a culture or more universal, has attractions which can hardly be said as yet to have been investigated. But if one looks at the simplicity, which though a mark of ingenuity is none the less extreme, of the schemata used by Hymes (and it is of course admirable in its parsimony) one sees instantly how hopeless the task would be of constructing a generic system or a diagram of successive mediating terms adequate to the welter of obscurely related information in any novel, let alone a twentieth-century novel intensely aware of the generative powers of its own technology, intensely concerned to deface and transmute its structural données beyond recognition. The Chinook myth may be, as Hymes said, susceptible to multiple interpretation, but there is a difference between that and a novel *designed* to prevent any but incomplete and multiple interpretations.

The question, how did the novel, unlike other varieties of narrative, come to be like this, is too large to embark on now, but one or two reasons so obvious as to escape frequent notice may be mentioned. One is simply that it is characteristically quite long, and length breeds redundancies, another is that its technologists, in handling the structural problem created by length, have developed many different ways of endowing redundancy [6] with meaning, so that redundancy not so endowed intentionally may nevertheless, by a reader familiar with the techniques, be granted it as an addi-

---

[6] It is worth adding that the length of novels is in part determined by forces, social and economic, which the author does not control.

tional grace. There are, in novels we value, inexplicit relations and suggestions which grow simply out of the writer's love for his material, his dislike of loveless sequence. These types are self-generated, but obviously differ from Farrer's in that they have no external referents, and also in that they cannot be placed in some order of importance or authority, as his typologies must submit to the overriding importance of the gospel narrative. You cannot say of a gospel that if you read it for the story you would be so impatient as to hang yourself, but you can say it of many novels from *Clarissa* to yesterday's avant-garde success. Most novelists hate noise about as much as readers do, and are as much concerned to reduce it, and to have information instead. They have great powers in this matter, greater than any dreamt of by the Chinook narrator, so great that to emulate them would be impiety in an evangelist. They are putting flesh on some disgorged diagram, and that flesh, though it may take the general shape dictated by the book's physique, has its local whorls and irregularities. They can milk an incident, a figure, a word, or let them go. They can 'fake' relations: also they occur as they occur, for novelists to see them and exploit them or not. Such relations may be only very deviously and unsystematically related to whatever is taken to be the anatomical structure of the novel. They may not be related at all. They may he held to constitute a relationship for which a novelist would be unwilling to vouch. Certainly he can do things as striking as the ending of St. Mark's Gospel, and founded on relations equally recondite; certainly he can invent the equivalent of the young man in the linen cloak. But he is not obliged to include or suggest typological evidence. He can thrust his verticals into the horizontal system of the novel, but what he really does is to offer a licence for typological explanations rather than an account of them or a guarantee that they exist. The conversion of narrative events from *historisch* to *geschichtlich* need be his affair only randomly. The hint that it is going on somewhere around is enough to establish the kind of reading the book requires. In theory there seems no limit to the number of verticals that might in these circumstances be dropped into a story established as susceptible to them; and this is a degree of enforced liberty of interpretation that none of the methods described could countenance.[7]

[7] A critical method that goes closer than most to coping with this kind of problem is outlined by Avrom Fleishman, 'The Criticism of Quality,' *The University [of Kansas City] Review* (1966), 1-10.

It appears then that the deep structures of novels, in so far as they can be said to possess them, will always elude description. The extremely complex system of redundancies might be described by techniques similar to those of Farrer, though of course much adapted; and it is conceivable that very much more complicated methods than those used by Hymes might, at the cost of great labour, isolate something resembling a socio-anthropological structure, or a period grammar, common to a whole sample of books written, say, in the first decade of the present century. My guess is that this would be unhelpful simply because of its gross reductiveness; and analyses which begin by abandoning interest in horizontal sense of 'secondary elaboration' are clearly, in a situation which makes redundancy an essential, even less instructive. One may think of 'the novel' as actually trying to conceal its structures, to create a haze of indeterminacy between them and the reader, to seduce him with counter-structures; what in ordinary communication is only noise becomes the *raison d'être* of the whole enterprise.

It does appear that many who are capable themselves of developing complex and hardly reducible structures of plot, of the kind I've discussed with examples from Conrad, are capable also, in theoretical or homiletic commentary, of greatly oversimplifying the problems of the veracity and good faith of such structures. It might be possible, at best, to work out some dialectical relation between fictions characteristic of novels and those characteristic of myth, of gospel, of history; it might be possible to discover, at bedrock, some useful analogies between different modes of legitimation in institutions of increasing levels of complexity, assuming that they are all finally concerned to legitimate the same things, such as death and endings. But the puritanical imperative, the insistence that redundancies merely obscure the one thing necessary, is a much simpler and much falser operation than any that might be involved in such a programme. The structures of fiction are plural, inaccessible without severe instrumental interference, and possessing no validity or interest except in union with acts of idiomatic interpretation. The reason why it is wrong to distinguish as Barthes does between science of literature and criticism is that there is nothing of interest that the former can do without the intervention of the latter; the naked structure which we rush to clothe with meanings of our own is only a model, and a misleading one, since the only structures there are arise from those imported meanings and our attempts to hold them somehow in a single thought.

1969

II. Critical Profiles

Georg Lukács's *Theory of the Novel*

PAUL DE MAN ❦ The rather belated discovery of the work of Georg Lukács in the West and, most recently, in this country, has tended to solidify the notion of a very deep split between the early, non-Marxist and the later Marxist Lukács. It is certainly true that a sharp distinction in tone and purpose sets off such early essays as *Die Seele und die Formen* (1911) and *Die Theorie des Romans* (1914-15) from recently translated essays on literary subjects such as the *Studies in European Realism* (1953) or the political pamphlet *Wieder den mißverstandenen Realismus* (1957) published here under the title *Realism*. But the distinction can be overstated and misunderstood. It would be unsound, for instance, to hold on to the reassuring assumption that all the evil in the later Lukács came in as a result of his Marxist conversion; a considerable degree of continuity exists between a pre-Marxist work such as *Die Theorie des Romans* and the Marxist *Geschichte und Klassenbewußtsein*; it would be impossible for an admirer of the former to dismiss the latter entirely. There is a similar danger in an oversimplified view of a *good* early and a *bad* late Lukács. The works on realism have been treated very harshly on their American publication by such diverse critics as Harold Rosenberg (in *Dissent*) and Peter Demetz (in the *Yale Review*); on the other hand, *The Theory of the Novel* is being called by Harry Levin (*JHI*, January-March 1965, p. 150)

---

* Five of these articles were given, in substance, as papers at the *Yale Symposium on Literary Criticism* in the spring of 1965. Professor Jacques Ehrmann of Yale University was the Director of the Symposium.

" possibly the most penetrating essay that ever addressed itself to the elusive subject of the novel." If the blanket condemnation of the books on realism is clearly unjustified, especially if one bears in mind the considerable amount of debatable but interesting theoretical justification offered in Lukács's late *Ästhetik* (1963), the almost unqualified endorsement of *The Theory of the Novel* seems equally unwarranted. Whatever one may think of Lukács, he is certainly an important enough mind to be studied as a whole, and the critical interpretation of his thought has not been helped by the oversimplified division that has been established. The weaknesses of the later work are already present from the beginning, and some of the early strength remains operative throughout. Both weakness and strength, however, exist on a meaningful philosophical level and can only be understood in the larger perspective of nineteenth and twentieth-century intellectual history: they are part of the heritage of romantic and idealist thought. This stresses again the historical importance of Georg Lukács and rejects the frequent reproach made against him that he remains overconcerned with nineteenth-century modes of thought (a reproach that appears in both the Demetz and the Rosenberg reviews). Such criticism is inspired by an ill-conceived modernism or is made for propagandistic reasons.

I certainly do not intend to address myself to the complex task of defining the unifying elements in Lukács's thought. By a brief critical examination of *The Theory of the Novel,* I hope to make some preliminary distinctions between what seems to remain valid and what has become problematic in this very concentrated and difficult essay. Written in a language that uses a pre-Hegelian terminology but a post-Nietzschian rhetoric, with a deliberate tendency to substitute general and abstract systems for concrete examples, *The Theory of the Novel* is by no means easy reading. One is particularly put off by the strange point of view that prevails throughout the essay: the book is written from the point of view of a mind that claims to have reached such an advanced degree of generality that it can speak, as it were, for the novelistic consciousness itself; it is the Novel itself that tells us the history of its own development, very much as, in Hegel's *Phenomenology,* it is the Spirit who narrates its own voyage. With this crucial difference, however, that since Hegel's Spirit has reached a full understanding of its own being, it can claim unchallengeable authority, a point which Lukács's novelistic consciousness, by its own avowal, is never allowed to reach. Being caught in its own contingency, and being indeed an expression of this contingency, it remains a mere phenomenom without regulative power; one would be lead to expect a reductive, tentative and cautiously phenomenological approach rather than a sweeping history asserting its own laws. By translating the work in a less exalted language, one loses its moving and impressive philosophical pathos, but some of the preconceptions become more apparent.

Compared to a formalistic work such as, for instance, Wayne Booth's *Rhetoric of Fiction*, or to a work grounded in a more traditional view of history such as Auerbach's *Mimesis, The Theory of the Novel* makes much more radical claims. The emergence of the novel as the major modern genre is seen as the result of a change in the structure of human consciousness; the development of the novel reflects modifications in man's way of defining himself in relation to all categories of existence. Lukács is not offering us, in this essay, a sociological theory that would explore relationships between the structure and development of the novel and those of society, nor is he proposing a psychological theory explaining the novel in terms of human relationships. Least of all do we find him conferring an autonomy on formal categories that would give them a life of their own, independently of the more general intent that produces them. He goes instead to the most general possible level of experience, a level on which the use of terms such as Destiny, the Gods, Being, etc. seems altogether natural. The vocabulary and the historical scheme is that of later eighteenth-century aesthetic speculation; one is indeed constantly reminded of Schiller's philosophical writings on reading Lukács's formulation of the distinctions between the main literary genres.

The distinction between the epic and the novel is founded on a distinction between the Hellenic and the Western mind. As in Schiller, this distinction is stated in terms of the category of alienation, seen as an intrinsic characteristic of the reflective consciousness. Lukács's description of alienation is eloquent, but not strikingly original; the same could be said of his corresponding description at the beginning of the essay of a harmonious unity in the ideal Greece. The original unified nature that surrounds us in " the blessed times . . . when the fire that burns in our souls is of the same substance as the fire of the stars"[1] has now been split in fragments that are "nothing but the historical form of the alienation (Entfremdung) between man and his works (seine Gebilden)." And the following text could take its place among the great elegiac quotations of the early nineteenth century: "The epic individual, the hero of the novel, originates in the alienation from the outside world. As long as the world is inwardly one, no real qualitative distinctions occur among its inhabitants; there may well be heroes and scoundrels, worthy men and criminals, but the greatest hero only rises by a head's length above his fellow-men, and the noble words of the wise can be understood even by the fools. The autonomy of inwardness becomes possible and necessary only when the differences between men have grown to be an unbreachable gap; when the gods have grown silent and no sacrifice or prayer is capable of loosening their tongues; when the world of action loses contact with that of the self, leaving man empty and powerless, unable to grasp the real meaning of his deeds . . . : when inwardness and adventure are forever distinct." We are much closer here to Schiller than to Marx.

A definitely post-Hegelian element is introduced with Lukács's insistence on the need for totality as the inner necessity that shapes all works of art. The unity of the Hellenic experience of the world has a formal correlative in the creation of closed, *total* forms, and this desire for totality is an inherent need of the human mind. It persists in modern, alienated man, but instead of fulfilling itself in the mere expression of his given unity with the world, it becomes instead the statement of an intent to retrieve the unity it no longer possesses. Clearly, Lukács's idealized fiction of Greece is a device to state a theory of consciousness that has the structure of an intentional movement. This implies, in turn, a presupposition about the nature of historical time, to which we will have to return later.

Lukács's theory of the novel emerges in a cogent and coherent way out of the dialectic between the urge for totality and man's alienated situation. The novel becomes "the epic of a world from which God has departed" (p. 87). As a result of the separation between our actual experience and our desire, any attempt at a total understanding of our being will stand in contrast to actual experience, which is bound to remain fragmentary, particular and

[1] All quotations from *Die Theorie des Romans*, Zweite Auflage, Berlin 1963. The first edition is from 1920.

unfulfilled. This separation between life (Leben) and being (Wesen) is reflected historically in the decline of the drama and the parallel rise of the novel. For Lukács, the drama is the medium in which, as in Greek tragedy, the most universal predicament of man is to be represented. At a moment in history in which such universality is absent from all actual experiences, the drama has to separate itself entirely from life, to become ideal and otherworldly; the German classical theater after Lessing serves Lukács as an example for this retreat. The novel, to the contrary, wishing to avoid this most destructive type of fragmentation remains rooted instead in the particularity of experience; as an epical genre, it can never give up its contact with empirical reality, which is an inherent part of its own form. But, in a time of alienation, it is forced to represent this reality as imperfect, as steadily striving to move beyond the boundaries that restrict it, as constantly experiencing and resenting the inadequacy of its own size and shape. " In the novel, what is constituted is not the totality of life but rather the relationship, the valid or mistaken position of the writer who enters the scene as an empirical subject in his full stature, but also in his full limitation as a mere creature, towards this totality." The theme of the novel is thus necessarily limited to the individual, and to this individual's frustrating experience of his own inability to acquire universal dimensions. The novel originates in the Quixotic tension between the world of romance and that of reality. The roots of Lukács's later dogmatic commitment to realism are certainly to be found in this aspect of his theory. However, at the time of *The Theory of the Novel*, the insistence on the necessary presence of an empirical element in the novel is altogether convincing, all the more so since it is counterbalanced by the attempt to overcome the limitations of reality.

This thematic duality, the tension between an earth-bound destiny and a consciousness that tries to transcend this condition, leads to structural discontinuities in the form of the novel. Totality strives for a continuity that can be compared with the unity of an organic entity, but the estranged reality intrudes upon this continuity and disrupts it. Next to a " homogeneous and organic stability " the novel also displays a " heterogeneous and contingent discontinuity " (p. 74). This discontinuity is defined by Lukács as irony. The ironic structure acts disruptively, yet it reveals the truth of the paradoxical predicament that the novel represen*s.

For this reason, Lukács can state that irony actually provides the means by which the novelist transcends, within the form of the work, the avowed contingency of his condition. "In the novel, irony is the freedom of the poet in relation to the divine . . . for it is by means of irony that, in an intuitively ambiguous vision, we can perceive divine presence in a world forsaken by the gods." This concept of irony as the positive power of an absence also stems directly from Lukács's idealist and romantic ancestors; it reveals the influence of Friedrich Schlegel, of Hegel and most of all of Hegel's contemporary Solger. Lukács's originality resides in his use of irony as a structural category.

For if irony is indeed the determining and organizing principle of the novel's form, then Lukács is indeed freeing himself from preconceived notions about the novel as an imitation of reality. Irony steadily undermines this claim at imitation and substitutes for it a conscious, interpreted awareness of the distance that separates an actual experience from the understanding of this experience. The ironic language of the novel mediates between experience and desire, and unites ideal and real within the complex paradox of the form. This form can have nothing in common with the homogeneous, organic form of nature: it is founded on an act of consciousness, not on the imitation of a natural object. In the novel " . . . the relationship of the parts to the whole, although it tries to come as close as possible to being an organic relationhip, is in fact an ever-suspended *conceptual* relationship, not a truly organic one " (p. 74). Lukács comes very close, in statements of this kind, to reaching a point from which a genuine hermeneutic of the novel could start.

His own analysis, however, seems to move in a different direction; the second part of the essay contains a sharp critical rejection of the kind of inwardness that is associated with a hermeneutic theory of language. In the 1961 preface which Lukács added to the recent reissue of his essay, he scornfully refers to the phenomenological approach as a " right-wing epistemology," that runs counter to left-wing ethics. This criticism was already implicit in the original text. When he comes closest to dealing with contemporary developments in the novel and with moments in which the novel itself seems to become conscious of its real intent, a revealing shift in the argument takes place. He shows us, convincingly enough, how inwardness for its own sake can lead to an evasion of the novel into a falsely

Utopian realm "a Utopia which, from the start, has a bad conscience and a knowledge of its own defeat " (p. 119). The romantic novel of disillusion (Desillusions-romantik) is the example of this distortion of the genre, in which the novel loses contact with empirical reality; Lukács is thinking of Novalis, who was attacked in similar terms in an essay from the earlier book *Die Seele und die Formen*, but he also gives examples from Jacobsen's *Niels Lyhne* and Gontcharov's *Oblomov*. He fully realizes, however, that these examples do not account for other developments in European fiction in which the same theme of disillusion is obviously present and which he neither can nor wishes to dismiss. Flaubert's *Sentimental Education*, of course, is the most striking instance, a truly modern novel shaped by the overpowering negativity of an almost obsessive inwardness but which nevertheless, in Lukács's own judgment, represents the highest achievement of the genre in the nineteenth century. What is present in Flaubert's *Sentimental Education* that saves it from being condemned together with other post-romantic novels of inwardness?

At this moment in the argument, Lukács introduces an element that had not been explicitly mentioned up till now: temporality. In the 1961 Preface, he points with pride to the original use of the category of time, at a moment when Proust's novel was not yet known to the public. For the decadent and belated romantic, time is experienced as pure negativity; the inward action of the novel is a hopeless " battle against the erosive power of time." But in Flaubert, according to Lukács, this is precisely not the case. In spite of the hero's continuous defeats and disappointments, time triumphs as a positive principle in the *Sentimental Education,* because Flaubert succeeds in recapturing the irresistible feeling of flow that characterizes Bergsonian *durée*. " It is time which makes possible this victory. The uninterrupted and irrepressible flow of time is the unifying principle that gives homogeneity to the disjointed parts, by putting them in a relationship that, although irrational and ineffable, is nevertheless one of unity. Time gives order to the random agitation of men and confers upon it the appearance of organic growth . . ." (p. 128). On the level of true temporal experience, the ironic discontinuities vanish and the treatment of time itself, in Flaubert, is no longer ironic.

Can we admit Lukács's interpretation of the temporal structure of the *Sentimental Education*? When Proust, in a polemical exchange with Thibaudet, discussed Flaubert's style in terms of temporality, what he emphasized was not homogeneity but precisely the opposite: the manner in which Flaubert's use of tenses allowed him to create discontinuities, periods of dead and negative time alternating with moments of pure origination, complexities in memory structures comparable to those achieved by Gérard de Nerval in *Sylvie*. The single-directed flow of mere *durée* is replaced by a complex juxtaposition of reversible movements that reveal the discontinuous and polyrhythmic nature of temporality. But such a disclosure of authentic temporality demands reductive moments of real inwardness in which a consciousness confronts its own true self; and this moment is precisely the one at which the organic analogy between subject and object reveals itself as false.

It seems that the organicism which Lukács had eliminated from the novel when he made irony its guiding structural principle, has reentered the picture in the guise of time. Time in this essay acts as a substitute for the organic continuity which Lukács seems unable to do without. Such a linear conception of time had in fact been present throughout the essay. Hence the necessity of narrating the development of the novel as a continuous event, as the fallen form of the archetypal Greek epic which is treated as an ideal concept but given actual historical existence. The later development of Lukács's theories on the novel, the retreat from Flaubert back to Balzac, from Dostoevsky to a rather simplified view of Tolstoi, from a theory of art as interpretation to a theory of art as reflected imitation (Wiederspiegelung) should be traced back to the reified idea of temporality that is so clearly in evidence at the end of *Theory of the Novel*.

1966

Hugo Friedrich and the Modern Lyric

BY LEO SPITZER Hugo Friedrich's book, *Die Struktur der modernen Lyrik von Baudelaire bis zur Gegenwart*,[1] is intended as one link in a chain of publications of " Rowohlts Deutsche Enzyklopädie," destined to enlighten the general German public about the present status of research in the different fields of scholarship. While easily readable for a public of high intellectual capacities, it represents also a scholarly achievement in its own right, as we might have expected it from Hugo Friedrich who, now that death has claimed Ernst Robert Curtius, is unquestionably the greatest German literary critic in Romance. Having begun with a comparative study (*Abbé Prévost in Deutschland*, 1929), he conquered one Romance literature after the other, writing about anti-romantic thought in France (1935), Descartes (1937), Stendhal, Balzac and Flaubert (1939), later branching out into Italian (*Die Rechtsmetaphysik der Göttlichen Komödie*, 1941) and then into Spanish literature (*Der fremde Calderón*, 1955). His great master work is his *Montaigne* (1949) which seems to me the most intelligent comprehensive appraisal of that elusive philosopher which I know.

At the end of a short *vita* appended to the present volume, Professor Friedrich characterizes his whole activity as showing " predilection for unsentimental poets " and aversion against the method called *Erlebnis und Dichtung*. The same sympathy and the same aversion have inspired the author in this book. Whoever is aware of the dangers of emotionalism and intuitionism for German literary scholarship will appreciate the work of a scholar who, by his choice both of subject matter and method, shows a deep affinity with the intellectualism of Romance literature and Romance literary criticism. A book of Friedrich's is always distinguished by clear concepts, elegant definition, serene judgment and terse, unemotional writing. He shows similar equipoise in the skilful dosage of the historical and the descriptive approach: in his *Montaigne*, for

[1] (Hamburg, Rowohlt, 1956), 214 pp.

instance, all the possible ' sources ' used by the essayist are duly displayed and gauged, but the protagonist of the book remains Montaigne in his uniqueness. This tendency had led to serious disagreement with Curtius whose inclination, growing with the years, toward dissolving the great literary figures by what Friedrich calls " Kontinuitätsdenken " met with his strong opposition.

The title of the book under discussion first filled me with misgivings given the manifold anarchic tendencies of modern lyricism, would it be possible for a critic to succeed in the attempt to master the change and to discover that intellectual unity implied by the term " structure "? But in fact, Friedrich's work splendidly fulfills the promise of his title. Indeed, undisturbed by labels such as Expressionism, Dadaism, Futurism, Unanimism, Hermetism, Surrealism, etc., Friedrich convincingly shows, as only a literary historian of his width of horizon could have done, a relative unity in all these movements—a unity which can be traced back to only one particular period and country in which the archetype of contemporary lyrics first appeared. Thus Friedrich has done for European poetry something similar to what was achieved by Diez for the Romance languages: the reconstruction on the basis of a comparative study of the existing variants, of their historical archetype (only here the archetype can be grasped more easily because, contrary to Vulgar Latin, it exists in the clear light of history) whose milieu Friedrich defines as the late nineteenth century in France. Thus it was France that in the nineteenth century established, so to speak, the lyrical mother tongue for Europe just as it had provided the " epic tongue " par excellence in the twelfth century. It would be possible to reword a famous adage by saying (au XIXe siècle) le Français a la tête lyrique. Such a discovery will displease the chauvinist littérateurs in certain countries, especially the Spaniards who, according to Friedrich, are only too ready to assert their national independence (or dependence only on the Spaniard Góngora). But Friedrich has shown beyond doubt that the triangle

$$\text{Baudelaire} < {\text{Mallarmé} \atop \text{Rimbaud}}$$

in nuce contains all subsequent discoveries and experiments as they appear in the twentieth-century poetry of England (America), Spain, Italy, Germany.

Friedrich's method consists in working, as it were, from both ends toward the middle; thus he will, in the chapters on the three great Frenchmen, anticipate the developments that they have initiated while in the crowning chapter on twentieth-century Western lyricism taken as a whole, he reminds us of what it owes to that French ancestry. As for the antecedents of Baudelaire, Rousseau, Diderot, Novalis, and other romantics are treated in an introductory chapter, whereas Baudelaire's indebtedness to Poe is woven into the chapter about the former. Since Friedrich excludes from his book all poetry that is not " modern " in his sense (that is poetry asking for the consensus of the reader, a Goethean or Hugoesque tradition which survives in Germany, for instance, in George, Hofmannsthal and the early Rilke, in Italy in the oratory of D'Annunzio) , Baudelaire comes to a position, comparable to that of Goethe in his time, as the initiator of all " modern " lyrics (and this term includes " contemporary " lyrics) , the parallelism with Flaubert's influence on European prose fiction being duly noted. The *stupide XIXᵉ siècle* proves after all not to have been as " stupid " as its amateurish detractors wished it to be: this is one of the insights one gains from Friedrich's book. From Baudelaire as a starting point, there branch off then two main directions embodied in Mallarmé and Rimbaud, the one the form-respecting destroyer of the things of the outward world (which he replaces by attractions, contrasts, tensions) , the other the form-destroying destroyer of all aggregates of things (who delights in " sensuous irrealism") , both having in common, with each other and with their ancestor, the profound hatred against things-as-they-are and things-as-they-are-commonly-represented—a reflection of the isolation of the poet in the midst of leveling political, technical, and rationalizing processes in the society around him. The poets of today who generally, and often to a higher degree, share this situation, and the attitude toward it, with their predecessors fall into the two main categories of Mallarméism or Rimbaudism. Also in modern art, whose connections with modern poetry Friedrich consistently points out, we witness the same two main tendencies which have been defined by Kandinsky as the striving toward " the great abstraction " and " the great reality." Professor Friedrich has found an ingenious device in order to make the reader grasp the basic unity between the " French triangle" and contemporary lyricism: he offers in each of the three first chapters subdivisions entitled according to those abiding features that will characterize the lyrics to come and conversely, in the final chapter on contemporary lyrics, subdivisions and titles that to a certain degree recapitulate those of the preceding chapters. Thus we are asked to gauge the unity of the lyricism of the last hundred years by comparing the subchapters of the section on Baudelaire (the poet of modernity—concentration and awareness of form—lyricism and mathematics—modernity as an end-product—the aristocratic pleasure of displeasing—precarious Christianity—void idealism— magic of language—creative imagination—decomposition and deformation—abstraction and arabesque) with some of the subchapters of the chapter on twentieth-century lyricism (feast of the intellect, collapse of the intellect—incongruent style of the new lyrical language—Apollo, not Dionysos—twofold relationship toward modernity and the literary heritage—dehumanization—isolation and anguish—magic of language and suggestion—alogical poetry—reality—dictatorial imagination—fusion technique and metaphors) .

One will notice the " twofoldness " of the titles in the latter chapter (which comprehends Mallarméism and Rimbaudism) while Baudelaire appears more unified. It must be also noted that form and content are taken together in both series of titles. Certain titles are perhaps traditional (Ortega!), others are coinages of Friedrich himself (for instance, the title " void idealism " ably characterizes Baudelaire's enmity against the given world which is, however, not coupled with a positive creed) . In addition to his anticipative-recapitulative method and to his fusion of form and content Friedrich resorts in all chapters to *explication de texte* as illustration for his characterization of general trends. In the last chapter that has to deal with the enormous masses of contemporary international lyricism we find in the titles of sub-divisions names of great poets (which I have left out in the diagram quoted above) alternating with the definitions of general tendencies: Apollinaire and García Lorca (obviously a diptych that reproduces the previous diptych Rimbaud-Mallarmé) ; Paul Valéry—Jorge Guillén—García Lorca again (exemplification by one poem, *Romance sonámbulo*)— T. S. Eliot—Saint-John Perse. (No German or Italian poét of today receives from Friedrich's hands the honor of a separate subchapter.) Thus with Friedrich, historical treatment does not crowd out the great poetic individualities. Neither are the latter subordinated to national categories (only the Spaniards are seen within their particular national framework). The comments on all the poets are based on the original texts (generally accompanied by translations) which are found either in the text of the author or in an appendix. The last two lines of the work reveal Friedrich's general attitude toward modern lyrics: "One may love it or reject it, but this must be a love or a rejection based on an intellectual act" (*Erkennen*). Mr. Friedrich has *erkannt* modern lyrics and has in the end not come out with a rejection, an attitude to be highly praised if we remember his statement at the beginning of his book that he is no "avant-guardist by principle" and feels "more at home" with Goethe than with T. S. Eliot. It was then not with emotional bias, but with intellectual empathy that he has been able to study with so much love and labor those phenomena which at first sight are the most disconcerting that poetry has ever produced. When faced with so unprejudiced a historical treatment of contemporary subject matter, we cannot withhold from the author our deep-felt homage. He may serve as an example of "personal culture without resentments," especially to us in this country where I so often feel that scholars study, for example, the medieval literature because they like its theocratic thought and dislike the freethinking side of the Renaissance or, conversely, study Renaissance literature because they dislike medieval theocracy, being in other words, not equipped to study both the Middle Ages and the Renaissance because of some fanaticism (pro or con) lurking behind their scholarly endeavors.

Very helpful indexes (particularly a most welcome index of subject matter which sometimes suggests to us new *rapprochements*), a bibliography reduced to the most essential data and a chronological table (with such witty juxtapositions as: "1885 Death of Victor Hugo in Paris"—"1885 birth of Ezra Pound in Haily, U. S. A.," or "1926 Rilke's death in Val-Mont, Switzerland" —"1927 T. S. Eliot becomes an English citizen") conclude the volume, so slight in appearance, so strong in impact.

This does however not imply that the work is beyond criticism. As to material included, an Anglo-Saxon public will be surprised to find missing such great names as G. M. Hopkins (with his "realism of disrealization") or Walt Whitman (the discoverer of what I called in a book mentioned in Friedrich's bibliography "chaotic enumeration"). Furthermore, among the ancestors of

" sensuous irrealism " surely Rabelais, Quevedo and Gracián would
have deserved an outstanding place. It is also regrettable that, for
reasons probably connected with publisher's economies, not *all* the
poems commented on in detail can be read in the appendix and,
conversely, that not all the poems printed in the appendix have
been commented upon in the text (and also that no poem of the
late Rilke has been analyzed).

A more essential weakness of our book is due to the occasional
inability of the author, as of so many literary critics endowed with
a keen sense for linguistic innovation, to present his pertinent
observations within the proper linguistic framework. For example,
Friedrich infers (p. 129) from the final line of Gottfried Benn's
poem " Welle der Nacht ": " die weisse Perle rollt zurück ins
Meer " that since no pearl had been mentioned before, rather a
general movement of rolling, the definite article is meant to be
" a phonetic sign of the absolute movement " (of the rolling back)
and to give this " determinant " an " indeterminate," mysterious
connotation. But if we consider the whole stanza:

> Welle der Nacht—, zwei Muscheln miterkoren,
> die Fluten strömen sie, die Felsen her,
> dann Diadem und Purpur mitverloren,
> die weisse Perle rollt zurück ins Meer,

we see the forward rolling movement (" miterkoren ") embodied in
two (worthless) shells, while we lose to the receding waves
" diadem and purple " as well as " the white pearl "—the idea
obviously being that the wave takes back much more than it brings
to the shores. ." Diadem and purple " are the insignia of past
grandeur (of the Istrian palace now vacant, mentioned in stanza 1—
the whole poem is centered on the wave-like passing of majesty) —
a grandeur climaxed by the final mention of the white pearl.
" Diadem and purple " are in this context as unexpected (or
mysterious) as the pearl. The definite article that accompanies
the latter, just as in expressions like ' the best, the top,' may thus
be considered as the article of superlativity (the final position
of the pearl also serves the visual effect of whiteness in the night).

In the poem " Genazzano " by M.-L. Kaschnitz:

> Genazzano am Abend
> Winterlich
> Gläsernes Klappern
> Der Eselshufe

5   Steilauf die Bergstadt.
    Hier stand ich am Brunnen
    Hier wusch ich mein Brauthemd
    Hier wusch ich mein Totenhemd
    Mein Gesicht lag weiß
10 Unterm schwarzen Wasser
    Im wehenden Laub der Platanen.
    Meine Hände waren zwei Klumpen Eis
    Fünf Zapfen an jeder
    Die klirrten

Friedrich finds that while the first five lines with their nominal sentences contain " something like a real event " in " empirical time " the following verbs, in the preterite, render unreal, dreamlike events and since some of these are future events the preterite becomes in truth a " supratemporal tense " that ignores the " Zeitstufen." This analysis leaves out line 6 which shows a preterite expressing a real event and, in its pivotal rôle, must influence our understanding of the meaning both of what precedes and of what follows it: by the preterite *hier stand ich* we understand retroactively that the upward movement which has come to an end in line 6 (*Klappern der Eselshufe steilauf . . .*) must have been meant to be in the preterite (= *die Eselshufe klapperten steilauf . . .*). Again, line 6 ushers in also the vision which has for the poet the same reality (therefore the preterite) as the factual standing at the well (witness the anaphora *hier* that similarly bridges the gap between reality and dream). The following preterites do not include a future (of planned suicide) nor are they meant " supra-temporally," but they indicate a past that was lived through in the dream. The effect of the poem resides in the gradual passage from a reality that includes cold of winter and glasslike clatter to a vision of death that contains similar elements: cold and clattering ice. Between these two states stands the well, the end of the journey in reality, the potentiality of death in the dream. Death moves into reality imperceptibly or magically—and the uninterrupted preterites render precisely this gradual invasion.

At times Friedrich may stress a linguistic point overly much while omitting one a linguist would find all-important. In Benn's poem " Bilder," according to Friedrich, the articulation achieved is due, not to syntax, but to variation of emphasis or tone: he is led to the negative part of his statement by what he calls the " veiled " character of the hypothetic period. But in reality the period that takes up the whole poem is most clearly articulated by syntactic means: the thrice repeated *siehst du* . . . (ll. 1, 13, 15) is as clearly a hypothetic clause as the *du siehst* is a clear apodosis, for the feeling of a German, and the use of the same word material, *siehst du—du siehst*, rather enhances the stringency of the conclusion drawn (cf. the even more identical and therefore even more conclusive wording in Chamisso: "*Du fragest* nach den Riesen, *du findest* sie nicht mehr"). In contrast to his overemphasis on the hypothetic period, Friedrich says nothing of the extraordinary syntactical fact that in the list of the features of old age (depicted in modern paintings) two are clearcut nominatives, not accusatives as the verb *siehst du* would normally require it: . . . *käsiger Bart . . . ein Lebensabend* . . . : it is as though the ugly things painted emancipated themselves from the syntactic texture, achieving a kind of destructive autonomy as they often appear to the bewildered beholders of modern paintings, while, on the contrary, the firmly organized period *siehst du—du siehst* presents a framework (syntactical, as well as mental) by which order (in this case the correct evaluation of pictures, however ugly, as works of the "great genius") is re-established.

Mr. Friedrich seems at times fascinated by the boundless power of language as such (if I may thus translate his term "eigenmächtige Sprache"): often, he claims, the modern lyrical poet is "alone with his language," and allows it to go where it wishes, defying any rational interpretation. For example, in Ungaretti's poem *L'Isola*:

A una proda ove sera era perenne
Di anziane selve assorte, scese,
E, s'inoltrò
E lo richiamò rumore di penne
Ch'erasi sciolto dallo stridulo
Batticuore dell' acqua torrida.
E una larva (languiva
E rifioriva) vide;
Ritornato a salire vide
Ch'era una ninfa e dormiva
Ritta abbracciata a un olmo.
In sé da simulacro a fiamma vera
Errando, giunse a un prato ove
L'ombra negli occhi s'addensava
Delle vergini come
Sera appiè degli ulivi;

Distillavano i rami
Una pioggia pigra di dardi,
Qua pecore s'erano appisolate
Sotto il liscio tepore,
Altre brucavano
La coltre luminosa;
Le mani del pastore erano un vetro
Levigato da fioca febbre

the final " metaphoric dissonance " (hands like glass), coming as a climax after so many " hermetic " features such as the pronoun ' he,' an " indeterminate determinant," and statements evoking rather " lines of movement " (arrival, encounter, rest) than pastoral things and beings (island, woods, nymph, shepherd, sheep), points to a level of " eigenmächtige Sprache." Here, it seems to me, the literary critic, more overawed by the mystery of language than a linguist would be, has abdicated too early and concedes too much to meaningless language. The ' he,' a generic pronoun serving as an " exemplifying " device just as much as, in all lyrical poetry through the ages, an ' I ' or ' you ' would do, is shown in the beginning of our poem engaged in a movement downward (to the shore of the island and to ancient forests located on the shore) when he is called back to the heights (*lo richiamò*—' called him back,' not ' attracted him '; *ritornato a salire* ' he turned again to the ascent ')— and there, proceeding from " appearances " (the ghost who becomes a nymph) to the " true flame," he finds a meadow with virgins in whose eyes shadows have gathered just as " the evening [*sera* = nominative, not ' in the evening'] gathers around the olive-trees " —obviously the only trace of darkness in this dazzling landscape— with trees emitting a " lazy rain of arrows," with animals asleep in the " smooth " (not " soft ") tepid atmosphere or grazing on the " shining cover " of the lawn—and then finally there appears the glass-like hands of the shepherd " polished by dull fever." It seems clear that we have here the picture of a Southern island made of heat, torpor, laziness, light, consuming sensuous love: the hands of the shepherd have become " polished glass " (a motif anticipated by the epithet *liscio* ' smooth ') through the scorching flame of love in that torrid climate in which the amorous fever, never exploding, but persistent, has burnt all organic living matter in the lover. We have here what I would call in German a *Verdinglichung*, a materialization of the pastoral themes of the flame of love and

of the island of love (and this *Verdinglichung*, also to be observed
in the end of Lorca's *Romance sonámbulo* and Kaschnitz's poem
quoted above, is a foil to the *Entdinglichung* or disrealization
characteristic of modern poetry—both tendencies leading away from
the observable model in the outward world). This *Verdinglichung*
is the modern, more radical counterpart to *préciosité* in which
metaphors were *suivies jusqu'au bout*.[2] Once this is understood
all motifs in the poem become clearly visualizable and the language appears in strict accord with the dictation of imagination—
which is not of a verbal, but of a "materializing" kind.

Similarly, I believe that Friedrich (p. 75) is overrating language
when he states that in Mallarmé's poem *Sainte* (which was first
called *Sainte Cécile jouant sur l'aile d'un chérubin*) the *Entdinglichung* has brought the poet to the point where events and things
described exist "not in reality, but only in language" ("nicht
in der Sache, sondern in der Sprache"). While I am in full agreement with Friedrich's judgment as to disrealization (the old instruments *viole, flûte, mandore* and the missal with the Magnificat
serve no longer), I must point the absolute reality of the Saint
who is still that Saint Cecilia who dropped her own musical instruments in order to listen to celestial music and who is played upon,
as if she herself were an instrument, by the angel. She has thus
become an active-inactive *musicienne du silence* (notice that according to Pythagorean ideas the silence of the spheres is only their
music which human ears are unable to hear). Thus the spiritual,
physically unhearable music that plays within the saint is a "real"
fact, no *flatus vocis* of language. While there exists no actual mass
in which the Magnificat might be sung there develops, at the
window where the Saint is sitting, a spiritual mass (as the expression *vitrage d'ostensoir* shows) in which the Saint may repeat the
vows of Hannah and Mary: *Magnificat anima mia*. Notice also the
pallor of the Saint which indicates the approach of death which
brings her close to martyrdom and Paradise. The poem with its
overtones of Pythagorean-Christian world harmony stands much

---

[2] Or to the conceits of a Quevedo whose "logique conceptuelle" Amédée Mas
in his recent book *La Caricature de la femme . . . dans l'oeuvre de Quevedo*
(Paris, 1957) has duly emphasized. For example, when Quevedo assures us
that his soul, his veins, his marrow burning of love will, when death comes,
become "feeling ashes" and "loving dust," this is the same extreme of "materialization within the logic of a conceit" as in Ungaretti's poem the hands
of the love-burnt shepherd which have become "polished glass."

more in a long tradition than Friedrich seems to have realized.

Again, in the sonnet *Éventail* (*de Madame Mallarmé*), which Friedrich takes mainly as an *ars poetica* dealing not with the fan but with Mallarmé's poetry or the poetry of the future, he stresses *Entdinglichung* (disrealization) because things in this poem exist only in their absence, "are present only in language." But I disagree first with the statement that, in opposition to former *poésie galante*, "tender feelings or gallantry" are missing in the poem (this would be the *dehumanización* of Ortega) : on the contrary all in it (that is the long sentence which takes up these stanzas) tends toward the final wish and compliment *Cet éventail . . . limpide . . . toujours tel il apparaisse/entre tes mains sans paresse.* Secondly, while I do not deny that, as always with Mallarmé, delicate relationships appear between art (or an *objet d'art*) and poetry, I am convinced that the first stanza is already concerned with the fan (and contains a compliment to its user) :

> Avec comme pour langage
> Rien qu'un battement aux cieux
> Le futur vers se dégage
> Du logis très précieux.

"Language" and "verse" refer here not truly to poetry, but to the poetic utterance implied in the flickering of the fan by the lady (notice: "avec *comme* pour language"—the language of the fan is only a metaphoric one) : the poet follows with his eyes the actualization of the potential in the fan, which actualization will produce its effect (*le futur vers*) each time it will move away from its *très précieux logis*, the body of the precious person who builds it (a *précieux* compliment in its traditional form: *très précieux*). *Un battement aux cieux* introduces the identification of the fan with the wing (of an angel? again a compliment!) which will be followed up by *aile tout bas la courrière* in the next stanza. This line is taken by Friedrich as an apostrophe lacking syntactical ties with the rest, *tout bas*, translated 'ganz leise,' being the "boldest possible" apostrophe. I would rather analyze *aile-la-courrière* [que] *cet éventail*, the emotional syntactical form for an assertion: the fan *is* the wing of an angel, a "messenger from heaven that flies low [on this earth]," *tout bas* belonging to the *voler* implied in *aile*: with this identification of the fan with a heavenly wing our eyes are lifted beyond the earthly figure of the lady. Now we see

behind the lady the mirror in which a bright movement of the fan
flickers so that fan and reflection of fan become one: *limpide* at the
beginning of stanza 3 can then refer as well to the mirror as to
the fan. And now the Ronsardian idea of the frailty of the earthly
being who owns the fan appears:

> . . . où va redescendre
> Pourchassée en chaque grain
> Un peu d'invisible cendre
> Seule à me rendre chagrin.

"Redescendre"—before and after the momentary shining of the
fan in the mirror a mist of ashes veils the body of the lady, ashes
invisible at the moment, but for ever feared by the poet (*pour-
chassée en chaque grain*, mistranslated by Friedrich 'in jedem
Körnchen verjagt,' means '[ashes whose traces are] anxiously followed by the poet's eyes in each grain of the lady's skin') : the poet
is watching the face of the lady for any sign of the approach of old
age and death. The moment of beauty when she was flicking her
fan against the background of the mirror is seized upon by the
poet who wishes for her indirectly, by way of the fan and the
mirror—each of which he would have forever "limpid" (un-
altered) —immortality, and this as ardently as any poet of the
Pléiade could have done. Indirection (a tribute to a woman by
means of a tribute to beautiful things with which she surrounds
herself) has always been more effective in lyrics than direct statement: it has been multiplied in our poem written in an age when
the poet fears more than ever the *cliché*.

Again in Mallarmé's sonnet that begins *Surgi de la croupe et du
bond*, Friedrich sees opaqueness of meaning, "singing mystery,"
etc. Remembering Mallarmé's utterances about "juggling of
words" in his poems, he believes that in the first stanza:

> Surgi de la croupe et du bond
> D'une verrerie éphémère
> Sans fleurir la veillée amère
> *Le col ignoré s'interrompt*

the two words *croupe* and *bond* are inspired by two other words
that are not there: *coupe* and *fond*. Apart from the assumed in-
congruence of the word *fond*, which expresses something resting at
the bottom, supposedly replaced by *bond*, the equivalent of an
upward leap, it seems to me more likely that in this stanza there is

described the wide-bellied, thin-necked form of a vase without flowers in terms of an animal movement, that of a beast crouched in order to leap, interrupted by the absence of flowers which would prolong and carry to its end the initiated movement. By means of the expressions *ignoré* (that should be translated not ' unrecognized,' but ' ignored ') and *veillée amère* (which suggests the waking at a death-bed) a bridge is built to *veuvage*, which symbolizes sterility, frustration, death, and will be the theme of this as of many other poems by Mallarmé. This theme explains the " ephemeral " character of the " glass substance " that can never form a true vase. In the next stanza the vase-that-is-not-a-vase becomes the drinking glass from which the Sylph's parents have failed to drink the drink of true love, that is a drinking glass that is not a true glass. The Sylph himself can be no true human being, only a vague homunculus, born as he is from the ambivalence of chastity (purity— sterility) : he is doomed (*froid plafond* indicating a tomb). The atmosphere of death is condensed even more in the last two stanzas (*agoniser—expirer—funèbres—ténèbres*) where the flower image (the " rose ") returns only to be denied any existence. Friedrich is right in calling this poem " a poem about negations " (neither vase nor flower nor Sylph exist, what exists is sterility and death), but if he is right language has excellently expressed the " negative category ": why then should the poet, in our poem, by the symbol of the nonexistent rose, have deplored the impossibility of " Sprachwerdung," the impossibility for the language to find the " erlösende Wort "? Our poem deals with the negativity, not of language, but of a sterile poetic imagination. Cicero's use of " flower " for " poetic expression " has no bearing on our poem, which contains no allusion to " poetry."

At times it happens that failure to sense the importance of a particular word prevents Friedrich from seeing the full meaning of a poem. Thus for him in *Addii* of Montale (p. 144) the indeterminate *tu* of the second stanza represents only a " remainder of humanity," the main emphasis resting on the inhuman " automatons." But in reality the poet is complaining about a suspected personal attitude of the *tu*, his beloved, in a moment (the farewell) when inner tensions usually become articulate. After having described tersely the mechanical side of a train departure at a railway station, expressing by the line " Forse gli automi hanno ragione " a sceptic submissiveness on his part of the overpowering

mechanization of our modern lives, he concludes with the sharp,
almost accusing question:

> —Presti anche tu (!) alla fioca
> litania del tuo rapido quest' orrida
> e fedele cadenza di carioca?—

" will you too lend that horrible, submissive rhythm of the (well-
known) dance song *carioca* to the hoarse litany of your express
train? "—where we obviously have an allusion to the habit of
travelers of hearing the rhythm of the train according to their own
favorite melody. The poet is horrified by the possibility that his
beloved too (*anche tu = et tu, mi fili Brute?*) may lend her tacit
support, and in a trivial way (by hearing the trivial *carioca* in
the rhythm of the train), to the mechanization of our modern
world. Surely a general cultural question is underlying the poem,
but this is centered on a personal concern about the beloved's reaction to the cultural situation (had she herself been " mechanized
and trivialized " thereby?) —a concern which is " modern " in that
love today searches into strata of the soul which formerly would
have been irrelevant for love. Thus the poem does not show only
a remainder of humanity, but is pervaded by humanity (by a
human concern about a human attitude). Mr. Friedrich has not
paid sufficient attention to the most important word (*anche*) in
the poem and this, in his hands, has become, like that of Mallarmé
about the fan of Mme Mallarmé, too strongly " dehumanized."[3]

---

[3] There are a few observations of detail which have not found their place in
the preceding discussion. P. 123: to the excellent analysis of Lorca's *El Grito*
as a perfect example of " disrealization " and " dehumanization " I should like
to add a comment on the clever procedure of the poet who introduces into the
poem the cry itself: ¡ay! Though we are told at the beginning that the cry
goes from mountain to mountain, this cry is not yet formed; it is only in
stanza 2 that we are told of the starting point of the cry or rather where
(in the olive trees) the cry *will start*: *será*. Only after this announcement
can the cry be heard (¡ay!). In stanza 3 it *has begun* its acoustic existence
(*ha hecho vibrar*), continuing as an echo so that again we must hear ¡ay!
In stanza 4 it has passed by " the people in their caves " (that it has passed
above their heads in its passage from mountain to mountain is indicated by
the parenthesis), yet still lingers as a vibration in the ether after the poem
itself has ended: the last ¡ay!—which is placed outside of the parenthesis.
It is true that, as Friedrich has felt, human beings here are only a parenthesis
in the life of the self-sufficient " ellipsis " of the cry. P. 138: *Ciudad de los
estíos* is incorrectly translated ' Wesensstadt ' (confusion with *estar?*). P. 151:
the *por* in the refrain line of G. Diego's *Insomnio: Tú por tu sueño y por
el mar las naves* should not be translated ' through ' (' *durch* '), but ' along '

All the poems discussed in this overlong review would seem to bear out the truth that modern lyrics, because of their difficult structure, semantic ambiguities, incoherence, and arbitrariness, require to a greater degree than did previous poetry (even medieval poetry) the collaboration with the critic of the philologist who will not abandon prematurely the search for meaning and will warn the critic against explanations that are linguistically impossible. This is, of course, only a consequence of the other truth that modern poets are more " philological," that is, *closer* to language and its requirements (not " *alone with* the language," as Friedrich believes) in their disrealization and dishumanization of poetry than were former poets who concerned themselves mainly with the imitation of things and man. After these have receded to the background language has become paramount—but language is still addressed to the fellow man!

1957

(cf. the common phrases *andar por esos mundos, por esas calles,* etc.) —the idea being that the sleeping beloved proceeds on her particular well-defined route (of sleep) as do the ships that ply the sea. The line is an imitation of Lorca's *Romance sonámbule*: " El barco sobre la mar / y el caballo en la montaña " (again, the whole poem reflects the motif of " la regarder dormir " treated by Proust and Valéry). P. 162: " [tes mains] nées dans le miroir clos des miennes " (Eluard): *miroir clos* should not be translated ' umschlossener ' but ' umschliessender Spiegel.'

ERICH AUERBACH'S CRITICAL THEORY AND PRACTICE: AN ASSESSMENT ✎ WOLFGANG BERNARD FLEISCHMANN

✎ In the course of his introduction to his last, and perhaps greatest book, *Literary Language and its Public in late Latin Antiquity and in the Middle Ages,* Erich Auerbach refers to Vico's conception of the total phenomenon of history as an eternal Platonic state in spite of constant change displayed by the historic process. If one were to seek a phrase to describe the contours and perspectives of Auerbach's accomplishments as a philologist and critic, Vico's metaphor yields a clue. Early and late, Auerbach's work is permeated by a genial, though limited, set of ideas on literary process which serve to illuminate and explain a kaleidoscopic variety of literary phenomena. His republic of letters is a Platonic state, in which the multiplicity of appearances, the flux of languages, styles, and texts is, through Auerbach's skill, continually made relevant to structures of ideas which, by dint of serving in many instances to show order in diversity, help define the nature of historic process.

Any attempt to seize upon and describe Auerbach's set of structures, as they illuminate his work with literature, would send one to the "Epilogue" of *Mimesis.* For it is here that we find a kind of genetic development for three of these: From an apposition of Plato's ranking *mimesis* as third after truth, in Book 10 of *The Republic,* with "Dante's assertion that in the *Commedia* he presented true reality," and from a keeping in mind of this apposition as he proceeded to a wide study of the interpretation of human events in European literature, Auerbach states having crystallized out " three closely related ideas " which in turn form the methodological base for *Mimesis*. These are, first and second, the two " breaks with the doctrine of stylistic levels " in the literary history of the West—the breakthrough to realism in the early nineteenth century with its representation of random individuals in the context of " serious, problematical, and even tragic " situations being paralled earlier in the tradition by a " first break with the classical theory . . . (through) . . . the story of Christ, with its ruthless mixture of everyday reality and the highest and most sublime tragedy." Unlike the Romantic breakthrough, however, the Christ story did not foreshadow realistic representation in literature. Much rather, New Testament theology gave rise to what Auerbach terms figural interpretation, the seeing of one occurrence in terms of the new, " the connection between occurrences . . . (being) . . . not regarded as primarily a chronological or causal development but as a oneness within the divine plan, of which all occurrences are parts and reflections." The " figural . . . conception of reality in late antiquity and the Christian Middle Ages " is Auerbach's third key idea for the intellectual dimensions of *Mimesis*.

A fourth guiding concept in Auerbach's work is his notion of deriving insight into the nature of a literary audience through the exploration of key phrases having to do, within a given stage of linguistic and literary developments, with author-reader relationships, with social status in relation to readership, or with the description of readers, as such. Here, Auerbach's early study on the phrase " La Cour et la Ville " as revelatory of the nature of reading publics in late seventeenth-century France is paradigmatic, as to method, for the interconnecting series of essays on late classical and medieval reading publics which constitute *Literary Language*.

It will be noticed that all four of Auerbach's key concepts for approaching literary phenomena are firmly grounded in a historic process. Three of these—the notions of breaks in traditional stylistic conventions through the literary portrayal of commonplace persons in the *New Testament* and in the Romantic novel, as well as the concept of assessing a literary public through a study of its habituated language—are deeply concerned with the relationship between literature and society. Auerbach's thoughts on " figural interpretation " are, by contrast, less historical and societal in conception, than they are historical and theological. While the

methodological part of his essay "Figura" purports to be the analysis of an idea strongly represented in medieval modes of literary
interpretation and useful for a modern interpretation of medieval
literature, the terms of its applicability are visualized along theological lines. Having demonstrated the often complex ways in
which the "prophetic" writings of the Church fathers had interpreted the Old Law as foreshadowing the New by means of
endowing *figurae* in the former with eschatological significance for
the latter and by way of anticipating his own "figural" approach
to the *Divine Comedy,* Auerbach admits: "There is something
scholarly, indirect, even abstruse about . . . [figural interpretation]
. . . , except on the rare occasions when a gifted mystic breathes
force into it."

Is the Auerbach of *Mimesis* a "gifted mystic" on this order? In
part, my answer would be "yes"; in part, "no." My positive answer would be strongest for a case like Auerbach's interpretation
of Virginia Woolf's *To the Lighthouse,* in the chapter of *Mimesis*
entitled "The Brown Stocking," where a misreading of the novel
as fragmented and disorganized is presented with such force of conviction that even a reader objectively certain that Auerbach is
wrong is carried along by his argument. There is, secondly, an almost uncanny quality about Auerbach's choice of texts for inclusion
in *Mimesis*: Why do seemingly random passages from texts often
of doubtfully representative quality for the period of literary history
envisaged work so well in bringing not only the work from which
they are taken but also the whole period of their origin to life?
Finally, a reading of *Mimesis,* especially when it is done at one sitting, will give one the illusion of having recapitulated, in that series
of essays acknowledged by their author to have been presented on
eclectic and fragmentary principles, the whole of the Western tradition in literature. There is no doubt that *Mimesis* is infused with
a kind of providential spirit, seeming effortlessly to make the chaos
whole, which is hard to find in twentieth-century literary criticism
and which is, besides, explicitly prefigured in the author's methodological assumptions.

Yet in other, equally important contexts, *Mimesis* is by no means
a theological work and Auerbach, the sum total of his writings
considered, no theologian. For one, Auerbach's commitments to
eminently secular notions of history and society (discussed below)
would qualify any purely theological, let alone mystical stand. For

another, Auerbach suffers too strongly from the " philological conscience " of his academic generation to be less than skeptical of
metaphysical commitment. He feels compelled to justify his genial
ideas on " figurative interpretation " by prefatory excursions on a
strictly etymological order. An attempt is made to anchor every
chapter of *Mimesis* in the grounds of accepted literary history, by
means of a comparative epilogue. When Auerbach writes either
for students or for the public presumed to be beyond his field, he
takes distance from ideas to which he confesses elsewhere being
very close, and assumes a stance of scholarly " objectivity." No student using Auerbach's textbook *Introduction aux Études de Philologie Romane* could feel that the discussion of Leo Spitzer's
philological methods, to which Auerbach admits on many occasions
having been signally indebted, was written by any but the most
dispassionate knowledgeable observer. Readers of the *Journal of
Aesthetics and Art History,* seeing Auerbach's cool and uncommitted
discussion of "Vico and Aesthetic Historicism " could get no sense
of the author's strong intellectual attachment to Vico, which
amounts to a discipleship.

Auerbach seems thus, in communicating to a student or general
public, to be able to stand outside his own commitments, to act as
a distant, dispassionate commentator upon ideas very close to his
scholarly life and work. For a critic as interested as is Auerbach in
levels of literary understanding as these related to the place of
authors and readers in their social and educational structure, such
a pronouncement of exoteric doctrine, with one's own working essentials viewed from an objective distance, is not very surprising.
" Philosophy," says Vico in enunciating the sixth element of his *New
Science,* " considers man as he should be and so can be of service to
but very few, who wish to live in the Republic of Plato, not to fall
back into the dregs of Romulus."

Wish to live in the Republic of Plato, where the essentials of his
quest are concerned, Auerbach does. What he has in mind is a
Geistesgeschichte which understands, through a seizing upon of all
phenomena possibly relevant to it, the totality of its spiritual, intellectual, aesthetic, political, and social essence. Studying the portrayal of reality in a given era, on the one hand, and the relationship between literary language and its reading public, on the other,
defines the character of the era. Breaks in stylistic levels signify
demarcation points between eras. Ways of interpreting events from

one era through significations derived from another, the Old Law in terms of the New, create a dynamic in the inter-relationship of historic process which, all at once, prevents one from a static view of literary " periods " anchored in the past and also permits the flow of history to emerge into the present and thence into the future. All phenomena are studied in relation to phenomena of their own era as well as to those of eras in their past. At the same time they stand ready, as it were, to be reinterpreted by future eras and in terms of these.

While the critic reasons, the present shifts; the future becomes the past. The task of what Auerbach calls, in *Literary Language,* his " radical relativism " is thus unending—" a task of infinite dimensions which everyone must attempt for himself, from his own point of observation." In the process of the critic's study, all "extrahistorical and absolute categories" vanish; legitimate categories of cognition are derived from the historical process itself, but they are, by reason of the nature of this process, necessarily " elastic " and temporary." Nothing is final or absolute *except,* when it comes to the flow of history and to its beholder, the relativity of the process itself.

Plato, in replacing *mimesis* third from truth assumed truth, in the context of the tenth book of *The Republic* to be absolute. The maker of the painted bed in question here, i. e. the carpenter, is second from truth. The true maker of the archetypal bed is God. Divine Providence was, for Vico, the moving force behind the historic process. Historical relativity was a function of divine decree. To quote Auerbach, " Divine Providence makes human nature change from period to period; the distinction between human nature and human history disappears; as Vico puts it, human history is a permanent Platonic state." Auerbach's Platonic state finds what permanency lies behind it in the dialogue of the historic process itself. " The general image," he says, " which seems to me capable of representation, is the view of a historic process; something like a drama which contains no theory but a paradigmatic exposition of human fate. Its subject, in the broadest sense, is Europe; I try to seize upon this in a number of individual critical attempts." Yet Auerbach hints, elsewhere, that the end of the process he is concerned with is in view. Civilizations will either be destroyed, in short order, or become as one. In the latter case, consciousness of the diversity of historic process will disappear. By an implication

not stated by Auerbach, the disappearance of historical consciousness would mean the end of a continuation of historic process, as
he understands this. Past history could be looked at from a static
point of observation; what had been discovered about it would assume permanence. The drama of European literature would cease
to be part of a shifting dialectic, subject to modification by future
participants; its different acts would assume the nature of perennial
human paradigms.

In the time immediately preceding Auerbach's early death, we
know that he engaged in the study of minute and technical problems
in Dante. By way of personal reading, he was intensively preoccupied with the *Essais* of Montaigne. It seems almost as if he wished
to convince himself, and perhaps posterity, of the absence either
of theological concern or commitment on his part. I cannot but
believe, however, that the strength and momentum needed by Auerbach in attempting over and again to seize the variety of Occidental
literary phenomena in structures were based upon an intimation
either of a cessation of historic process which would give these
structures permanence or of a hope, on a theological order, that
these were part of a meaningful plan. At the same time, the nature
of Auerbach's work makes it abundantly clear that the difficulties
of maintaining a radical relativism, uninformed by a certain belief
in the eventual relevance of the historic patterns discovered upon
a plane of absolute truth, took their toll in denying the work
eventual coherence. What unifies the work is its method. Once this
is understood, the hard covers placed about either *Mimesis* or *Literary Language* could melt, revealing a series of brilliant individual
essays, of fragments yielding luminous insights into the varied eras
of literary history their topics connote.

We can learn much from the work of Erich Auerbach, but not
the sort of literary historiography which will allow students and
teachers a working knowledge about any given era. If the synthetic
survey of Romance literatures in Auerbach's *Introduction aux
Études de Philologie Romane* fails to relate the author's scholarly
ways to the student, this lack of contact may be due not only to
Auerbach's consciousness for the need of simplified generalizations
in a manual of this sort but also to an inability to relate, on a broad
canvas, the highly specific insights his discoveries convey. If *Mimesis,* for all its semblance of unity, presents no "coverage" in the
sense of historic continuity, this is due less to the great intrinsic

difficulty of coping with the Occidental tradition from Homer to Virginia Woolf within the scope of one volume than to the fundamental lack of belief, on Auerbach's part, in either the possibility or relevance of such an attempt.

Again, it would be folly to use Auerbach's method as a dogma. By his own admission, some of the essentials required of a philologist cannot be taught. Breadth of cultural horizon, wealth of personal experience, power to re-experience imaginatively the work of art, ability to seize upon what is important—these are, for Auerbach, necessary but personal accomplishments, on this order. Whether or not a teacher can do anything to further these factors is a matter for debate but the fact that Auerbach considers them unteachable points to a view of his own work, which I share, as a highly personal, creative achievement. To send graduate students to *Mimesis,* as is occasionally done, with a view of having them hunt for Auerbach's specific structures in texts not treated by him seems a dubious undertaking. " *Mimesis,*" as its author says, " is quite consciously a book written by a certain kind of man, in a certain kind of situation at the beginning of the 1940's." What students and critics can learn from Auerbach's method, however, is a lesson in the possibility of combining essentially structural criticism with the most detailed philological study, of keeping form in mind without needing to forget the ever present multiplicity of detail.

On the practical level this means that a critic learning from Auerbach can make stylistic studies without wedding himself beforehand to a system of categories. Much rather, the categories his critical exposition necessarily must contain can evolve, as it were, from the text, the probability of their truth being assured by a vigilant exercise of those scholarly virtues Auerbach considers teachable— " grammar and lexicography, the use of sources and textual criticism, bibliography . . . (and) . . . careful reading." What will emerge will have the advantages of creative originality and of relevance to the text, without for a moment sacrificing that accuracy and exactitude only the application of linguistic and historical insight can achieve—in short, the advantage of Auerbach's own work, at its very best.

1966

Ernst Robert Curtius: Topology and Critical Method ❧ Alexander Gelley

ERNST ROBERT CURTIUS: TOPOLOGY AND CRITICAL METHOD ❧ ALEXANDER GELLEY ❧ On the one hand Curtius belongs to that tradition of literary essayists, German in language but European in outlook, that has its source in the Schlegel brothers.[1] Here the critical essay was cultivated as a distinct literary genre. Adapting a *mot* of Friedrich Schlegel, Curtius has written, "Criticism is the literature of literature. Or more specifically: criticism is that form of literature whose subject matter is literature " (KE, 33) .[2] Curtius's own style is personal yet authoritative; capable of fine nuances of thought and feeling in the course of rapid, compressed exposition. He knows how to use quotations to the best effect: they are as important to the critic as illustrations to the art historian, he maintains; without them the critical concepts would remain "void" (FG, 342) . But he can also perceive the large design in a figure, show the temper of an artist or an epoch crystallized in a trope.

At the same time Curtius proudly acknowledges himself a pupil and disciple of Gustav Gröber, one of the masters of the historical

---

[1] In the preparation of this essay I have had the friendly advice of Dr. Michael Kowal of Queens College and of Mr. Richard Mackler.

[2] The translations from the German are mine except for *European Literature*, where I have used Willard R. Trask's published translation. Following are the editions cited and the abbreviations by which they are identified in my text: *Balzac*, 2nd ed., Bern, 1951; *Büchertagebuch*, Dalp-Taschenbücher, Bern and Munich, 1960; *Deutscher Geist in Gefahr* (DG), Stuttgart and Berlin, 1932; *European Literature and the Latin Middle Ages* (EL), trans. Willard R. Trask, New York, 1953; *Französischer Geist im zwanzigsten Jahrhundert* (FG), 2nd ed., Bern and Munich, 1960; *Gesammelte Aufsätze zur romanischen Philologie* (GA), Bern and Munich, 1960; *Kritische Essays zur europäischen Literatur* (KE), 3rd ed., Bern and Munich, 1963, a translation of which, by Dr. Michael Kowal, is to be published shortly by The Princeton University Press.

and positivistic scholarship of the later nineteenth century. In a long essay on Gröber written in 1952 [3] Curtius characterizes those qualities of concreteness, precision, and impersonality that distinguish Gröber's work. One of the mottoes for *European Literature and the Latin Middle Ages* (1948; English trans., 1953) is taken from Gröber and might stand as an exemplary precept for traditional historical scholarship: it emphasizes the painstaking accumulation of details that must precede any attempt at synthesis; even so, the scholar must be prepared to abandon premature syntheses over and over until all parts finally fit into place in an unassailable totality. Gröber, Curtius tells us, was the first to give due weight to the Latin tradition in the study of medieval literature; but Curtius himself was not to take up this theme until the early thirties, over twenty years after his period of study under Gröber.

It was through his pioneering interpretations of modern French literature that Curtius initially made his name in European belles-lettres. This first period of scholarly-critical activity extends from *Die literarischen Wegbereiter des neuen Frankreich* (1st. ed., 1919) to *Einführung in die französische Kultur* (1930). The finest products of this decade are the *Balzac* (1923) and *Französischer Geist im neuen Europa* (1925) with its long study of Proust.

In the Proust essay we find one of the most personal statements of Curtius's notion of criticism, a statement based on Proust's own views in his essay on Ruskin. Curtius writes, " If the practice of philosophy is rooted in wonder, then the premise of all criticism is that the critic notices certain things. Both activities are realized only through an expectant surrender to the subject matter. The fundamental attitude of the critic must be one of pure absorption, passive and at rest. Reception is the preliminary condition for perception, and this in turn leads to conception " (FG, 278 f.). It is such a state of spiritual receptivity that Curtius often denotes as intuition. But this faculty implies much more than simply a personal aesthetic sensitivity. For Curtius any proper apprehension of artistic forms reveals the fragmentary pattern of an immutable realm of spirit. In an essay on T. S. Eliot we read, " The fundamental act of criticism involves irrational contact. True criticism never seeks to prove but only to disclose. Its metaphysical assump-

---

[3] " Gustav Gröber und die romanische Philologie," *ZRPh*, LXVII (1951), 257-288. Reprinted in GA, pp. 428-455.

tion is a conviction that the world of mind [die geistige Welt] is organized round patterns of affinities" (KE, 317). The critic's intuition, then, is akin, if not equal, to the artist's creative vision. In the Proust essay Curtius writes, "All things are potent with unfathomed codes. We pass by without attending to them, without being even aware of them." In an art like Proust's, he continues, "the mute traces are endowed with meaning and reality" (FG, 336). The artist fashions his work through insight into an ideal unity, a kind of Platonic order, for which he offers a system of symbolic approximations. The critic's task, in turn, is to delineate the network of forces and forms implicit in a work. He should discern "the components of spiritual form [die seelische Formelemente] of an author" (which are never simply his opinions or feelings, Curtius cautions), and to proceed from these "in a synthetic process toward a reconstruction of the author's total spiritual position" (FG, 278 f.).

These "components of spiritual form" undoubtedly determined the organization of both the Balzac and the Proust studies. The Balzac book is organized around such topics as Secrecy, Magic, Energy, Passion, Love, Power, Knowledge, Society, Politics, and Religion; the Proust essay into sections on Art and Perception, Music, Intuition and Expression, Transience and Recollection, Will, Sensibility, and Contemplation. What Curtius has done is to apply key metaphors and themes of a poet to the whole of his work, demonstrating in this manner, from a variety of perspectives, the unity of the creative intuition.

Already in 1916 Curtius had written to Friedrich Gundolf, then a close friend, about a chapter of Gundolf's Goethe study, "Here you have realized something that is perhaps more valuable, and certainly rarer, than depth, ingenuity, insight: Totality. Totality as the willing and pious vision of a whole. You have achieved a relation to the figure of Goethe such as Goethe had to the world." [4] Although Curtius was strongly attracted by Gundolf's interpretation of works in terms of a poet's decisive inner experiences, he nonetheless possessed a sense of logical discrimination and a respect for historical patterns that was far removed from Gundolf's monumental approach to the literary tradition. It was in the Paris of

---

[4] *Friedrich Gundolf—Briefwechsel mit Herbert Steiner und Ernst Robert Curtius*, eds. Lothar Helbing and Claus Victor Bock, Amsterdam, 1963, p. 261. The next quotation is from p. 251.

that period, among such figures as Gide and Charles du Bos, that
the young Curtius found a more congenial milieu than among the
George circle, to which the friendship with Gundolf had drawn him
for a time. From France he could accept those visionary and in-
tuitionist principles which, if derived from George, would have involved too great a sacrifice of formal and historical values. While
working on the *Wegbereiter* Curtius still struggled with this issue,
and he wrote to Gundolf in 1916 upon completing that book,
" Thus the work has become, in a personal sense, a confrontation
between two of my spiritual attitudes: French spirit and Georgean
commonwealth [französischer Geist und georgischer staatswille]."
But there could be little doubt what the outcome of this inner
conflict would be. George's sharp rejection of the *Wegbereiter* [5]
indicates how little Curtius was already then attuned to his demands.
And, as it appears from the correspondence, the relationship to
Gundolf declined in the succeeding years.

We can appreciate now why Curtius was the first to grasp the
importance of the visionary side of Balzac and to demonstrate the
dynamic and totalizing impulses at work in the *Comédie Humaine*.
His study is remarkable not only as an exegesis of Balzac's work
but as a demonstration of that intuition of unity that Curtius saw
in Balzac. Du Bos, in an admirable appreciation of Curtius's criticism, notes that the Balzac study proceeds not in a rectilinear
manner but in the form of widening, interlocking circles which
parallel the pattern of Balzac's own creation.[6] Thus Curtius could
maintain that ". . . Balzac was endowed with an intuition of the
world as a totality which is a unity," (*Balzac*, 41) and again,
" Unity is for Balzac a mystic principle, the seal of the absolute "
(*Balzac*, 45) . Such an impulse is basic to Curtius's own thought.
He termed it " Theory of the unity of the All " (*All-Einheits-
Lehre*) and understood it as a perennial philosophy some of whose
traces are to be found in those occult and magical beliefs that
Balzac utilized. " It apprehends reality as an infinite, multi-dimen-
sional All, which is a living Unity, a single, active continuity of
being " (KE, 190) , Curtius writes in an essay which links Emerson
and Balzac as expositors of the *All-Einheits-Lehre*. Although this

---

[5] Cf. George's letter to Gundolf, quoted in *Briefwechsel*, ibid., p. 259, note 1.
[6] Charles du Bos, " Ernst Robert Curtius " in *Approximations*, 5° Ser., Paris,
1932, p. 125.

principle may find expression in philosophical terms, it is in essence both suprapersonal (irreducible to an author's personality or mind) and suprahistorical. We touch here on what may be called the religious horizon of Curtius's thought. It helps us to understand the temper of the man, what Rudolf Alexander Schröder has characterized as the "truly Leibnizian optimism, the pre-established inward harmony upon which are founded the energetic serenity and urbanity of [Curtius's] style." [7]

At the same time, we can now better understand the reason for certain limitations of sensibility in Curtius. Beside the vitalism of Balzac, he dismissed Flaubert's aestheticism straightway as "nihilism" (KE, 177). And Joyce, to whose *Ulysses* Curtius devoted a pioneer study in 1929, called forth only slightly less revulsion. Nor had Curtius any interest in realism as a phenomenon of nineteenth century literature. In 1950 he wrote, "The rendering of quotidian reality is not an artistic accomplishment of the nineteenth century. It can be found in the poetry of Hellenism, in the novels of imperial Rome, in the Icelandic sagas of the twelfth century, and also in Chaucer, in Rabelais, in Cervantes, in Fielding. . . . There are dozens, if not hundreds of realisms . . ." (KE, 176 f.). Coming after the appearance of *Mimesis*, such a passage appears certainly to have been directed against Erich Auerbach. It is noteworthy that Curtius was antagonistic to Auerbach's work; he rejected not only Auerbach's concept of *mimesis* but also that of *figura*. This latter could have been highly relevant to Curtius's own medieval studies, but he refused to accept Auerbach's differentiation between the historically-prophetic figural allegory characteristic of the Hebraic-Christian tradition and the more abstract allegorical mode stemming from Classical and pagan sources. It is not surprising that Auerbach's dialectically historical viewpoint should have been antipathetic to Curtius, with his transhistorical, unifying, implicitly Platonic orientation. [8]

By 1930, after over a decade of work on modern French litera-

---

[7] In *Die Neue Rundschau*, LXVII (1956), 531.

[8] Curtius attacked the *figura* concept in a note to "Gustav Gröber und die romanische Philologie," ZRPh, loc. cit., p. 276, note 2; or see in GA, p. 445, note 18. A critique of an aspect of *Mimesis* may be found in "Die Lehre von den drei Stilen im Altertum und Mittelalter," *RF*, LXIV (1952), 57-70. Auerbach's reply is in "Epilegomena zu Mimesis," *RF*, LXV (1954), 1-18, see esp. pp. 10-13.

ture, Curtius moved into a new area. His justification is characteristic: "A compelling intellectual necessity forced me to a change
in my field of scholarship. I felt the need to move back to older
epochs, speaking symbolically, I would say today, to archaic levels
of consciousness: and first of all to the Romanic Middle Ages"
(KE, 439). In 1949 he wrote to Ortega y Gasset, who had expressed
dismay at what he saw as a cooling in Curtius's attitude toward
him, "It is not from you that I have estranged myself, but rather,
to a certain extent, from philosophy. In consequence I have moved
closer to history, to an extra-philosophical notion of history whose
masters for me are Goethe, Ranke, Burckhardt. I am well aware
of this alteration; it represents an unfolding of my entelechy. I
cannot help expressing this." [9]

This zeal to remain true to his "entelechy" is typical of Curtius.
He frequently speaks of the path his own development as a scholar
took, but in no sense apologetically or as a qualification of his
achievements as an essayist and scholar. Rather, these discussions—
with their fascinating glimpses of the circles in which he moved
as a youth: Berlin and the George circle in the first decade of the
century, Alsatia just prior to the war, or Paris in the twenties—all
these self-revelations are offered, I believe, as evidence of an exemplary process, of such an interfusion of life, history, and intelligence
as could still bring forth a fully-rounded European consciousness
in this day and age.

It is one of Curtius's finest achievements to have made fully
clear the personal grounds upon which his assessments rest; and
more important: to have made it an ideal that the critic's and
scholar's personality must be an adequate organ of his age, capable
of both apprehending and expressing its significant intellectual
forces. This ideal is adumbrated in a passage like the following on
Proust: "For such an artist, his life signifies nothing else than the
indispensable organ of perception: precisely what the experimental
apparatus is to the research scientist. It is this sacrifice of one's life
in the service of perception and formation that constitutes the
morality of the artist" (FG, 279 f.). If the artist's morality is
related to his manner of perceiving, the critic's is no less so. Curtius
focuses on the moral issue not in terms of any ulterior ideology but
of the very consciousness with which the scholar apprehends texts.

[9] In *Merkur*, XVIII (1964), 914.

But inevitably, this has ramifications on a political-cultural level and it is necessary to understand Curtius's career under this aspect too.

In the early fifties Curtius wrote this of his *Wegbereiter* of 1919: " The ' new France ' in which I believed dissolved in the very moment in which my book appeared. But it would never have been written without the idealistic faith that possessed me and many others of my generation: the faith in the possibility and the necessity of a new Europe " (*Büchertagebuch*, 108) . This new Europe, he goes on to say, could have emerged only out of a creative renewal of the relations between France and Germany; and he hoped that his own book would contribute to such a renewal.

When Curtius began his systematic investigation of medieval literature in the early thirties he was still concerned to establish a basis for a pan-European consciousness, but he now saw a new way of justifying the idea of Europe as a unified historical phenomenon, an " intelligible field of study " in Toynbee's sense. He undertook to study the Latin sources of the various national literary traditions and by linking these, to disclose a pattern that would testify to a perennial humanism. In that admirable polemic of 1932, *Deutscher Geist in Gefahr*, he called it " Humanism as Initiative." It was Viacheslav Ivanov's defence of humanism in 1920 (in his letters to Mikhaïl Gershenzon) that inspired this formulation. Thus in the early period of the Nazi threat Curtius took upon himself a task prefigured by Ivanov's response to the Russian Revolution. Curtius argued that initiation in its ritual sense involves an orientation toward the future arising out of a dedication to the past: it is thus both restorative and initiatory. Humanism today, he hoped, might fulfill a similar function by revealing a collective memory, stored in the literary tradition, " by which the European mind preserves its identity through the milleniums " (EL, 395) . To achieve this goal he put forward the following programme in *European Literature*:

> European literature is coextensive in time with European culture, therefore embraces a period of some twenty-six centuries. . . . To see European literature as a whole is possible only after one has acquired citizenship in every period from Homer to Goethe. This cannot be got from a textbook, even if such a textbook existed. One acquires the rights of citizenship in the country of European literature only when one has spent many years in each

of its provinces and has frequently moved about from one to
another. One is a European when one has become a *civis Ro-
manus*. (EL, 12)

Unquestionably, this is an immense and inspiring goal that Curtius proposes for literary scholarship. But we must ask whether his
conception of a European totality can serve as the basis for a viable
and secure methodology for historical criticism. Or is it no more
than a heuristic principle, the humanist's passionate effort to reor-
ganize and preserve his inheritance against the threat of disintegra-
tion? It might be said that Curtius makes no claim for any general
method, that what he offers in *European Literature* is only a propae-
deutic for further historical and critical studies. On one occasion
he does indeed write that topology (*Toposforschung*) represents
for him simply "a heuristic, an *ars inveniendi*" (GA, 106). In
European Literature he notes that that work may be viewed as a
Nova Rhetorica (EL, 128), a *thesaurus* (EL, 394) whose function
it is to preserve what may be of use in a forthcoming period of
cultural rebirth. He likens the present situation to the cultural
eclipse of the early Middle Ages: "Even in times of educational
atrophy and of anarchy the heritage of the European mind, which
is bound up with language and literature, can be fostered, as was
the case in the monasteries of the early Middle Ages under the
assaults of barbarians and Saracens" (EL, 394). But the limitations of such a justification are clear enough, and Curtius was not
blind to them. He saw that the cultural storehouse always has a
touch of the sepulchral: it can easily decline into a repository of
dead monuments. Thus, though the collecting, the antiquarian
instinct was strong in him, it represented only part of a more complex and ambitious endeavor. "A medieval scholarship which went
no further than philology could never satisfy me," he wrote, "Out
of the detailed labor of philology there must be formed a historical
viewpoint that will disclose new structures of the mind" (GA, 118).
It was through topology that Curtius sought a new synthetic method
firmly grounded upon the data of philology.

The notion of topoi derives from the art of rhetoric. Topoi are
defined as "storehouses of trains of thought," Quintilian's "argu-
mentorum sedes" (EL, 70). In the rhetoric of Antiquity they were
primarily aids in argumentation: patterns of organization and at
the same time ideas conventionally associated with such patterns.

With the breakup of the Roman judicial and political organization, the rhetorical system that had evolved in it comes to penetrate other areas, particularly that of the literary genres. It becomes in late Antiquity, Curtius tells us, "the common denominator of literature in general," and consequently, ". . . the topoi too acquire a new function. They become clichés, which can be used in any form of literature, they spread to all spheres of life with which literature deals and to which it gives form" (EL, 70). This development suggests an altogether new category, what Curtius calls "historical topics." These can no longer be derived from rhetorical forms and are, in effect, themes characteristic of specific epochs. To view them as topoi emphasizes their historically determined nature, though ultimately they may derive from universal and timeless themes such as the beauty of nature, love, friendship, transience. Curtius argues that by tracing the "genesis of new topoi" we can uncover "indications of a changed psychological state" in the history of the West, "indications which are comprehensible in no other way" (EL, 82), and he suggests further that Jung's theory of archetypes provides a confirmation for such an approach.

This summary in no way does justice to the dense, subtly differentiated fabric that emerges from Curtius's assemblage and grouping of the topoi themselves. The scope, the discrimination, and modernity of his synthesis have been often acknowledged. If I concentrate here on his theoretical statements rather than on the over-all design of *European Literature*, it is to examine whether such a reservation as Leo Spitzer's is justified: "Personally, I am not convinced that topology is a new *method*—it is only a new, a very rich, source of historical information which finds its place within the age-old inquiry into outward sources—it represents indeed a more systematic approach to the ultimate outward sources." [10] By examining Curtius's justifications for topology we may be better able to assess what it can mean for us, that is, for criticism at this time.

Two qualities recur repeatedly in Curtius's discussion of the topoi—their *concrete* nature and their function as *constants*, as signs of endurance. The distinctive virtue of topology for Curtius may be summarized in this way: The topoi represent concrete, empirically verifiable data which can reveal of themselves—through their

[10] From Spitzer's review of *European Literature*, in *AJP*, LXX (1949), 429.

survival in successive periods—certain constants of all literary forms.

In one sense this ideal of concreteness represents a reaction to the tradition of *Geistesgeschichte*. At the beginning of this century this movement was itself a reaction, fed by neo-Idealist and neo-Romantic impulses, against the positivistic historicism of the later nineteenth century. It did not so much reject the historical and methodological achievements of positivism as seek to integrate them with a new spirit in psychology and aesthetics. But later in its development, particularly in the twenties, *Geistesgeschichte* came increasingly to signify, in the words of a recent historian of the movement, " an absolute autonomy of the spiritual, which functions in terms of an ahistorical or phenomenological typology and thus continually moves into an ' Expressionistic ' sphere." [11] It is against this tendency that Curtius polemicizes in the first chapter of *European Literature* (see esp. pp. 11-12). He attacks *Geistesgeschichte* for being reductive, for subsuming a mass of diverse phenomena under a few qualities or essences. He feels that it tends to view historical epochs as closed systems, their general terms being derived from aesthetics, metaphysics, national character, or a combination of these and yet other categories. The uniqueness of historical and aesthetic phenomena is obliterated in favor of an all-encompassing, homogeneous *Weltanschauung*. The very connotation of this last term for many Anglo-American readers—grandiose, inflated, amorphous—conveys something of the spirit of Curtius's own reaction to *Geistesgeschichte*.

In its place he wants to evolve a historical method that will preserve the material of literature, leaving it " in whatever form it found it," but at the same time " unraveling " and " penetrating " it; a method that will " ' decompose ' the material (after the fashion of chemistry with its reagents) and make its structures visible " (EL, 15). The necessary point of departure for such a procedure, he continues, " can only be discovered empirically." Thus, certain rhetorical conventions (like " affected modesty "), certain themes (like the Muses), certain stylistic attitudes (like Mannerism) are chosen as " phenomena so concrete in themselves and so clear genealogically that they resist any attempt at wire-drawn interpretation on the part of *Geistesgeschichte* " (EL, 292). In spite of their

[11] Jost Hermand in *Literaturwissenschaft und Kunstwissenschaft*, Sammlung Metzler, Stuttgart, 1965, pp. 28-9. My translation.

obvious diversity, even their difference of kind, Curtius considers such phenomena significant for their facticity, their concreteness: "When we have isolated and named a literary phenomenon, we have established one fact. At that one point we have penetrated the concrete structure of the matter of literature" (EL, 383).

As a reaction against *Geistesgeschichte*, then, Curtius's position is understandable. Yet we must seek for a more positive justification as to why topology offers a concreteness hitherto unavailable to literary studies. The most sustained argument on this point comes in the course of a distinction which Curtius draws between literary texts and other aesthetic phenomena, notably those studied by art history:

> . . . [literature] has an autonomous structure, which is essentially different from that of the visual arts. . . . [it] has different forms of movement, of growth, of continuity, from art. It possesses a freedom which is denied to art. For literature, all the past is present, or can become so. . . . I can take up Homer or Plato at any hour, I "have" him then, and have him wholly. . . . Works of art I have to contemplate in museums. The book is more real by far than the picture. Here we have a truly ontological relationship and a real participation in an intellectual entity. (EL, 14)

What Curtius is attacking specifically here is the widespread tendency of *Geistesgeschichte* to combine the methods of literary and art history, an approach inspired to a large degree by Heinrich Wölfflin and given its most famous formulation by Oskar Walzel as "wechselseitige Erhellung der Künste" (reciprocal illumination of the arts). However pertinent Curtius's point may be here— and criticism of recent decades has, of course, been predominantly on his side—Curtius is still very far from having demonstrated the unique concreteness in any ontological sense of a literary text.

Curtius's notion of a text remains too inert, too undifferentiated to serve the purpose that he envisaged, such as his aim of charting changes in the "psychological state" of Western history by means of topology. It is true that he has reminded us that certain texts presuppose other texts, that literature is part of the experience of literature. But the relationships of texts to each other are not the whole of literature, and the *how?* and *how much?* regarding these relationships remain relatively undeveloped in *European Literature*.

Furthermore, the idea that one can "have" an author, and "have him wholly" in taking up a volume of his works, though of course consciously overstated by Curtius, suggests nonetheless a reified conception both of the act of understanding and the process of creativity. The act of interpretation would seem to become super- fluous. The collected texts of an author are presumed to be the wholly adequate and transparent embodiment of his thought. In another passage Curtius writes, "Only in words does mind speak its own language. Only in the creative word is it in its perfect freedom: above concept, above doctrine, above precept" (EL, 394). Certain assumptions in Curtius's argument need to be brought out here. First, that the mind's "own language" is in fact language; second, that "texts" have preserved a comprehensive or at least adequately representative record of human thought; and third, that these texts yield their full meaning in juxtaposition with each other without the illumination of ancillary disciplines such as philosophy and history.

By distinguishing the "creative word" from "concept, doctrine, precept" Curtius wants to establish a delimited, readily accessible segment of language, a kind of equivalence of the thought process that reflects it more accurately, more concretely, than any such systematic disciplines as metaphysics or theology. This "creative" element represents for him essentially no more than the successive variations which certain forms or themes undergo in the course of time. Now it is true that such series of variations may reveal innate patterns of their own. This, in effect, is the life of topoi. But Curtius does not sufficiently allow that the successive stages of such a process are more than simply variations or mutations of earlier ones. Each stage, insofar as it is truly creative, represents an inten- tional articulation that transcends the antecedent structure. And this intentional articulation, by going beyond the word, is subject to the same problems of interpretation as "concept, doctrine, precept."

Thus, while rejecting *Geistesgeschichte* and seeking to introduce a new concreteness into literary studies, Curtius did not really come to terms with the issues of historical interpretation. In spite of his preoccupation with historical method, his conception of a text is remarkably ahistorical. Fundamentally, he viewed literary texts as coextensive and timeless. This assumption served as a guarantee of the truth of tradition and more especially of its availability, its preservation. It was thus a cornerstone of Curtius's humanistic faith, but it failed to account for that historical moment in which a text enters the cultural heritage and makes manifest a truth hitherto unavailable to it, a truth which both adds to and transforms that heritage. Curtius viewed the topoi as concrete in a double sense: first, as authentic remnants of a historical moment and then as constants of literature, symbols of the endurance of man's mind. But the discrepancy between these two levels did not seriously occupy him. His greatest concern was with the latter, and he viewed the former, the topoi in their historical limitation, primarily as illustrations for a level of enduring spiritual reality, thus slighting the problem of how the topoi become stages in an autonomous historical process.

When Curtius does look at historical change, when he speaks of a "vast passing away and renewal" of tradition (EL, 393), he is concerned not so much with the substance of literature, its forms or themes, as with its material bases (manuscripts, books) or, more important, with what he calls "the transmissional techniques," in short, the humanistic labor of preservation and transmission. In the essay "Humanism as Initiative" he had already introduced the notion of a "biology of tradition," whereby he meant a cycle of barbarism and enlightenment, the alternating loss and recovery of the literary forms.[12] In *European Literature* we read,

> . . . [the creative word] is safeguarded, but it is also emptied and externalized by the transmissional techniques of grammar, rhetoric, the "liberal arts," the schools. These techniques are not an end in themselves, nor is continuity. They are aids to memory. Upon memory rests the individual's consciousness of his identity above all change. The literary tradition is the medium by which the European mind preserves its identity through the milleniums. (EL, 394-95)

Between the two levels—the "transmissional techniques" and the storehouse of memory—there would seem to be no possibility of organic relationship. It is a dichotomy that must virtually paralyze the study of historical process in literature.

Admittedly, I am bearing down strongly on a passage that makes no pretensions to logical precision, one that is in fact a fine example of Curtius's impassioned, metaphorical mode of argumentation.

[12] Cf. DG, p. 114.

But it is clear that what guided his scholarly investigations was the vision of what Hofmannstahl (quoted by Curtius) has called, " a certain eternal European mythology: names, concepts, structures linked to some higher meaning, personified forces of the moral or mythical order " (KE, 151). Criticism, Curtius believed, could draw together from poets of all times the elements of such a mythological system and thus " contribute to the great task that has fallen to mankind since the destruction of the tower of Babel: restoration of unity " (KE, 409). From such a passage it is evident that Curtius's topology is not so much a means of investigating the transformations of literary forms as a compendium that might testify to an ultimate, mystically irreducible level of intellectual reality. Thus he could write, " A topos is something anonymous. It flows into the author's pen as a literary reminiscence. It has a temporal and spatial omnipresence like a sculptural motif. Topology resembles an ' art history without names ' in contrast to the history of individual masters. It can advance to the impersonal stylistic forms. In these impersonal stylistic elements we touch on a layer of historical life which is more deeply imbedded than that of individual invention." [13] A critic may well believe in such a " deeper layer of historical life " and he unquestionably must at times concern himself with " impersonal stylistic forms." But the question at issue is whether Curtius has found a way of converting this belief into a working method adequate to the present age.

Spitzer has written that when one reads some of Curtius's demonstrations of the endurance of topoi through centuries, " one feels as though the world-clock stood still; man appears here as a being consisting in continuity." But then he goes on to consider what motivated Curtius to abandon the approach of his earlier work and to devote himself to medieval studies and the elaboration of the topological method in the thirties and forties: ". . . is not the insight into such a basic conservatism of man an antidote against the feeling of helplessness engendered by the vista of chaotic dismemberment and of the crumbling of tradition that the world of today offers us? " Spitzer asks.[14] That Curtius should have undertaken so rigorously disciplined an approach as a response to the cultural barbarism of the Nazi period is, of course, all to his honor.

---

[13] " Zur Literarästhetik des Mittelalters II," ZRPh, LVIII (1938), 139.
[14] Spitzer, loc. cit., p. 428.

But one wonders with Spitzer whether in doing so he did not too harshly repress the superbly intuitive approach of his work of the twenties and return to the source studies of an older positivism, even though his motive for such studies was a new one.

Curtius discerned value in literature with an artist's intuition; he collected and treasured such excellence with a humanist's zeal. These are remarkable enough qualities in a critic. But his aim in *European Literature* goes further. The book was conceived as much more than a compendium. It was meant to demonstrate that a thematics and a typology of literature can serve as a history of the human spirit in an exceptionally pure and direct fashion. Yet one feels that Curtius's preservative humanism was not congenial to such a task; it kept him aloof from the contingent and fluid quality of historical processes. Maurice Merleau-Ponty, though writing in a different connection, gives a helpful analysis of the issue at stake:

> S'il y a un humanisme aujourd'hui, il se défait de l'illusion que Valéry a bien désignée en parlant de "ce petit homme qui est dans l'homme et que nous supposons toujours." . . . Le "petit homme qui est dans l'homme," ce n'est que le fantôme de nos opérations expressives réussies, et l'homme qui est admirable, ce n'est pas ce fantôme, c'est celui qui, installé dans son corps fragile, dans un language qui a déjà tant parlé, dans une histoire titubante, se rassemble et se met à voir, à comprendre, à signifier. L'humanisme d'aujourd'hui . . . ne parle plus de l'homme et de l'esprit que sobrement, avec pudeur: l'esprit et l'homme ne *sont* jamais, ils transparaissent dans le mouvement par lequel le corps se fait geste, le langage œuvre. . . .[15]

Aesthetic thought in recent decades has been intensely concerned with the ways in which the flux of personal and historical experience is distilled into "works" of art, into literary "texts." The notion of a work or a text is no more self-evident than, as Merleau-Ponty suggests, is that of spirit and of man, and any critical method that aims at a comprehensive view of literary forms needs to show fullest awareness of the historical genesis of such forms.

Curtius was filled by regret for the loss of a humanistic canon, Through his investigations of analogies and continuities he sought to recover such a canon—one that might be accepted in this age not through the authority of precedent but because of patterns inherent in the very processes of literary creation. But one feels

[15] Maurice Merleau-Ponty, *Signes*, Paris, 1960, p. 305.

that he was temperamentally disinclined to dealing with these processes in the full complexity and multiplicity of their historical horizon. He sought to meet the demands of this age by validating in historical terms the kind of canon he envisaged. But for himself this canon had always been an article of faith, fundamentally beyond history.

Bibliographical Note. A bibliography of Curtius's writings can be found in *Freundesgabe für Ernst Robert Curtius*, Bern, 1956, pp. 213-34. In addition to the du Bos and Spitzer pieces already cited, the following have proved valuable to me:

General essays on Curtius: Leo Cavelti, "Ernst Robert Curtius als Kritiker," *Neue Schweizer Rundschau*, N. F. XVIII (1950-51), 467-72; Karl August Horst, "Zur Methode von Ernst Robert Curtius," *Merkur*, X (1956), 303-13; F. P. Pickering, "On Coming to Terms with Curtius," *GLL*, XI (1957-58), 335-45; Otto Pöggeler, "Dichtungstheorie und Toposforschung," *Jb. f. Ästhetik u. allgm. Kunstwissenschaft*, V (1960), 89-201. (This study, basing itself not only on Curtius but on Auerbach and others, seeks to establish topology as a general critical method. Its chief value lies in an imposing collection of quotations on the subject by various critics. But its terminology is so imprecise as to make it of little value as a theoretical discussion.) The only substantial study of Curtius that I have seen since the original publication of the above essay is one by Arthur R. Evans, Jr., in *On Four Modern Humanists—Hofmannsthal, Gundolf, Curtius, Kantorowicz*, edited by A. R. Evans, Jr., Princeton, 1970, pp. 85-145— a study particularly valuable for its biographical data on Curtius.

Some reviews of *European Literature*: Erich Auerbach in *RF*, LXII (1950), 237-45, and in *MLN*, LXV (1950), 348-51; Walter Bulst in *Wirkendes Wort*, III (1952-53), 56-58; H. Kuhn in *DVLG*, XXIV (1950), 530-44, see esp. 531-33; Arno Schirokauer in *JEGP*, IL (1950), 395-99; Max Wehrli in *Anzeiger f. dt. Altert.*, LXIV (1950), 84-91; Paul Zumthor in *ZRPh*, LXVI (1950), 151-69.

1966

INTRODUCTION TO GASTON BACHELARD ❧ JACQUES EHRMANN ❧

Before dealing with Bachelard, the literary critic, it seems relevant to recall that he was formerly a philosopher of sciences. He had already spent an important part of his career writing books and essays on scientific topics when, in 1938, he undertook his first "literary" work. This change, which appears so radical and of which there are very few examples in our modern times of intense specialization, concerns only the object of his inquiry (literature instead of science), but not his method. It is only later—during what one might consider his third phase—that the method changed. Leaving aside his work on science, we shall limit ourselves to an exposition and analysis of the phases related to Bachelard's literary career.

How did this shift from science to literature occur? When he undertook the investigation of "the formation of scientific thought," Bachelard's intention as indicated in the subtitle of his book, was to psychoanalyze objective knowledge. He wished to purify it of all possible remnants of the magical, the irrational, the "literary," and the theological which were at the core of such pre-scientific disciplines as astrology, alchemy, and medecine and which unconsciously persisted through the centuries in the minds of the scientists in spite of their claims to absolute objectivity. To illustrate his point, Bachelard wrote a psychoanalysis of fire, which was to be the first of his four psychoanalyses of the basic Elements of alchemy (fire, water, air, earth).

This first psychoanalysis is still clearly addressed to men of science. It is meant to serve a curative function in as much as it warns the scientist against his own unconscious reactions which may falsify,

or tarnish, a " purely " scientific (i. e. rational) outlook: " Ces convictions non discutées sont autant de lumières parasites qui trou-
blent les légitimes claretés que l'esprit doit amasser dans un effort
discursif. Il faut que chacun s'attache à détruire en soi-même ces
convictions non discutées." In other words, Bachelard's intention is
to " wise up " (déniaiser) the scientist, to warn him against his own
naïveté.

In the course of this small volume, this critic identifies and
studies four major fire complexes: the Prometheus complex, defined as " the Oedipus complex of intellectual life," a desire to know
as much as or more than our fathers, our masters; the Empedocles
complex, the urge to renew life by destroying it; the Novalis complex, fire as sexual heat rather than as light; and finally the Hoff-
man complex, the punch, that is to say, water as fire. These
complexes help Bachelard identify the " valorized image " that, he
feels, lies at the origin of one's imagination and gives it, so to speak,
a particular dye. Hence, for example, the different " value " of
alcohol for Poe and Hoffmann.

After studying these complexes with the extreme sensitivity and
subtlety that characterizes all of his writings, Bachelard concludes
his essay by arguing that such a method might be useful in the study
of literary texts. A psychoanalysis of this kind, he says, would open
up a new route to an objective literary criticism.

His next book, L'eau et les rêves, deals, from the start, with
problems of literature and literary criticism. Science is not even
used any more as a pretext. Bachelard's purpose is to reveal the
relationship between formal imagination (l'imagination formelle)
and material imagination (l'imagination materielle) that is to say
the imagination of matter, of substances: " Pour qu'une rêverie se
poursuive avec assez de constance pour donner une œuvre écrite,
pour qu'elle ne soit pas simplement la vacance d'une heure fugitive,
il faut qu'elle trouve sa matière, il faut qu'un élément matériel lui
donne sa propre substance, sa propre règle, sa poétique spécifique."

Thus, to a certain type of rêverie corresponds a certain type of
image, or the opposite. The psychoanalysis of the images of the
work that Bachelard practices, consists in the discovery of the
guiding image, or the guiding substance, with which other images,
or images of other substances mix.

Such a position leads Bachelard to express a new cogito which
could be formulated thus: I imagine, therefore I am; or, in the
critic's own words: " Je suis fait de la matière de mon rêve." I do

not, however, *know* this matter. It is given to me, *through* my imagination and *with* my dream; at the same time form and content of my dream, "attitude irréfléchie qui commande le travail même de la réflexion."

Bachelard shows, for example, in the case of Edgar Poe (one of his favorite poets) the rare unity (*la monotonie géniale*) of this poet's dreams: "Sous ses mille formes, l'imagination cache une substance privilegiée, une substance active qui détermine l'unité, la hiérarchie de l'expression." This substance is "heavy water" (*l'eau lourde*) and Bachelard procedes to show that "toute eau primitivement claire est pour Edgar Poe une eau qui doit s'assombrir, une eau qui va absorber la noire souffrance. Toute eau vive est une eau dont le destin est de s'alentir, de s'alourdir." And it never goes the other way around. A dark, heavy water never becomes clear and light.

This investigation of the unconscious zones of our "material imagination" is pursued in *L'air et les songes*. It is now the mobility of imagination which seeks the attention of the critic, a mobility characterized by a double sublimation: discursive when the dreamer is in quest of an "*au dela*" (the City of God); dialectic when in quest of an "*à côté*" (utopia, imaginary voyage). But what interests Bachelard is neither the "*au dela*" nor the "*à côté*" in their unavoidable immobility, it is the itinerary (*le trajet*) which leads imagination from here to there, "ce trajet continu du réél à l'imagination."

Two volumes on the imagination of the earth complete Bachelard's psychoanalysis of the Elements. In one of them, *La terre et les rêveries de la volonté*, he studies the *rêveries* which induce to act upon matter, and calls this type of imagination the extrovert imagination; in the other volume, *La terre et les rêveries du repos*, he analyzes the images of intimacy or introvert imagination.

If we do not go into a detailed analysis of each of Bachelard's psychoanalyses of the Elements, it is because we feel it less important to make a complete and detailed inventory of the themes of imagination revealed by such a method (we can always go back to the particular book dealing with the kind of images we are concerned with in our particular project) than to see what kind of relationship Bachelard establishes between imagination (*l'imaginaire*) and reality (*le réél*). To the preeminence of reality over imagination that can be found in all psychologies which base the imagination process on perception of images, and thus automatically impoverish imagination by turning the image into a weakened perception; to the preeminence of reality over imagination which grants imagination only the power to re-produce, Bachelard opposes a productive imagination: " A elle appartient cette *fonction de l'irréél* qui est psychiquement aussi utile que la fonction du réél." He inverts the established relationship between perception and image. To " bien voir " he opposes " bien rêver."

Having reached this stage in the development of Bachelard's system, we should pause for a moment and ask ourselves a few questions on its validity.

By taking the four Elements of alchemy as his tools for a literary investigation; and using psychoanalysis as his method, Bachelard believes he has found the ideal position. He can stand at the crossroads where myth and knowledge, poetry and science, meet. According to him, both the tool (the imagination of Elements) and the method (psychoanalysis) belong to both the domain of imagination and of science. Therefore, cumulating the advantages of the two, the subtlety of the former and the rigor of the latter, the study of literature would gain in precision and in depth.

It is true that literary criticism in France gained a lot from the kind of investigation started by Bachelard. He helped—maybe more and certainly earlier than any other single critic—to rid French criticism of the dogmatic rules of the historical school, by opening new vistas on the examination of texts. And there is not one critic today in France who does not owe something to Bachelard.

Though it may be attributed to the Prometheus complex labeled by Bachelard, we would like to show that, in spite of the qualities of inventiveness and sensitivity manifest in his work, which can still be of great profit to all, this critic failed on two counts to surmount a contradiction resting at the root of his endeavor.

On the one hand, by assuming he can use psychoanalysis as a method of objective knowledge, Bachelard assimilates his object (i. e. the *rêverie,* or matter as it is dreamed by the poet) to a " natural " object without making any point of the particular intentionality which is to be found in any " artistic " object. In other words, the flame, water, earth, air *in the work* cannot be the same Elements as the ones observed and manipulated by the scientist. The poetic flame is a flame already made language. And although Bachelard studies it *in* and *through* language, this fact never constitutes a problem for him. Such a distinction is conjured away.

On the other hand, and inversely, when he writes: " under its thousand forms, imagination hides a privileged substance, an active substance which determines the unity and hierarchy of poetic expression," he believes he can, behind a specific expression, dig out a specific substance. We are then entitled to ask him: which substance, if not the one offered in and by the expression? Thus, it is precisely at the very moment when the object (i. e. the substance) can only be interpreted through its expression (i. e. poetic language) that this object loses its "objectivity." Consequently, this method, failing to reach the goal it had set, is reduced to a merely subjective commentary lacking the guarantee of the objectivity it pretended to offer.

Such is the vicious circle in which Bachelard is led through his psychoanalytical study of the Elements. In spite of such shortcomings, Bachelard's contribution to literary criticism would already have been of exceptional significance, had he stopped writing then. But, growing aware of the problems raised by his method, he switched to a radically different one with his next book, *The Poetics of Space*, and opened the third phase of his intellectual career.

In 1957, having reached an age when most do not bother to question their own work and methods, Bachelard has the courage to change and re-evaluate their efficiency. Psychoanalysis, he says, is no longer appropriate to his purpose. It presupposes that the origin of the image can and has to be found outside the image itself, depriving the critic of a genuine intimacy with the poetic image and/or imagination. It is precisely this intimacy that Bachelard seeks and finds now in a phenomenology of imagination. " By this should be understood a study of the phenomenon of the poetic image when it emerges into the consciousness as a direct product of the heart, soul and being of man apprehended in his actuality."

Instead of looking for a causal relationship between the image and what makes it such, instead of going from the present of the image to its past, as he used to, Bachelard prefers "l'écouter dans son retentissement."

> Par ce retentissement, en allant tout de suite au dela de toute psychologie ou psychanalyse, nous sentons un pouvoir poétique qui se lève naïvement en nous-mêmes. . . . Cette image que la lecture du poème nous offre, la voici qui devient vraiment nôtre. . . . Elle devient un être nouveau de notre langage . . . elle est à la fois un devenir d'expression et un devenir de notre être. Ici, l'expression crée de l'être.

The communion of the poet and his reader, sought by Bachelard, inclines him to examine the images of space primarily for their potential of happiness found in the remembrance of space lost and its recapturing. Thus, the feeling of space is a feeling of harmony, peace, intimacy; it calls to mind images of the house, with its protective corners, the hut, the nest, the shell, finally and *essentially* the circle which delimits the inside from the outside.

In his last books, *La Poétique de la rêverie* and *La Flamme d'une chandelle* the personal, intimate and at the same time cosmic character of *rêverie*, grows and allows the author to reach a plane of perfect detachment and identification of reading and *rêverie*, of memories and *rêverie*, of the candle and the *rêverie*, of the world and the work, of the author and the reader:

> Voici alors l'image simple, le tableau central dans le clair-obscur des songes et du souvenir. Le rêveur est à sa table; il est en sa mansarde; il allume sa lampe. Il allume une chandelle. Il allume sa bougie. Alors je me souviens, alors je me retrouve: je suis le veilleur qu'il est. J'étudie comme il étudie. Le monde est pour moi, comme pour lui, le livre difficile éclairé par la flamme d'une chandelle. Car la chandelle, compagne de solitude, est surtout compagne du travail solitaire. La chandelle n'éclaire pas une cellule vide, elle éclaire un livre.

However moved we may be by Bachelard's genuine serenity and wisdom we cannot help feeling that such a critical process (if the term " critical " still applies?) involves as much risk as the one represented by his previous method, although inverted. Bachelard's ontology is untenable. The poetical image that he places at the origin cannot be original. When he writes that " the poetic image . . . emerges into the consciousness, as a direct product of the heart, soul, and being of men," he cannot explain to us how it emerges, and in whose consciousness. We are not told if it is in the poet-dreamer's consciousness (that is, the dreamer who *produces* the poetical image) or in the reader-dreamer who re-produces it through the experience of reading, even if, as Bachelard would like us to have it, the reader-dreamer re-creates the image. How then can this phenomenology be applied if the reader-dreamer-critic dissolves into the object of his inquiry, into the image?

Such a method supposes a pure adherence or a complete fusion of one subjectivity (the reader's) to another (the poet's), regardless of the cultural and historical differences which cannot, in our opinion, be set aside without falsifying the act of criticism.

Furthermore, when he asks the following rhetorical question: "When a dreamer speaks, who speaks, he or the world?" Bachelard admits the possibility of a fusion between the subject and the object of *rêverie*. This fusion, I am afraid, leads to confusion. Thus, at last, in spite of this double assimilation of the reader-dreamer to the poet-dreamer, and of the dreamed to the dreaming, Bachelard is compelled to promote *rêverie* to an unquestioned and unquestionable status, to make of it a category of judgment and being, as a matter of fact, *the* unifying category; he is compelled to endow it with a particular objectivity, which is however impossible to do since it is, as we have just seen, stuffed with subjectivism. The dangers of adopting Bachelard's method, uncritically, lie in a fragmentation of points of view on poetic imagination (the imagination of fire, water, air, space, etc.), with, as its consequence, a fragmentation of the object of criticism. The work, the poem, as totalities, are lost for the sake of identification and description of specific images singled out as illustrative but not related to the whole.

This atomistic conception of the critical activity forces the critic to adopt categories uncritically (however *basic* they may appear), as the frame through which poetic imagination is channeled and sifted. We could be asked why, then, pursue this critic with our criticism; why bother at all with his methods and findings if they are so untrustworthy? In spite of our reservations, we owe a great debt to Bachelard. As we stated before, it is he who broke for the first time with the tradition of historical criticism prevailing among French critics. Bachelard's inestimable contribution was to force the critic to turn to the work itself.

This does not mean, however, that he satisfied himself with the analysis of the merely "visible" forms of the work, as once did the New Critics. More radically, his primary concern was to reach, through and in literary creation, the very structure of imagination, and give to *l'imaginaire* the priority it ought to have in the appraisal of any work of art.

If it were only on these two counts, our debt to Bachelard would already be great. But there is in him, also, a rare quality of modesty in the act of reading, and a devotion for the thing read, that demands our admiration. Bachelard is the exemplary poet-reader that too few critics bother to be.

1966

SARTRE'S CRITICISM ❧ BY OTTO HAHN ❧

To understand—such is Sartre's project. But what does he seek to understand and how does he go about it? By describing the successive stages of his thought and method, from his first critical essays in the *N. R. F.* to his *Flaubert* in progress, we shall seek the answers he has given and the techniques he has used. And in so doing we shall follow the different directions of his interest and his various attempts to work out the nature of understanding, which he reviews in his *Critique de la Raison Dialectique.*

For the sake of simplicity one can divide his critical work into two parts, separated by the Korean war of 1951: the study of consciousness on the one hand, the study of history on the other.

All of the first part is governed by an almost Heideggerian question: How is thought possible? But the German philosopher poses the problem very abstractly and in general terms: How did thought arise? How did being one day become conscious of itself? Sartre poses the problem in more realistic terms: How does consciousness function? Right through his *Baudelaire* [1947] the study of the mode of being of consciousness is the ultimate question that dominates his critical enterprise.

The organization of Sartre's critical work reveals itself from the time of "Une Idée Fondamentale de Husserl" [1939], in which he describes the ontological mode of consciousness and proposes a phenomenological and anti-subjectivist interpretation. Appealing to Husserl, he empties consciousness of its "content" and, taking psychologism as foil to his own views, he proposes a consciousness projected "onto the road, into the city, into the midst of the crowd. . . ." "Here we are, liberated from Proust," he announces, "and at the same time liberated from the *inner life.*"

At this period the young Sartre wants to go beyond subjective

This essay has been translated from the French by Catherine and Richard Macksey. The works by Sartre treated in this essay are *Situations I* (1947); *Baudelaire* (1947); *Saint-Genet, Comédien et Martyr* (1952); and *Critique de la Raison Dialectique* (1960), all published by Gallimard.

attitudes. To do this, he turns away from human " conduct," seeking only to determine the intelligibility of phenomenological structures and proposing to constitute " a new treatise on the passions " which will study " the properties of things and of beings." This objectivist realism, which permits him to escape from the idealism which has dominated his training, is all the easier for him because, having enjoyed a privileged childhood, he is not encumbered by the morbid universe of infantile attachments—so he doesn't believe in its existence. Optimistically, then, he organizes universal ideas with a view to some future phenomenological encyclopedia. And immediately, as though this imaginary status of reality were already established, he considers particularities (infantile fixations, contradictions, anguish) to be realities falsely assumed, inauthentic attitudes. This position was to turn him away from what constitutes the very stuff of the novelistic universe.

And yet he is drawn to certain novels, even admires them, but without believing in them. How can one love without believing? Sartre has the impression that his assent is cozened from him— seduced by appearances, he is taken in. He wants to find the secret of this seduction so as to rip off the mask, and he scrutinizes novels looking for the trick, the treachery, the artifice. In his first literary article, devoted to *Sartoris* [1938], he tries to catch Faulkner red-handed. Falling back on the description of consciousness (consciousness, according to Sartre, is always consciousness of something), he analyzes the characters. Finding nothing in the consciousness of old Bayard Sartoris, Sartre has the impression that Faulkner is hiding a secret which does not exist. " Is he the dupe of his art? Is he lying to us? " asks Sartre. Thanks to a bad novel, he thinks he has exposed the mystification. But studying other novels from the point of view of the ontology of the consciousness, he encounters the same problem and tries to solve it with an appeal to the vague notion of beauty: " The world of Dos Passos is impossible—like that of Faulkner, of Kafka, of Stendhal—because it is contradictory. But that is why it is beautiful: beauty is a veiled contradiction " [1938].

In his essay on Mauriac [1939] Sartre proceeds forthwith to develop the implications of his formula: the excellence of the novelist bears no relation to his errors; inauthenticity and partiality of viewpoint are of little importance if the author respects the structures of consciousness and its temporal openness toward a free future.

Sartre, who seemed in the beginning to be implicitly wondering " How does it happen, since there is *one* objective reality, that there are also novels? " goes beyond the notion of veiled contradiction and writes: " Art lives by appearances alone." And at the conclusion of his Mauriac essay, he specifies: " There is no room for a privileged observer." In recognizing the partiality of viewpoint Sartre leads up to the notion of " situation," which he broaches for the first time in his review of Nabokov's *La Méprise* [1939]. Here the understanding of the book, for the first time in Sartre, is joined to the understanding of the author. By linking the situation of the author with the subject of the novel, with its particular stylistic devices and tics, Sartre demonstrates its organic unity. The understanding of the author comes from the revelation of this unity.

In his " Temporality in Faulkner " [1939], written at the same period, Sartre defines the critic's task: first to delineate the author's metaphysics, then to evaluate [*apprécier*] his technique. By " evaluate " Sartre means: compare the construction of the novel with the particular mode of being of consciousness, a mode of being related to the author's metaphysical concepts. Then in conclusion Sartre pronounces judgment on Faulkner's implicit metaphysics, which leads him back to the contradiction already experienced with regard to most authors: " I like his art; I don't believe his metaphysics." [1]

Three years later, in 1943, Sartre takes up the notion of the absurd and of existence, that is, the position of man in the world, his relation to others. Camus's *L'Etranger* gives him the opportunity to develop his own concepts. His method remains the same. Taking the *Myth of Sisyphus* as his basis, he defines Camus's metaphysics, then evaluates the technique of *L'Etranger* (grammatical construction and narrative plot).

The relationship between Being and Existence leads him to consider Bataille [1943]. At this point Sartre still believes in the

---

[1] Instead of "metaphysics " Sartre would now say " sense of the world" [*conception du monde*]. For support, compare two definitions: " a novelistic technique always reflects the novelist's metaphysics," which he wrote in 1938, was rephrased in 1957: "The style of an author is directly linked to a sense of the world," [*Critique de la Raison Dialectique*].

transcendence of existential structures, and Bataille is, it so happens, a man in search of a transcendence. But for Sartre, transcendence is the abstract framework of our existence, " the fundamental absurdity, the *facticity*, that is, the irreducible contingency of our *being-there*, of our purposeless and groundless existence." For Bataille transcendence would be the coincidence of Being and Existence—an unattainable desire. Perhaps, through Bataille, Sartre attempted to discover how a man launches into, and sticks doggedly to, an enterprise which is metaphysically unrealizable. It is here for the first time that Sartre probes the inner life of one of the authors he is studying; he does this on the level of the direction and the quality of inner experiences, but he stops just short of psychoanalysis.

" A New Mystic," the essay on Bataille, marks the conclusion of Sartre's first stage of development. He broadens his field to take in the problems of language ("Aller-Retour " on Brice Parain, 1944), and in " Man and Things," a study of Ponge (1944), he reaffirms his belief in the possibility of an objective knowledge reducible to existential qualities. But his method and the motivation which guides his criticism remain identical: a general problem concerns Sartre; he discovers this problem in an author; he determines the particular dialectic of the author and compares it with the dialectical structure of the problem (for example, the Absurd for Camus, as related to the phenomenology of the Absurd; Being and Existence for Bataille, compared to the real dialectic of Being and Existence).

This procedure casts onto the author studied the light of a *relative comprehension*. Sartre analyzes the author's central preoccupation, the form or the structures of his Project [*Projet*], but neglects the causes which have given birth to the Project. Why does Ponge turn away from History and confine his interest to Things? Why did Bataille involve himself in his impossible dream of transcendence? Sartre is more concerned with fitting the Project into a phenomenological description, as though he expected the phenomenological description to lead him to certainties and to lead men to authentic behavior.

The study of Bataille concludes with " the rest is a matter for psychoanalysis," while the study of Descartes [1947] poses the question of freedom. The *Baudelaire* [1947], takes up again the question of freedom and the question of psychoanalysis, left in abeyance at the end of the Bataille essay. This synthesis moves the Sartrian method further toward a broader totalization.

Sartre's *Baudelaire* proposes to retrace the history of a consciousness grappling with freedom; it is an attempt to relive a man's history from the inside. It is here, in Sartre's critical writings, that the notion of "original choice" [*choix originel*] appears. The study is divided into five parts: [2]

1. Baudelaire described objectively with reference to his choices (EN SOI).
2. Baudelaire as he felt himself to be (POUR SOI).
3. The World of the IMAGINATION, or the Baudelairian mind with reference to behavior.
4. Relationships with OTHERS.
5. The act of poetry [*Le fait poétique*].

In the first four stages Sartre describes Baudelaire at four different levels; the first two concern the *choices* of Baudelaire, the following two, his *conduct*.

1. Beginning with the original choice, the rift [*fêlure*], Sartre seeks the objective signification of Baudelaire; he describes his character and the way in which he manifests his singularity. This description is reinserted into the general context of childhood. It is in relation to a phenomenology of childhood and to a "transcendence of existential structures" that Sartre determines the situation and the objective signification of Baudelaire. The study moves forward on two planes—the particular and the general. Passing from the one to the other, Sartre proceeds by differential notations. In passing Sartre touches on general themes—Action, the Creative Act, the Revolutionary, and the Rebel. When he speaks of Baudelaire's attitude in the face of Christian principles, he compares it directly with the attitude of Gide. The discussion proceeds *by comparisons*. As in his preceding studies, Sartre inscribes an individual dialectic in the framework of a broader phenomenology.

2. Next Sartre comes back to Baudelaire's childhood and under-

---

[2] First section: pp. 17-59. Second section: pp. 59-114. Third section: pp. 114-53. Fourth section: pp. 153-99. Fifth section: pp. 199-224. Elsewhere the categories EN SOI, POUR SOI, etc., are used in the margin to characterize divisions, to define a general area rather than strict limits. [Page references are to the French text.]

takes a subjective description: how Baudelaire understands himself, understands Good and Evil; the impression he seeks to make on Others; the face Others present to him. To bring out the subjective attitude of Baudelaire, Sartre recreates the ambiance—the " insignificant " mother, " good old Ancelle "—and he gives his view of the Judges and persecutors Baudelaire has chosen for himself. The understanding of Baudelaire from the inside is possible only if reality is described to us at the same time, or at least given its proper weight by the critic.

3. After he finishes the portrait of Baudelaire, Sartre carefully examines traits of character, linking to them the structures that dominate the *constituting* [*constitution*] of the imaginary universe—horror of nature, cold, etc. Sartre places this constituting of the imaginary universe in the anti-naturalistic current of the nineteenth century. He studies in addition the existential qualities of the reality structured by Baudelaire: (a) Nature for Baudelaire—Plants, captive water, fecundity; and (b) The body and Woman for Baudelaire—love of artifice, theatrical dress, cult of frigidity, of whiteness, etc. By linking these qualities together in a synthesis, Sartre gives unity to the general movement of the Baudelairian Spirit [*l'Esprit Baudelairien*] and fixes its extreme limits.

4. Sartre then takes up dandyism, Baudelaire's social conduct. He first reviews the position and attitude of nineteenth-century artists in relation to the aristocracy, the bourgeoisie, the proletariat. Baudelaire affirms the singularity of his own behavior, and Sartre defines Baudelaire's singularity in relation to that of Flaubert, of Gautier, of Mérimée. Then Sartre returns to qualities already considered—affectation, fancy dress, mystification—and analyzes them as relationships with Others. Finally he explains briefly the significance of Time and Progress for Baudelaire.

5. Last, Sartre takes up the making of poetry [*le fait poétique*], linking it to Baudelaire's relationship with his past. He describes how Baudelaire seeks the synthesis of Being and Existence; then the level on which he wants to appropriate things and to bring about his fusion with them; and finally the way in which Baudelaire uses significations. The last ten pages of the book are devoted to a *living* portrait of Baudelaire.

Before drawing the final portrait, Sartre has made four cross-sectional cuts the internal framework of which is organized according to the same pattern; character traits are linked one with another and generate one another, while being continually confronted, as they develop, with reality or value judgments. The rhythm of dispersion-reconcentration, which characterizes Sartrian criticism, animates the work. And yet the four sections overlap, the same elements reappearing in each. Masochism, which is Baudelaire's concrete attempt to recover Being (first part, EN SOI), becomes, in the second part (POUR SOI), the search for Judges, the "consciousness in Evil" ["consicence dans le Mal"], self-punishing; manifests itself, in the third part (the IMAGINARY WORLD), in the accentuation of the notion of sin, the search for authority and frigidity in women—for "the frigid woman is the sexual incarnation of the Judge"; and is transformed, in the fourth part, into the seeking of punishment through provocation and sinking into Evil.

The look [le regard] is dealt with by turns as the reflexive look, the seeking of the look of Others, the gaze of the frigid woman, the pleasure of looking at Others, the look as possession by Others. The desire to horrify (second part) overlaps the desire to scandalize (fourth part). The series White-Frigid-Lunar is assimilated to Lucidity of Gaze [la Lucidité du regard], which in turn involves relations with Others, and these relations permit Sartre to go into the matter of eroticism.

This churning into the depths shows Sartre's determination to restore the unity of the character whose mechanisms he has dismantled. More than once he insists on this notion of dismantled mechanisms, because for Sartre not the EN SOI nor the POUR SOI nor the IMAGINARY WORLD can exist independently of the other levels. "The description we have attempted is inferior to a portrait in being successive, whereas the portrait is simultaneous," he writes. "The features mentioned here one after the other in fact overlap in an indissoluble synthesis in which each of them expresses at the same time both itself and all the others"; he speaks of "the interdependence of all instances of behavior. . . ."

To understand Baudelaire's character [personnage] means for Sartre, at this stage of his evolution, to understand Baudelaire's way of being, his relationship with himself, with the world—to understand a situation "transformed by an original choice." Sartre brings out the choices open to Baudelaire and indicates the reasons which led the poet to choose one way rather than another. Further, to understand a work means to recover the Baudelairian signification of language; in other words, to re-interpret language as Baudelaire's means of recovering Being.

Up to this point, through the works he studies, Sartre has one aim in view: to describe the way of being of consciousness, to define the contingent and the absurd. In writing his *Baudelaire,* Sartre's aim is not to show why the *Flowers of Evil* has an artistic value or causes an aesthetic emotion but rather to show that a consciousness clouded by an infantile fixation is not thereby alienated from its freedom, and that " the free choice of himself that a man makes is absolutely identifiable with what is called his destiny." In spite of this clarification, Sartre was roundly attacked by eminent critics, such as Bataille, Blanchot, Georges Blin, who accused him of having drawn up an indictment against the inauthentic conduct of Baudelaire without taking into consideration the authentic success of the *Flowers of Evil.*

In effect, art locates itself at an imaginary level which is not the carbon tracing of life. The imaginary does constitute itself on the basis of the lived, and in this order of ideas the description of the lived serves toward the understanding of the imagined, *but* the one does not totally account for the other. Hence the inauthentic conduct of an author does not automatically impugn the authenticity and the scope of his work.

So Sartre undertakes his *Saint-Genet, Comedian and Martyr,* published five years after the Baudelaire study in 1952, with the intention of offering a complete comprehension of a man and his work. At this point Sartre has already definitively abandoned his belief in the existence "of essences and types, artificially isolated." Having, with his *Baudelaire,* psychoanalyzed metaphysics, he no longer believes in it. This development, linked to the Korean war and to the failure of the Liberation, introduces into his work historical concerns. Thus the Genet study takes on a breadth which was lacking in the preceding book. The infantile fixation is no longer only a shock, a rift, but a fact which occurs against the background of a social conditioning—a sort of reflexive blow of the social milieu. The social milieu, moreover, is seen in a historical perspective and as alienation.

At the beginning of the work Sartre reveals the thrust of his method: " If we wish to understand this man and his universe, there is no other way than to reconstruct carefully, using the mythic representations which he gives us, the original event. . . . This method is obligatory: through the analysis of the myths to re-establish the facts in their true signification." In order to follow the progress of understanding according to Sartre, we shall give the schematic structure of his *Genet*. For the sake of clarity we are leaving aside Sartre's judgments, with the understanding that as he is speaking of Good, Evil, Beauty, of the Criminal, or of Masochism, he is redefining these notions, giving them values and fitting into them Genet's progress. We must emphasize that these value judgments are not peripheral, that they form an integral part of the process of comprehension; it is only through such judgments of general applicability that the adventure of Genet becomes comprehensible.[3]

I. CHILDHOOD: AT SEVEN

1) " *The melodious child dead in me long before the axe chops* Category [4] of *off my head."* * Sartre describes how the first " devi-
EN SOI and
POUR SOI   ation " came about. First he studies Genet EN SOI and situates him in society: the motherless child, the bastard, finds himself a misfit in the peasant community which is attached to the soil and to legitimate possession (Being and having). Then Sartre takes up the POUR SOI, describing the ecstasy of the bastard who challenges his bastardy by identifying with Sainthood (Being) and who on the other hand identifies himself with property through Theft (Having).

2) " *A vertiginous word."* Sartre studies the child-thief in the POUR AUTRUI perspective of the POUR AUTRUI: the bastard, surrounded and the relationship be- by suspicion, suddenly caught in the act; a word, which
tween the
POUR SOI and reflects the social order, gives the unconscious little
the POUR
AUTRUI   thief a special place in society. Sartre then goes into the rapport between the POUR SOI and the POUR AUTRUI: the child who steals is ˅going through the motions of a dreamer; caught, labeled in a single word, he becomes conscious and submits to his

---

[3] Readers not interested in the purely technical outline of the Genet may want to skip to page ——.

[4] These categories, noted under a number or a letter, indicate the general theme of the whole section designated by the number or letter, as in the *Baudelaire*.

* Italicized, quoted paragraph headings here are phrases taken from Genet's own works and used by Sartre in chapter titles. To avoid rebarbative approximations, the privileged terms of Sartre's "phenomenal ontology" are here left in the original French—EN SOI, the " opaque " being of things; POUR SOI, the intentionally active being of consciousness; POUR AUTRUI, being of the self reified by the consciousness of the Other. [Ed.]

POUR AUTRUI. Thenceforward he is metamorphosed by others into an Object.

II. THE THIEF—BETWEEN TEN AND FIFTEEN, FROM EIGHTEEN TO TWENTY-TWO, AND FROM TWENTY TO TWENTY-TWO

1) *"I will be the Thief."* Metamorphosed by others into an EN SOI Object (childhood is evoked for the second time), Genet accepts himself as such, and proposes thievery to himself as his activity: " I will be the Thief." Sartre studies the objective significance of Genet's formal decision and its objective implications. Then he shows how, in transforming a concrete situation into a revindication, Genet is at once both Realist and Idealist.

2) *"I have decided to be what crime has made of me."* This POUR SOI chapter takes up the inner experience: Sartre studies the subjective significance of Genet's decision, that is, his consciousness of it as well as its objective implications. Genet accepts himself, then, as an Object, fixed [*figé*] by Others. " I have decided to be what crime has made of me." Sartre examines the contradictory postulates implied by this decision to Be Evil: since the realm of Being is the realm of predetermination, Genet thus arrives at innocent nonresponsibility. But Genet is led into Doing Evil, for the Doing implies a free decision. Genet appeals then to two value systems, which leads Sartre to study the categories of Being and Doing. He explains his method:

> To be perfectly logical, we should have to pursue our study of the two points of view simultaneously; but were we to do so, we should inevitably fall into confusion. So we shall examine separately the intention of being and that of doing . . . , we shall take the conversion of Genet at its source and make a cross-section of these two intentions in the instantaneity of their emergence; it will be, if you will, a *static* description. But, as we must not lose sight of the fact that these intentions co-exist . . . we shall indicate, in a third section, the immediate and confused relationship that unites them.

Sartre then gives, still on the level of the POUR SOI, a static description of: (a) *The intention of Being* Thief, Culprit, of Being the incarnation of Evil; (b) *The intention of making himself* [i. e., *doing*] Thief, Culprit, Incarnation of Evil; and (c) the relations which unite the intention of Being and that of Doing: to Do in order to Be. In this last section Sartre reviews the dialectic of

Being and Doing from childhood (which is evoked for the third
time) and he arrives at a double postulate which, from Genet's
perspective (POUR SOI), expresses itself in this way: If Evil is Fated,
I am a Martyr, a Victim, a Saint [fem.]; if I freely choose Evil, I
am the Prince of Crime, the Black Archangel.

3) *" The Eternal Couple: criminal and [fem.] saint "—from*
fifteen to eighteen. Up to this point Sartre has described
the character. Now he puts it into a historical perspective. The double postulation of Being and Doing (of

Rapport of
the POUR
SOI and the
POUR AUTRUI

Saint and Criminal) is not inert, says Sartre, who adds: " it lives,
it changes, it grows richer with the years, it is transformed by
contact with experience and by the dialectic of each of its elements—
we shall have to follow its evolution." Sartre studies the evolution
of the intention of Being a Saint, then the intention of Making
himself a Criminal through relationships with Others. To elucidate the rapport between the POUR SOI and the POUR AUTRUI Sartre
chooses the area of sexuality, for in this activity man, through the
Other, affirms himself as desire and as wish to be; further, this
individual adventure is easily describable. Sartre uses the intentional pattern of Being in order to study the child violated by the
look of the Other who decides to interiorize his POUR AUTRUI by
making his POUR SOI coincide with his POUR AUTRUI. Sartre studies
pederasty and crime as choices of Being, then as Doing. This
double postulate manifests itself in the desire to *be* loved and in the
desire to *make* oneself the tormentor of the other. Masochism and
assumption of abjection. The chapter ends with the failure of the
pederastic enterprise, which Genet had invested with the mission
of justifying Being. Genet finds himself alone again.

4) *" I is another"—from eighteen to twenty.* Sartre describes
Genet as " non-thetic consciousness (of) Self." He describes
Genet's consciousness of his Being reflected by Others and

Dialectic
of Being

also the form taken by the search for Being through the mediation
of Others. Then he describes the circular movement of Genet, who
cannot apprehend himself as Other, and the adventure of the consciousness which can grasp itself only as freedom, that is to say,
Non-Being [*Néant*], Void.

5) *" A daily labor, long and disappointing. . . ."* Sartre comes
back to the moment at which " the child has made simultaneously the decision to *be* wicked and to *do* Evil." He

Dialectic
of Doing

traces the path that leads from Being to Existence, that is, the problems posed for Genet at the time he decides to do Evil. This chapter is divided in two: Genet's formal determinations and his material determinations; in other words, the dialectic of the possible at the level of consciousness and at the level of society.

Formal determinations. Genet gives the world a status, gives it rules; but first, what is Evil? Sartre indicates Genet's place in the dialectic of Good and Evil and his relationship to Being and Non-Being; Evil for Others, for Genet, is the relationship of the consciousness with Good and Evil. Sartre shows that the decision to do Evil is in fact a payment of homage to the Good; only the unconscious beast can do Evil in ignorance of the Good. Genet then would have to attain lucidly the abject state of the unconscious beast.

Material determinations. "What is the most criminal act?" Evil in society, in religion, with regard to other men, with regard to the original crisis. Sartre concludes the impossibility of doing absolute Evil. He then describes the reasons which lead Genet to choose betrayal. He inserts betrayal into the dialectic of Good and Evil for Genet.

6) *" To succeed in being all, strive to be nothing in anything."* Sartre comes back to childhood and to the intention of Being. He establishes the formal determinations of saintliness (sanctity as a social fact, its objective function in a consumer society) and the subjective determinations (sanctity as direction of the inner life— Jouhandeau, Saint Theresa of Avila; to be a saint, to Make oneself a saint; the use Genet makes of saintliness) .

<small>Rapport of the POUR SOI and the EN SOI; Rapport of the POUR SOI and the POUR AUTRUI; Rapport with AUTRUI</small>

7) *Caïn—eighteen.* Sartre proposes to do a syncretic portrait of Genet "as he appears to himself around the age of eighteen." This chapter takes up again all of the preceding analyses and synthesizes them. It is divided into five sections which can be regrouped and summarized as follows:

<small>Concrete TOTALITY OF INNER EXPERIENCE</small>

a) Affective climate—Genet's tastes, his desires; his reflective nature—masochism and reflective pleasure, how the universe appears to Genet; what he wants to represent in the world; how he experiences his Being.

b) Genet confronting the external World and the meaning of Genet's World; attitude of Genet before the world (this section is divided into three parts) —Genet and tools, Genet and Nature, Genet and Miracles—that is, the events in which Genet recognizes his " destiny." Sartre again analyzes the Sacred and arrives at aesthetic contemplation.

c) Genet and language: twenty to twenty-two. After a brief consideration of the function of language, Sartre describes the attitudes of Francis Ponge, of Michel Leiris, of Georges Bataille, and of Brice Parain towards language. Then he situates Genet with regard to language and we find again dynamic themes already studied at other levels—guilt, silence, theft—all of which Sartre relates to language. Genet uses language to disguise meanings; betrayal and unnatural love are linked to the unnatural use of language. Sartre shows thus how a situation manifests itself in language. He then considers language as the expression of self, as desire to be. Finally, Sartre analyzes an image of Genet's ["Moissoneur des souffles coupés."—Ed.] and brings out both its meaning and its natural sonant quality.

d) The rejection of History. Sartre studies the way in which Genet " lives " an event and goes back to the analysis of " becoming an object." Genet, being a repetition, a reaffirmation of his own past, has no history.

e) The rejection of Reason, the vicious circle. Sartre takes to pieces Genet's circular sophistry. Thought against-nature is added to the analysis of love against-nature. Sartre returns to his analyses of the Saint [fem.], of the pederast, of the criminal, and of the traitor. After determining the path of the vicious circle—of the circular prison—Sartre links it with the delirium of double images, delirium of lucidity, dream of conflict; and also with the hidden enchantment surrounding the footsteps of the unpunished thief, and with the _drama_ of the thief caught red-handed. And thus Sartre gets to the poetry.

III. THE AESTHETE—FROM TWENTY TO TWENTY-SIX

1) " *The strange hell of Beauty. . . .*" This chapter is divided into three parts:

a) The Image (EN SOI). Genet, craving Evil, transforms an Act EN SOI into an Image and a conflict. Sartre goes back to the analysis of Evil, on the level of the imaginary, of the dream, and of the desire to be. He is led back to sexuality, the privileged locus of the imagination—onanism.

b) The Gesture (POUR SOI). The dream transforms the Act into POUR SOI Gesture. Sartre describes how an Image is reconstituted and transformed into a manifestation. Next he turns to relationships between Evil and Beauty; and, finally, how Genet uses Beauty to make the Gesture unreal.

c) The unity of the EN SOI in praxis—the Word. Sartre explains why Genet achieves a unity of image and gesture by resorting to Words. The operation of magnification and derealization through words is described.

2) *"I went to theft as to a liberation"*—*twenty-six.* Sartre describes the contradictions that come with growing older; evolution of sexuality; theft as affirmation of self and liberation; how Genet is led toward the realization of imaginary situations through writing.

IV. THE WRITER—THIRTY

1) *"A mechanism having the exact rigor of verse"*—from the POUR SOI and Rapport with OTHERS word to the work. The metamorphosis of the aesthete into a writer repeats the general patterns of conduct which Sartre has brought out in the child-adult relationships— oppression, exclusion, demand for solitude, provocation, exhibitionism. Sartre analyzes the elaboration of the first poems and links the poetic moment to passive sexuality, which is only one point in Genet's evolution toward prose and activity sexuality.

2) *"And I gentler than a wicked angel. . . ."* Sartre analyzes the form of self-awareness realized through the creative process in three sections:

a) The artist's creations. Sartre describes the process which POUR SOI directs the choice of characters and points out the significance of this choice: the beings he creates harbor the onanistic dreams of Genet; they have the same organization as his dreams and reconstitute his desires. The analysis of his characters coincides with the analysis of his sexuality.

b) Words. Sartre analyzes Genet's relationship to words and Rapport with OTHERS the rapport he seeks to esablish, through words, with his reader. This analysis overlaps the analysis of the relationships with others.

c) Images—the affective pattern of the image and the choice of being it contains. Through the image Genet reconstructs the form of his desires. Sartre describes, then, the sense of the world reflected by Genet's reconstruction of the universe. The interrelationships of his creations point to the desire for a certain social order.

3) *"On the fine arts considered as a murder."* Sartre studies

the form of communication proposed by this art and the artifice used by Genet to achieve it. Sartre goes back to the analysis of Genet transformed into an Object by the gaze of others and raises this attempt (which had ended in failure) to a higher level— through the book Genet transforms himself into an Object and can apprehend himself as an Object delivered up to the gaze of others. Finally, by analyzing the composition and the internal structure of Genet's work, Sartre describes the path along which Genet seeks to draw the reader.

4) *"My victory is verbal. . . ."* This last chapter describes Genet as he transcends his situation by realizing objectively the imaginary pattern of his infantile crisis. Sartre then draws up the balance: the moral-intellectual content of Genet's work; its effect on the reader.

V. PLEA FOR THE PROPER USE OF GENET

Sartre reconsiders the significance of Genet's work in our society: action on the reader; perspective which the reader should adopt; the self-awareness to be found in Genet's work.

With the *Genet* Sartre's method is almost fully developed. His regressive-progressive method analyzes the past in the light of later events (sexuality at fifteen is explained on the basis of sexuality at twenty-five or thirty-five) ; then the synthesis is made on the basis of the infantile crisis.

Sartre's aim is to rediscover the " pluridimensional unity of the act." To arrive at this he proceeds schematically through Analysis, (1) deciphering of the significance of a work through objective consideration of it as an act and (2) relocation of this act and its meaning with reference to the original choice, and through Synthesis, (3) reconstruction of the act as subjective on the basis of the original choice, in the framework of its formal determinations and (4) relocation of this subjective reconstruction in the framework of society's material determinations.

Since the interaction of these elements is indissociable each part overlaps the next, and Sartre repeats at every opportunity that the demands of comprehension force him to establish artificial categories and to step outside the process of totalization in order to examine static ensembles.

In describing a man from the inside Sartre does not involve himself in the description of a subjectivity, for to describe from within is to describe the movement which interiorizes the external world and makes objective the inner world. So there is a perpetual movement to-and-fro between outside and inside, man and society, subjective meanings and objective meanings, and through the description of these exchanges each area enriches and illuminates the others. The analyses moreover are differential; events are always related to a general judgment (Evil for Genet is studied in connection with objective structures of Evil).

Sartre's technique then is a phenomenological and differential analysis, followed by a spiraling totalization which constantly passes back through the same points, and each progression leads to totalization on a higher level, from which new perspectives are visible, so that totalization could continue to unfold indefinitely.

What Sartre seeks to understand is the particularity of a work, which reflects the particularity of a man. And the particularity of the man is " his totality in his process of being objectified."

To understand a work is for Sartre, then, to reproduce, in a way translucent to itself, the activity of the author against the background of human activity. By reproducing the totality in the process of its objectification, one restores life to the author's aggressivity, his frustrations, his struggle, the meaning he attributed to language, and thus one discovers the significance of the work.

The Sartrian technique, at the same time as it proposes to men a certain way of becoming aware of themselves, aims at unifying the present state of the knowledge of man (sociology, psychoanalysis, history, linguistics, anthropology). Conjointly, Sartrian critical understanding, which seeks to give an account of the depth of experience [*du vécu*], is an unlimited exploration in depth.[5] The Flaubert of the *Critique de la Raison Dialectique* encompasses areas even more vast than those of the *Genet*. The concept of the infantile crisis, for example, which was only a rift in the *Baudelaire*, then a displacement [*décalage*] in the *Genet*, covers, in the *Flaubert*, the notion of class apprehended as reality and the pathology of the family (" Flaubert's father, who felt injured by his

[5] Does the ordinary reader's understanding of Genet or another author require this limitless study in depth? Yes and no. It is not necessary to recognize and analyze all of the author's own ins and outs, for the reading of the work turns us back toward ourselves. It is we who confer a reality on the situations evoked—conflict, remorse, hate, love. Our own situations and our own problems, then, become the object of the limitless study in depth. To understand oneself and to understand others is one and the same thing.

' boss' Dupuytre, terrorized everybody with his worth, his repu-
tation, his irony . . ."). The pathology of the family reflects the
irreligiousness of the father (" petit bourgeois intellectual and son
of the French Revolution. . . .") while the notion of class reflects
a point in History ("repression of rising family capitalism, return
of the landlords, contradictions in the régime, misery of the still
underdeveloped proletariat. . . ."). And the point in History takes
its place in the movement of History.

Understanding, for Sartre, does not aim at the establishment of
a definitive " Knowledge." Sartre does not believe in that, any
more than he believes in the Eternal Verities. For him there is only
an understanding which questions itself and evolves *ad infinitum*.

The original French text appeared in MLN *80 (1965).*

THE LITERARY CRITICISM OF JORGE LUIS BORGES ✌ THOMAS R. HART ✌

Outside the Spanish-speaking world, Jorge Luis Borges is known almost exclusively as a writer of short stories. His books of essays, with a few exceptions, have not yet been translated.[1] Yet the short stories, as Ana María Barrenechea has pointed out, form a relatively small part of Borges's work; most of them were written during a period of some fifteen years, from the middle thirties to the early fifties.[2] Borges's career as an essayist, on the other hand, begins with the publication of *Inquisiciones* in 1925 and continues without a break down to the publication of *El hacedor* in 1960. Though he has written, or at least published, hardly any new works of fiction in the past ten years, he remains active as a poet and essayist.

The value of Borges's essays has been, and continues to be, hotly debated by critics. There is surely much less agreement about their worth than about that of his short stories.[3] While the lasting value

[1] The exceptions are *Otras inquisiciones*, translated by Paul and Sylvia Bénichou as *Enquêtes*, 1937-1952 (Paris, 1957), and *Historia de la eternidad*, trans. Roger Caillois and L. Guille, *Histoire de l'infamie. Histoire de l'éternité* (Monaco, 1958). A number of essays are included in *Labyrinths*, ed. Donald A. Yates and James E. Irby (New York, 1962).

[2] *La expresión de la irrealidad en la obra de Jorge Luis Borges* (Mexico, 1957) pp. 9-11. Hereafter cited as *Irrealidad*.

[3] For César Fernández Moreno, Borges's essays are " la parte más débil de su obra; los defectos de Borges parecen resaltar y sus virtudes oscurecerse en este campo. . . . Los ensayos de Borges se apartan de [la] vocación de verdad inherente al género; buscan más bien el asombro, la paradoja, el funcionamiento del pensar como un fin y no como un medio." (*Esquemas de Borges* [Buenos Aires, 1957], p. 27.) Adolfo Prieto, in a generally hostile book, declares that Borges " rara vez ha corrido la aventura de la crítica con todas las precauciones y supuestos que ésta implica. Las numerosas notas que ha publicado hasta ahora son, en

of the essays may well be largely in the light they throw on the mind of the artist who created the stories, they are, nevertheless, of considerable interest in themselves. Many of the themes found in Borges's poems and stories appear also in the essays; some, already present in his youthful writings, recur again and again in his later books. Borges's thought, however, has not remained static. In this paper I shall attempt to trace the development of some of his central ideas on the nature of literature and of literary criticism.[4]

*   *   *   *   *

The most important influence on Borges's literary criticism is doubtless that of Benedetto Croce. Borges, however, has not followed Croce slavishly. Some superficially Crocean passages in his essays reveal important differences in point of view, and Borges has not hesitated to make explicit his disagreement with Croce on particular issues. It is, nevertheless, true that Croce is mentioned in Borges's essays more often than any other critic; true, too, that, while Borges's attitude toward certain features of Croce's doctrine has changed with the years, his critical practice has remained consistently true to Crocean principles.

Borges's first book of essays, *Inquisiciones,* published in 1925, presents an apparent exception. Croce is not mentioned and the idea of poetry which Borges defends does not seem specifically Crocean. There are, however, as we shall see, a number of passages in the book which, if not drawn from Croce himself, do suggest substantial agreement with his views.

buena parte, comentarios circunstanciales de un lector hedonista. Abunda en observaciones agudas. [Pero] los puntos de vista valen aislados del contexto, mejor dicho, valen mucho más que el contexto." (*Borges y la nueva generación* [Buenos Aires, 1954], p. 33.) For Marcial Tamayo and Adolfo Ruiz-Díaz, on the other hand, " la personalidad de Borges se mantiene idéntica tanto cuando aborda notas o ensayos críticos como cuando redacta un relato. [Si] hemos preferido como punto de vista los relatos . . . nada debe a un criterio valorativo. No es que juzguemos al Borges inventor de ficciones como el más alto o el más auténtico." (*Borges enigma y clave* [Buenos Aires, 1955], pp. 13-16.) Señorita Barrenechea, a sympathetic and perceptive student of Borges's work, also finds that in it " poesía, ensayo, cuento son las diversas manifestaciones de un mismo espíritu." (*Irrealidad,* p. 11.) See also Allen Phillips's review of Borges's *Leopoldo Lugones* in *NRFH,* X (1956) , 449; for Phillips, too, " el Borges crítico sigue siendo el Borges creador."

[4] For an account of the evolution of Borges's ideas on language, see Ana María Barrenechea, " Borges y el lenguaje," *NRFH,* VII (1953) , 551-569; for the development of his poetry, see Juan Carlos Ghiano, " Borges y la poesía," *CA,* LXXXV (enero-febrero, 1956) , 222-250.

Borges explicitly declares his adherence to Croce's theory of art as expression in an essay, " La simulación de la imagen," first published in the Buenos Aires newspaper *La Prensa* on December 25, 1927, and incorporated in his second book of essays, *El idioma de los argentinos*, in the following year: " Indagar ¿qué es lo estético? es indagar ¿qué otra cosa es lo estético, qué única otra cosa es lo estético? Lo expresivo, nos ha contestado Croce, ya para siempre. El arte es expresión y sólo expresión, postularé aquí " (p. 83).[5] In another essay included in the same collection, " Indagación de la palabra," Borges is just as explicit in *dissenting* from Croce's theory that the ultimate unit of speech is not the word but the sentence and that the latter must be understood, not in the usual grammatical way, but as an expressive organism whose meaning is complete, and which, therefore, may extend from a single exclamation to a long poem.[6] Such a view, Borges insists, is " psicológicamente . . . insostenible [y] una equivocación psicológica no puede ser un acierto estético. Además, ¿no dejó dicho Schopenhauer que la forma de nuestra inteligencia es el tiempo, línea angostísima que sólo nos presenta las cosas una por una? Lo espantoso de esa estrechez es que los poemas a que alude reverencialmente Montolíu-Croce alcanzan unidad en la flaqueza de nuestra memoria, pero no en la tarea sucesiva de quien los escribió ni en la de quien los lee. (Dije espantoso, porque esa heterogeneidad

[5] The dates of publication of the individual essays are taken from the very useful bibliography by Nodier Lucio and Lydia Revello, " Contribución a la bibliografía de Jorge Luis Borges," *Bibliografía argentina de artes y letras,* number 11 (abril-septiembre, 1961), 43-112. Citations from Borges's writings will be incorporated into my text; wherever possible, they are to the *Obras completas* (Buenos Aires, 1953-60). The full titles of the books cited, together with the date of publication in this edition, are as follows: *Historia de la eternidad* (1953); *Ficciones* (1956); *Discusión* (1957); *Otras inquisiciones* (1960); *El hacedor* (1960). Citations from *Inquisiciones* (Buenos Aires, 1925) and *El idioma de los argentinos* (Buenos Aires, 1928) are to the first editions.

[6] I have paraphrased the argument presented by Croce in his *Estetica come scienza dell'espressione e linguistica generale,* 9th ed. (Bari, 1950), p. 159. See Gian N. G. Orsini, *Benedetto Croce: Philosopher of Art and Literary Critic* (Carbondale, 1961), p. 68; my treatment of Croce is heavily indebted to Professor Orsini's excellent book. We may note, in passing, that, while Borges correctly attributes to Croce the idea that " la oración . . .es indivisible y las categorías gramaticales que la desarman son abstracciones añadidas a la realidad " (p. 15), he mistakenly considers the extension of the concept of the sentence to include an entire poem to be the contribution of Croce's Spanish disciple, Manuel de Montolíu, in his book *El lenguaje como fenómeno estético* (Buenos Aires, 1926).

de la sucesión despedaza no sólo las dilatadas composiciones, sino
toda página escrita.)" (*Idioma*, pp. 16-17). Twelve years later, in
the short story "Tlön, Uqbar, Orbis Tertius," we find Borges writing that on his imaginary planet Tlön, "hay poemas famosos com-
puestos de una sola enorme palabra. Esta palabra integra un *objeto
poético creado* por el autor" (*Ficciones*, p. 21).

Croce's identification of art with expression which Borges accepts
in this essay is questioned in "La postulación de la realidad," published in the review *Azul* in 1931. The difference in tone between
the two essays is striking. "Hume notó para siempre," Borges
begins, "que los argumentos de Berkeley no admiten la menor
réplica y no producen la menor convicción; yo desearía, para elim-
inar los de Croce, una sentencia no menos educada y mortal. La
de Hume no me sirve, porque la diáfana doctrina de Croce tiene
la facultad de persuadir, aunque ésta sea la única. Su defecto es
ser inmanejable; sirve para cortar una discusión, no para resolverla.

"Su fórmula—recordará mi lector—es la identidad de lo estético
y de lo expresivo. No la rechazo, pero quiero observar que los
escritores de hábito clásico más bien rehúyen lo expresivo" (*Discusión*, p. 67).[7]

"Classical" here, as Borges goes on to explain, does not designate the writers of a particular historical period. The classical
writer is one who has confidence in the power of the accepted
language to say anything he may wish to say: "Distraigo aquí de
toda connotación histórica las palabras *clásico* y *romántico*; entiendo por ellas dos arquetipos de escritor (dos procederes). El
clásico no desconfía del lenguaje, cree en la suficiente virtud de
cada uno de sus signos."[8] The classical writer "no escribe los prime-
ros contactos de la realidad, sino su elaboración final en conceptos" (p. 68); as examples, Borges cites Gibbon, Voltaire, Swift,

---

[7] Borges's exposition may be confusing to a reader unfamiliar with Croce's
thought. He is not so much attacking the identification of art and expression
as the related premise that literature—Croce would say, "poesia"—is built up,
not from abstract propositions, but from "intuizioni." See the excellent discussion of Croce's use of the latter term in Orsini, pp. 31-36.

[8] For a more elaborate definition of classicism conceived in similar terms, cf.
Idioma, p. 67: "Entiendo por clasicismo esa época de un yo, de una amistad,
de una literatura, en que las cosas ya recibieron su valoración y el bien y el
mal fueron repartidos entre ellas. [Las voces] son designación de las cosas, pero
también son elogio, estima, vituperio, respetabilidad, picardía. Poseen su entonación, su gesto."

and Cervantes. Such a view is obviously very different from the Crocean doctrine of intuition, as Borges himself makes clear: "Pasajes como los anteriores, forman la extensa mayoria de la literatura mundial, y aun la menos indigna. Repudiarlos para no incomodar a una fórmula, sería inconducente y ruinoso. Dentro de su notoria ineficacia, son eficaces; falta resolver esa contradicción" (p. 69). Borges attempts to resolve it with the argument that "la imprecisión es tolerable o verosímil en la literatura, porque a ella propendemos siempre en la realidad. . . . El hecho mismo de percibir, de atender, es de orden selectivo: toda atención, toda fijación de nuestra conciencia, comporta una deliberada omisión de lo no interesante. . . . Nuestro vivir es una serie de adaptaciones, vale decir, una educación del olvido" (pp. 69-70). Readers of Borges's stories may recall the case of Funes *el memorioso,* who was incapable of forgetting anything he had once experienced and equally incapable of grouping his experiences—we might say, in Crocean language and not without a certain malice, his *intuizioni*—into any more general categories. As a result poor Funes "no era muy capaz de pensar. Pensar es olvidar diferencias, es generalizar, abstraer. En el abarrotado mundo de Funes no había sino detalles, casi inmediatos" (*Ficciones,* p. 126) [9]

One consequence of Croce's theory of poetry as a perfectly realized expression of an immediate intuition is his rejection of allegory as a literary form. "For Croce," as Orsini explains, "allegory is essentially a kind of cryptography. . . . By an act that is purely arbitrary, and therefore belongs to the sphere of the practical will and not that of the imagination, a writer decides that a certain sign shall stand for a certain thing with which it is not usually connected." [10] Borges presents Croce's argument, with appropriate quotations from the *Estetica* and from *La poesia,* in an essay of 1949, "De las alegorías a las novelas." To Croce's denial that allegory can ever be aesthetically successful, Borges opposes Chester-

---

[9] In the prologue to his recent *Antología personal* (Buenos Aires, 1962), Borges returns once more to Croce's theory: "Croce juzgó que el arte es expresión; a esta exigencia, o a una deformación de esta exigencia, debemos la peor literatura de nuestro tiempo. . . . Alguna vez yo también busqué la expresión; ahora sé que mis dioses no me conceden más que la alusión o mención." One might equally well say, using the term in Borges's special sense, that his own writing has become increasingly "classical." An analysis of the evolution of Borges's prose style would surely confirm this view.

[10] Orsini, p. 234.

ton's view that language is not an adequate instrument for the representation of reality: "Declarado insuficiente el lenguaje, hay lugar para otros; la alegoría puede ser uno de ellos, como la arquitectura o la música" (*Otras inquisiciones*, p. 213). Though Borges begins his essay with the assertion that he believes Croce to be in the right (p. 211), he later shifts his position and declares that "no sé muy bien cuál de los eminentes contradictores tiene razón; sé que el arte alegórico pareció alguna vez encantador . . . y ahora es intolerable" (p. 213). Borges's explanation of how allegory came to lose favor with both readers and writers need not concern us here. It will be enough to remark that his sympathy with Chesterton's position is probably greater than it appears to be in this essay; we shall return to this point a little later in connection with Borges's views on the nature of language.

Another, more detailed exposition of Croce's attack on allegory and Chesterton's defense of it may be found in the long essays on Nathaniel Hawthorne, also of 1949. Here again Borges's own position is somewhat ambiguous, though he is, I think, rather more sympathetic to Chesterton than to Croce: "La alegoría, según esa interpretación desdeñosa [that of Croce,] vendría a ser una adivinanza, más extensa, más lenta y mucho más incómoda que las otras. Sería un género bárbaro o infantil, una distracción de la estética. Croce formuló esa refutación en 1907; en 1904, Chesterton ya la había refutado sin que aquel lo supiera" (*Otras inquisiciones*, p. 74). Borges, however, still refuses to commit himself fully: "No sé si es válida la tesis de Chesterton; sé que una alegoría es tanto mejor cuanto sea menos reducible a un esquema, a un frío juego de abstracciones" (p. 75). There are, he declares, two kinds of writers: those who think in images (Shakespeare, Donne, Victor Hugo) and those who think in abstractions (Julien Benda, Bertrand Russell). Neither group is inherently superior to the other, but difficulties arise when a writer attempts to change groups: "Cuando un abstracto, un razonador, quiere ser también imaginativo, o pasar por tal, occure lo denunciado por Croce. Notamos que un proceso lógico ha sido engalanado y disfrazado por el autor. . . . Es, para citar un ejemplo notorio de esa dolencia, el caso de José Ortega y Gasset, cuyo buen pensamiento queda obstruído por laboriosas y adventicias metáforas" (p. 76). Hawthorne is an example of the opposite tendency. It is worth noting that Borges's division of writers into two groups may not be simply a matter of difference in temperament; indeed, his choice of examples suggests that the distinction is rather between creators of imaginative literature and writers who cultivate discursive forms, with the implicit corollary that what is appropriate in one kind of writing will be out of place in another.[11]

Croce's sharp distinction between the poetic and the 'practical' personality of the writer has fared much better in Borges's hands than his summary dismissal of the aesthetic possibilities of allegory.[12] There is, however, no evidence that Borges considers the distinction peculiarly Crocean.[13] We find it already in an essay of 1922, "La nadería de la personalidad," in which Borges declares that "yo, al escribir [estas inquietudes,] sólo soy una certidumbre que inquiere las palabras más aptas para persuadir tu atención. Ese propósito y algunas sensaciones musculares y la visión de la límpida enramada que ponen frente a mi ventana los árboles construyen mi yo actual.

". . . Fuera vanidad suponer que ese agregado psíquico ha menester asirse a un yo para gozar de validez absoluta, a ese conjetural Jorge Luis Borges en cuya lengua cupo tanto sofisma y en cuyos solitarios paseos los tardeceres del suburbio son gratos" (*Inquisicones*, p. 85). Borges here insists that many things a writer has said and done may have no bearing at all on his work. There are, however, some books in which the reader's interest is centered on the personality of the writer himself. Whitman is a case in point; another, less obvious perhaps, is Valéry. In an essay, "Valéry como símbolo," written on the occasion of the French poet's death in 1945, Borges compares him with Whitman and declares that although the two seem wholly unlike each other, they are,

[11] Borges had drawn a similar distinction as early as 1925: " El pensativo, el hombre intelectual vive en la intimidad de los conceptos que son abstracción pura; el hombre sensitivo, el carnal, en la contigüidad del mundo externo. Ambas trazas de gente pueden recabar en las letras levantada eminencia, pero por caminos desemejantes. El pensativo, al metaforizar, dilucidará el mundo externa mediante las ideas incorpóreas que para él son lo entrañal e inmediato; el sensual corporificará los conceptos " (*Inquisiciones*, pp. 148-149).

[12] For an exposition of Croce's views, see Orsini, pp. 159-160, and Lienhard Bergel, " Croce as a Critic of Goethe," *CL*, I (1949), 352.

[13] It is, of course, an article of faith for a great many modern critics; see, for example, T. S. Eliot, " Tradition and the Individual Talent," in his *Selected Essays 1917-1932* (New York, 1932), pp. 7-9, and Paul Valéry, *The Art of Poetry*, trans. Denise Folliot (New York, 1951), p. 86.

nevertheless, linked by the fact that "la obra de los dos es menos preciosa como poesía que como signo de un poeta ejemplar, creado por esa obra" (*Otras inquisiciones,* p. 105. In a later essay, "Nota sobre Walt Whitman," of 1947, Borges returns to the same theme and develops it in considerably more detail. His point of departure is Robert Louis Stevenson's remark that "the whole of Whitman's work is deliberate," an observation which, as Borges is careful to point out, has also been made by a number of other critics. The protagonist of *Leaves of Grass* must not be equated with the poet: "Imaginemos que una biografía de Ulises . . . indicara que éste nunca salió de Itaca. La decepción que nos causaría ese libro, felizmente hipotético, es la que causan todas las biografías de Whitman" (*Otras inquisiciones,* p. 99). Borges has recently returned to the same theme of the distinction between the writer as a man and as a figure in his own works in a brilliant and witty essay, "Borges y yo," where he asserts that "al otro, a Borges, es a quien le ocurren las cosas. . . . Me gustan los relojes de arena, los mapas, la tipografía del siglo XVIII, el sabor del café y la prosa de Stevenson; el otro comparte esas preferencias, pero de un modo vanidoso que las convierte en atributos de un actor. Sería exagerado afirmar que nuestra relación es hostil; yo vivo, yo me dejo vivir, para que Borges pueda tramar su literatura y esa literatura me justifica. . . . Poco a poco voy cediéndole todo, aunque me consta su perversa costumbre de falsear y magnificar. . . . No sé cuál de los dos escribe esta página" (*El hacedor,* pp. 50-51).

Both in his theoretical writings and in his practical criticism, Croce lays great stress on what he calls "characterization" (*caratterizzazione*).[14] In his studies of individual writers, "the method," as René Wellek has remarked, "is always one and the same. Croce selects what he considers poetry, pushes aside what is something else, and tries to define a leading sentiment, something like Taine's *faculté maîtresse,* which allows him to characterize by constant qualification."[15] Here again, Borges's critical practice is much like Croce's, though, as with the distinction between the poetic and the practical personality of the writer, there is no reason to speak of the influence of Croce on Borges. Borges himself sets forth the critic's problem in an essay, "Menoscabo y grandeza de Quevedo,"

[14] Orsini, pp. 151-164.
[15] "Benedetto Croce: Literary Critic and Historian," *CL,* V (1953); 78.

published in 1924 in the *Revista de Occidente*: " Aquí está su labor [that of Quevedo], con su aparente numerosidad de propósitos, ¿cómo reducirla a unidad y curajarla en un símbolo? La artimaña de quien lo despedaza según la varia actividad que ejerció no es apta para concertar la despareja plenitud de su obra. Desbandar a Quevedo en irreconciliables figuraciones de novelista, de poeta, de teólogo, de sufridor estoico y de eventual pasquinador, es empeño baldío si no adunamos luego con firmeza todas esas vislumbres " (*Inquisiciones,* pp. 39-40). He concludes that the unity of Quevedo's work lies not in its subject matter, which is immensely varied, but in the author's constant preoccupation with exploiting the resources offered him by language: " Casi todos sus libros son cotidianos en el plan, pero sobresalientes en los verbalismos de hechura " (*Inquisiciones,* p. 40). The same method is employed in many of Borges's later essays. Thus, the essay on Whitman, to which we have already referred, is centered on the conception of Whitman as a conscious artist who deliberately creates his own personality as poet in the same way that a novelist might create a personality for his protagonist. Nor is the method limited solely to studies of individual writers; the *caratteristica,* to use Croce's term, of the *gaucho* poetry of the nineteenth century is that it presents the life of the cowboy as it appeared to a sophisticated observer from Buenos Aires or Montevideo: " Derivar la literatura gauchesca de su materia, el gaucho, es una confusión que desfigura la notoria verdad. No menos necesario para la formación de ese género que la pampa y que las cuchillas fue el carácter urbano de Buenos Aires y de Montevideo. . . . De la azarosa conjunción de esos dos estilos vitales, del asombro que uno produjo en otro, nació la literatura gauchesca " (*Discusión,* p. 12).

Since, for Croce, art is a perfect realization of the artist's intuition, form and content are inseparable. Croce has no interest in the forms of poetic language, since the forms—not only metrical and stanzaic forms, but also such things as metaphor and simile—are not poetic in themselves; they become so only when they are used to express the artist's intuition, that is, when they are combined with an appropriate content.[16] Borges's position is identical with Croce's, and he does not hesitate to acknowledge his debt. In *El idioma de los argentinos,* surely the most consistently

[16] See Orsini, pp. 64-95.

Crocean of all his books, he declares that "la metáfora no es poética
por ser metáfora, sino por la expresión alconzada. No insisto
en la disputa; todo sentidor de Croce estará conmigo" (pp. 69-70).
In an essay of 1931, "La supersticiosa ética del lector," Borges
returns to the same point and develops it at much greater length.
Most readers today, he argues, "entienden por estilo no la eficacia
o la ineficacia de una página, sino las habilidades aparentes del
escritor: sus comparaciones, su acústica, los episodios de su punc-
tuación y de su sintaxis" (*Discusión*, p. 45).

If those who insist that "la numerosidad de metáforas [es] una
virtud" (*Idioma*, p. 69) are in the wrong, so are those who consider the number of words in a particular language a valid index
of its possibilites as an instrument of aesthetic expression, a fault,
incidentally, which Borges finds particularly common among pen-
insular Spanish critics. Here again, just as with metaphors, "la
numerosidad de representaciones es lo que importa, no la de
signos" (p. 170), and we find Borges once more proclaiming the
unity of form and content: "la sueñera mental y la concepción
acústica del estilo son las que fomentan sinónimos: palabras que
sin cambiar de idea cambian de ruido" (p. 172).

The same point, combined with another which is of great importance for Borges's thinking about the nature of literary language, is made in the essay, "Indagación de la palabra," of 1927:
"Es una sentencia de Joubert, citada favorablemente por Matías
Arnold. . . . Trata de Bossuet y es así: *Más que un hombre es
una naturaleza humana, con la moderación de un santo, la jus-
ticia de un obispo, la prudencia de un doctor y el poderío de un
gran espíritu.* Aquí Joubert jugó a las variantes no sin descaro;
escribió (y acaso pensó) *la moderación de un santo* y acto con-
tinuo esa fatalidad que hay en el lenguaje se adueñó de él y
eslabonó tres cláusulas más, todas de aire simétrico y todas relle-
nadas con negligencia. Es como si afirmara . . . *con la moderación
de un santo, el qué sé yo de un quién sabe qué y el cualquier cosa
de un gran espíritu.* . . . Si la prosa, con su mínima presencia de
ritmo, trae estas servidumbres, ¿cuáles no traerá el verso?" (*Idioma*,
pp. 22-23).

Borges here sees language as a dangerous invitation to the
writer to exploit the resources which it offers him without regard
for what he himself wishes to say. The danger is obviously greater

in verse than in prose, a point to which Borges returns again and
again. In his prologue to *Índice de la nueva poesía argentina,* of
1926, we already find him saying that " la rima es aleatoria. Ya
don Francisco de Quevedo se burló de ella por la esclavitud que
impone al poeta." [17] In " La supersticiosa ética del lector," he
declares that " ya se practica la lectura en silencio, *síntoma venturoso*
[italics mine]. Ya hay lector callado de versos. De esa capacidad
sigilosa a una escritura puramente ideográfica—directa comunicación
de experiencias, no de sonidos—hay una distancia incansable, pero
siempre menos dilatada que el porvenir" (*Discusión,* p. 49) .[18]
The danger, however, is present in prose, too, as Borges demonstrates in his analysis of the sentence he quotes from Joubert;
it is a consequence, not simply of the need to fit one's thought
into a given metrical scheme, but of the need to express it in a
pre-existing language.

Every language, Borges insists, represents an attempt to inject
some order into our perceptions of the reality which surrounds us,
to simplify it and make it intelligible; we should not be too much
surprised if this collective vision, the product of centuries of development, should fail to correspond exactly to the pattern imposed
upon reality by the will and needs of any individual.[19] Here
Borges, by stressing the writer's subservience to language, his inability to say precisely what he wants to say, differs sharply from
Croce, who contends that the writer creates his own language
anew, on the basis of his private intuitions.[20] Borges's conception
of language as a check upon the writer's freedom has important
consequences for his theory of literature. Since the writer's ability
to create something wholly new is, for Borges, limited by the language he uses, he may as well resign himself to repeating, with
minor variations, things others have said before him: " Ni [Spinoza]

[17] Cited by Ghiano, p. 232.
[18] In an earlier essay, Borges had discussed the attempt of the seventeenth-
century clergyman John Wilkins to create a universal language and made the
significant remark that " esa su música silenciosa no comportaba obligatoria-
mente ningún sonido. Esa es ventaja máxima y qué más quisiera yo que hablar
de ella " (*Idioma,* p. 171) .
[19] For a fuller discussion, see Barrenechea, *Irrealidad,* pp. 75-82.
[20] Croce, of course, would not limit this creative power to writers, but would
consider it the property of every speaker of a language; see Orsini, pp. 70-73.
For a more moderate statement of a position rather similar to Croce's see Leo
Spitzer, *Linguistics and Literary History* (Princeton, 1948) , pp. 10-11 and note
5, p. 31.

con su metafísica geometrizada, ni [Lulio] con su alfabeto traducible en palabras y éstas en oraciones, consiguió eludir el lenguaje. . . . Sólo pueden soslayarlo los ángeles, que conversan por especies inteligibles: es decir, por representaciones directas y sin ministerio alguno verbal.

" ¿Y nosotros, los nunca ángeles, los verbales, los que
en este bajo relativo suelo

escribimos, los que sotopensamos que ascender a letras de molde es la máxima realidad de las experiencias? Que la resignación, virtud a que debemos resignarnos—sea con nosotros. Ella será nuestro destino: hacernos a la sintaxis, a su concatenación traicionera, a la imprecisión, a los talveces, a los demasiados énfasis, a los peros, al hemiferio de mentira y de sombra en nuestro decir. . . .

" No de intuiciones originales—hay pocas—, sino de variaciones y casualidades y travesuras, suele alimentarse la lengua. La lengua: es decir humilladoramente el pensar " (*Idioma*, pp. 26-27) .

The idea that the writer cannot hope to create anything wholly new becomes increasingly frequent in Borges's later essays. In *Inquisiciones*, he had defined the creation of a metaphor as " la inquisición de cualidades comunes a los dos terminos de la imagen, cualidades que son de todos conocidas, pero cuya coincidencia en dos conceptos lejanos no ha sido vislumbrado hasta el instante de hacerse la metáfora " (p. 156) . In an essay on Norse poetry, " Las kenningar," first published as a separate book in 1933 and later included in the collection of essays *Historia de la eternidad,* he adopts a somewhat different position. Though he praises certain kennings because they can awaken a sense of wonder in the reader ("nos extrañan del mundo "), he is aware that the kennings do not in most cases represent original poetic intuitions, but simply the use of a learned language; their apparent originality is an illusion created by our ignorance (*Eternidad,* pp. 65, 44). In the lecture on Hawthorne, of 1949, we find him doubting whether a really new metaphor can be found at all: " es quizá un error suponer que puedan inventarse metáforas. Las verdaderas, las que formulan íntimas conexiones entre una imagen y otra, han existido siempre; las que aún podemos inventar son las falsas, las que no vale la pena inventar " (*Otras inquisiciones*, p. 71) . " La esfera de Pascal," of 1951, begins with the suggestion that " quizá la historia universal es la historia de unas cuantas metáforas " and ends with a slightly more precise statement of the same theme: " quizá la historia universal es la historia de la diversa entonación de algunas metáforas " (*Otras inquisiciones,* pp. 13, 17). Borges thus reaffirms his adherence to a point of view fundamentally identical with that he had expressed in " Indagación de la palabra " nearly a quarter of a century earlier: " No de intuiciones originales —hay pocas—, sino de variaciones y casualidades y travesuras, suele alimentarse la lengua " (*Idioma,* p. 27).

* * * *

Borges's criticism has been attacked on the ground that it rarely aims primarily at the interpretation of a given work but rather uses the work as a point of departure for reflections on all sorts of philosophical problems.[21] The charge is not without foundation; one might perhaps counter it by saying that Borges is less a literary critic than a theorist of literature.[22] Indeed, I think it can be argued that the remarks on books and writers scattered throughout Borges's essays do add up to some clearly definable and coherent ideas on the nature of literature and the function of criticism. These ideas may be expressed in the form of three postulates, though, of course, any such schematization of Borges's thought, expressed in dozens of essays and over a period of almost forty years, runs a grave risk of distorting it by making it seem more systematic than it really is.

The first postulate is that a work of literature is an indivisible whole; the critic cannot profitably consider form and content in isolation from one another. But this does not mean that the union of form and content is always perfectly realized; Borges's objection to the sentence from Joubert, already cited, is that the four parallel phrases do not correspond to a fourfold development of the writer's thought. It does mean that the critic must be concerned, not with form in itself, but in its relation to the whole work.[23]

[21] See Adolfo Prieto, *Borges y la nueva generación,* pp. 33-34.

[22] I have in mind here the distinction drawn by René Wellek and Austin Warren, *Theory of Literature* (New York, 1949), p. 30.

[23] Cf. Northrop Frye, *Anatomy of Criticism: Four Essays* (Princeton, 1957), p. 77: " ' Every poem must necessarily be a perfect unity,' says Blake: this, as the wording implies, is not a statement of fact about all existing poems, but a statement of the hypothesis which every reader adopts in first trying to comprehend even the most chaotic poem ever written." In pointing out analogies between Borges's critical position and that of Frye, I do not, of course, wish

The second postulate is that a work of literature is self-contained; its critical corollary is that the critic's interest should be centered on the work itself. From this comes Borges's distinction between the writer as a man and as a 'mask' in his own writings. (I use this somewhat unsatisfactory term rather than 'character' since I wish it to include the implicit 'speaker' of an essay or lyric.)

The last, and most important, of the three postulates is closely bound up with the second; it is that a work of literature may best be understood, not as an assertion about something outside itself, but as a hypothesis about something whose existence is neither affirmed nor denied. Borges's critical position here comes quite close to that of Northrop Frye, for whom literature is "a body of hypothetical creations which is not necessarily involved in the worlds of truth and fact, nor necessarily withdrawn from them, but which may enter into any kind of relationship to them, ranging from the most to the least explicit." [24]

Borges's theory of the autonomy of the literary work is a consequence of his more general theory that man can never truly know reality: "Notoriamente no hay clasificación del universo que no sea arbitraria y conjetural. La razón es muy simple: no sabemos qué cosa es el universo. . . . Cabe sospechar que no hay universo en el sentido orgánico, unificador, que tiene esa ambiciosa palabra. Si lo hay, falta conjeturar su propósito; falta conjeturar las palabras, las definiciones, las etimologías, las sinonimias, del secreto diccionario de Dios" (*Otras inquisiciones,* pp.

to suggest that either critic is dependent upon the other. Borges had not heard of *Anatomy of Criticism* when I mentioned it to him in August, 1962, and the ideas which I have tried to sum up in my three postulates are found, admittedly with important differences of emphasis, in all Borges's books of essays, some of which antedate the *Anatomy* by thirty years or more. I refer to Frye simply because his work seems to me the most comprehensive, and in some ways the most successful, recent attempt to construct a general theory of literature.

[24] *Anatomy of Criticism,* pp. 92-93; see also pp. 350-354. The analogy between literature and mathematics which Frye develops in these two passages is especially suggestive in the light of Borges's often-expressed interest in mathematical problems. See, for example, his note on Kasner and Newman's *Mathematics and the Imagination (Discusión,* pp. 165-166); the discussion of number systems in *Otras inquisiciones,* p. 140; or the passage in *El idioma de los argentinos* where Borges argues that the number of words in a given language is no indication of its richness or poverty in concepts, since "el solo idioma infinito—el de las matemáticas—se basta con una docena de signos para no dejarse distanciar por número alguno" (p. 170).

142-143). Borges's philosophical position is thus fundamentally skeptical, as he himself recognizes. In the epilogue to *Otras inquisiciones* he declares that in reading the proofs he has noted " una [tendencia] a estimar las ideas religiosas o filosóficas por su valor estético y aun por lo que encierran de singular y de maravilloso. Esto es, quizá, indicio de un escepticismo esencial " (p. 259).[25] Borges surely would agree with those librarians mentioned in his story " La biblioteca de Babel " who "repudian la supersticiosa y vana costumbre de buscar sentido en los libros y la equiparan a la de buscarlo en los sueños o en las líneas caóticas de la mano " (*Ficciones,* p. 88). He is like the metaphysicians of his own imaginary Tlön who " no buscan la verdad ni siquiera la verosimilitud: buscan el asombro. Juzgan que la metafísica es una rama de la literatura fantástica " (*Ficciones,* p. 23). The remark applies with equal force to Borges's own, often fantastic, stories, and to his criticism of other men's writings, of whatever kind. But it is worth stressing that Borges's critical principles, despite the fanciful way in which they are usually presented, are sound enough, and that they do form a coherent, if not a comprehensive, theory of literature.

1963

[26] Barrenchea, *Irrealidad,* p. 76, gives a convenient list of similar passages from Borges's other works.

L ANGUAGE, VISION, AND PHENOMEN- OLOGY: MERLEAU-PONTY AS A TEST CASE ❧ BY EUGENIO DONATO ❧

> Le moment de la crise
> est toujours celui du
> signe.
>
> J. Derrida

To question at our present intellectual juncture the relationship of phenomenology to literature implies beyond a re-elaboration or an extension of familiar concepts the re-examination of a relationship which is essentially problematical.[1] To circumscribe the problem, let us start from the following observation: Literature is a linguistic phenomenon and as such has to partake of the nature, attributes, and properties of language. Whatever implicit or explicit intentions it may sustain, whatever ends it may strive for or achieve, literature is first and foremost a stringing together of words. Such a statement is more than the reiteration of a platitude if we are willing to take into account that French thought of the last decade as exemplified by Foucault, Lévi-Strauss, Lacan, and Derrida has been openly hostile to phenomenology and that the conceptual break they have introduced has been achieved by placing language in a fundamental and primary position and by carrying to their logical extreme the radical consequences that such an undertaking might entail. It is from such a discontinuous perspective that today we must look back at what phenomenology might have had to say about language and meditate on its literary consequences. Phenomenology was not indifferent to language, far from it; from Husserl to Sartre and Merleau-Ponty the problem of language recurs persistently. Yet it recurs as a problem, as a phenomenon to be described, or at times as something with an inherent opacity which blurs the contemplation of the essences

---

[1] This text was originally read at the section on "Phenomenology and Literature" of the 1969 meeting of the Society for Phenomenological and Existential Philosophy at Northwestern University.

revealed to the phenomenological consciousness. For phenomenology, language has always been a *problem* rather than that primordial element that governs the articulation of problems. Within the scope of this paper not only would it be an impossible undertaking to treat the problem of the relationship of phenomenology to language in its entirety but it would also be in part a futile exercise since we would find ourselves for the major and more complex part of the problem—namely that which concerns Husserl—repeating some of the brilliant analysis that Jacques Derrida has undertaken in his *La Voix et le Phénomène*.[2]

We shall instead limit ourselves to Merleau-Ponty. We shall study the problem of language and by extension the problem of literature through Merleau-Ponty for two reasons. The first is of a purely practical nature. The technical vocabulary that Merleau-Ponty uses in speaking of language is very close to that which we might use ourselves today. To describe the phenomenon of language he uses expressions such as signifier, signified, sign, and signification. In this context, the fact that late in his career he became interested in the works of Saussure, when the latter was becoming important on the French intellectual scene, might make it easier for us to define what is specific to Merleau-Ponty's conception of language.

The second reason is more fundamental. If Merleau-Ponty became interested in the problem of language, and if he talked about it at great length throughout his entire philosophical undertaking, his conceptualization, or more exactly his attitude towards language, did not remain constant. May it suffice for us to recall that his work does not end with a meditation on language or literature but with a meditation on painting which refers us to the more primordial phenomenon of vision; and vision coextensive with silence, does not find an easy adequation with the vocation of language. Besides, the careful reading of his work notes collected in *Le Visible et l'Invisible* might lead us to believe that had Merleau-Ponty ever finished his work he would have gone even further to assert that vision and language are by essence mutually exclusive and that it is to the former and not to the latter that we ought to give ontological primacy.

Nous voyons les choses mêmes, le monde est cela que nous voyons: des formules de ce genre expriment une foi qui est

[2] Derrida, J. *La Voix et le Phénomène*, Paris, 1967.

commune à l'homme naturel et au philosophe dès qu'il ouvre les yeux, elles renvoient à une assise profonde 'd'opinions' muettes impliquées dans notre vie. Mais cette foi a ceci d'étrange que, si l'on cherche à l'articuler en thèse ou énoncé, si l'on se demande ce que c'est que *nous,* ce que c'est que *voir* et ce que c'est que *chose* ou *monde,* on entre dans un labyrinthe de difficultés et de contradictions. (*V. I.* p. 1) [3]

There is no clearer statement of Merleau-Ponty's view of the discontinuity of vision and language than the very first sentence of *Le Visible et l'Invisible.* Vision partakes of the undivided unity of Subject and Object, Self and Other, whereas the universe of discourse is one of contradictions. That is to say a world of dualisms incapable of resolving themselves in an original, forever lost unity and if we are to take the metaphor of the labyrinth seriously, language provides us with a space whose beginning and end are lost, whose rationality escapes him who has the misfortune of being in it and who will have to submit to the cipher of its meanderings without the hope of ever unravelling it. In a word, and to use concepts dear to Derrida, the world of language is a world without *arche* or *telos.*

To underscore the primacy of vision over language in the latter works of Merleau-Ponty is not only to make explicit an attitude which runs throughout his complete work but also to characterize the dynamic factor which determines the progression of his thought. For, from a certain perspective—a teleological perspective which I believe to be implicit in Merleau-Ponty's concept of vision—it could be said that all of Merleau-Ponty's philosophical enterprise is centered around the problem of explicitating at the level of a philosophical consciousness—and therefore a reflexive consciousness —the original vocation of phenomenology which is a visual, specular, and painterly vocation rather than a linguistic, conceptual, and literary one.

From the vantage point offered to us by *L'Oeil et l'Esprit* one might say that one of the characteristics of the *Phenomenology of*

[3] For convenience we shall give our references to the works of Merleau-Ponty directly in the text using the following notation:

Ph. P.   *Phénoménologie de la Perception,* Paris, 1945.
S. N. S.   *Sens et Non-Sens,* Paris, 1963.
O. E.   " L'Oeil et l'Esprit " in *Les Temps Modernes,* Vol. XVII (1961) no. 184-185, pp. 193-227.
V. I.   *Le Visible et l'Invisible,* Paris, 1964.
All italics are in the original texts.

Perception consists in the recasting of the phenomenological concepts in visual metaphors and the systematic elaboration into a coherent web of these same metaphors. It would be a tedious and unnecessary task to do an elaborate analysis of the visual metaphors used by Merleau-Ponty. Let us simply give a few examples.

If phenomenology rejects certain scientific positions it is because:

> C'est moi qui fais être pour moi (et donc être au seul sens que le mot puisse avoir pour moi) cette tradition que je choisis de reprendre ou cet horizon dont la distance à moi s'effondrerait, puisqu'elle ne lui appartient pas come une propriété, si je n'étais là pour la parcourir du regard. *(Ph. P.* p. iii)

If the idealist position is unsatisfactory it is because: "Il est essentiel à ma vision de se référer non seulement à un visible prétendu, mais encore à un être actuellement vu." *(Ph. P* p. 429)

The act of vision is in fact so primary and so fundamental that upon it rests the bond that will join in an unresolvable fashion, subject and object: "Je pense fermer les yeux, me boucher les oreilles mais je ne peux pas cesser de voir, ne serait-ce que le noir de mes yeux." *(Ph. P.* p. 453)

If the being of consciousness is being conscious of itself, it is because: "L'apparence est réalité en moi, l'être de la conscience est de s'apparaître." *(Ph. P.* p. 432) And if consciousness is adequate to the object it intentionalizes it is because: "La vision s'atteint en elle et se rejoint dans la chose vue." *(Ph. P.* p. 432) And phenomenological reduction is fundamentally a problem of distance and perspective:

> . . . nous ne pouvons pas soumettre au regard philosophique notre perception du monde sans cesser de faire un avec cette thèse du monde, avec cet intérêt pour le monde qui nous définit, sans reculer en deçà de notre engagement pour le faire apparaître lui-même comme spectacle. . . . *(Ph. P.* p. ix)

The task of philosophy then is not to elucidate the world, for nothing could become more transparent than our original position, or as he puts it: "La philosophie ne peut que le replacer sous notre regard, l'offrir à notre constatation." *(Ph. P.* p. xiii)

That consciousness should be equated with vision or to be more exact, that vision should be made the archetypal form of all perception is not without having a certain number of consequences with regard to the problems concerning the nature of the perceiving subject, the world that it inhabits, or its inter-subjective relationship to other perceiving subjects. We shall not in this context attempt to try to analyze what are the unique characteristics of Merleau-Ponty's treatment of these problems or to what extent he remains faithful to the Husserlian project. It would not be out of place, however, to attempt a characterization of the dominant features of a world constructed around the ontological properties of vision. Such a world is dominated by the law of identity where, for example, between an object and its appearance there does not exist the division that language introduces in the form of signifier and signified, or signifier and referent. Thus: "L'esprit sort par les yeux pour aller se promener dans les choses, puisqu'il ne cesse d'ajuster sur elles sa voyance." (O. E. p. 200-1)

The seeing subject is continuous with its own vision and not divided against itself, the way the subject as enunciator and the subject of the enunciation are in a linguistic context. For:

> Il se voit voyant, il se touche touchant, il est visible et sensible pour soi-même. C'est un soi, non par transparence, comme la pensée, qui ne pense quoi que ce soit qu'en l'assimilant, en le constituant, en le transformant en pensée—mais un soi par confusion, narcissisme, inhérence de celui qui voit à ce qu'il voit, de celui qui touche à ce qu'il touche, du sentant au senti. (O. E. p. 197)

Between the seeing subject and the world it intentionalizes there is no discontinuity; at best they are one, at worst subject and object are simply at a distance. The problem is not one of discontinuity or of difference but of perspective: "Voir c'est avoir à distance, et que la peinture étend cette bizarre possession à tous les aspects de l'Etre, qui doivent de quelque façon se faire visibles pour entrer en elle." (O. E. p. 200)

And since the problem is only one of perspective, inter-subjectivity is not a problem, for we all come to inhabit the same visual and pictorial space. There is a no more eloquent description of such a pictorial universe than Merleau-Ponty's own:

> Essence et existence, imaginaire et réel, visible et invisible, la peinture brouille toutes nos catégories en déployant son univers onirique d'essences charnelles, de ressemblances efficaces, de significations muettes. (O. E. p. 204)

If now we turn to Merleau-Ponty's treatment of language, we should not be very far off the mark in saying that at least in his early works language is conceived on the model of vision. For the author of the *Phenomenology of Perception* the most outstanding feature of the linguistic sign does not reside in the fact that the signifier and the signified constitute two discontinuous orders, nor that the former comes to break the continuity between consciousness and its ' object,' but on the contrary that the two are continuous, that the corporeity of language disappears in the very act of its utterance: " La merveille du langage est qu'il se fait oublier: je suis des yeux les lignes sur le papier, à partir du moment où je suis pris par ce qu'elles signifient, je ne les vois plus." (*Ph. P.* p. 459)

The linguistic sign is never treated as an end in itself. It is either regarded as a graphic sign which dissolves as visual perception or else under its phonetic aspect which itself dissolves in the act of communication which it sets up between two subjects.

Language then, like vision, is a medium which unites the conscious subject to his world, and the self to other selves:

> Le langage n'est plus un instrument, n'est plus un moyen, il est une manifestation, une révélation de l'être intime et du lieu psychique qui nous unit au monde et à nos semblables. (*Ph. P.* p. 229)

> La pensée se transcende dans la parole, que la parole *fait* elle-même cette concordance de moi avec moi et de moi avec autrui sur laquelle on veut la fonder. (*Ph. P.* p. 449)

The imperatives of the order of the signifier with the host of consequences that it entails do not exist. The primordial order for Merleau-Ponty is the semantic order of the signified, or in his words: " La signification dévore les signes." (*Ph. P.* p. 213)

The materiality of language is an exterior and secondary envelope, for: " Le sens est pris dans la parole et la parole est l'existence extérieure du sens." (*Ph. P.* p. 212)

It should not seem paradoxical to us if Merleau-Ponty confronted with language assigns to us the task of uncovering the silent world that it hides.

> Notre vue sur l'homme restera superficielle tant que nous ne remonterons pas à cette origine, tant que nous ne retrouverons pas, sous le bruit des paroles, le silence primordial, tant que nous ne décrirons pas le geste qui rompt ce silence. La parole est un geste et sa signification un monde. (*Ph. P.* p. 214)

The original moment of language lies in the spatial properties
of a gesture, a gesture that indicates the separation of subject and
object yet at the same time postulates their spatial continuity. " Il
faut bien qu'ici le sens des mots soit finalement induit par les
mots eux-mêmes, ou plus exactement que leur signification conceptuelle se forme par prélèvement sur une *signification gestuelle*,
qui elle, est immanente à la parole." (*Ph. P.* p. 209)

At this point it is impossible to refrain from noticing how close
such an attitude can come to some eighteenth-century theories of
language so admirably commented upon by Foucault,[4] where the
origin of language was again seen as a gesture, since that was the
closest that one could come to conceiving the continuity of self
and nature without the alienating intermediary of the social world
which is a world of representational discontinuities. Yet whereas
for the eighteenth century the gesturality of language remained a
hypothetical, forever lost origin, for Merleau-Ponty its recovery
remained the teleological aim of any valid philosophical endeavor.

Before asking ourselves whether philosophy or literature is the
proper activity—both being linguistic activities—by which to approach this original moment, let us stop to draw some empirical
consequences implicit in Merleau-Ponty's early theory of language.

For the author of the *Phenomenology of Perception* there does
not exist any fundamental difference between literature and painting, or, for that matter, music. " Un roman, un poème, un tableau,
un morceau de musique sont des individus, c'est-à-dire des être où
l'on ne peut distinguer l'expression de l'exprimé." (*Ph. P.* p. 177)

Each of them through its own medium of words, colors, or sounds
expresses the intentional unity of a subject with its surrounding
world. The artistic or philosophical act *is*—and does not represent—
this intentional unity. If an author writes, his activity is not
essentially different from any other undertaking, since any activity
is the positional relationship of a subject to his surrounding world.
" Il s'est toujours agi dans les ouvrages de l'esprit, mais il s'agit
désormais expressément, de fixer une certaine position à l'ègard du
monde dont la littérature et la philosophie comme la politique ne
sont que différentes expressions." (*S. N. S.* p. 47) The medium then
is indifferent. What counts is the inevitable unity of the subject
to its surrounding world.

[4] See in particular Michel Foucault, *Les Mots et les Choses*, Paris, 1966, pp.
119-136.

As a by now established critical tradition—inaugurated by Merleau-Ponty himself in *Sens et Non-Sens*—has demonstrated, the task of the literary critic redoubles in a way that of the author. The function of the critic is to elucidate the web of significations imminent to the literary work. Since vision is continuous with the world it represents and since language is continuous with vision, then one could expect language, in its representational relationship to the world, to maintain the identity necessary to safeguard the truth value of the universe of discourse and manifest itself by the objectivity of phenomenological description; and since language is capable of being completely adequate to the objects it describes, a second degree critical language does not raise any particular problem since a second degree critical language is to its object-language in exactly the same relationship as ordinary language is to vision. Hence the 'objectivity' of a second degree critical language is of the same nature as that of ordinary language. If phenomenological description can claim to be 'scientific and objective' it is by renouncing any finality to language and by letting language offer a mirror image of the objects of its discourse. It is for this reason that in a phenomenological perspective the discourse of the critic is not problematical. The literary critic elucidating the signification of a work can assume to be describing the 'objective reality' of the work. On the other hand, however, the critic's discourse is itself the imminent manifestation of *his* relationship to his world, thus partaking of his subjectivity; and whatever the critic may find is, in the last analysis, as much dependent on him as on his object of study. To quote Merleau-Ponty: "Nous ne trouvons dans les textes que ce que nous y avons mis." (*Ph. P.* p. ii) I believe most phenomenological literary criticism can be said to oscillate between these two poles of the inevitable subjectivity of the critic and the necessary objectivity of the work.

Such a statement is banal in itself. What is interesting is the particular attitude towards language that it implies. I do not believe that such an attitude to language can open the latter to a genuinely hermeneutical problematic. If in fact a certain number of statements of Merleau-Ponty and if some of the phenomenological critical activity with its capacity of producing various discourses on the same literary object tend to point in that direction, it is not because phenomenological critics are willing to assume the hermeneutic nature of language, but because the phenomenological reduction which in the last analysis supports the objectivity of discourse is itself a never ending act. As Merleau-Ponty himself states, phenomenological reduction can never be a complete reduction: " Le plus grand enseignement de la réduction est l'impossibilité d'une réduction complète." (Ph. P. p. viii)

Or to put it in perceptual terms: " On peut dire de la perception intérieure ce que nous avons dit de la perception extérieure: qu'elle enveloppe l'infini, qu'elle est une synthèse jamais achevée et qui s'affirme, bien qu'elle soit inachevée." (Ph. P. p. 439)

Merleau-Ponty will give us a moving and touching commentary of this fundamental incompleteness of reflection and the subject it constitutes in L'Oeil et l'Esprit. With L'Oeil et l'Esprit he shows that the Cartesian total adequation of a reflected vision to the vision of its objects is equivalent on the one hand to an unconscious subject and on the other hand to postulating one's vision identical to that of God. The perceiving subject can only be constituted by an ever repeated attempt at making vision adequate to itself.

The same dialectic applies, of course, to language. No philosophical description will ever be able to exhaust its object and in the same way no critical discourse will ever exhaust its literary object.

It may be objected at this point that Merleau-Ponty did see that language had its own rationality which sets it apart from painting or music. It is in fact true that in the Phenomenology of Perception he will say:

> . . . l'on peut parler sur la parole alors qu'on ne peut peindre sur la peinture, et qu'enfin tout philosophe a songé à une parole qui les terminerait toutes tandis que le peintre ou le musicien n'espère pas épuiser toute peinture ou toute musique possible. Il y a donc un privilège de la Raison. (Ph. P. p. 222)

I think, however, that such a statement rather than being consistent with the rest of the statements about language given in the Phenomenology of Perception instead points to the irrevocable break between the linguistic and the painterly which is going to characterize Merleau-Ponty's later meditation.

For the late Merleau-Ponty language will not be any more the silent accomplice of vision. The two modes will be discontinuous and as we have already suggested the ontological priority will have to go to the painterly rather than to the linguistic with all the anguish that such a position entails for a philosopher who has only words to describe the world. "Notre état de non-philosophie. La crise n'a jamais été aussi radicale." (*V. I.* p. 219)

It could be said that in a way the last works of Merleau-Ponty constitute a final inevitable conceptualization of that which was implicit through the whole phenomenological tradition. Descartes in founding his subject in the *cogito* had to have recourse to the visual mode. All the examples in the first two *Meditations* are taken from the visual domain. The subject that remains identical to itself does so through visions, dreams, or visual perception. Descartes when required to conceive of a mode of representation based on identity also referred himself to painting. No matter how imaginative a painter can be, his constructs, either through their individual parts or through the use of colors, refer us to an outside reality. "Toutesfois il faut au moins avoüer que les choses qui nous sont representées dans le sommeil, sont comme des tableaux et des peintures, qui ne peuvent estre formées qu'à la ressemblance de quelque chose de réel et de véritable." [5]

To admit a mode of representation based on difference rather than identity constitutes no less than madness and madness has to be expelled as Foucault has shown, from the universe of discourse.[6] We can even go further and say that the truth value of the Cartesian discourse is founded on this very expulsion outside of its realm of the world of non-identity. It is curious to note already in Descartes the suspicion that language could disturb the quiet, oneiric properties of vision. "Cependant je ne me sçaurois trop étonner, quand je considère combien mon esprit a de foiblesse, et de pente qui le porte insensiblement dans l'erreur. Car encore que sans parler je considère tout cela en moy-mesme, les paroles toutes-fois m'arrestent, et je suis presque trompé par les termes du langage ordinaire; car nous disons que nous voyons la mesme cire, si on nous la presente, et non pas que nous jugeons que c'est la mesme, de ce qu'elle a mesme couleur et mesme figure: d'où je voudrois presque conclure, que l'on connoist la cire par la vision des yeux, et non par la seule inspection de l'esprit." [7]

Yet Descartes was too concerned with sight, with the eye of the mind of the third *Meditation*,[8] or with that fantastic eye-machine of

---

[5] Adam and Tannery, eds. *Oeuvres de Descartes*, Paris, 1964, Vol. IX, part I p. 15.

[6] See in particular Foucault, *Histoire de la Folie*, Paris, 1961, pp. 54-57.

[7] Adam and Tannery, eds. *Oeuvres de Descartes*, Paris, 1964, Vol. IX, part I p. 25.

[8] "Sed quoties haec praeconcepta de summâ Dei potentiâ opinio mihi

the sixth discourse of the *Dioptrique* (upon which Merleau-Ponty will comment with nostalgic irony in *L'Oeil et l'Esprit*) to concern himself with what language might do to the subject of the *cogito*. Derrida has shown, and there is no need to return to the argument, how important vision and sound were for Husserl and how for the founder of phenomenology language was a secondary phenomenon which simply came to represent a reality other than itself.[9]

The preceding digression was necessary if we are to appreciate Merleau-Ponty's originality to its fullest and to accept the radical consequences of his philosophical enterprise. With *L'Oeil et l'Esprit*, as we have already suggested, not only does Merleau-Ponty's phenomenological project come to its inevitable conclusion but it also shows the impossible contradiction implied in any linguistic enterprise and, by extension, any philosophical enterprise.

In *L'Oeil et l'Esprit* the task that originally had been assigned to the philosopher falls to the painter. " L'oeil voit le monde, et ce qui manque au monde pour être tableau, et ce qui manque au tableau pour être lui-même." (*O. E.* p. 200)

We shall not at this point attempt to follow him further in his analysis of painting. Let us simply note that having recognized the impossibility of a direct philosophical discourse, all the working notes of *Le Visible et l'Invisible* attest to the search for a new mode of discourse sometimes qualified as indirect and sometimes

---

occurrit, non possum non fateri, siquidem velit, facile illi esse efficere ut errem, etiam iniis quae me puto mentis oculis quàm evidentissime intueri."
Unfortunately the expression *mentis oculis* in the French version has been rendered by " présente à ma pensée."

[9] It might be of interest at this point to quote some of Derrida's comments:
C'est à la condition de cette proximité absolue du signifiant au signifié, et de son effacement dans la présence immédiate que Husserl pourra précisément considérer le médium de l'expression comme ' improductif ' et ' refléchissant '. C'est aussi à cette condition qu'il pourra, paradoxalement, le réduire sans dommage et affirmer qu'il existe une couche pré-expressive du sens. C'est à cette condition que Husserl se donnera le droit de réduire la totalité du langage, qu'il soit indicatif ou expressif, pour ressaisir l'originalité du sens.
...... il faut bien le reconnaître, le mouvement qui, depuis longtemps amorcé, aboutit à l'*Origine de la géométrie,* confirme, par sa face la plus évidente, la limitation profonde du language à une couche secondaire de l'expérience, et, dans la considération de cette couche secondaire, le phonologisme traditionnel de la métaphysique. Si l'écriture achève la constitution des objets idéaux, elle le fait en tant qu'écriture phonétique: elle vient fixer, inscrire, consigner, incarner une parole déjà prête. Et réactiver l'écriture, c'est toujours réveiller une expression dans une indication, un mot dans le corps d'une lettre qui portait en elle, en tant que symbole qui peut toujours rester vide, la menace de la crise. La parole déjà jouait le même rôle à l'égard de l'identité de sens telle qu'elle se constitue d'abord dans la pensée.
Derrida, *op. cit.,* pp. 90-91.

qualified as negative, which could rejoin that undivided prelinguistic region of being to which the painter had direct access: " *On ne peut pas faire de l'ontologie directe.* Ma méthode ' indirecte' (l'être dans les étant) est seule conforme à l'être—' φ négative' comme 'théologie négative.' " (*V. I,* 233) [10] Merleau-Ponty ascribes to the painter the prerogatives that Heidegger had ascribed to the poet,[11] for Merleau-Ponty, as far as we can gather, was not willing to grant even to the poet a capacity of returning to the origins to enter into communion with the world. Language has forever lost its origins and is doomed never to regain a proximity with things. Merleau-Ponty opened *l'Oeil et l'Esprit* with an indictment of science: " La science manipule les choses et renonce à les habiter." (*O. E.* p. 7) And what is said about science is certainly also true about language: " Car, devant la pensée critique, il n'y a que des énoncés, qu'elle discute, accepte ou rejette; elle a rompu avec l'évidence naïve des *choses*." [12]

It is at this juncture perhaps that our ways depart from those of Merleau-Ponty, yet we owe him our admiration for having carried his project through and for having remained faithful to the very end to his phenomenological commitment. In so doing Merleau-Ponty marks perhaps the end of a particular mode of thought, yet we owe him a heavy debt for having cut loose language from its original meta-physical complicity. Henceforth it is language that will occupy the center of a new meditation with its concomitant categories of discontinuity, discreteness, and difference. The notion of the subject will not be seen any more as the result of a form whose function it is to generate a unifying unity but from the primacy of language will emerge a subject whose main characteristic is, to use Lacan's expression, " to be in internal exclusion of itself." As for literature, liberated from its meta-physical, political, or psychological ties, it will be set free to attempt the impossible adventure of its linguistic finality.

1970

[10] φ of course stands as a shorthand notation for philosophy.
[11] The parallel is suggested by Merleau-Ponty himself:
Le monde perceptif ' amorphe' dont je parlais à propos de la peinture,— ressource perpétuelle pour refaire la peinture—qui ne contient aucun mode d'expression et qui pourtant les appelle et les exige tous et re-suscite avec chaque peintre un nouvel effort d'expression,—ce monde perceptif est au fond l'Être au sens de Heidegger. . . . (*V. I.,* p. 223)
[12] " Un inédit de Maurice Merleau-Ponty" in *Revue de Métaphysique et de Morale,* Vol. 67 (1962), p. 401.

THE CONSCIOUSNESS OF THE CRITIC: GEORGES POULET AND THE READER'S SHARE ᕫ BY RICHARD MACKSEY ᕫ

> —Read, read, read, read, my un-
> learned reader! read,—or by the
> knowledge of the great saint *Para-
> leipomenon*—I'll tell you before-
> hand, you had better throw down
> the book at once; for without *much
> reading*, by which your reverence
> knows, I mean *much knowledge*,
> you will no more be able to pene-
> trate the moral of the next marbled
> page (motly emblem of my work!)
> than the world with all its sagacity
> has been able to unravel the many
> opinions,. transactions and truths
> which still lie mystically hid under
> the dark veil of the black one.
> *Tristram Shandy*, vol. 3, chap. 36

Critics and novelists both must attend to the strategies of reading and to the problems that they raise. *Tristram Shandy* is a novel, perhaps above all others, that concerns itself with the reciprocal and highly suspect relations of author and reader. The reader is again and again invited to participate in the subversive act of the book's creation. And the author, insofar as he is embodied as a character within the book, albeit a dead character (who may, in-deed, have begot the narrator himself), is "read" by his own creations.

Trim, but one of the many eccentric readers within the novel, was caught by Hogarth in his plate for the second edition as the Corporal adjusted himself to the "laws of gravity" and began to read that text of a sermon just fallen from a copy of Stevinus (vol. 2, chap. 15). But what is the text that Trim begins, twice, to read? We learn that it is a sermon from the pen of Yorick,

memorialized some chapters earlier by the famous " black page."
At least Tristram's father definitively recognizes Yorick's " stile
and manner." And yet the authorship of the text within the text
is further confounded, since the narrator tells us that this very
sermon was " preach'd at an assize, in the cathedral of York, before
a thousand witnesses, ready to give oath of it, by a certain prebendary of that church, and actually printed by him when he had
done,—and within so short a space as two years and three months
after *Yorick's death* " (vol. 2, chap. 18).

The prebendary of York was, of course, Laurence Sterne, who
preached the sermon at the close of the summer assizes on July 29,
1750, and who did indeed publish it " at the request of the High
Sheriff and Grand Jury " on August 7 of the same year. He published it again in 1776, for the third time, under his *nom de pupitre*,
as the final sermon in the fourth volume, *The Sermons of Mr.
Yorick*, remarking by way of apology that it had already appeared
in a " certain moral work " but had been misconstrued by its
readers. And yet within the fictional time of the narrative, Trim
sets about reading the sermon on the very day of Tristram's birth,
in 1718, and some thirty years before Yorick's lamented death. As
an instance of Sterne's deliberate intercutting of fictional and historical time, the case is hardly unique. It may remain, however, as
an emblem of the ambiguities of authorship (and paternity) that
haunt the novel. Further, both the fictional reader and his fictional
audience complicate the text with their own narratives—of Trim's
brother Tom, of Slop's Romish apologetics, and of the Shandy
brothers' contrary readings.

But the preacher's text itself is a commentary on text which
further impinges on the act of reading and, behind that, on the
very act of self-apprehension: " For we *trust* we have a good Conscience " [*Hebrews* 13: 18]. Within the polysemous fabric of Sterne's
narrative, the reader is invited to read with the fictional readers, to
supply the final identification of yet another author, and to participate in the complex game of literary creation.

Within the text of Yorick's (Sterne's) sermon, with all its
dubieties about the assurance of our own " conscience," there is
yet another invitation to confirm or correct our self-awareness
through reading: " How readest thou? " he asks by way of qualification of the individual conscience. The preacher's *tolle lege*
invites the sinner to test his conscience, like that " British judge "

appealed to in the chauvinistic peroration, against that "which he knows already written." The reader's consciousness must engage in a reciprocal relationship with text, like that of the interpreter of Common Law or of the Bible.

That which is "hidden" in Sterne's novel lies in time somewhere between the infinite possibility of the *blank* page and the final, finitely determined "*black* one" that concludes Yorick's ambiguous career. All of the narrator's desperate will to live is concentrated on keeping the story going, somehow, before the final closure of that impending black page.

And yet, to continue the reading of our epigraph, it is the *marbled* page concluding volume 3, chapter 36, that becomes the "motly emblem" of the work. For it is in the space between the conventional marbled pages of the physical book that the act of reading—and of creation—transpires.

Within this potential space Sterne insists *two* consciousnesses must be at work. Their shaping collaboration, within the shifting relationships and misapprehensions of the novel, must remain active. Speaking of the gap between what any author can say and what his reader must supply, Sterne insists "the truest respect which you can pay to the reader's understanding is to halve this matter amicably, and leave [the reader] something to imagine, in his turn, as well as yourself" (vol. 2, chap. 11). Sterne is all too well aware that the reader's imagination can be illusory and digressive as well as veridical and progressive. What follows our epigraph and its marbled page is, in fact, the elaborately sophistic preamble to "Slawkenbergius's Tale." And the tale itself, after the bookish interruption between volumes 3 and 4, proceeds, in the double key of its punning Latin and Shandy *père*'s erratic English translation, to destroy the autonomy of the written word itself. The word "nose," like "whiskers" in the "dangerous chapter" of Book 5 or Toby's "proper end of woman," suffers a "wound." It eludes the "intended" use despite all the author's protestations and abortive attempts at definition: "For by the word *Nose*, throughout all this long chapter of noses, and in every other part of my work, where the word *Nose* occurs—I declare, by that word I mean a Nose, and nothing more or less." But for the obsessed imagination, whether of Walter Shandy or of the rival universities of Strassburg or of the book's reader, the word "nose" can never again mean quite that.

The act of reading, then, " creates " a world, the presentational form of the work itself, erected *between* the determinations or ellipses of the text and the responses of the reader. As John Dewey observed, in a Shandean vein, without the act of *recreation* the text cannot be perceived as a work of art. The reader supplies, from clues within the text, the dimensions of anticipation and retrospection. But he must supply as well the search for coherence within apparent chaos, something to fill the " holes " in the text (whether asterisks or dashes or missing chapters or interrupted conversations) , and, finally, he must participate in the animating double awareness of the imagination of another and the complementary imagination that receives and completes it.

Sterne's novel thus becomes an extended meditation on these reciprocal relations that so thoroughly enmesh both author and reader in the " timeless time " of the imagination. The " real " and the " fictive " interpenetrate; identification and analysis reciprocate. And thereby the novel can become a model for a certain kind of *critical* involvement and complicity in the act of reading.

That the text must be relived, and thus completed, is the first assumption in Sterne's problematics of the novel. Yet as the text is being read, in all its meanderings, both author and reader are establishing a " metatext " that disposes those ambiguous relations, concatenating events, and intersecting times and places so deliberately skewed in the original. The reciprocating interplay of readings and readers, time and arrest, " real " and " imagined " gives us a model for the interpretative act and, thereby, the invention of a new time—that of the interpretation: first, a naive, open, and " participatory " reading, like that of the generous Trim, tracing—diachronically—the " digressive, progressive " course of the narrative; then a paradoxically synchronic " reading " of the " hidden " elements and reconstituted structures in their dialectical relations, not unlike Walter Shandy at work on the differentials of language; and, finally, a synthetic rereading of both, like that of the author comprehending the life he has discovered, a movement turning in the familiar critical circle back to the marbled page that begins, ends, and emblematizes the book. Those other physically intercalated pages, at once signifiers and signifieds, the potential blank one and the completely determined black one, remain as troubling reminders of the ' two kinds of absence that always escape the asymptote of the critical reading.

*   *   *   *   *

Willst du dich selber erkennen, so sieh, wie die andern es treiben,
Willst du die andern verstehn, blick in dein eigenes Herz.
  Schiller (quoted by Scheler, *Wesen und Formen der Sympathie*)

Georges Poulet, a dedicated admirer of *Tristram Shandy*, perhaps
stands alone among the critics of our time in his insistence on the
peculiar hazards and rewards of the act of reading. To a generation
that would approach all literary texts as formal, autotelic objects
or social totems or elaborated sign systems, he has continued to
emphasize the relationship of author and reader as one of *process*,
a reciprocal and demanding experience. He conceives this act of
reading in very Shandean terms as a collaboration between author
and reader whereby the actual *presentation* of the literary work is
achieved through a process of identification and participation between consciousnesses. The authorial presence *in* the work is quite
other than the historical figure who created it; and the attention of
the reader is freed from most of the local dispositions and historical
concerns left behind in the act of sympathetic reading. In a sense,
both "author" and "reader" are created and continue to exist
only in the process of reading itself.

This notion of reading, for Poulet as for Sterne, accepts the
inadequacy of the determined text and aims instead at a convergence of "mental worlds" normally separated by time and space.
To read is to abandon much that normally defines the empiric
self, but it is also to discover a faculty for identification and participation that, for Poulet, defines the critical self in the very act
of shaping as well as perceiving the thought of another. This
faculty of identification is not simply a "community of feeling"
of "fellow-feeling," much less a kind of emotional "infection"
as Plato might have conceived it. It seems much closer to Max
Scheler's notion of *Einsfühlung*, true affective identification. And,
as for Scheler, the importance of this experience seems to suggest
that full knowledge of the critical self cannot precede the knowledge of others. For Poulet the privileged access to this kind of self-
knowledge is through the attentive "openness" of the reader to
his text. As in Scheler, however, this initial moment of identification can be succeeded by something like authentic "sympathy,"
in which it is not simply a question of "fusion" but of an encounter that recognizes, respects, and, in a sense, completes the

subjectivity of another human being. The time of the text and its author thereby becomes the time of the reader. Like Yorick's sermon, the reading becomes a convergence of past and present.

The duty of the critic, then, is to participate in a process—one in which he seems at first to have only the most passive of rôles. The " self " that lies open and available to the thought of another is very far removed from the Kantian self that judges in a normative aesthetic sense or from the intentional self that realizes itself in the " shaping up " of the literary work. It is, rather, constituted in an intersubjective relationship between author and reader that at first seems to allow only a minimal self-awareness to the latter in the act of apprehending the mental activity of the former. Yet Poulet, like Sterne, would emphasize the inevitable participatory rôle of the reader, once the primordial access is opened, a rôle that ultimately involves the ordering, clarifying, and shaping of the spiritual " adventure " of the author.[1]

Thus, the first moment of access is, in Poulet's recurrent phrase, one of a *prise de conscience* of the consciousness of another, wherein the author becomes virtually the " reader " of his own human " text." And yet this is succeeded by the necessary contribution of the critic-reader in organizing the spiritual itinerary and completing the mental world of both the author and his own progressive self-awareness. The nature of this organization and completion involves both an initial " mimetic " recreation of the author's experience and a subsequent dialectical ordering of the elements in this experience. Latent relationships are revealed, and thematic patterns are analyzed.

The experience of the critic thus leads from a recreation to a reordering that can demonstrate what Poulet sees as the essential

[1] Now such notions of "self" and "identity" seem to imply an assumption of purely spiritual substance, a concept subjected to extensive criticism in the classic discussions of the perplexes of identity by Locke (*Human Understanding*, chap. 27) and Hume (*Human Nature*, I, iv, 6). In our time, the problems of a purely mental subject, rather than a psychophysical person, have been elaborated by Gilbert Ryle (*The Concept of Mind*, chap. 6) and P. F. Strawson (*Individuals*, Chap. 3). Clearly, Poulet descends from a very different philosophic tradition, but one that inherits the difficulties of demonstrating verifiability and unity, even when the problem is limited to the special case of the "personal identity" of different works by the same author (a case where the " objective traits " of the texts could be analogized to the physical aspects of the changing person).

unity of the author's work, the narrative structure of his adventure. Reading in this sense implies something very like Sterne's "meta-text," which can be disengaged from the elaborate interpenetrating layers of time and levels of fictionality. The story that Sterne's self-conscious narrator has to tell is, in a sense, the story of his own consciousness. But this cannot be adequately situated in the nine volumes of the tortured mutually interfering narratives. It resides, rather, in the history that Sterne has first to discover within himself and then to communicate in the shifting relationships internally between characters and publicly between Tristram and his audience. For Sterne the author, as for Poulet the critic, the problem is not one of invention but of *discovery*, self-discovery of the text within oneself and then its enactment in the complex ordering of perceptions, themes, and perspectives in the apprehended architecture of a critical "rereading."

What is too seldom suggested by his critics is the experience, the peculiar compulsion of reading an achieved essay by Georges Poulet. Although artfully constructed out of quotations from the author himself (a little like that ideal essay Walter Benjamin dreamed of, in which the critic would supply only the art of juxtaposition), it can convey the sense of a new literary text of considerable complexity, nuance, and passion. A number of such essays read together allow the reader access to a mediating literary imagination that, even while striving for the utmost transparency before the original text, reveals its own contours and pressures. That the distinctive signature of the critic can be communicated through such a literary relationship is hardly a unique experience in the French critical tradition, where an essay by Baudelaire or Mallarmé or Blanchot— to limit the examples to "creative writers" away from their lasts —can have the architectonics and emotional density of a poem or novel. In Poulet's case, however, the literary texture appears almost despite the author's efforts to elide language in his quest of thought, to refuse rhetorical flowers in his quest to gain the perspective of another's garden. Thus, a critical text by Poulet is actually conceived as a necessary means to the convergence of *three* mutually interpenetrating subjectivities.[2]

---

[2] Despite a stylistic limpidity remarkable in an age where many critics seem to confuse density with depth, Poulet feels that all his writing falls far short of an ideal transparency. Thus he can speak with impatience of his own

* * * * *

The critic, to interpret the artist must be able to get into the mind of his artist; he must feel and comprehend the vast pressure of the creative passion.

H. L. Mencken, *Prejudices: First Series*, vol. 1

In an age when critical fashions change almost with the rapidity of *haute couture*, the critical work of Georges Poulet shows a remarkable persistence of purpose and method. His first volume of *Etudes sur le temps humain*, published in 1949 when the author was already in his middle years, is a work of achieved maturity, firm control, and exceptional scope. Yet, as Paul de Man has demonstrated in a subtle essay,[3] this first collection and its successors gather together preoccupations already apparent in the essayist and novelist of a quarter-century earlier. That Poulet's initial concerns sprang from the experience of a writer of fiction as well as from his first encounter with Bergson is not surprising in a critic so intensely involved with establishing narrative origins and discovering continuity in apparent discontinuity. How to begin and where to begin inevitably implicate those fictions that must precede formal beginnings.

Yet, to emphasize the problem of origins implicit in Poulet's notion of a critical " point of departure "—where point is conceived either spatially or temporally—at the expense of the development of his notions of the critical experience and its possible extrapolation into a larger narrative of consciousness would be to falsify some of the presiding concerns of Poulet's enterprise.

It is easier, in a heuristic sense, to begin with the act of reading as his own critical point of departure than to approach his work through the much vexed question of writing and its originary paradoxes. In the first volume of the *Etudes* and in the nine volumes of essays and " presentations " that have succeeded it, the initial duty and recompense of the critic is that of a reader open, like the

---

critical language as " ce voile, cette enveloppe opaque qui s'oppose toujours chez moi à l'expression pure, c'est-à-dire complètement invisible, de ce qui devrait être dit. C'est pourquoi écrire est toujours pour moi une expérience humiliante. Elle me montre à moi-même, non dans ma subjectivité que je rêve cristalline, mais engagé dans la semi-objectivité de mon propre corps " (from an unpublished letter).

[3] Paul de Man, " The Literary Self as Origin: The Work of Georges Poulet," *Blindness and Insight* (New York: Oxford University Press, 1971), pp. 79-101.

disposition of those seventeenth-century Quietists Poulet so admires, to the experience of another, of the author constituted however partially in his text.

In the case of favored authors, Poulet has been able to return more than once, as his own concerns and techniques have evolved, and on each occasion the initial apprehension has developed into a quite distinct critical essay. Thus Proust, perhaps for Poulet the model interpretative text, has been revisited four times: first in the remarkable retrospective *summa* that concludes the first volume on " human time "; then in the shift to the perspective of space, or better, " place," and the present moment in *L'Espace proustien*; subsequently to a Proust oriented not toward the past but toward the future in *Mesure de l'instant*; and finally in a treatment of Proust as the originator of " thematic criticism " in *La Conscience critique*. These shifts of emphasis and presentation with respect to Proust derive not from a change in the basic reading experience or the way in which the critic participates in the act of completing the texts but rather from alterations within continuity, a movement in the concern of the reader from one category to another, or from phenomena of memory to the experience of the moment, or from the novelist's task to that of the critic.

Even while his concerns, more " categorical " than " thematic," have shifted from time to space, and even to relation and causality, Poulet has increasingly sought to resume the historical perspective suggested in the introduction to the first volume of the *Etudes*. This has not been a search for a history of " forms," much less a " history of literature " in the traditions of Taine or Thibaudet. Inasmuch as it admits of radical discontinuities, ruptures, and anachronisms, it is not really a history at all but rather a gallery of modes of consciousness that, through a kind of " family resemblance," characterize periods or moments in Western time since Augustine. Thus it is not the proprieties of language and conventions of literature that are in question but rather the subjective event that Poulet identifies as the *Cogito* or point of departure for each author in his apprehension or self and world. This initiating act can be very far removed from the clarity of the Cartesian *Cogito*, as in the confused, perceptual awareness of a Rousseau, and Poulet can further broadly discriminate what he sees as the underlying concerns of entire eras: in the seventeenth century, the primacy of the moment and the idea of continuous creation; in the eighteenth, the primacy of perception and the genesis of mind through a stress on continuous feeling; and in our own century, the anxious concern for a continuous grasp of consciousness that inherits some of the attitudes of these preceding centuries in a new context. Just as he insists, echoing Proust, that the comprehensive reader can extract from the totality of an author's works an identity not immediately apparent in any separate work, Poulet suggests the possibility, through the identification of such characteristic mental attitudes, of describing the "consciousness of an age." Drawing some obvious parallels with the ambitions of the history of ideas, he speaks of the prospect of reading an individual author in the light of an ideal "history of human consciousness." Here, as elsewhere in his methodological statements, one feels a tension between his immediate, sympathetic access to an author and a nostalgia for the coherence of an inclusive philosophic framework.

It is perhaps inevitable that Georges Poulet, a generous and compelling teacher as well as a sympathetic friend to other critics, should in time have come to be associated with a "school" and "method." Now the generic taxonomy of critical movements is, it could be argued, among the least rewarding of intellectual activities. Too many critics, when they attend to such concerns, are reduced from flexibility and awareness to rigid and defensive postures. Still, the lines of filiation as well as the subtle differences between Poulet and those critics with whom he has been associated are worth some attention. In an age when it seems to be a reflex of mind to call anything that moves either "structuralist" or "post-structuralist," it could be useful to consider the problems of naming an older (and richly productive) critical tradition that dates back at least as far as the first, seminal critics of the *N.R.F.* In recent years the term "School of Geneva" has sometimes been used, pointing to the pioneer rôle of Marcel Raymond (*De Baudelaire au surréalisme*, 1933) and the persistence of his work through students and successors at Geneva, such as Albert Béguin, Jean Rousset, and Jean Starobinski. Such a partial denomination might better be styled, however, the "Second School of Geneva," since the title was first applied to the linguistic circle around Ferdinand de Saussure and Baudouin de Courtenay before the turn of the century. In fact nothing could be farther from the immediate concerns of the second "School" than the differential nature of language, and Saussure would seem to be the posthumous father of

precisely those formalistic critics who would abandon any consideration of authorial subjectivity for the study of the text as a
synchronous sign system.

Poulet himself has used a number of different terms to describe
the critical tradition he has done much to define. Each reflects at
least one aspect of his presiding concerns. Thus, early in his career
he would speak of " la critique interne," emphasizing the goal of
penetrating the " inner space " of the author's consciousness. Somewhat later, in *Le Point de départ*, he speaks of " genetic criticism,"
underscoring the critic's quest for an initial, constituting act of the
mind (though this sort of " genetics " would have to be immediately
distinguished from the collective subject of Lucien Goldmann's
" genetic structuralism "!). In *Trois essais de mythologie romantique*, Poulet joins others in speaking more generally of " thematic criticism " (at a far remove, however, from the " the-
matology " of nineteenth-century positivist critics). Since Poulet's
own concerns, like those of many of his colleagues, seem larger and
more categorial than thematic, there is an added possibility for
misunderstanding in this term. While some of his interpreters, for
example, Sarah Lawall, have emphasized the status of the work as
an experience rather than an object by speaking of " existential "
criticism or " the criticism of consciousness," Poulet himself in his
most recent book, *La Conscience critique*, returns us to the privileged act of participatory *reading* in describing his tradition as
that of " the criticism of identification."

It is one of the hometruths of the academy that critical movements are most clearly outlined against the polemical dissent of
rival critical schools. The clarity of outline, of course, often
obscures the subtlety of detail, while polemical slogans may suggest
polarities where none exist. By the same token, definition by means
of contrasting rival sacred texts and shibboleths can also be initially
tempting and ultimately deceptive. Still, it is easy to see why
the kind of critical activity so energetically practiced over the
past quarter-century by Georges Poulet has about it at the moment a resolutely unfashionable aura. When so many critical
groups have almost convinced themselves that they have banished
all traces of subjectivity from the " object " or " system " they are
studying, it is clear why the critics of identification are viewed as
" the others." Much of the critical energy of our time seems, in
fact, to have been dedicated precisely to the " deconstruction " of

the traditional notion of consciousness, of the idea of "presence" on which it seems to depend, as well as of the mimetic adequacy of language and "points of departure" taken as origins.

To turn Merleau-Ponty's phrase slightly, there can be no criticism without its shadow. And at the moment, the shadows cast by the optimistic view of a critic's access, through an essentially transparent medium, to another consciousness can be said to haunt us all. These shadows of absence, discontinuity, and difference were, in fact, already figured in Sterne by the not-yet and the too late of the blank page and the black one. To take only those names most frequently invoked as the terrible parents of contemporary critical activity—Hegel, Marx, Nietzsche, Freud, and Saussure—one can immediately sense how alien these lines of thought are to Poulet's enterprise. He may have expanded the notion of the *Cogito* beyond any application Descartes would have recognized, but in a larger sense he has remained faithful to the Rationalist tradition, its cognitive assumptions, and metaphysics of presence.[4] For a critic who feels such a close sympathy with Leibniz and his conception of the perceiving monad constituting a universe in the dual awareness of a mirrored world and self, the ambitions of the Hegelian dialectic and Absolute Mind could only be repellent; put another way, Poulet's concern is with individual *thought* and not the *idea*. Similarly, the Marxian analysis of the collective at the expense of the individual subjectivity, whether in orthodox or anthropological formulations, is quite alien to his notion of consciousness. This is not to deny a certain surprising sympathy, especially in his later work, for the sort of collective or general consciousness described by Goldmann. The difficulty for Poulet, however, in accepting the Marxist formulation rests in the internal

---

[4] The very notion of the self-constituting *Cogito* has, for instance, been subjected to successively destructive critiques, contesting both its priority (Heidegger) and indubitability (Merleau-Ponty). Heidegger would substitute the hermeneutics of the *Sum* that, through a *Rückbezogenheit*, seems to link his philosophy of language in *Holzwege* with the initial analysis of *Dasein* in *Sein und Zeit*; Merleau-Ponty proposes a "new" *Cogito*, the *être-au-monde*, which in its psychophysical ambiguity could hardly appeal to Poulet. An equally sweeping revision of the possibility of interpersonal cognition could be found in Emmanuel Lévinas's notion of the "asymmetry of the interpersonal"; "La pensée et la liberté nous viennent de la séparation et de la considération d'Autrui—cette thèse est aux antipodes du spinozisme" (*Totalité et Infini*, p. 28).

relations between the individual and collective "levels" and his
adamant refusal of dialectical "objectifications." [5]

Again, Nietzsche clearly undertakes his celebrated deconstructions at the expense of the metaphysics from which Poulet descends;
the consequences of the demythologizing of origins (and their rôle
in the interpretative process, echoed in our time by Foucault's
"refus de commencement") weigh heavily on any assumption of a
privileged critical "point de départ"—although Poulet, like Leibniz, has no particular logical horror of infinite regress. Freud, in
positing the radical gap between the unconscious and consciousness,
the mechanism of repression and desire, raises yet another thesis
basically untenable to a criticism of immediacy, identification, and
copresence. Finally, Saussure and subsequent philosophies of language grounding the very possibilities for thought on the *differential*
relationships of a sign system that never corresponds precisely to
the things signified erect one more obstacle to a coincidence of
minds and the primacy of consciousness. (But it should be noted
that in our own time Piaget and others have, in turn, raised serious
objections to the so-called Whorfian hypothesis that language
generates and determines thought.) It has been largely on the
linguistic model (whose inadequacy we are just beginning to realize)
that critics such as Barthes have attacked traditional notions of
mimesis, from which Poulet inherits at least the assumption
that language "reflects," even if imperfectly, antecedent thought.
Jacques Derrida's use of the differential notions figured above in

[5] Poulet, writing in an unpublished letter of the relations between the collective and the individual consciousness in any given historical period, describes
his points of tangency and divergence with respect to Goldmann more precisely: " J'aime de concevoir les consciences individuelles comme baignant dans
une conscience commune, qui, dans une certaine mesure, les forme et les
détermine. Mais je rejette, bien entendu, l'assez grossier déterminisme que les
marxistes en déduisent. J'imagine plutôt chez chacun de nous la simultanéité
de différents niveaux de conscience, les uns plus étendus que les autres, et de
l'un à l'autre desquels, comme dans certaines mines, il est permis de passer. Mais
le problème alors consiste dans le fait qu'il n'est précisément possible de se
déplacer de l'un à l'autre de plusieurs niveaux de conscience, que si ceux-ci se
trouvent voisins ou quasi de plein-pied. D'un état de conscience à un autre
on ne peut passer que par participation, c'est-à-dire en ne sortant pas de la
subjectivité. Il ne peut donc y avoir influence de la conscience collective sur
la conscience individuelle que par un acte de l'esprit par l'entremise auquel la
conscience collective se fait partie intégrante de la conscience individuelle.
Alors le premier est saisi et assimilé par le second dans une expérience tout
interne. En d'autres termes, ce qui me sépare des marxistes, c'est que je me
refuse à admettre l'intrusion de l'objectif comme tel dans les relations entre le
général et l'individu."

his critique of the sign and its temporal structure has led to even more far-reaching conclusions aimed at the concepts of plenitude and presence, where the *trace* of meaning points to absent meaning and a *supplément* yet to be produced. In every case, a discourse seeking guarantees in the copresence of consciousness to consciousness is in this climate beset by discontinuities, errancy, and empty spaces. The laureate of these philosophical metaphors of defeat is, of course, the most modern of our literary ancestors, Stéphane Mallarmé.

In one sense Poulet, who has read the philosophers as well as the philosophic critics, would seem to embrace Leibniz's dictum that the only such way to refute a philosophical theory is to replace it. One should quickly add, however, that Poulet is too faithful a reader to remain long insensitive to those shadows when they are visible in a writer of genius. He has written two richly suggestive essays on Mallarmé and, surprisingly, has discovered in the highest achievements of Victor Hugo a paradoxically "negative poetry" that anticipates these very gulfs of vacancy threatening to swallow any emergent sense of reality. In fact, he sees in his friend Maurice Blanchot, at the opposite extreme from his own optimism about language and access, an exemplary criticism of silence and distance. Poulet would not deny the hazards of reading and the existence of a negative face to many texts. He obviously is drawn, however, to a theory of cognition and to a kind of writing able to sustain his own more positive impulses.

While those who dissent from the basic assumptions of Poulet's critical undertaking may help to define its first principles and risks, probably the best way to comprehend both its ambitions and achievements is to look with some care at the tradition to which it *belongs,* a tradition that eludes most of the earlier attempts at simple taxonomy. Fortunately, Poulet has himself made this task much easier by gathering, in *La Conscience critique,* his own readings of this tradition.

* * * * *

The house was quiet and the world was calm.
The reader became the book . . . .
Wallace Stevens

Almost half a century after his apprentice essays as critic and novelist, Georges Poulet has gathered together in *La Conscience critique* a kind of testament in reverse—a document wherein he

describes a tradition from which his critical work descends and a
full acknowledgment of his debts to ancestors and contemporaries.
Although its scope—from 1800 to the present—suggests a history
of modern French criticism, it is a history only in a highly personal
sense, a highly selective history relived within the critical life of
the author. The most satisfying of these " metacritical " essays
resemble markedly the method and tone of Poulet's " literary "
essays. They consist of rich and sensitive readings of elected critics
for whom he has especial sympathies, read in such a way as to
describe their spiritual itineraries and to provide an inventory of
their chosen methods and a narrative of the attainments and frustrations of their " quests."

Although a few critics who are strangers to Poulet's " criticism of
identification " are included, they exist either as paradigmatic
examples, like Blanchot, of the " other way," a criticism of distance
and silence, or, like Sartre and Barthes, as mere sketches of alien
sensibilities. The book is haunted, like any such enterprise, by those
critical travelers who are absent and by the roads not taken. But it
is nevertheless a remarkably full and varied critical voyage of
exploration.

The first part of the volume, after a brief introduction considering critics like Sainte-Beuve and the impressionists (Lemaître,
France, Faguet), who are sometimes mistakenly associated with the
" criticism of identification," consists of fifteen chapters dedicated
to eighteen critics—from Mme. de Staël to the generation of Richard
and Starobinski. The second, shorter part of the book consists
of two essays directly concerned with situating Poulet himself
within this tradition. The first attempts a " phenomenology of
the critical consciousness " and along the way reviews the critical
postures of a number of the authors discussed earlier. The second,
more personal in its address, describes the evolution of his own
work in terms of " the consciousness of the self and the consciousness
of the other."

In dismissing Sainte-Beuve and the impressionist critics from
the tradition of identification that he seeks to define, Poulet argues
that they never lend themselves freely to their authors and consequently achieve only a false identification simulated through
stylistic mimicry and a masquerade of sentiments and thoughts
handled as commodities. Poulet's somewhat startling image for
Sainte-Beuve is that of a cuckoo insinuating itself into the nest

of an author and usurping his identity.[6] Lemaître he sees as a detached actor playing his effects against an ironic screen that he maintains between his critical self-awareness and the consciousness of the author.

The positive line of a criticism of identification begins with an essay on Mme. de Staël (1766-1807). Poulet characteristically turns first to her early *Lettres sur les écrits et le caractère de Jean-Jacques Rousseau* (1788). The journey thus begins close to Geneva—and to the figure of Rousseau, whose example haunts so many of the succeeding critics in the narrative, not the least among them Poulet himself. It was Rousseau who could describe (for the first time in literature as a lived human experience, Poulet had asserted in his first book) the natural plenitude of a consciousness open to the moment and the *non-moi*, an affective *totum simul* not unlike the initial one of the critic's ideal reader: " Je remplissais de ma legère existence tous les objets que j'apercevais. Tout entier au moment présent . . . je n'avais nulle notion distincte de mon individu." (And perhaps from this one side of Rousseau's paradoxical imagination, the transparency of an almost emptied consciousness to the world, may be traced Poulet's persistent optimism about the critic's access to a primal thought constituting both the author's self and his world.)

For Mme. de Staël the experience of reading Rousseau evokes the intense pleasure of " le *souvenir* et l'impression de mon *enthousiasme*." This sense of recollected admiration grounded in a sympathetic act of identification, a convergence of experience and a joining of two moments in time, becomes for Poulet the genuine point of departure and key to all critical reading. External judgment on an objective work, the traditional notion of " criticism," is replaced by the enthusiastic participation in the " purely subjective movement that the work reveals and communicates " (23). But participation does not mean submersion, and Poulet develops the notions of " supplement " and " echo " to suggest that in the

6 Some qualification of the familiar charge of invincible " egoism " brought against Sainte-Beuve might be found in a recent essay by Jean-Pierre Richard, who argues that the critic despaired of any direct access to the consciousness of another and resignedly elected the devices of stylistic and biographical evidence as a second-best route (*Essais sur le romantisme* [Paris: Seuil, 1971]). It is a commonplace that Sainte-Beuve achieves the greatest authority when the temptation to confound the author in the work with his historical counterpart was not available to him.

interaction of emotion and reflection, with its own temporality, a new critical method is born whose aim is to reveal " the inner man," and to reveal him " is to cause him to reappear in what could precisely be called the ' critical ' consciousness with the very traits he possessed in the depth of his own past " (23). Criticism through the apprehension of an experience already lived by another has thus for its express mission, in the words of Mme. de Staël: " faire revivre le génie créateur."

Poulet sees in his countryman Charles Baudelaire (1821-67) an extension of this affective reiteration and reconstitution of the interiority of another. Exploring Baudelaire's privileged poetic emblems of the prostitute and the actor, he describes identification, whether in the poetic or the critical imagination, as a double experience, in which the subject can at once be " hors de chez soi " and still feel himself " partout chez soi " (29). The reciprocal movement of dispossession and possession is, no doubt, intimately related to the central Baudelairean impulses of condensation and expansion that Poulet studied under the existential image of the circle. " Correspondences " between the inner life and the exterior, between past and present experience, and finally between two interior lives—where the poem or novel is a form of verbal repetition between experiences—form the paradigmatic events for Baudelaire, whether as poet or as reader of Poe, Flaubert, or Gautier. The resonances in the reader allow him to achieve experiences analogous to the " double life " of creation. Baudelaire's " hypocrite lecteur " is in a real sense the double of the author, though the thought of the poet is the *cause* of the process and that of the reader the *effect*. The poet's intentional thought and the critic's interpretative recreation are mediated by the verbal poem itself, " a simple intermediary between two thoughts " (39), thanks to which an experience is realized that is never completely achieved in ordinary human contacts—genuine *intersubjectivity* where the means of the poet and the responses of the critic reciprocate. (Poulet draws freely on Baudelaire's criticism of music and painting, which also communicate to the listener or viewer the same " shudder " or " start " of shared experience, suggesting thereby that the literary work does not have a privileged status in this intersubjective process.) Finally, Poulet relates this phenomenon to the temporal dimension of Baudelaire's poetics, where echo and reflection represent the way experience can be *recognized* through memory and recreated through the "translation" or mirror of art in the life of the critic.

Proust (1871-1922), whose immense novelistic quest had its origins, we now realize, in a critical meditation, the *Contre Sainte-Beuve*, represents for Poulet an almost inexhaustible model for both the literature and the criticism of our century. He recalls that the novelist did not abandon his attempt to comprehend the literary response as he immersed himself in the act of creating it. Like the naive Marcel before the hawthorns or the spires of Martinville, Proust's reader attempts to recreate through a kind of mental mimicry the "gestures" of the creator. At this precritical stage, the reader's mimetic response conforms to one of Proust's favorite exercises, the *pastiche*, the same sort of imitation which, at the lowest point in the spiritual trajectory of the novel, in the "unpublished pages from the Goncourts' journal," forms the overture to the final affirmation of his own literary vocation. Yet Poulet argues that it was only a second critical discovery that saved Proust from foundering in the chaotic and essentially mediocre flux of imitation. This was the discovery, articulated in the introduction to his Ruskin text of 1900, that to read only one book by an author is to have only the most casual encounter with his imagination. All of his works must be attentively revisited and reread: "c'est seulement par [la] répétition [de certains traits singuliers] dans des circonstances variées qu'on peut les reconnaître pour caractéristiques et essentiels" (*Pastiches et Mélanges*, p. 107). What is in question is a form of *recognition* across the local contexts and concerns of a naive reading, and in this comprehension that is a recognition, the author, like Bergotte at his death, achieves a kind of immortality revealing the peculiar signature of his imagination. Proust speaks, in the same essay, of the power of the reader as a "mémoire improvisée." To criticize, then, is to remember through rereading. "As there is a time *recaptured*, there is then a reading *redone*, an experience *relived*, a comprehension *rectified*" (53). In the totality of a favorite author's work, in all the canvases of a Vermeer or an Elstir, there is a retrospective unity, present to us in its volume and density, of the imaginative life of the artist. Proust thus becomes for Poulet the "founder of thematic criticism" (55).

In his fifth chapter Poulet considers as a group those critics of the *N.R.F.* who are, in their sympathetic, unreserved adhesion to literary texts, his own immediate precursors in the criticism of identification—Albert Thibaudet (1874-1936), Jacques Rivière (1886-1925), Ramon Fernandez (1894-1944), and Charles Du Bos (1882-1939). One might initially observe that at least three of this remarkable group of colleagues, like Poulet himself, share, along with the traumatic discovery of Bergson's thought, a view of French culture seen at least partially from the outside: Thibaudet taught at Uppsala and Geneva; Ramon Fernandez was born in Mexico; and Du Bos was by birth and sympathy partly Anglo-American. Poulet begins his discussion by separating Thibaudet, in his desire to situate authors, genres, and epochs in some sort of geographic or historical tableau, from the other three critics, who remain " concentric " in their fidelity to the intimate identification of their reading. He sees Thibaudet as turning his back on this " feminine side " of his own critical instinct in order to pursue, under the " anxiety of influence," synoptic social and psychological explanations of literary history. Poulet's derogation of this latter movement as " excentric " to account for what today would be called " intertextuality " and for lines of historical filiation could be indicated as partial, since in his own later work he has increasingly felt the need to account for " periods " and a possible " historical development of consciousness." Thibaudet, in his best *N.R.F.* essays, remained a sensitive reader of texts, and sought, in his notion of literary " generations," to avoid some of the rigidities of positivistic historical determinations.

Poulet contrasts the suppleness and " availability " of his " concentric " critics—Rivière, Fernandez, and Du Bos—with the self-indulgent " impressionism " of a Lemaître. The contrast is especially sharp in the case of the partial and hesitant approximations of Jacques Rivière, whose sense of personal insufficiency before the work stems from what he calls " mon effroyable plasticité." Poulet feels that this almost tactile hesitation before the texture of the work to be criticized is at once the signature of Rivière's critical openness and the cause of his tendency always to stop short of the fully realized intersubjective experience. In contrast with this insecure " groping " toward contact Poulet places the sureness and clarity of Ramon Fernandez's vision, the " rage for order " of Stevens' Key West poem. Fernandez seeks to apprehend in the " troubled vision " of an author what can be rigorously reformulated in the analytic intelligence of the critic. Identification becomes a means of comprehending and organizing, by a willful act of the intelligence, the confused thought of the writer in the critic's *mise au point*, "la vision d'une vision." The extreme volontarism of Ramon Fernandez's enterprise, already so fully articulated in his extraordinary first book, *Messages*, perhaps deserves fuller development within the tradition Poulet is describing.[7]

The fourth of the *N.R.F.* critics, Charles Du Bos, although he shares Rivière's remarkable openness and malleability before the subjectivity of another, stands in striking contrast to his friend's uncertainties. With an extraordinary and fluid ease he is able to empty himself of personal concerns and become "a pure receptacle" for the spiritual life of another. He is able to become, in the words of Bergson, who affected his thought so deeply, a *"lieu de passage,"* or theater for the subjectivities of his favorite authors. Poulet develops his initial sketch of Du Bos in the succeeding chapter, an essay of exceptional sensitivity that moves easily back and forth between the journals of Du Bos and his *Approximations* and other critical essays. The chapter admirably displays the older critic's *"disponibilité"* and digressive flexibility before the richness of another's mind. But it is also organized in terms of a dialectical development much more characteristic of Poulet's own thought. Thus, Du Bos is presented as moving from an initial moment of almost complete vacancy to one of overabundance as the first receptivity is successively filled with the events for which it has passively become the *lieu de passage*, a gallery of doubles "approximated" in what Du Bos called his "*moi double*." This *Stimmung* of resonances and intersecting streams of thought constituted what Du Bos himself called his perilous "*multiplicité étalée*," borrowing the phrase from Ramon Fernandez. The danger, of course, in the case of such a passive and immobile center at the heart of such absolute mobility is that absence will be succeeded by glut and the place of passage will become a place of obstruction. Poulet movingly describes this "peril of the inexhaustible" confronted by possession in terms of the thought of meditative writers in a tradition equally dear to the younger critic, from Augustine to Fénelon, Joubert, Guérin, and Proust. To move from "interpretation" to "criticism" requires an additional act of elevation, of

---

[7] Poulet has recently supplemented his discussion of Ramon Fernandez in *La Conscience critique* with an essay in *MLN* 87 (Edelman Memorial Number): 53-57.

"raising oneself up," but Poulet ultimately pays the tribute of an inheritor to a precursor who made of himself "un lieu qui doit se transformer en temple," the interpreter who first revealed the seminal possibilities of those terms dear to the younger critic: a critical *point de départ* that can give access to the author's inmost *foyer*, or vital core of experience.

In Marcel Raymond (b. 1897), Poulet next describes both a major successor to the critics of the *N.R.F.* and the titular founder of that "Geneva School" to which he himself has such strong ties. The economy and rigor of Raymond's critical address may seem at the opposite pole from the abundance and confusion of Du Bos's "pre-critical" thought. Yet he shares with Du Bos a remarkable receptivity to the "awakening consciousness." Again, like Du Bos, he has an alert sympathy for the meditatives of the "interior life," many of them also natives of the *Suisse romande*, as well as a fondness for the devotional writers of the Baroque. In fact, he seems to find some of his own secular methodological principles prefigured in their treatises of devotion or spiritual exercises. Thus he cultivates an attitude of almost religious receptivity to the slightest movements and preverbal substructures of the contemplative experience. And, again like Du Bos, he also seems to have acquired from the German cultural tradition of Dilthey and Gundolf a sense of literature as "lived experience" and an awareness of the bonds between poetry and metaphysics in the creative act. (Raymond, who lectured in Leipzig from 1926 to 1928, retained from his reading there the first lesson of existential phenomenology, an insistence on the intentional nature of consciousness.) He emphasizes the critic's task as one of *participation* (a term borrowed from Lévy-Bruhl) in a dual act of comprehension that is at once ontological and noetic. But for Poulet the most important aspect of Raymond's critical method is the identification of the author's first distinctive moment of consciousness in a reciprocal awareness of self and world, a moment at once constitutive of the writer's being and the beginning of that cognition from which his creative "lignes de force" emanate. While Raymond styles this "sentiment de l'univers" the *Cogito*, a term central in Poulet's own development, it is very far removed from the clarity and distinctness of the Cartesian *Cogito*. In the tradition of writers Raymond has studied (Renaissance-Baroque, Romantic, Modern), the *Cogito* is, rather, while differing with each individual, always an obscure and confused first stirring at the very border between the conscious and the subconscious, a kind of "*conscience-minimum*" (120) anterior to its articulation in language, its eventual "mise en forme." (It is important to note that Raymond, in the Bergsonian tradition rather than the Freudian, sees no opposition or fissure between the "unconscious" and the barely conscious.) And from these primary spiritual events Raymond is able to suggest, as in his influential masterpiece of 1933, *De Baudelaire au surréalisme*, an anticipation of that "history of consciousness" to which Poulet's own later work aspires. Like each "personal history," these larger lines of development are generated by the dialectical opposition of existential constants. As in the career of Senancour, to whom he devotes a later essay dedicated to Georges Poulet (1965), the individual effort to resolve these tensions may end with a personal *échec* and yet serve to prefigure a central crisis of modern literature. Finally, for all Raymond's fondness for dialectical oppositions, Poulet sees at the heart of his enterprise a reapparition of the Plotinian myth of unity, a transcendent, originary state before the fall into division and separation. This resolution of the subject-object opposition is thus the secularized myth behind the critic's quest for participation.

Poulet next devotes a moving chapter to the spiritual itinerary of Albert Béguin (1901-57), Raymond's friend and pupil. Elsewhere Poulet has written of the regret with which he watched earlier literary loves replaced by bitter criticism in the "insatiable" moral quest that drove the author of *L'Âme romantique et le rêve*.[8] And yet in this present essay he describes with remarkable sympathy and coherence the stages that led Béguin from an initial sense of inner isolation and aridity to the unreserved literary immersion in the lives of others and, finally, beyond to a highly eclectic doctrine of presence and incarnation. From within their characteristic critical experiences Poulet contrasts the contemplative in Raymond with the urgent need for engagement in Béguin, an opposition echoed in their careers. For Béguin, to understand is to feel, and to feel fully means for the critic to seize, to lay hold of "reality," to apprehend "the things of this earth" through the poet's primary possession. He poses his elected poets of "carnal presence" (from

[8] "Albert Béguin, l'Insatiable," *in Albert Béguin: Étapes d'une pensée . . .* (Neuchatel: Éd. de la Baconnière, 1957), pp. 263-66.

Maurice Scève to Hugo, Claudel, and Péguy) against a Mallarméan, idealist poetry of absence. But these concrete presences that the poet, and through him the critic, loves are inexorably fallen into time and degradation. Thus Béguin, having rejected the sterile ideal fixity of Mallarmé's swan, seeks to preserve the presence of fugitive terrestrial things in the oneiric imagination of the Romantic dream. The myth of the soul having access in the freed space of the unconscious to the memory of a golden age is yet one more version of the ascent to sources, of the route from exile to harmony. This oneiric movement is coupled with the related myth of childhood, in which the poet is able to express his nostalgia for another version of the lost paradise of immediate presence. To understand this literature is "to remember." The language of poetry thus becomes the locus of both the *here* and the *elsewhere*, what Poulet calls a "poésie de l'absence dans la présence" (147). The contemplation of things leads to the creation of linguistic signs, marks of this present absence and reminders of that past presence. Poulet thus relates Béguin's poetics to his apologetics where the poet, unlike the mystic abolishing sensible objects, finds and remembers vestiges of the Creator present in the world of creation. And this poetic presence is also incarnate in historic reality, a continual act of presence realized between men in human time. Poulet quotes an admirable letter from Béguin to Raymond after the death of the latter's father and then summarizes the progressive stages of the ascent: "the presence of things, the presence of God in things, the presence of time and men, the presence in time and among men [leading to a final eschatologic stage], the presence of God in the Communion of Saints" (156-57). Béguin expresses this theology of continuous presence in a Pascalian phrase: "Toucher dans le concret à la présence de l'Invisible." Poulet, however, sees a final *échec* at this point in Béguin's quest, since the ultimate object of contemplation annihilates what had preceded it. "As there is a final retreat of all objective reality in the presence of God, there is a corresponding retreat of subjective reality" (157). All that the critic sought in the immediacy of shared experience is finally superseded by the contemplative's goal of a transcendent Presence. At all stages of its progress Poulet can speak of Béguin's participatory approach to the literary consciousness as "une critique de confiance," secure in its humble power to "see into" both the author's secondary world and the presence of things. Even when

Béguin attempts to see *beyond* both of these, which for Poulet is to abandon criticism, there is a certain aptness in the former's own words describing the ambition of poetic witness and its limits: " Serait-il vrai que la poésie trouve sa grandeur dans son échec? "

In a brief chapter Poulet next considers two critics who seem, in their cultivation of objectivity before the text, at the opposite extreme from the engagement of Béguin's personal quest. Jean Rousset (b. 1910), another friend and disciple of Raymond now teaching at Geneva, inherits the latter's contemplative attitude and taste for the literature of the Baroque. But more than any other of the Genevan critics he practices an apparently disinterested objectivity in approaching the literary text, its images, and its forms. He is drawn to the theatricality, fluidity, and metamorphic effects of the self-conscious imagination and describes stylistic, rhetorical, and mythic structures with the care of a formalist. Yet Poulet argues that Rousset is always intent upon moving *through* the " life of forms " to the " life of the consciousness " that generated them. His colleague Jean Starobinski has asserted that there is no structure "sans une conscience structurante," and Rousset seems to echo this formulation: " L'oeuvre désigne un au-delà de l'oeuvre " (163). In a version of the hermeneutic circle, the formal qualities of the text have their genesis and are reconciled in the consciousness that is realized in them. Gaëton Picon (b. 1915) seems even further removed from the " critics of identification," with his strong ties, through an insistence on the autonomy of the text, to the Russian Formalists and the American New Critics. Yet for him the work has an entelechy the process of which it is the critic's task to trace: " L'oeuvre est une origine, non une terme " (165). Thus, while he neglects the initial consciousness so important to Poulet's tradition, Picon (especially in his magisterial reading of Proust) ends by describing it through the guise of the intentional self revealed in the " shaping up " of the author's project. It is at this point that the programmatically formalist critic still attentive to the literary text as process joins the critics of consciousness.

Another short chapter is devoted to Georges Blin (b. 1917), who, despite his succession to Béguin's post at Basel, must stand some-what apart from the tradition of identification that Poulet has been describing. Blin shares with a number of the other critics a " phenomenological " approach to reading. But more than any

of the others he can speak of his criticism, with its direct links to
Husserl and Merleau-Ponty, as " une critique intentionnelle." His
chosen authors—Stendhal and Baudelaire—so acutely afflicted with
analyzing and revising their own multiple intentions, richly lend
themselves to Blin's ceaseless interrogation. Poulet relates the
peculiar density of this criticism—and its ultimate tragedy—to the
extraordinary acuity of Blin's intelligence and the vertiginous expansion of teleological speculation to which he submits the work.
Instead of the transparency of access that recommends the sort of
reading Poulet celebrates, the " pensée repensée " of Blin generates
an endless chain of propositional deductions from the evidence of
the text and becomes a kind of intellectual " tremplin" or
critical hall of mirrors. (Perhaps his incisive early Baudelaire
essay for the N.R.F. edition manages to escape this fate.) The
victim of his own intelligence and of an analysis that begins before
" participation " is achieved, Blin remains for Poulet a kind of
Sisyphus of unresolvable intentional speculation.

    The essay dedicated to Gaston Bachelard (1884-1962) is the
longest and one of the most rewarding in La Conscience critique.
In view of Bachelard's rôle as a pioneer, it could in fact be asked
why his appearance had been so long delayed in the architecture
of the book. (The answer, no doubt, has to do with his relative
independence of the tradition traced to this point, as well as his
more direct influence on younger critics like Jean-Pierre Richard,
who is discussed in the succeeding chapter.) Still, Poulet can speak
of Bachelard's discovery of the " material imagination " at work
in poetry as a " Copernican revolution " (174) for criticism and
can confidently style him " the greatest explorer of mental life since
Freud " (though, one should quickly add, his conception of consciousness is radically different from Freud's) .

    Poulet initially opposes in Bachelard the thinker and the dreamer,
the two sides of his personality that answer to the scientific and
poetic axes of his career. It is the former, the philosopher of
science, who attempts to describe a thought of extraordinary
objectivity, detached both from objects and from the thinker himself, a kind of anti-Cogito. But, in a telling passage from La
Formation de l'esprit scientifique (p. 248), Bachelard manages in
the very act of describing the " nudity " of scientific objectivity to
give birth to its psychic counterpart: " Vivre et revivre l'instant de
l'objectivité, être sans cesse à l'état naissant de l'objectification."

Along with the scientific "objectification" there is a "nascent
state" of consciousness that constitutes itself reflexively; behind
the nascent science there is an "instant de la connaissance nais-
sante" (L'Intuition del 'instant, p. 9). Thus the lived moment of
the scientific quest for the objectified concept gives birth to the
subjective experience of what Bachelard calls "une prise de conscience rationalisée." And, just as scientific thought has for its
goal the concept, subjective reverie generates the poetic image, the
two poles of Bachelard's reciprocating speculative activity: "Entre
le concept et l'image, pas de synthèse" (La Poétique de la rêverie,
p. 45). Poulet thence conducts a subtle exploration, too detailed
to suggest here, of Bachelard's emergent epistemology of the "material imagination," which he first conceived as a kind of therapy
or catharsis for the scientific spirit. Thus, the first volume in his
"inner cosmology," La Psychanalyse du feu (1938), is a transitional
work, an attempt to "psychoanalyze" those subjective elements,
images, of mental activity that have been the source of scientific
myths and "errors." Yet even within this book the initial ironic
stance toward such subjective phenomena is gradually succeeded by
one of increasing sympathy. And the volumes that follow, devoted
to the imagery of the elements, clearly move to a phenomenological
description of the intimate way one "thinks matter" and "ma-
terializes the imaginary." (The importance for Bachelard of
Eugène Minkowsky's notion of "retentissement" might have been
useful here in describing the "a-causal" dimension of the image in
the poetic imagination.) Poulet relives the drama of the Bache-
lardian Cogito, "an autonomous act of the spirit that launches the
existence of the image" (207), a movement from emptiness to
plenitude, and an experience of the "malleability" of the stuff
underlying both form and dreams. This Cogito is obviously much
closer to Rousseau's marginal vision than to Descartes' lucidity,
and the reader can share both its exaltation and its power to create
myths: "The poet and the critic pursue together the same dream"
(209).

Poulet next considers Jean-Pierre Richard (b. 1922), a critic
who clearly descends from Bachelard's phenomenology of the "concrete tissue" of material reality, but who, in his single-minded
adhesion to the primal images, leaves behind most of the latter's
epistemological concerns. The first part of the chapter is the
sympathetic preface that Poulet contributed to Richard's first

book, significantly titled *Littérature et sensation* (1954). From his earliest criticism Richard displayed an unguarded welcome to sensation apprehended through the literary image and his own astonishingly rich language for rendering this experience. (Although he is also a friend and disciple of Poulet, it is interesting to contrast the almost tactile density of his lyric prose with the exceptional limpidity of the latter's criticism.) In the second half of the chapter Poulet develops some revealing contrasts between Richard and Bachelard, notably the former's "*passive* power to refeel emotions and sensations" as opposed to his master's "*active* power to engender images" (215). Although he does not consider Richard's most recent work, Poulet underlines the persistent happiness that illuminates the younger critic's generous abandonment, early and late, to this adventure of elemental, "thematic" reading: "The return to the elementary is a return to happiness" (218).

As already noted, the criticism of Maurice Blanchot (b. 1907) represents, in detached and chilly lucidity, the opposite pole to the critical identification and intimacy of the Geneva School—and *a fortiori* to that of Richard. It remains, however, very much a criticism of consciousness, even if it is a consciousness of isolation, distance, and silence. Poulet's chapter on Blanchot deals almost interchangeably with his criticism and his fiction as testimonies to the alienating power of language; the maximum of intelligible communication here inevitably implies distance and a refusal of expression. Language assumes a profoundly negative power of "derealizing" being, and literature is always in a sense a "posthumous" activity, whose "task is to confer a sense on that which has ceased to exist" (221). The reader becomes a kind of critical vacuum pump. Poulet traces the way death (or absence) is the "initial castrophe" that defines the situation of both the author and the critic; for the author of *Thomas l'obscur*, as for Kafka, Melville, or Mallarmé, writing is the means of making this absence visible. Although Poulet perhaps neglects the significance of formal developments in Blanchot's successive fictions, he justly demonstrates the lucid ascesis and endless, empty renewal in both the theory and the practice. From the great distance that separates their opposed notions of reading, Poulet finally pays an eloquent tribute to the serene heroism of Blanchot's separated consciousness.

More than any other critic of the Geneva group, Jean Starobinski (b. 1920) has established bridges to other schools and methods—to psychoanalytic and Heideggerian thought through his reading of Ludwig Binswanger, to the more traditional *Literaturwissenschaft* as well as to the History of Ideas, to more recent " structuralist " approaches through his study of Saussure and synchronous relations in stylistics and linguistics. Significantly, Poulet is drawn throughout this discussion of his friend and former colleague at Johns Hopkins to images of reciprocation and alternation—emblems of oscillation between methodological postures as well as between modes of consciousness. Poulet begins his chapter on Starobinski, however, with an acute consideration of the latter's earliest, least systematic writings. These essays—a number of them devoted to supremely " negative " authors, Mallarmé and Kafka— reveal in the initial critical moment an isolated spectator constituting an intentional world but separated both from his own interiority and from others, whom he perceives at a distance. The overwhelming desire is, in Starobinski's words, " rejoindre l'existence . . . rejoindre le monde extérieur," but the only means of such union would be through the coincidence of consciousness, a coincidence denied by the distance that separates the spectator and his world. Thus, *le regard* becomes the emblem of this desire, a " view of what exists," in which the quest for being seems baffled by the opacity of exterior appearances. The dream, however, for the critic is one of perfect *transparency*: " a dream . . . of an intelligence to which the universe gives itself over without resistance and reveals itself thereby as precisely identical to mind " (242). The myth is one of a sovereign look that would render accessible and intelligible all existence open to the gaze like a universal " palace of crystal." This myth of penetrating vision is also the dream of Starobinski's central author, Rousseau, and it becomes supremely a myth of literature, of universal transparency and penetrability before the author's imagination. But, as both Rousseau and Starobinski realize, a world so purified to the point of transparency loses its material density, " delivers man from the state of incarnation," and risks foundering in lifeless abstraction. For both, this escape from carnal reality can only mean the sin of angelism. Poulet suggestively explores the compensatory images in Starobinski's thought of *obstacle*—veil, mask, hidden witness, pseudonym—in the play of which the critic can achieve some *detachment* and release from the dangers of a pellucid and penetrating intelligence. Between the two presiding images of transparency and obstacle can be established a complex dialectic of liberty and limitation that ultimately qualifies the conception of the reader-critic's task. And, as Poulet then suggests, the critic (who is also a physician) succeeds in introducing another counter-weight to that of intellectual distance, that of the mediating presence of the body and the implicit possibility of intimacy. Throughout Starobinski's criticism the metaphor's of sight persist, but the views alternate between the most penetrating and the most obstructed, between the most intellectually panoramic and the most sympathetically restricted. (Similarly, the category of perception that most marks his method in this oscillating world is that of *relation* or *rapport.*) His critical activity thus moves successively between "absolute distance and absolute intimacy" (258). Starobinski himself comprises these dual goals in a formula from *L'Oeil vivant* (p. 27): "La critique complète n'est peut-être ni celle qui vise à la totalité, ni celle qui vise à l'intimité; c'est un regard qui sait exiger tour à tour le surplomb et l'intimité."

The two concluding essays on those critics who stand farthest removed from the criticism of consciousness—Jean-Paul Sartre (b. 1905) and Roland Barthes (b. 1915)—give some external perspective on the tradition but are probably the least satisfying in Poulet's gallery. Perhaps the most obvious reason for this is the exigency of his own demonstration, which requires him to abandon the open and generously sympathetic reading of an author for a more polemical and public stance. The essay on Sartre should be supplemented by Poulet's own more extended reading of *La Nausée* (in *Le Point de départ*). Poulet resolutely begins his discussion here with Sartre's early tirade against what he styles the "omnivorous" view of the consciousness, "Une Idée fondamentale de la phénoménologie de Husserl" (1939). ("O philosophie alimentaire!") In an argument more marked by panache than by technical precision, Sartre pushes his conclusion—the folly of the mind "digesting" external objects and the impossibility of any penetration "into" the consciousness of another: "La conscience n'a pas de dedans" (*Situations I*, p. 33). Thus, for Sartre any intentional analysis must renounce the myth of mental interiority. Poulet asserts the ensuing paradox of any attempt to capture an author's *projet*: "One can occupy the 'inner thought' only by turning one's back on it and by concentrating on what is external to thought" (263). Consciousness is an insubstantial nothingness, a void oriented toward an external plenitude. But even more alarming to Poulet than Sartre's initial metaphysical assumptions about the way the nothingness of thought "makes itself," with its consequences for a metaphorics of interiority, is the existentialist's progressive movement on the practical level away from his early "open" criticism to an increasingly dogmatic posture. Poulet takes "open" criticism to mean something analogous to Sartre's concept of the "open" novel, open to surface vagaries and to the future, free to collaborate with the texts in the solution of local problems. Sartre's "dogmatism" comprises every tendency that would enclose the reading within previously assumed sociological, ethical, and political constraints. The specter for Poulet is, of course, Sartre's difficult mistress, Marxism. The difference, however, between the "open" and the "dogmatic" is already marked in the distance that separates the supple and attentive literary essays of *Situations I* from the normative, "historical" judgments of the *Baudelaire*.

Roland Barthes is, understandably, beyond the pale for a critic of consciousness; his "simulacra" and operational vocabulary define "the least subjective criticism possible" (271) in which both the subject and the signified dissolve before the abstracted interplay of linguistic signifiers. Yet "the logic of signifiers" would ultimately account not only for structure but for the other basic element in the system, desire, as well. Language, in fact, becomes the subject: "Le langage n'est pas le prédicat d'un sujet inexprimable ou qu'il servirait à exprimer, il est le sujet" (*Critique et vérité*, p. 70). (We have, in Poulet's response to such a reduction, the antinomy between hermeneutic depth and semiotic surface.) Poulet does allow that the *degré zéro* of the impersonal Barthean critic is well adapted to describe the structural games of a Robbe-Grillet (even as Sartre's brand of intentional analysis lends itself to the poetry of Ponge). This brief essay does not, however, try to account for the methodological development within Barthes's career or for the highly personal idiosyncrasies of his style. (Poulet would, in fact, seem to conflate at one point "le degré zéro de l'écriture" with what Barthes himself calls "le style.") Yet even at this extremity of criticism, so far removed from a sustaining consciousness and presence, Poulet sees in the work of Barthes's most accomplished disciple, Gérard Genette, the ghost of dispossessed consciousness, "the negative but active presence of an unrecognized subjectivity . . . is there, but incognito, written in the margin and *en blanc*" (272).

*   *   *   *   *

The two synoptic essays that comprise the short second section of *La Conscience critique* differ in kind from the critical profiles that precede them. Taken together they form a summary of the tradition that has been described and a programmatic statement of Poulet's own critical *appui*. " Phénoménologie de la conscience critique," beginning somewhat paradoxically with Mallarmé and the open book of *Igitur*, establishes an interpretative model for reading and follows this with a succinct review of a number of the critics already discussed. (Rousset seems to occupy a privileged place as a resolution of conflicting claims of form and content.) The essay ends with a moving account of the critic's own experience among the Tintorettos in the Scuola di San Rocco, a critic possessed by a transcendent mind in the shape of an artist whose defining mental activity seems to surpass all the individual forms that are reflected in it. The experience becomes, in this final achievement of identity with another, an access to " a subjectivity without objects" (299)! The final essay describes in personal terms the evolution of Poulet's own critical method, from an initial and chaotic Bergsonian flux in the act of reading to the stage in middle years where the collaborative mind of the critic can, through the introduction of a point of departure in the *Cogito*, organize a Leibnizian sort of harmony within his " borrowed consciousness." He concludes that while the artist's thought is born in solitude, all the variations of consciousness in its interpretation and recontruction of the universe depend upon the vital contact established between minds in the act of reading. " All criticism is initially and fundamentally a criticism of consciousness."

*   *   *   *   *

Bedar, the Watchman, caught the Mulla prising open the window of his own bedroom from the outside, in the depths of night.
" What are you doing, Nasrudin? Locked out? "
" Hush! They say I walk in my sleep. I am trying to surprise myself and find out."
The Exploits of the Incomparable Mulla Nasrudin

It remains only to suggest a few of the figures absent from Poulet's panorama, absences who cast their shadows, and then to review and perhaps rectify a few of the objections that have been raised against Poulet's conception of critical reading.

There are a number of figures who might be styled ancestors and fellow travelers of the criticism of consciousness. As a reader who struggles to define himself in the act of reading, Montaigne stands, of course, as an attentive and skeptical patron. He assures the reader that "je suis moy-mesmes la matiere de mon livre": but then quickly adds, "ce n'est pas raison que tu employes ton loisir en un subject si frivole et si vain." Rousseau also presides over the criticism of Poulet (and that of Raymond, Starobinski, and many of their colleagues), and it was he who first inspired the enthusiasm of Mme. de Staël. But Rousseau, too, embodies enough paradoxes to explode a number of critical systems—as the recent fortunes of his speculations on the origins of language would indicate.

Poulet has limited himself then, in *La Conscience critique*, to a gallery that excludes those philosophers and historians who may have contributed to the kind of reading he is describing. Still, it would be instructive to have essays on Jean Wahl, whose thought so well equipped him to glide into the intuition of another and to seize those "thoughts" that precede philosophy, or on Gabriel Marcel, who in all his writing explored the nature and conditions of "intersubjectivity." Among the historians it might be useful to have portraits of the Abbé Bremond and A. O. Lovejoy, who, in their very different ways left a mark on Poulet and some of his fellow critics. It would also be interesting to situate a few critics from outside the French tradition who are attentive to the same kind of participatory reading—say, Walter Pater and Gundolf, or G. Wilson Knight and Hillis Miller, to take early and late examples.

Among the shadows of those critics who are alien to a criticism of identification, as Poulet himself suggests, none is more important than Mallarmé, though his "negative consciousness" is represented within the book by Blanchot. (The linguistic inheritance of Mallarmé might also have been represented by Valéry and Jean Paulhan, the latter continuing some of the judgments of the earlier *N.R.F.* critics while shifting the focus from identification to the paradoxes of rhetoric.) The critical traditions emanating from those "terrible parents" of nineteenth-century thought alluded to earlier—Hegel, Marx, Nietzsche, Freud—are for the most part obvious in their absence from *La Conscience critique*, though a perversely original critic like Georges Bataille seemed to descend from an odd crossing of Hegel and Nietzsche, in some ways a diabolic version of Blanchot. Among the critics primarily concerned with the text as a linguistic or rhetorical structure in the Barthean tradition, Gérard Genette would afford a challenging topic for Poulet to situate; their respective readings of Proust might afford points of tangency.

To turn very briefly to some of the objections raised by Poulet's critics to his " participatory reading," perhaps the most familiar is that posed by his former colleague Leo Spitzer: the passage to the authorial *Cogito* neglects or dissolves the forms and structures of literary text.[9] Poulet has replied to this indictment on a number of occasions, but perhaps the clearest indication of his own concerns is given in a questionnaire appearing in *Les Lettres Nouvelles*. There he asserts that literature is not primarily language, nor even a structure composed of language: " A literary text is above all a living and conscious reality, a thought that thinks itself and which, in thinking itself, becomes thinkable to us; a voice that speaks itself and which, in so speaking, speaks to us from within. . . . It is the nature of the [literary] work at once to invent structures and to destroy them. Thus the work of an author is really the ensemble of all the works he has written, but in the sense that, succeeding one another, they displace one another and reveal thereby a movement that is the liberation from structures." [10]

Other common objections, for example to Poulet's attitudes toward history or the unconscious, have already been encountered; but one might consider one claim most persuasively put by Hillis Miller, his most articulate interpreter, in an *MLN* article,[11] that is, the familiar assertion that Poulet's attitude before the text is one of total disinterestedness. This claim would have to be qualified for even so " open " a critic as Richard, and Poulet, though he surely does not have the *parti pris* of a Béguin, is obviously more attentive to some resonances than to others. In fact, one could argue that the recurrent drama of the attempt to escape

---

[9] " A propos de la *Vie de Marianne* (lettre à M. Georges Poulet)," *Romanic Review*, April 1953, pp. 102-26. In this exchange it should be noted that Spitzer is talking about *Marianne*, and Poulet about " Marivaux."

[10] " Réponse de Georges Poulet," *Les Lettres Nouvelles*, June 1959, pp. 10-13.

[11] " The Literary Criticism of Georges Poulet," *MLN* 78, 5 (December 1963): 471-88.

from the fugitive moment of transience to some sort of temporal or spatial stability coincides with the critic's own quest. In this sense the optic chosen to read the text may help to determine the character of the narrative.

In his " Beyond Formalism " [reprinted in this volume], Geoffrey Hartman raises some other objections. Perhaps the easiest to deal with is that Poulet is importing formalism into his project through some Hegelian notion of literary history. Now in any strict sense Poulet is not concerned with *literary* history at all, as we have seen, and the last philosopher of history to whom he would turn is surely Hegel. On the other hand, Hartman's comments about the partial insight achieved in Poulet's brief essay on Henry James come much closer to the point. In its insistence on the epistemological and relational aspects of the author's concern to the neglect of the ontological and moral ambiguities, Poulet's reading does seem to erase the shadows from the Jamesean consciousness. At a purely practical level, one might observe that Poulet relies in this essay on an unusually high proportion of quotations from one text, the Prefaces to the New York edition of the novels, and this may account for the emphasis on problems of representation and the masking of the fearful costs of the Jamesean consciousness. More generally, however, Hartman's comments do illuminate the optimism of Poulet's address and the tendency to elide or reconcile zones where the negative imagination—absence, emptiness, guilt—presides. Consciousness, like Sterne's language, can suffer wounds.

Finally, Paul de Man, a friend and former colleague of Poulet, manages with great subtlety in his essay to borrow the latter's own technique of situating a virtual point of departure in early texts that do not immediately seem to give up the secret of the later work. He concludes his essay, however, by leading the critic to an impossible (and " blinded ") choice between either the self or language as the " source " or point of origin: " Self and language are the two focal points around which the trajectory of the work originates. . . . Each is the anteriority of the other. If one confers upon language the power to originate, one runs the risk of hiding the self. . . . But if the subject is, in its turn, given the status of origin, one makes it coincide with Being in a self-consuming identity in which language is destroyed." [12] In search of apocalyptic paradox

[12] " Literary Self as Origin: The Work of Georges Poulet," in *Blindness and Insight* (New York: Oxford University Press, 1971) , pp. 79-101—the quotation

and confirmation of his dialectic of critical blindness and insight,
de Man here concludes a sensitive essay by falsifying the rôle of
language in Poulet's work. The latter scrupulously avoids granting
any priority to language, which is always falling short, even in the
most achieved literature, of capturing the fugitive activity of
thought. Poulet alludes to that which is in fact anterior to
language in his tradition, thought, in the course of an exchange
with Jean Hyppolite after a paper on " Hegel's Philosophic Language "; the exchange underlines Poulet's actual priorities but it
also brings us back to the constantly self-qualifying text with which
we began, *Tristram Shandy*:

> GEORGES POULET: . . . And then we find ourselves in the
> presence of a problem which . . . we might call the *implication*
> and *explicitation* in and through language. Leibniz's thought,
> as expressed by Leibniz, is a form of language which always
> remains as condensed as possible. This is the category of maxi-
> mum density. On the contrary, a thought like Hegel's can satisfy
> itself only to the degree that it develops itself through language.
> There seems to be an extremely curious paradox here, in that
> Hegel's philosophy begins as the story of unhappy *consciousness*
> and ends as the story of happy *speech*. Don't we find the opposite
> in philosophies such as that of Leibniz? Isn't that also what we
> would find if we considered poetry briefly? Poetry is generally

---

appears on pp. 100-101. Elsewhere in the volume, de Man proposes to rescue
the New Critics from their own peculiar fallacy of reifying the literary
" work " into a natural object; the rescue is through a partial application of
Heidegger's hermeneutic circle.. De Man speaks of the interpretation of the
text as a disclosure of what is already there: " No new set of relationships
is added to an existing reality, but relationships *that were already there* are
being disclosed, not only in themselves (like the events of nature) but as they
exist *for us*. We can only understand that which is in a sense already given
to us and already known, albeit in a fragmentary, inauthentic way that cannot
be called unconscious. Heidegger calls this the *Forhabe* [sic], the forestructure
[sic] of all understanding " (29-30). For Poulet, the *Vor-Struktur* of the author's
intentional act would seem to reside not in the text but in the attitudes of
mind that he derives from the *Cogito* (very different from the Cartesian *Cogito*
that Heidegger himself subjects to such a destructive critique and closer to
the " questioning " that lies behind the syntax of the latter). These attitudes
must remain implicit until they are disclosed by the explicitation of interpretative reading. (The implicit " forestructure" could perhaps be analyzed into
the component parts of the Heideggerian triad—*Vorhabe, Vorsicht, Vorgriff*—
but the question in Poulet's case is not really an ontological one, and the
status of the mediating language is hardly privileged. " Poetic speech " for
Poulet lags behind thought.)

speech [*parole*] which seeks to remain as far as possible in its *implicitation,* so much so that if it develops itself, it is lost. It deteriorates to the degree that it develops, to the degree that it abandons itself to its "gift of speech." This is especially true for, let us say, the poetry of Victor Hugo. Let us oppose to this sort of poetry a poetry like that of Char. This is a poetry in which density of language corresponds to a sort of immediate grasp of poetic truth in a sort of *prélocution* or *pro-locution* which is the opposite of elocution—of a certain philosophical elocution which might be the Hegelian type. Therefore, alongside the success of philosophical speech which you have proposed, with Hegel as example, there is a failure of *explicit* speech. We can see an example of this in a work which is somewhat earlier than Hegel's, namely Sterne's *Tristram Shandy.* What is *Tristram Shandy?* It is the story of somebody who, just as in the *Phenomenology of the Mind,* wants to present the story of the very fluctuation of his thought. He finds himself, however, in conditions that make it more and more impossible for him to tell this story. This is because speech is too slow while, on the contrary, thought is too fast; and the initial lag between thought and speech grows steadily worse while speech is progressing, so much so that the progression becomes a digression. Here we see the passage from the triumph of language to the failure of language.[13]

1973

THE CRITICISM OF GEORGES POULET

Etudes sur le temps humain. Edinburgh: Edinburgh University Press, 1949; Paris: Plon, 1950. English translation, Baltimore, 1956.

La Distance intéreure. Paris: Plon, 1952. English translation, Baltimore, 1959.

Les Métamorphoses du cercle. Paris: Plon, 1961. English translation, Baltimore, 1967.

L'Espace proustien. Paris: Gallimard, 1963.

Le Point de départ. Paris: Plon, 1964.

Trois essais de mythologie romantique. Paris: Corti, 1966.

Les Chemins actuels de la critique (editor). Paris: Plon, 1967.

[13] Richard Macksey and Eugenio Donato, *The Languages of Criticism and the Sciences of Man: The Structuralist Controversy* (Baltimore: The Johns Hopkins Press, 1970), pp. 176-77.

Mesure de l'instant. Paris: Plon, 1968.
Benjamin Constant par lui-même. Paris: Seuil, 1968.
Qui était Baudelaire? Geneva: Skira, 1969.
La Conscience critique. Paris: Corti, 1971.

THE CRITICS OF GEORGES POULET

Hartman, Geoffrey. " Beyond Formalism," *MLN* 81, 5 (December 1966) :
    550-55. Reprinted in this volume.
Lawall, Sarah. In *Critics of Consciousness: The Existential Structures of
    Literature.* Cambridge, Mass.: Harvard University Press, 1968.
Man, Paul de. " Vérité et méthode dans l'oeuvre de Georges Poulet."
    Critique 25, 266 (July 1969) : 608-23.
Miller, J. Hillis. " The Literary Criticism of Georges Poulet." *MLN* 79,
    5 (December 1963) : 471-88.
————. " The Geneva School." *The Virginia Quarterly Review* 43,
    3 (Summer 1967) : 477-82. Reprinted in *The Critical Quarterly*, 8,
    4 [Winter 1966]: 313-16.
————. " Georges Poulet's ' Criticism of Identification.' " In *The Quest
    for the Imagination*, ed. O. B. Hardison, Jr. Cleveland: Case
    Western Reserve Press, 1971.

"LITERATURE" / LITERATURE ❧
BY ALAN BASS ❧

—"... pourqoui 'littérature' nommerait
encore ce qui déjà se soustrait à la
littérature—à ce qu'on a toujours conçu
et signifié sous ce nom—ou, ne s'y dé-
robant pas seulement, la détruit im-
placablement?" (la Dissémination)[1]
—"La littérature s'annule sans son illimi-
tation." (la Dissémination)[1]

If the question "What is literature?" has never satisfactorily
been answered, it may be time to scrutinize the question itself.
Does "literature" have any status as an "object," as something
about which the question "what is it?" can be asked? Or if the
question cannot be answered, how does literature affect the rest
of what is, everything—excluding, perhaps, literature—which the
question "what is it?" is pertinent to? And in what discipline can
these questions be situated? Science? Philosophy? Literature itself?
Our traditions tell us that science has the most immediate, the most
potentially "truthful" relationship to the question "what is it?",
that is, to an object outside itself. Philosophy, we know, aspires to
"scientific" truthfulness, often constituting itself as the path from
naive non-scientificity to science itself.[2] Literature is seemingly

---

[1] Jacques Derrida La dissémination, Seuil, Collection "Tel Quel," Paris, 1972
"... why is 'literature' still the name for that which already withdraws itself
from literature—withdraws itself from what has always been conceived and
signified by this name—or, not only eluding it, implacably destroys it?" (p. 9)
"Literature annihilates itself through its illimitability." (p. 253) La dissémination consists of three previously published essays and a new text entitled
"Hors-livre." To facilitate access to these essays and to make apparent which
essay is being referred to, the following are their first places of publication
and their placement in La dissémination: "La pharmacie de Platon" first
published in Tel Quel, Nos. 32 and 33, pp. 69-197 in La dissémination; "La
double séance," Tel Quel, Nos. 41 and 42, pp. 199-317; "La dissémination,"
Critique, Nos. 261 and 262, pp. 319-407. "Hors-livre—Préfaces" occupies pages
9 to 67.

[2] This description has Hegel most specifically in mind, at very least because
of his powerful treatment of the progression from intuitive, naive certitude
to scientific truth. The "vehicle" upon which Hegel proposes to take us from

excluded from answering this most basic of questions, because it never gets beyond its own textuality, is not concerned with determining the "essence" or "truth" of objects outside itself. This framework could even be recapitulated as degrees of textual transparency: accepted values indicate that the text of science should be totally transparent in relation to the "reality" it deals with; that philosophy, in quest of "truth," proceeds from an opaque to a transparent text, or is a "transparent" text insofar as it is scientific; and that literature is all opaque textuality, somehow in relation to "reality" only through its use or disregard of the imitative techniques that always imply a distance from reality.[3] The analysis, and possible breakdown, of this traditional framework would have to have as its focus the possibility of the *presence* of truth in science and its *non-presence* in literature. In other words, is there a text (for science is as textual, as written-down as literature) in which truth can be made present? What is the relationship between truth, presence, and textuality? This question is the brunt of the work of Jacques Derrida, a "philosopher" whose texts are "literary" because they have attacked the fundamental notion of "scientific" truth. As Derrida has written, the question "what is literature?" can make the authority of the question "what is—?" tremble, because this question is "located" between literature and truth, between literature and the presence of anything that is.[4] The possible subversion of the oppositions truth/non-truth or presence/absence is to be sought between each term of the opposition, and the question of literature has always been the question of the "between."[5]

certitude to truth is the *Aufhebung*, the idealization of a given stage of mental development through its negation and conservation that permits us to go on to the next stage. Derrida has defined the "deconstruction of metaphysics" as "indefinite explications with Hegel." Cf. *L'écriture et la différence*, Seuil, Collection "Tel Quel," Paris, 1967, p. 371.

[3] There is an obvious similarity between the hierarchy "science"—"philosophy"—"literature" and "Plato's" paradigm (in *The Republic*) god-artisan-painter as degrees of direct relationship to Forms, specifically the form of the bed. (God creates the form, the artisan manufactures the object, approximating the form, and the painter imitates the object. The painter is thus the furthest from the original truth.) However, it is not my intention to assimilate one scheme to the other, disregarding all specificity. The point to be made is that there is a correspondance between the theories of imitation regarding painting and those regarding literature. Cf. *La dissémination*, pp. 158-160.

[4] *La dissémination*, p. 203.

[5] Again, an anticipation, another philosophical example, may be of assistance.

The first question that would have to be examined in the analysis of the relation between text and truth is that of the sign. All texts—scientific, philosophical, literary—are apparently made of signs, linguistic signs which have two faces: the *signifier*, the acoustic material making up the sign, and the *signified*, the conceptualization of the referent, the thing outside language. That which makes a text a text, distinguishing it from spoken discourse, is writing, and in the case of Occidental culture, phonetic writing; the function of writing, the "analysis" and fixing of the (acoustic) signifier, would apparently make it the signifier of the signifier, the sign of the sign. At least since the *Cratylus* of Plato, philosophy has grappled with the relationship between the signifier and the signified, the question usually bearing on whether or not they are intrinsically related; and also, at least since Plato, writing has been defined as exterior to the sign itself, precisely because it is the signifier of the signifier, the sign of the sign. Spoken discourse is always associated with presence—it is "alive." Its written "representation" signals non-presence—the author of the discourse is silent, or even dead insofar as his text is concerned.

This valuation of spoken discourse over the written text, the association of writing with exteriority, is at work in one of the most influential texts of modern linguistics, *le Cours de linguistique générale* of Ferdinand de Saussure. The essence of Saussure's work in linguistics is his doctrine of the arbitrary or unmotivated relationship between signifier and signified. According to Saussure, there is no intrinsic relationship between signifier and signified because of the differential character of language: the concept signified by the signifier is never present in and of itself because signs are made possible through the *differences* between sounds. That is, there is nothing to link any particular sound to any

Artistic creations, literature included, are often deemed creations of the "imagination," the faculty that produces works that are neither in nature, nor in some other world, mediating *between* "intelligence" and nature. This particular articulation of what might be called *between-ness* belongs at least to Kant and to Jean Rousset, a contemporary French critic. Derrida discusses this formulation of Kant's in an essay on Rousset; cf. *L'écriture et la différence*, p. 16. The underlying question is the relationship of form and content, specifically of the imagination which can "fill" mental "forms" with "content" from the world because it mediates between them. For a further discussion of the possibility of confining a text to the realm of the imagination cf. *La dissémination*, p. 266, where the text in question is precisely *l'Univers imaginaire de Mallarmé* by Jean-Pierre Richard.

particular concept, but the perception of differences between combinations of sounds permits one group of sounds (signifier) to
stand for, or take the place of a thing, which itself is engaged in
a system of differences.[6]

It can be inferred then (although Saussure does not state so
explicitly) that the possibility of conceptuality depends upon a
silent system of differential references: one concept refers to
another in their difference; one signifier refers to another in their
difference.[7] If, as Saussure says, language is a classificatory system
that did not fall from the sky, these silent differences were somewhere produced, have somewhere a point of origin: that which
makes speech possible—a system of differential reference—must obviously precede speech and speakers, what Saussure calls " *le sujet
parlant* " (which has the larger signification of being consciousness
in general). But this immediately leads to a logical contradiction,
a contradiction that contradicts logic itself, for the concepts of
" cause " and " effect," " before " and " after " here become confused. If all causes are localized points of presence, if every " after "
is preceded by a " present " that came before it, how can the pre-
requisite for speech—difference, which is never present itself, but is
always *between* two " presences "—be its origin? How can the *sujet
parlant,* the consciousness of presence, be constituted by what
never was or will be present? Further, this concept of " original
difference " (how can a difference be original?) has a fundamental
bearing on the (metaphysical) concepts used to determine being
(what is) : time and space. First, the possibility of the sign itself,
the substitution of the sign for the thing in a system of differences,
depends upon the temporal concept of *deferral,* the putting-off into
the future of the present grasping of the thing itself. That a system
of differences permits a sign to stand for a thing, to replace it,
always implies a future relationship to an element from the past.
Which brings us to the second point, and the significance of the

[6] It goes without saying that within the field of linguistics Saussure does not
represent the final word on the problem of the motivation of the sign. Saussure's disciples themselves have modified his original conceptions. The obvious
stumbling blocks are imitative words, e. g. onomatopoeias, which are not arbitrarily connected to their referent.

[7] This implication of Saussure's work, and the discussion of it to follow are
taken from Derrida's essay " *La différance* " in *Théorie d'ensemble*, Seuil, Paris,
1968; the reference here is to pp. 49-54. This question is covered more fully,
with reference to many linguistic thinkers in *De la grammatologie*, Editions
de Minuit, Paris, 1967, pp. 42-108.

fact that etymologically *defer* and *differ* are the same word: this temporal *interval*, which separates the thing present from itself in time, also irreducibly divides all "spatial" presence; for the system of differential reference requires that each present element refers to an element *other* than itself, the perception of objects depending upon the perception of their differences. The sign is thus constituted by the *trace* of a past element that was never fully present, because it must always refer to something other than itself; and this trace refers to a future that will never become present, because the interval separating sign from thing must always reconstitute itself. Any other alternative, any attempt to save the value of full presence would lead to the postulation of a point of origin not different from itself (an in-different origin), thus destroying the essentially differential quality of language. This concept of the *trace* is the production of intervals in both time and space, "is" a kind of writing before writing as we know it, for writing has never been concerned with anything but tracing and leaving the trace of speech. "Is" must be in quotation marks because the trace, the original difference, the writing before speech, destroys the idea of a simple presence, of the presence of a being as the simple origin of beings.

Thus, the origin of "alive" spoken discourse "is" an enlarged conception of "dead" silent writing. Silence is not exterior to speech, writing is not the signifier of the signifier, the sign is neither motivated nor arbitrary. The philosophical gesture which devalues writing, because speech always implies presence, can be construed as the principle common to all metaphysics, the system that always prefers presence to non-presence. Derrida has named this epoch of metaphysics (our own) "logocentrism," and one could say that it always writes to devalue writing.[8] Speaking of the philosophical desire to devalue writing that always leads to this contradictory logic, Derrida says, in *De la grammatologie*:

[8] Derrida has often used the Freudian concepts of denegation and the logic of dreams, which "illogically" ignores negation, as indices of this evidently contradictory logic of writing so that writing may be devalued (or presence constituted as an ultimate value). Cf. *La dissémination*, p. 126. In *The Interpretation of Dreams* (Standard Edition, Vol. IV, p. 120) Freud uses the case of the kettle as an analog to dream-logic: the man charged by his neighbor with having returned a borrowed kettle in damaged condition retorts 1. that he gave back the kettle undamaged; 2. that the kettle had a hole in it when he borrowed it; 3. that he never borrowed the kettle at all.

To what zone of discourse does this strange functioning of argumentation belong . . . ? How is this functioning articulated with
the ensemble of theoretical discourse, throughout the history of
science? Rather, how does it work upon the concept of science
from within it? . . . this index and several others (generally
speaking, the treatment of the concept of writing), provide us
with an assured means of commencing the de-construction of the
greatest totality—the concept of *epistémè* and logocentric metaphysics—in which were produced all Occidental methods of
analysis, explication, reading or interpretation without ever
posing the radical question of writing. What must now be
thought is that writing is simultaneously more exterior to speech,
because it is not the 'image' or 'symbol' of speech, and that it is
more interior to speech which in and of itself is already writing.
Before even being linked to a . . . signifier referring in general
to a signifier signified by it, the concept of *graphie* implies, as the
possibility common to all systems of signification, an *instituted
trace* . . . The instituted trace cannot be conceived without
conceiving the retention of difference in a referential structure
in which difference appears *as such* and permits a certain freedom
of variation between full terms. The absence of an *other* here
and now, of an other transcendental present, of an *other origin*
of the world appearing as such, presenting itself as irreducible
absence in the presence of the trace is not a metaphysical formulation substituted for a scientific conception of writing. This
formulation, besides being *the* objection to metaphysics itself,
describes the structure implied by the 'arbitrariness' of the sign.
The 'unmotivated' quality of the sign requires a synthesis in
which the completely other is announced as such—without any
simplicity, identity, resemblance or continuity—in that which is
not itself. . . . The trace, in which the relationship to the other
is marked, articulates its possibility on the entire field of being
that metaphysics has determined on the basis of the occulted
movement of the trace. The trace must be conceived as coming
before being. But the movement of the trace is necessarily
occulted, produces itself as its own occultation. When the other
is announced as such, it presents itself as a dissimulation of itself.
(pp. 67-69)

The essential notion to be grasped from this analysis of Saussure
(who represents only one moment of the valuation of presence, of
the equivalence between truth and presence) is that all speculation
on the origin of being can always be deconstructed to show that
the point of origin is different from itself. Origin is always *other*

than itself, for the idea of origin depends upon the production of " spatial " and " temporal " difference that must *precede* any origin. Since writing, throughout the history of philosophy, has been associated with the values " non-origin," " secondariness," " exteriority " —in short, " otherness "—the treatment of writing by philosophy is a means of taking apart the fundamental oppositions upon which our thought is based—presence/non-presence, truth/non-truth, interior/exterior. The concept of " trace " forces us to think in ways proscribed by metaphysics, making us " conceptualize " an exterior within an interior, a presence constituted by non-presence, etc. Which is not to say that an anti-metaphysics that would assert non-presence as an absolute origin would escape the contradictions of metaphysics. It must be emphasized that this notion of an origin other than itself, here called " trace," makes it impossible to locate any origin, ever to constitute a full presence. The movement of the trace can never be stopped, or pinned down to a *point* of absence or presence.

The disappearance of an origin implied in this enlarged conception of writing (writing as *différance,* the word invented by Derrida to connote production of spatial and temporal difference), also entails an enlarging of the concept of repetition. In his analysis of Plato, Derrida comes to associate writing, the disappearance of a present origin of presence, with the Platonic concept of *epekeina tes ousias* (the beyond of all presence).[9] Derrida demonstrates that the presence of the *eidos,* the thing itself, the unity of the signified and the referent, cannot be separated from the concept of (grammatical) difference, since Plato defines the origin of the visible as that which cannot be viewed directly (the sun). If the invisible " beyond " of all presence is the origin of the thing itself, the thing itself can never be present. Derrida further proceeds to demonstrate the link between writing and the idea of that which is in excess of being, is " beyond " being, is *epekeina tes ousias.* Again, a generalized concept of writing can be shown to be the (non) origin of being. And if " truth " is absolute presence, the presence of the *eidos,* the disappearance of an original presence would simultaneously make truth possible and impossible. This simultaneity amounts to postulating that the thing itself, in its identical presence, is " duplicitous " (true and not-true), is doubled,

---

[9] For what is to follow, cf. *La dissémination,* pp. 192-195. The status of *epekeina tes ousias* was one of Derrida's first preoccupations: cf. *L'écriture et la différence,* pp. 86-88 and 126-128.

doubles itself, as soon as it appears, or rather it appears as the possibility of its own duplication: it *repeats* itself, its origin is its repetition. The menace that Plato ascribed to the Sophists—that, in their pre-occupation with combining signifiers they mechanically *repeat* things without any real knowledge of them—is what makes truth possible, thereby destroying truth. Truth and non-truth derive from repetition.

If, then, repetition is the production of unity, there can be no "full" unity, no unity without something missing, something that calls for the production of a supplementary "unity" that is similar enough to and different enough from the "faulty" original (which is thus *not* the original) to be added to it, as that which it is missing, *or* to replace it, as its double. Be added to *or* replace: this contradictory assertion is included in another of Derrida's "concepts," that of *supplementarity*. The verb *suppléer* in French has the double sense of adding for the sake of completion and of replacement—how can a *missing* element replace (take the place of, stand for) that from which it is missing? And the word *supplément* has a necessary link to writing: as Rousseau defines it, writing is the *supplément* of speech, completing it and standing for it. Derrida has used the supplementary status of writing—the addition that replaces, the part bigger than the whole—to deconstruct one of Rousseau's major contributions to thought, the opposition nature/ culture, as well as to deal, once more, with the strange phenomenon of the philosopher who writes to attack writing. The philosophical attack upon writing is perhaps always motivated by the danger of mechanical repetition that Plato first associated with writing, the fear of the machine gone out of control, producing double after double of the same thing with no attempt to master its product.[10] But it is obvious that philosophy needs this machine as much as it fears it, and thus the incessant attempts to circumscribe it, to

---

[10] The analysis of the fear of automatic, mechanical repetition is one of the richest strata of Derrida's thought. For one, it opens new perspectives in charting what might crudely be called the "philosophic unconscious," which would first require a systematic confrontation of the Freudian and philosophical (Hegelian) concepts of negativity, as already implied in note 8, above. For the machine in Hegel, Cf. "*Le puits et la pyramide*," in *Hegel et la pensée moderne*, P. U. F., Paris, 1970, p. 82, where what is in question is again the relationship of signified to signifier. The machine in Freud—an automaton— concerns the relationship of fiction to reality and the concept of castration in an essay called "*Das Unheimliche*" ("The Uncanny"—Standard Edition, Vol. XVII). Derrida has written that his essay on Mallarmé, "*La double séance*" constitutes a rereading of this essay of Freud's. Cf. *La dissémination*, p. 300, n. 56.

make writing a simple *means* for the presentation of truth. Philo-
osphy has even provided itself with an adjunct whose job is to keep
watch over the machine, to keep the means in control by separating
good writing from bad so that it can express the truth as *adequately*
as possible: rhetoric.[11] But these attempts, which inevitably link
writing with difference, repetition, supplementarity allow us to turn
them against themselves.

What then does one call the writing, the text in which philosophical concepts turn against themselves, explode themselves in order
to demonstrate their own (im)possibility, their irreducible doubleness? Since they obey no philosophical regulations of truth, these
texts have a certain "fictive" or "literary" quality; but since they
must rigorously explode the truths by which philosophy aspires to
scientificity, they have an intimate relationship with what philosophy has construed as "science." Thus, Derrida proposes to
elaborate a "double science," [12] a "science" in which each concept,
each term carries within it the principle of its own death. Once
one has determined the totality of what is as "having been" made
possible by the institution of the trace, "textuality," the system of
traces, becomes the most global term, encompassing all that is and
that which exceeds it. The "double science" is then the "science
of textuality," giving a privileged place to what was formerly called
"literature," but can no longer be called such when the relationship
to truth and reality that allegedly distinguished literary, scientific
and philosophical texts from each other breaks down as we are
forced to rethink the metaphysical concept of "reality" in terms
of textuality. What becomes particularly revelatory for the "double
science" are the ways of reading "literary" texts that are governed

---

[11] Ever since Aristotle, in the *Poetics*, distinguished good metaphors from bad
on the basis of adequation *(homoiosis)*, similarity to a natural model, rhetoric
has been concerned with keeping discourse truthful. For an analysis of the
Aristotelean concept of metaphor and the role of metaphor in science and in
the creation of negative concepts, cf. *"La mythologie blanche"* in *Poétique*,
No. 5.

[12] Elsewhere, Derrida has proposed the name *"économie generale"* for this
science, cf. *"De l'économie restreinte à l'économie générale,"* in *L'écriture et
la différence*, pp. 369-406. In note 2, above, reference was already made to this
essay which concerns the relationship of Bataille to Hegel. This is perhaps
the place to cite the guiding question of the general economy or the double
science, the question that involves it in indefinite explications with Hegel:
". . . after having exhausted the discourse of philosophy, how can we inscribe,
in the lexicon and syntax of a language, *our* language, which was also the
language of philosophy, that which nevertheless exceeds the oppositions of concepts governed by its communal logic?"

by the classical, metaphysical concepts of interpretation. In other words, the deconstruction of "literary criticism" and the explosion of some of its key concepts play a crucial role in this "double science."

The word "criticism" derives directly from the Greek verb *krinein* and its adjectival form *kritikos*, meaning "able to discern or to judge." In other words, criticism *decides* (discerns, judges), and what it decides is the meaning of a text. "Meaning" is a value intrinsically associated with those of "truth" and "presence"—a text's meaning is the truth that is present "behind" or "under" its textual surface that criticism makes fully present by placing it before us. Since "truth," "presence," or meaning are made (im)possible by textuality, by writing as trace, we can foresee that a text is precisely always that which cannot be decided upon, and that the project of criticism is linked to the project of philosophy in its drive to efface writing before single *or* multiple meanings implicitly (immanently) "present" in it. Whether it falls under the rubric of "formalism" (attention to that which makes literature literature, the attempt to determine a specificity of "literariness"), or of "thematism" (attention to the combinations, juxtapositions, and recurrences of meaningful units within a text, usually stopping at the level of the word), all criticism as we know it depends upon the notion of the sign, of a signified (a meaning) behind the signifier and the pertinence of their opposition; [13] criticism is thus engaged in the system of values attached to the sign. The "double science," founded upon the incompatability of the notions "sign" and text, must explore the consequences of this incompatability as it deconstructs the project of deciding, of criticism.

For a text to be "undecidable" it must resist being consumed or exhausted by its semantic relationships, that is, it can never be fully "saturated" with meaning.[14] At some point its syntax—syntax being that which philosophically is always subordinated to semantics, because it is not concerned with the presentation of

---

[13] The opposition form/theme has been treated at length by Freud in his analyses of the *pleasure* to be taken from literature: the work of art obeys the pleasure principle, its "form" being the enticement to the release of tension found in the perception of the "theme" behind the form. For a brief discussion of this and the essential references to Freud, cf. *La dissémination*, p. 279, n. 44. The question of formalism cannot be raised without reference to Hegel, whose treatment of the complicity between formalism and empiricism is crucial to Derrida. Cf., among other places, *La dissémination*, p. 17.

meaning—must overflow its apparent meanings. This hypothesis is a direct result of the demonstration that the sign is dependent for its existence upon the production of (temporal and spatial) differ-ence, for syntax is the principle of textual arrangement, that is, of differentiation. The most obvious "index" of syntax is the space *between* words, what Mallarmé called the *blanc;* and it is upon the Mallarmean example of the *blanc* that Derrida has articulated some of his most important deconstructions of literary criticism. It is by now apparent that for Derrida words with irreducibly double meanings, (such as *supplément, différance* and others not mentioned here) ,[15] which are always connected to the concept of textuality, have a certain privilege. A crucial aspect of this pri-vilege is that these words are dependent upon syntax for their meaning. These words (and the *hymen* in Mallarmé: either wedding or hymen, that which is between consummation and non-consummation, signifying both) have no intrinsic meanings, there

[14] It is this resistance of the text to semantic saturation, the fact that some-thing always remains behind after every attempt to idealize a text into its meaning, that is the key to the deconstruction of the concept of *Aufhebung,* for the process of negation-and-conservation always implies an idealization so complete that no *trace* of that which is idealized is left behind. Cf. *La dis-sémination,* pp. 15-37. Thus, Derrida has called the concept of *Aufhebung* the "decisive target" in the deconstruction of metaphysics. (p. 280, n. 45) To say, then, that Derrida has interpreted Heidegger's destruction of humanism as "a strategy that allows for both a transcendence and a conservation of the inherited concepts [of metaphysics], in line with the Hegelian principle of *Aufhebung,*" or that the "chief lesson" that Derrida's work offers to criticism "is that it seeks to balance in scrupulous fashion both the conserving and the negating forces involved in the activities of reading and of interpretation" is to profoundly misconstrue the import of everything that Derrida has had to say about Hegel. (Cf. Alexander Gelley, "Form as Force" in *Diacritics,* Spring, 1972, pp. 9 and 13 respectively.)

[15] Two other particularly important examples: *pharmakon,* the Greek word which simultaneously means poison and remedy and is systematically associated with writing by Plato, especially in the *Phaedrus* (cf. *La dissémination,* pp. 108-133) ; and *usure,* the word implying both a process of impoverishment, using up, and of profit-taking, the too-large profits made by lending (usury). *Usure* covers the entire history of metaphor, the "lending" of a name to something other than itself (as it is defined by Aristotle- in the *Poetics*) , for the concept of metaphor always implies 1. that a word can etymologically be traced back to a primitive sense of which we no longer think in using the word, which thus has been impoverished through constant circulation, and 2. that the passage from a primitive sense of the word to a more abstract one corresponds to the passage from the physical to the metaphysical, the acquiring of a richer sense. This double sense of *usure* guides the analysis of the meta-phoricity of science in "*La mythologie blanche.*" Further, Freud's essay on "*Das Unheimliche*" concerns the conversion of one sense of a word to another (here, the "familiar" to the "unfamiliar") through the concept of castration.

is always the *space, veil* or *blanc* of syntax between them and their meanings. To simplify greatly, since all texts are dependent upon the silent, blank intervention of space between words in order to make meaning possible (similar to the way in which the supposedly acoustic sign is dependent upon silent differentiation), these " duplicitous " words, marking the points at which syntax overflows semantics, destroy, the possibility of semantic saturation, of a text's meaning or meanings being greater than its syntax. And since what these words mark is the *necessary* intervention of blank space in a text (" *indéfectiblement le blanc revient* . . ."—Mallarmé), we can postulate that a text's meaning or meanings are destroyed *and* produced by the principle of spacing—*espacement*. One immediate consequence of this essential openness of texts is the destruction of the idea of literature, if by " idea of " is meant something that has an essence, a truth, a, particular state of being, for all these values by definition exclude the openness of the undecidable. There is no quality, no assignable " literariness " that makes literature literature, rendering not pertinent the question " what is literature," which was our point of departure.[16] This too, is the " basis " upon which formalist or thematic criticism, which never accounts for the plus/minus of the space *between* words (that is, that which is *less* than meaningful, since it is by definition non-meaning, and is *more* than meaningful, since it includes within it the possibility of meaning) can be taken apart.[17]

That a text is undecidedly open does not mean that there is nothing to say about it. Rather, a " system " of textuality must be elaborated that does not rely upon reducing a text to its " meaning." Again, to undertake this task rigorously one would have to depend upon concepts that destroy themselves, that lead not to the presence of the singular, but to the division and silence of the differences that constitute the multiplicity that is textuality (one could say: the multiplicity that " is ") . All that " is " has as

Derrida's concept that covers irreducible doubleness—*la dissémination*—has important ties to the Freudian concept of castration, the cutting off of the ultimate model of unicity and presence—the phallus—, although the two are not interchangeable. Cf. *La dissémination*, pp. 32 and 300, n. 56.

[16] This is an over-simplification of the arguments found in *La dissémination*, pp. 249-253.

[17] Reasons of space and the necessary *closeness* to particular texts upon which these arguments are articulated prevent even a cursory summary of them. For the argument concerning thematic criticism, cf. *La dissémination*, pp. 276 ff., and for those on formalist criticism, *De la grammatologie*, pp. 86-88 and *L'écriture et la différence*, pp. 9-49 (the essay on Rousset) .

its *supplément*—the part that makes it whole, the part that replaces the whole—texts, the "appearance" of difference as such, that divides every "thing" from itself, *doubling* it, *repeating* it, *citing* it. The *supplément*, the part bigger than the whole, can be construed as a citation, a double that is not the thing itself, always referring backwards and forwards to an impossible present. Citation itself is the textual form of doubling, of transplanting or inserting part of another text into a text, making the citation slightly different from itself. And citations ultimately have no source or origin: they always refer to another text which refers to another text, etc.[18] Since any exhaustive attempt to find the source or origin of a text will always lead to another text, (or to other texts, since a single text as a punctual source would reinstate the metaphysical notions of textuality as secondary and derivative, as for instance in the theories of all books having their source in *the* Book—the Bible) all the theories of *mimesis*, of imitation, that have governed interpretation break down, for all these theories interpret a text according to its relationship to a referent outside textuality. Derrida has demonstrated that criticism has always been programmed by two propositions (and their consequences) concerning *mimesis*—it either produces the double of the thing, and is not qualitatively different from its model, or resembling its model or not, the vehicle of imitation exists, because there is *mimesis*—and that in either case *mimesis* is governed by a truth outside textuality.[19] The major acquisition of the "double science" is that there is nothing outside textuality, outside ". . . the temporalization of an *experience* which is neither *in* the world nor in an 'other world' . . . no more *in* time than *in* space, [in which] differences appear between elements or rather produce them, making them emerge as such and constitute *texts*, chains and systems of traces. . . ."[20]

The old name for textuality, "literature," is then the possibility of science, as it is the possibility of science's objects—being, in time and space. Because of its illimitability, literature must be seen as annihilating itself, exploding itself and thereby implacably subverting the metaphysical system that has *named* it such in order to confine the *letter*, which, as Rousseau has taught us, *kills*.

1972

[18] Again, an over-simplification. Cf. *La dissémination*, pp. 350-352.
[19] For the dissection of mimetology, cf. *La dissémination*, pp. 209-221.
[20] *De la grammatologie*, p. 95.

Other Critical Essays from *MLN*

On Beckett: Lawrence Harvey, "Samuel Beckett on Life, Art, and Criticism," *MLN* 80 (1965) : 545-62.

On Béguin: Jean-Jacques Demorest, "Albert Béguin, le salut par les poètes," *MLN* 78 (1963) : 453-70.

On Benjamin: Carol Jacobs, "Walter Benjamin: Image of Proust," *MLN* 86 (1971) : 910-32.

On Fernandez: Georges Poulet, "Le Volontarisme de Ramon Fernandez," *MLN* 87 (1972) : 53-57.

On Girard: René Girard, "Perilous Balance: A Comic Hypothesis," *MLN* 87 (1972) : 811-26; Carl Rubino, "René-Girard, *La Violence et le sacré*," *MLN* 87 (1972) : 986-98.

On Goldmann: Lucien Goldmann et al., "Microstructures dans les 25 premières Répliques des Nègres de Jean Genet—Avant Propos," *MLN* 82 (1967) : 531-48; Lionel Gossman, "Lucien Goldmann—1913-1970," *MLN* 86 (1971) : 453-55.

On Hartman: Edward W. Said, "What Is Beyond Formalism" *MLN* 86 (1971) : 933-45.

On Intention: Michael Hancher, "Three Types of Intention," *MLN* 87 (1972) : 827-51.

On Interpretation: Michael Hancher, "The Science of Interpretation and the Art of Interpretation," *MLN* 85 (1970) : 791-802.

On Lévi-Strauss: Eugenio Donato, "*Tristes Tropiques*: The Endless Journey," *MLN* 81 (1966) : 270-81.

On Lukács, Girard, and Goldmann: Anne-Marie Dibon, "Form and Value in the French and English 19th-century Novel," *MLN* 87 (1972) : 883-914.

On Mauron: Robert Greer Cohn, "Mauron on Mallarmé," *MLN* 78 (1963) : 520-26.

On Metaphor: Richard Macksey and Gerald Kamber, "'Negative Metaphor' and Proust's Rhetoric of Absence," *MLN* 85 (1970) : 858-83.

On Narrative Structure: Richard Macksey, "The Artist in the Labyrinth: Design or *Dasein*," *MLN* 77 (1962) : 239-56; also see special number on narrative structure, *MLN* 86 (1971), with contributions by A. J. Greimas, Eugenio Donato, Thomas M. Kavanagh, Gérard Bucher, Paul Bouissac, John Heckman, Gian-Paolo Blasin, Keith Ellis, and Silviano Santiago.

On Ortega: Nelson R. Orringer, "Ortega y Gasset's Sportive Theories of Communication," *MLN* 85 (1970) : 207-34.

On Poetics: Walter Albert, "Yves Bonnefoy and the Architecture of Poetry," *MLN* 82 (1967) : 590-603; Michel Deguy,· "La Poésie en question," *MLN* 85 (1970) : 419-33; idem, "Poésie et connaissance," *MLN* 81 (1966) : 255-69.

On Poulet: J. Harris Miller, "The Literary Criticism and Georges Poulet," *MLN* 78 (1963) : 471-88.

On Spitzer: Michel Baraz, "Leo Spitzer—*Romanische Literaturstudien, 1936-1956*," *MLN* 78 (1963) : 60-74; Elliot Coleman, "Leo Spitzer— *Essays on English and American Literature*," *MLN* 79 (1964) : 80-82; Leo Spitzer, "State of Linguistics: Crisis or Reaction?" *MLN* 61 (1946) : 497-502; idem, "Situation as a Term in Literary Criticism Again," *MLN* 72 (1957) : 224-28.

On Structuralism: René Girard, "Des Formes aux structures, en littérature et ailleurs," *MLN* 78 (1963) : 504-18; Teresa de Laurentis, "Metodi strutturali nella critica letteraria italiana," *MLN* 86 (1971) : 73-88.

On Valéry: Jacques Derrida, "Les sources de Valéry. Qual, Quelle," *MLN* 87 (1972) : 563-99; Gérard Genette, "Valéry et la poétique du language," *MLN* 87 (1972) : 600-615; Judith Robinson, "Words and Silence in L'Idée fixe," *MLN* 87 (1972) : 644-56; also see speical number, May 1972.

Contemporary Criticism: Selected Readings

The following bibliographic suggestions, drawn from an almost embarrassing array, are limited to works available in English and primarily to those published during the past decade.—Ed.

Adorno, Theodor W. *Prisms: Cultural Criticism and Society*. London, 1967.

Althusser, Louis. *For Marx*. New York, 1970.

Arvon, Henri. *Marxist Aesthetic*. Ithaca, 1973.

Babb, Howard S., ed. *Essays in Stylistic Analysis*. New York, 1972.

Baxandall, Lee. *Marxism and Aesthetics*. New York, 1968.

Beardsley, Monroe C. *The Possibility of Criticism*. Detroit, 1970.

Benjamin, Walter. *Illuminations*. New York, 1969.

Bloom, Harold. *The Anxiety of Influence: A Theory of Poetry*. New York, 1973.

Bloomfield, Morton W., ed. *In Search of Literary Theory*. Ithaca, 1972.

Boas, George. *The History of Ideas*. New York, 1969.

Bonnefoy, Yves. "Critics—English and French—and the Distance Between Them." *Encounter* 11 (1958) : 39-45.

Boon, James A. *From Symbolism to Structuralism: Lévi-Strauss in a Literary Tradition.* New York, 1972.

Brady, Frank; Palmer, John; and Price, Martin, eds. *Literary Theory and Structure.* New Haven, 1973.

Burke, Kenneth. *Language as Symbolic Action.* Berkeley & Los Angeles, 1966.

Casey, John. *The Language of Criticism.* London, 1966. On the Anglo-American critics and linguistic philosophy.

Cavell, Stanley. *Must We Mean What We Say?* New York, 1969.

Caws, Peter. " What Is Structuralism? " *Partisan Review* XXXV (1968) : 75-91.

The Critical Moment. London, 1964. Reprinted from *TLS* special issues, July 26 and September 27, 1963, with contributions by Dámaso Alonso, Barthes, Eco, Picard, and Staiger.

Deleuze, Gilles. *Proust and Signs.* New York, 1972.

Demetz, Peter; Greene, Thomas; and Nelson, Lowry, Jr., eds. *The Disciplines of Criticism.* New Haven, 1968.

Derrida, Jacques. " Positions." *Diacritics* 2, 4 (1972) : 35-43 and 3, 1 (1973).

Ehrman, Jacques, ed. *Structuralism.* Yale French Studies 36 and 37 (1966).

Erlich, Victor. *Russian Formalism: History—Doctrine.* 2nd ed. The Hague, 1965. Standard introduction to the Formalists.

Evans, Arthur R., Jr., ed. *On Four Modern Humanists.* Princeton, 1970. Essays on Hofmannsthal, Gundolf, Curtius, and Kantorowicz.

Fletcher, Angus. *Allegory: The Theory of a Symbolic Mode.* Ithaca, 1964.

Foucault, Michel. *The Order of Things.* New York, 1970. Translation of *Les Mots et le choses.*

Fowler, Roger. *The Languages of Literature.* New York, 1971.

Frye, Northrop. *The Stubborn Structure.* Ithaca, 1970. Essays on criticism and society.

————. *The Critical Path.* Bloomington, 1971. Essay on the social context of literary criticism.

Graff, Gerald. *Poetic Statement and Critical Dogma.* Evanston, 1970.

Guillén, Claudio. *Literature as System.* Princeton, 1971. Essays toward the theory of literary history.

Harrari, Josué. *Structuralists and Structuralisms.* Ithaca, 1971. Invaluable bibliography of recent French thought.

Hartman, Geoffrey H. *Beyond Formalism.* New Haven, 1970.

Hernadi, Paul. *Beyond Genre: New Directions in Literary Classification.* Ithaca, 1972.

Hirsch, E. D. *Validity in Interpretation.* New Haven, 1967.

Hobsbaum, Philip. *Theory of Criticism.* Bloomington, 1970.

Holland, Norman N. *The Dynamics of Literary Response.* New York, 1968. A Freudian approach.

Jameson, Frederic. *Marxism and Form.* Princeton, 1971.

——. *The Prison-House of Language: A Critical Account of Structuralism and Russian Formalism.* Princeton, 1972.

Kaelin, Eugen F. *An Existentialist Aesthetic.* Madison, 1966. Critical theories of Sartre and Merleau-Ponty.

Klein, Richard. "Prolegomenon to Derrida." *Diacritics* 2, 4 (1972) : 29-34.

Krieger, Murray. *The Play and Place of Criticism.* Baltimore, 1967.

Lacan, Jacques. *The Language of the Self.* Baltimore, 1968. Translation with extensive commentary by Anthony Wilden.

Lane, M., *Structuralism: A Reader.* London, 1970.

Lemon, Lee. *The Partial Critics.* New York, 1965. On the Anglo-American critics.

LeSage, Laurent, ed. *The French New Criticism.* University Park, Pa., 1967.

Lichtheim, George. *George Lukács.* New York, 1970.

Macksey, Richard, and Donato Eugenio, eds. *The Structuralist Controversy.* Baltimore, 1972. Contributions by Barthes, Derrida, Girard, Goldmann, Hyppolite, Lacan, Poulet, Rosolato, Todorov, Vernant, and others.

Man, Paul de. *Insight and Blindness.* New York, 1971. Essays on Derrida, Blanchot, Poulet, Lukács, and others.

Miller, J. Hillis, ed. *Aspects of Narrative: English Institute Essays.* New York, 1971. Contains essays on the reader's response by Wolfgang Iser and on time and narrative in Proust by Gérard Genette.

Osborne, Harold, ed. *Aesthetics in the Modern World.* London, 1968.

Palmer, Richard E. *Hermeneutics.* Evanston, 1968. Theory of interpretation in Schleiermacher, Dilthey, Heidegger, and Gadamer.

Piaget, Jean. *Structuralism.* New York, 1970. Translation of *Le Structuralisme.*

Poulet, Georges. "The Self and the Other in Critical Consciousness." *Diacritics* 2, 1 (1972) : 46-50.

Ricoeur, Paul. *Freud & Philosophy.* New Haven, 1970. Translation of *De l'interpretation.*

Said, Edward W. "A Sociology of Mind." *Partisan Review* 33 (1966) : 444-48. On Lucien Goldmann.

——. "The Totalitarianism of Mind." *Kenyon Review* 29 (1967) : 256-68. On Lévi-Strauss.

——. "Michel Foucault as an Intellectual Imagination." *Boundary* 2 (1972) : 1-27. On Michel Foucault.

——. "Eclecticism and Orthodoxy in Criticism." *Diacritics* 2, 1 (1972) : 2-8.

Sartre, Jean-Paul. *Search for a Method.* New York, 1963.
————. *Situations.* New York, 1965.
Scott, Nathan A. *Negative Capability.* New Haven, 1969.
Simon, John K., ed. *Modern French Criticism.* Chicago, 1972.
Singleton, Charles S., ed. *Interpretation: Theory and Practice.* Baltimore, 1969.
Spector, Jack J. *The Aesthetics of Freud: A Study in Psychoanalysis and Art.* New York, 1973.
Spiegelberg, Herbert. *The Phenomenological Movement.* 2 vols. The Hague, 1960.
Starobinski, Jean. "Considerations of the Present State of Literary Criticism." *Diogenes* 74 (1971) : 57-88.
Todorov, Tzvetan. *Poetics of Prose.* Translation of *Poétique de la Prose,* to be published in 1973 by the Cornell University Press.
Watson, George. *The Study of Literature.* New York, 1969.
Wellek, René. *Concepts of Criticism.* New Haven, 1963.
————. *Discriminations: Further Concepts in Criticism.* New Haven, 1970.
Wellek, René, and Austin, Warren. *Theory of Literature.* 3rd ed. New York, 1962.
Wilden, Anthony. *System and Structure.* London, 1972.
Williams, Raymond. *The Country and the City.* New York & London, 1973.
Wimsatt, W. K. *Hateful Contraries: Studies in Literature and Criticism.* Lexington, 1966.
Wollheim, Richard. *Art and Its Objects.* New York, 1968.

For additional entries, see the bibliography appended to Ezio Raimondi's essay.

About the Contributors

AMADO ALONSO (1896-1952), trained at the University of Madrid, was a leading philologist of his generation. He taught at the Centro Estudios Históricos, was the director of the Philological Institute and Professor of Romance Linguistics at the University of Buenos Aires, and taught at Harvard from 1947 until his death. Don Amado was the editor of the *Rivista de filología hispanica* and a number of scholarly series. His publications include *El problema de la lengua en América* (1935), *Castellano, español, idoma nacional* (1938), *Poesia y estilo de Pablo Neruda* (1940; 1951), *Estudios lingüisticos (temas hispano-americanas)* (1953), and *Materia y forma en poesia* (1955).

ROLAND BARTHES, born in Bayonne in 1915, is at present Directeur d'Études in the VIᵉ Section of the École Pratique des Hautes Études, where he conducts seminars on "semio-criticism and the sociology of signs, symbols, and collective representations." He participated in the Baltimore "Structuralist" Symposium and was a visiting professor at Johns Hopkins during 1967-68. His early essays in *Combat* were published in *Le Degré zéro de l'écriture* (1953), a landmark in contemporary criticism. During the same period he was one of the founders of Théâtre Populaire and an early champion of Brecht in France. His subsequent publications include *Michelet par lui-même* (1954), *Mythologies* (1957), *Sur Racine* (1963), a reissue of *Le Degré zéro* with *Eléments de sémiologie* (1964), *Essais critiques* (1964), *La Tour Eiffel* (1964), *Critique et Vérité* (1966), *Système de la mode* (1967), *S/Z* (1970), *L'Empire des signes* (1970), and *Sade, Fourier, Loyola* (1971).

ALAN BASS is a graduate student in comparative literature at Johns Hopkins. He is currently completing a translation of and critical commentary on Jacques Derrida's *L'Ecriture et la différence.*

EUGENIO DONATO was born on Cyprus and educated at Brandeis and Johns Hopkins, working in mathematics and Romance philology. He has taught at Cornell, Johns Hopkins, and Montréal and is currently a member of the comparative literature faculty at the State University of New York in Buffalo. He is the author of studies in French and Italian literature, critical theory, and the methodology of the *Sciences de l'homme* and is the co-editor of *The Structuralist Controversy* (1972).

JACQUES EHRMANN (1931-72) was educated at the Sorbonne and the University of California at Los Angeles and, at the time of his death, was a member of the French faculty at Yale. He was the author of *Un paradis désespéré* . . . and editor of *Yale French Studies* issues on "Structuralism," "Literature and Revolution," and "Game, Play, Literature."

WOLFGANG BERNARD FLEISCHMANN was born in Vienna and educated at St. John's College and the University of North Carolina. He has taught at North Carolina, Oklahoma, Emory, Wisconsin, Princeton, and Massachusetts and is currently Dean and Professor of Comparative Literature at Montclair State College. He has written on the classical background of European literature and was the general editor of the *Encyclopedia of World Literature in the Twentieth Century* (1967).

ALEXANDER GELLEY obtained his doctorate in comparative literature at Yale and has taught at a number of institutions, including the City College of New York, The Hebrew University, and Cornell. He is currently director of the Comparative Literature program at the University of California, Irvine. He has published essays on contemporary French and German critical theory and on the modern novel and is currently working on a study of landscape settings in the nineteenth-century European novel.

RENÉ GIRARD, born in Avignon in 1923, studied at the École des Chartes and took a degree in history at Indiana University. He taught there and at Bryn Mawr before coming to Johns Hopkins in 1957, where he served as chairman of the Romance Language department and general editor of *MLN*. He has also taught at the State University of New York in Buffalo and has recently accepted a post at Stanford. His publications include *Mensonge romantique et vérité romanesque* (1961; English translation, 1965), *Dostoïevski: du double à l'unité* (1963), and *La Violence et le sacré* (1972), as well as the Proust volume in the "Twentieth Century Views" series.

LUCIEN GOLDMANN (1913-70) studied law and letters at the Universities of Bucharest, Vienna, Zürich, and Paris. In 1958 he became a *directeur de recherches* in the VIᵉ section of the École Pratique des Hautes Etudes and, in 1961, began his association with the Institut de Sociologie of the University of Brussels. During 1966-67 he was a visiting professor at Johns Hopkins. His extensive publications include *La communanté humaine et l'univers chez Kant* (1948), *Sciences humaines et philosophie* (1952), *Le Dieu caché: étude sur la division tragique dans les Pensées de Pascal et dans le théâtre de Racine* (1956; English translation, 1964), an edition of the correspondence of Du Barcos (1956), *Recherches dialectiques* (1958), *Pour une sociologie du roman* (1964), and two posthumous collections, *Structures mentales et création culturelle* (1970) and *Marxisme et sciences humaines* (1970).

LIONEL GOSSMAN, educated at Glasgow, Paris, and Oxford, is currently Professor of Romance Languages at Johns Hopkins. His publications include *Men and Masks: A Study of Molière* (1963) and *Medievalism and The Ideologies of The Enlightenment* (1968).

OTTO HAHN is a French man of letters who has published on literary, philosophical, and social topics in *Les Temps Modernes*.

THOMAS R. HART was educated at Yale and has taught at Amherst, Harvard, Johns Hopkins, and Emory; he is currently Professor of Romance Literature at the University of Oregon. He has published on Spanish and Portuguese literature, edited an edition of Gil Vicente, and contributed to *The Disciplines of Criticism* (1968).

GEOFFREY H. HARTMAN, born in Germany in 1929, was educated at Queens College and Yale. He has taught at Iowa and Cornell and is currently Professor of English and Comparative Literature at Yale. He is the author of *The Unmediated Vision* (1954), *Wordsworth's Poetry* (1964), for which he received the Christian Gauss Prize, and *Beyond Formalism: Literary Essays* (1970).

FRANK KERMODE, born on the Isle of Man in 1919, was educated at Liverpool University and is currently Lord Northcliffe Professor of Modern English Literature and head of the literature program at the University College in London. He is a Fellow of the Royal Society of Literature and participated in the Johns Hopkins Humanities Seminars during 1968-69. He is the author of *Romantic Image* (1957), *Wallace Stevens* (1960), *Puzzles and Epiphanies* (1962), *The Sense of an Ending* (1967), and *Continuities* (1968) and is the editor of *The Living Milton* (1960) and the Fontana Modern Masters series.

RICHARD MACKSEY, who studied at Princeton, Oxford, and Johns Hopkins, is currently Chairman of the Humanities Center at Johns Hopkins and the comparative literature editor of *MLN*. He has published poetry and work in number theory, intellectual history, film, music, and hermeneutics, as well as critical studies of European and American authors; he has written a study of Proust (*La Lanterne Magique*), *Florilegium anglicum* (1964), contributions to three volumes in the Twentieth Century Views series and to *The Act of the Mind* (1965), and a forthcoming book on comedy; he is co-editor of *The Structuralist Controversy* (1972).

PAUL DE MAN, born in Belgium in 1920, was educated there and at Harvard. He taught at Cornell, Zürich, and Johns Hopkins and is currently Professor of Comparative and French Literature at Yale. A collection of his essays, *Blindness & Insight: Essays in The Rhetoric of Contemporary Criticism*, was published in 1971.

J. HILLIS MILLER was educated at Oberlin and Harvard and has taught at Williams College and Johns Hopkins (1953-73); he is currently Professor of English at Yale. He has published studies of Charles Dickens, of five nineteenth-century writers (*The Disappearance of God*, 1963), of six twentieth-century writers (*The Poets of Reality*, 1965), and of Thomas Hardy.

EZIO RAIMONDI, born in 1924, is currently Professor of Italian Literature at the University of Bologna. He participated in the Johns Hopkins Humanities Seminars in Baltimore and Zürich and, during 1968-69, was a visiting professor at Johns Hopkins. He has published widely on all periods of Italian literature and critical theory, including *Letteratura barocca* (1963), *Il lettore provincia, Anatomie seicentesche* (1966), *Techniche della critica letteraria* (1967), *Metafora e storia* (1970), and a critical edition of Machiavelli.

EDWARD W. SAID, born in Jerusalem in 1935, was educated at Princeton and Harvard. Currently Professor of English and Comparative Literature at Columbia, he is the author of *Joseph Conrad and the Fiction of Autobiography* (1966) and has published on critical theory and Arabic culture.

LEO SPITZER (1887-1960) studied Romance philology in his native Vienna under Meyer-Lübke; he became *Privatdozent* at the University there in 1913 and subsequently taught at Bonn, Marburg, and Cologne. With the accession of Hitler, he accepted a post in Istanbul and, in 1936, joined the faculty of Johns Hopkins—an association that continued until his death. For an evaluation of his career and a useful bibliography of his far-ranging publications, see René Wellek, *Discriminations* (New Haven: Yale University Press, 1970), pp. 187-224.

Index

Library of Congress Cataloging in Publication Data

Macksey, Richard, 1931–   comp.
  Velocities of change.

      CONTENTS: Macksey, R. Velocities of change.—
The fiction of criticism: Gossman, L. Literary
education and democracy. Said, E. W. Notes on the
characterization of a literary text. Alonso, A. The
stylistic interpretation of literary texts. Barthes,
R. The two criticisms. Girard, R. Critical reflec-
tions on literary studies. Goldmann, L. Genetic
structuralism and the history of literature. Hartman,
G. Beyond formalism. Raimondi, E. Symbolic criticism.
Miller, J. H. The antitheses of criticism. Donato, E.
Of Structuralism and literature. Kermode, F. The
structures of fiction. [etc.]
      1.   Criticism—Addresses, essays, lectures.
I.   Modern language notes.   II.   Title.
PN85.M24   801′.95′08   72-12343
ISBN 0-8018-1494-4
ISBN 0-8018-1495-2 (pbk.)

THE JOHNS HOPKINS UNIVERSITY PRESS

This book was composed in Baskerville text and display type by Maryland Linotype Composition Company, Inc. It was printed on Maple's 60-lb. Danforth stock and bound in Holliston Roxite by The Maple Press Company.